Accounting Best Practices

Second Edition

Accounting Best Practices

Second Edition

Steven M. Bragg

John Wiley & Sons, Inc.

New York • Chichester • Weinheim • Brisbane • Singapore • Toronto

This book is printed on acid-free paper. ∞

Copyright © 2001 by John Wiley & Sons, Inc. All rights reserved.

Published simultaneously in Canada.

This publication is designed to provide accurate and authoritative information in regard to the subject matter covered. It is sold with the understanding that the publisher is not engaged in rendering professional services. If professional advice or other expert assistance is required, the services of a competent professional person should be sought.

Library of Congress Cataloging-in-Publication Data:

Bragg, Steven M.
      Accounting best practices / Steven M. Bragg. — 2nd ed.
         p.   cm.
      Includes bibliographical references and index.
      ISBN 0-471-40914-6 (cloth : alk. paper)
      1. Accounting.   I. Title.   **3 2280 00728 2783**
   HF5635 .B818 2001
   657—dc21   2001017811

Printed in the United States of America.

10   9   8   7   6   5   4   3   2

To my wife, Melissa. Thinking of you always.

About the Author

Steven Bragg, CPA, CMA, CIA, CPM, CPIM, has been the Chief Financial Officer or Controller of four companies, as well as a consulting manager at Ernst & Young. He received a master's degree in finance from Bentley College and an MBA from Babson College. He has also written *Just-in-Time Accounting, Advanced Accounting Systems, Outsourcing, Financial Analysis, Accounting Best Practices, Cost Accounting,* and *Managing Explosive Corporate Growth,* and has co-authored *Controllership* and *The Controller's Function.* Mr. Bragg resides in Englewood, Colorado.

Acknowledgments

A special note of thanks to my managing editor, John Deremigis, who provided so much assistance in getting this project under way and seeing to it that it never strayed from its course.

Contents

Preface

The accounting department is a cost center. It does not directly generate revenues, but rather provides a fixed set of services to the rest of a company, and is asked to do so at the lowest possible cost. Consequently, the accounting staff is called upon to process transactions, write reports, create new processes or investigate old ones—while doing so as an ever-shrinking proportion of total expenses.

This cost-based environment is a very difficult one for most accountants, for their training is primarily in accounting rules and regulations, rather than in how to run a very specialized department in a cost-effective manner. They find a few ideas for improvements from attending seminars or perusing accounting or management magazines, but there is no centralized source of information for them to consult, which itemizes a wide array of possible improvements. Hence the need for the second edition of *Accounting Best Practices*.

This book is compiled from the author's lengthy experience in setting up and operating a number of accounting departments, as well as by providing consulting services to other companies. Accordingly, it contains a blend of best practices from a wide variety of accounting environments, ranging from very small partnerships to multi-billion-dollar corporations. This means that not all of the best practices described within these pages will be useful in every situation—some are designed to provide quick and inexpensive, incremental improvements to an operation that can be installed in a day, while others are groundbreaking events that require six-figure investments (or more) and months of installation time. Some will only work for companies of a certain size, and should be discarded as more expensive and comprehensive accounting systems are installed—it all depends on the situation. Consequently, each chapter includes a table that notes the ease, duration, and cost of implementation for every best practice within it. The best practices are also noted in summary form in Appendix B.

This second edition of *Accounting Best Practices* contains fifty additional best practices. They are skewed toward increased usage of the Internet, which now contains many new sites that provide valuable alternatives to more traditional ways to operate an accounting department. Wherever possible, specific web sites are mentioned alongside each of these best practices. There is also a new chapter on finance, which is an important topic for the accountants in smaller companies, where the accounting and finance functions are blended together.

Obviously, there is a great deal of innovation going on in a field that has been in existence for hundreds of years. In the future, I expect that more best practices will continue to be found on the Internet. In addition, there is a great deal of effort being expended on wireless and handheld computing applications that will probably result in advanced accounting best practices, such as remote data entry and document creation, as well as remote access to the central accounting database. The next edition of this book will undoubtedly include some precursors to these groundbreaking changes.

    If you feel the need to cut costs in the accounting department while still providing an advanced level of service to the rest of the company, then this is the book for you.

Englewood, Colorado
September 2000

Accounting
Best Practices

Second Edition

Chapter 1

Introduction

A chief executive officer (CEO) spends months deciding on a corporate strategy. The plan probably includes a mix of changes in products, customers, and markets, as well as demands for increased efficiencies or information in a number of existing areas. The CEO then hands off the plan to a group of managers who are quite capable of implementing many of the changes, but who scratch their heads over how to squeeze greater efficiencies or information out of existing departments in order to meet their strategic goals. This is where best practices come into play.

A best practice is really *any* improvement over existing systems, though some consultants prefer to confine the definition to those few high-end and very advanced improvements which have been successfully installed by a few world-class companies. This book uses the broader definition of any improvement over existing systems, since the vast majority of companies are in no position, either in terms of technological capabilities, monetary resources, or management skill, to make use of truly world-class best practices. Using this wider definition, a best practice can be anything that increases the existing level of efficiency, such as switching to blanket purchase orders, signature stamps, and procurement cards to streamline the accounts payable function. It can also lead to improved levels of reporting for use by other parts of the company, such as activity-based costing, target costing, or direct costing reports in the costing function. Further, it can reduce the number of transaction errors, by such means as automated employee expense reports, automated bank account deductions, or a simplified commission calculation system. By implementing a plethora of best practices, a company can greatly improve its level of efficiency and information reporting, which fits nicely into the requirements of most strategic plans.

One can go further than describing best practices as an excellent *contributor* to the fulfillment of a company's strategy, and even state that a strategy does not have much chance of success *unless* best practices are involved. The reason is that best practices have such a large impact on overall efficiencies, they unleash a large number of excess people who can then work on other strategic issues, as well as reduce a company's cash requirements, releasing more cash for investment in strategic targets. In addition, some best practices link company functions more closely together, resulting in better overall functionality—this is a singular improvement when a company is in the throes of changes caused by strategy shifts. Further, best practices can operate quite well in the *absence* of a strategic plan. For example, any department manager can install a variety of best practices with no approval or oversight from above, resulting in a multitude of beneficial changes. Thus, best practices are a linchpin of the successful corporate strategy, and can also lead to improvements even if they are not part of a grand strategic vision.

The scope of this book does not encompass all of the best practices that a company should consider, only those used by the accounting department. This area is especially susceptible to improvement through best practices, since it is heavily procedure-driven. When there are many procedures, there are many opportunities to enhance the multitude of procedure steps through automation, simplification, elimination of tasks, error-proofing, and outsourcing. Thus, of all the corporate functions, this is the one that reacts best to treatment through best practices.

Chapter 2 covers a variety of issues related to the implementation of best practices, such as differentiating between incremental and re-engineering changes, circumstances under which best practices are most likely to succeed, and how to plan and proceed with these implementations. Most important, there is a discussion of the multitude of reasons why a best practice implementation can fail, which is excellent reading prior to embarking on a new project, in order to be aware of all possible pitfalls. The chapter ends with a brief review of the impact of best practices on employees. This chapter is fundamental to the book, for it serves as the groundwork on which the remaining chapters are built. For example, if you are interested in modifying the general ledger account structure for use by an activity-based costing system, it is necessary to first review the implementation chapter to see how any programming, software package, or inter-departmental issues might impact the project.

Chapters 3 through 16 each describe a cluster of best practices, with a functional area itemized under each chapter. For example, Chapter 8 covers a variety of improvements to a company's commission calculation and payment systems, while Chapter 16 is strictly concerned with a variety of payroll-streamlining issues related to the collection of employee time information, processing it into payments, and distributing those payments. Chapter 13 is a catchall chapter. It covers a variety of general best practices which do not fit easily into other, more specific chapters. Examples of these best practices are the use of process-centering, on-line reporting, and creating a contract-terms database. Chapters 3 through 16 are the heart of the book since they contain information related to nearly 200 best practices.

For Chapters 3 through 16, there is an exhibit near the beginning that shows the general level of implementation difficulty for each of the best practices in the chapter. The exhibit notes the level of implementation ease, cost, and duration. This information gives the reader a good idea of which best practices to search for and read through, in case ease of implementation is a strong consideration. For each chapter, there are a number of sections, each one describing a best practice. There is a brief description of the problems it can fix, as well as notes on how it can be implemented, and any problems one may encounter while doing so. Each chapter concludes with a section that describes the impact of a recommended mix of best practices on the functional area being covered. This last section always includes a graphical representation of how certain best practices impact specific activities. Not all the best practices in each chapter are included in this graphic, since some are mutually exclusive. This chapter layout is designed to give the reader a quick overview of the best practices that are most likely to make a significant impact on a functional area of the accounting department.

The book ends with two appendices. Appendix A lists a number of references the reader can consult which describe specific best practices in greater detail, usually including real-life examples of implementations. These are mostly magazine articles, since no one has yet published a book that contains a significant number of best practices. Appendix B lists all of the best practices in each of the preceding chapters in alphabetical order. This list allows the reader to quickly find a potentially useful best practice. It is then a simple matter to refer back to the main text to obtain more information about each item.

This book is designed to assist anyone who needs to improve either the efficiency of the accounting department, reduce its error rates, or provide better information to other parts of a company. The best practices noted on the following pages will greatly assist toward attaining this goal, which may be part of a grand strategic vision or simply a desire by an accounting manager to improve the department. The layout of the book is extremely practical: to list as many best practices as possible, to assist the reader in finding the most suitable ones, and to describe any implementation problems which may arise. In short, this is the perfect do-it-yourself fix-it book for the manager who likes to tinker with the accounting department.

Chapter 2

How To Use Best Practices

This chapter is about implementing best practices. It begins by describing the various kinds of best practices and goes on to cover those situations where they are most likely to be installed successfully. The key components of a successful best practice installation are also noted. When planning to add a best practice, it is also useful to know the ways in which the implementation can fail, so there is a lengthy list of reasons for failure. Finally, there is a brief discussion of the impact of change on employees and the organization. Only by carefully considering all of these issues in advance can one hope to achieve a successful best practice implementation that will result in increased levels of efficiency in the accounting department.

TYPES OF BEST PRACTICES

This section describes the two main types of best practices, each one requiring considerably different implementation approaches.

The first type of best practice is an incremental one. This usually involves either a small modification to an existing procedure or a replacement of a procedure that is so minor in effect that it has only a minimal impact on the organization, or indeed on the person who performs the procedure. The increased level of efficiency contributed by a single best practice of this type is moderate at best, but this type is also the easiest to install, since there is little resistance from the organization. An example of this type of best practice is using a signature stamp to sign checks (see Chapter 3); it is simple, cuts a modest amount of time from the check preparation process, and there will be no complaints about its use. However, only when this type of best practice is used in large numbers is there a significant increase in the level of efficiency of accounting operations.

The second type of best practice involves a considerable degree of re-engineering. This requires the complete reorganization or replacement of an existing function. The level of change is massive, resulting in employees either being laid off or receiving vastly different job descriptions. The level of efficiency improvement can be several times greater than the old method it is replacing. However, the level of risk matches the reward, for this type of best practice meets with enormous resistance and consequently is at great risk of failure. An example of this type of best practice is eliminating the accounts payable department in favor of having the receiving staff approve all payments at the receiving dock (see Chapter 3); it involves the elimination of many jobs and is an entirely new approach to paying suppliers. A single best practice implementation of this sort can reap major improvements in the level of accounting efficiency.

Thus, given the considerable number and size of the differences between the incremental and re-engineering best practices, it is necessary to first determine into which category a best practice falls before designing a plan for implementing it. Given the difficulty of implementation for a re-engineering project, it may even be necessary to delay implementation or intersperse a series of such projects with easier incremental projects, in order to allow employees to recover from the re-engineering projects.

THE MOST FERTILE GROUND FOR BEST PRACTICES

Before installing any best practice, it is useful to review the existing environment to see if there is a reasonable chance for the implementation to succeed. The following bullet points note the best environments in which best practices can not only be installed, but also have a fair chance of continuing to succeed:

- *If benchmarking shows a problem.* Some organizations regularly compare their performance levels against those of other companies, especially those with a reputation for having extremely high levels of performance. If there is a significant difference in the performance levels of these other organizations and the company doing the benchmarking, this can serve as a reminder that continuous change is necessary in order to survive. If management sees and heeds this warning, the environment in which best practices will be accepted is greatly improved.

- *If management has a change orientation.* Some managers have a seemingly genetic disposition toward change. If an accounting department has such a person in charge, there will certainly be a drive toward many changes. If anything, this type of person can go too far, implementing too many projects with not enough preparation, resulting in a confused operations group whose newly revised systems may take a considerable amount of time to untangle. The presence of a detail-oriented second-in-command is very helpful for preserving order and channeling the energies of such a manager into the most productive directions.

- *If the company is experiencing poor financial results.* If there is a significant loss, or a trend in that direction, this serves as a wake-up call to management, which in turn results in the creation of a multitude of best practices projects. In this case, the situation may even go too far, with so many improvement projects going on at once that there are not enough resources to go around, resulting in the ultimate completion of few, if any, of the best practices.

- *If there is new management.* Most people who are newly installed as managers of either the accounting department or (better yet) the entire organization want to make changes in order to leave their marks on the organization. Though this can involve non-best practice items like organizational changes or a new strategic direction, it is possible that there will be a renewed focus on efficiency that will result in the implementation of new best practices.

In short, as long as there is a willingness by management to change and a good reason for doing so, then there is fertile ground for the implementation of a multitude of best practices.

PLANNING FOR BEST PRACTICES

A critical issue for the success of any best practices implementation project is an adequate degree of advance planning. The following bullet points describe the key components of a typical best practices implementation plan:

- *Capacity requirements.* Any project plan must account for the amount of capacity needed to ensure success. Capacity can include the number of people, computers, or floor space that is needed. For example, if the project team requires 20 people, then there must be a planning item to find and equip a sufficient amount of space for this group. Also, a project that requires a considerable amount of programming time should reserve that time in advance with the programming staff to ensure that the programming is completed on time. Also, the management team must have a sufficient amount of time available to properly oversee the project team's activities. If any of these issues are not addressed in advance, there can be a major impact on the success of the implementation.

- *Contingencies.* Murphy's Law always applies, so there should be contingencies built into the project plan. For example, if the project team is being set up in a new building, there is always a chance that phone lines will not be installed in time. To guard against this possibility, there should be an additional project step to obtain some cellular phones, which will supply the team's communications needs until the phone lines can be installed.

- *Dependencies.* The steps required to complete a project must be properly sequenced so that any bottleneck steps are clearly defined and have sufficient resources allocated to them to ensure that they are completed on time. For example, a project planning person cannot set up the plan if there is no project planning software available and loaded into the computer. Consequently, this step must be completed before the planning task can commence.

- *Funding requirements.* Any project requires some funding, such as the purchase of equipment for the project team or software licenses or employee training. Consequently, the project plan must include the dates on which funding is expected, so that dependent tasks involving the expenditure of those funds can be properly planned.

- *Review points.* For all but the smallest projects, there must be control points where the project manager has a formal review meeting with those people who are responsible for certain deliverables. These review points must be built into the plan, along with a sufficient amount of time for follow-up meetings to resolve any issues that may arise during the initial review meetings.

- *Risk levels.* Some best practices, especially those involving a large proportion of re-engineering activities, run a considerable risk of failure. In these cases, it is necessary to conduct a careful review of what will happen if the project fails. For example, can the existing system be reinstituted if the new system does not work? What if funding runs out? What if management support for the project falters? What if the level of technology is too advanced for the company to support? The answers to these questions may result in additional project steps to safeguard the project, or to at least back it up with a contingency plan in case the project cannot reach a successful conclusion.

- *Total time required.* All of the previous planning steps are influenced by one of the most important considerations of all—how much time is allocated to the project. Though there may be some play in the final project due date, it is always unacceptable to let a project run too long, since it ties up the time of project team members and will probably accumulate extra costs until it is completed. Consequently, the project team must continually revise the existing project plan to account for new contingencies and problems as they arise, given the overriding restriction of the amount of time available.

The elements of planning that have just been described will all go for naught if there is not an additional linkage to corporate strategy at the highest levels. The reason is that although an implementation may be completely successful, it may not make any difference, and even be rendered unusable, if corporate strategy calls for a shift that will render the best practice obsolete. For example, a fine new centralized accounts payable facility for the use of all corporate divisions is not of much use if the general corporate direction is to spin off or sell all of those divisions. Thus, proper integration of low-level best practices planning with high-level corporate planning is required to ensure that the correct projects are completed.

Given the large number of issues to resolve in order to give an implementation project a reasonable chance of success, it is apparent that the presence of a manager who is very experienced in the intricacies of project planning is a key component of an effective project team. Consequently, the acquisition of such a person should be one of the first steps to include in a project plan.

This section described in general terms the key components of a project plan that must be considered in order to foresee where problems may arise in the course of an implementation. We now proceed to a discussion of the impact of time on the success of a best practices implementation.

TIMING OF BEST PRACTICES

Both the timing of a best practice implementation and the time it takes to complete it have a major impact on the likelihood of success.

The timing of an implementation project is critical. For example, an installation that comes at the same time as a major deliverable in another area will receive scant attention from the person who is most responsible for using the best practice, since it takes a distant second place to the deliverable. Also, any project that comes on the heels of a disastrous implementation will not be expected to succeed, though this problem can be overcome by targeting a quick and easy project that results in a rapid success—and which overcomes the stigma of the earlier failure. Further, proper implementation timing must take into account other project implementations going on elsewhere in the company or even in the same department, so that there is not a conflict over project resources. Only by carefully considering these issues prior to scheduling a project will a best practice implementation not be impacted by timing issues.

In addition to timing, the *time* required to complete a project is of major importance. A quick project brings with it the aura of success, a reputation for completion, and a much better chance of being allowed to take on a more difficult and expensive project. Alternatively, a project that impacts lots of departments or people, or which involves the liberal application of cutting-edge technology, runs a major risk of running for a long time; and the longer the project, the greater the risk that something will go wrong, objections will arise, or that funding will run out. Thus, close attention to project duration will increase the odds of success.

IMPLEMENTING BEST PRACTICES

The actual implementation of any best practice requires a great degree of careful planning, as noted earlier. However, planning is not enough. The implementation process itself requires a number of key components in order to ensure a successful conclusion. This section discusses those components.

One of the first implementation steps for all but the simplest best practice improvements is to study and flowchart the existing system about to be improved. By doing so, one can ascertain any unusual requirements which are not readily apparent and which must be included in the planning for the upcoming implementation. Though some re-engineering efforts do not spend much time on this task, on the grounds that the entire system is about to be replaced, the same issue still applies—there are usually special requirements, unique to any company, which must be addressed in any new system. Accordingly, nearly all implementation projects must include this critical step.

Another issue is the cost-benefit analysis. This is a compilation of all the costs required to both install and maintain a best practice, which is offset against the benefits of doing so. These costs must include project team payroll and related expenses, outside services, programming costs, training, travel, and capital expenditures. This step is worth a great deal of attention, for a wise manager will not undertake a new project, no matter how cutting-edge and high-profile it may be, if there is not a sound analysis in place that clearly shows the benefit of moving forward with it.

Yet another implementation issue is the use of new technology. Though there may be new devices or software on the market that can clearly improve the efficiency of a company's operations, and perhaps even make a demonstrative impact on a company's competitive situation, it still may be more prudent to wait until the technology has been tested in the marketplace for a short time before proceeding with an implementation. This is a particular problem if there is only one supplier available who offers the technology, especially if that supplier is a small one or with inadequate funding, with the attendant risk of going out of business. In most cases, the prudent manager will elect to use technology that has proven itself in the marketplace, rather than using the most cutting-edge applications.

Of great importance to most best practice implementations is system testing. Any new application, unless it is astoundingly simple, carries with it the risk of failure. This risk must be tested repeatedly to ensure that it will not occur under actual use. The type of testing can take a variety of forms. One is volume testing, to ensure that a large number of employees using the system at the same time will not result in failure. Another is feature testing, in which test transactions that test the boundaries of the possible information to be used are run through the system. Yet another possibility is recovery testing—bringing down a computer system suddenly to see how easy it is to re-start the system. All of these approaches, or others, depending on the type of best practice, should be completed before unleashing a new application on employees.

One of the last implementation steps before firing up a new best practice is to provide training to employees in how to run the new system. This must be done as late as possible, since employee retention of this information will dwindle rapidly if not reinforced by actual practice. In addition, this training should be hands-on whenever possible, since employees retain the most information when training is conducted in this manner. It is important to identify in advance all possible users of a new system for training, since a few untrained employees can result in the failure of a new best practice.

A key element of any training class is procedures. These must be completed, reviewed, and available for employee use not only at the time of training, but also at all times thereafter, which requires a good manager to oversee the procedure creation and distribution phases. Procedure-writing is a special skill that may require the hiring of technical writers, interviewers, and systems analysts to ensure that procedures are properly crafted. The input of users into the accuracy of all procedures is also an integral step in this process.

Even after the new system has been installed, it is necessary to conduct a post-implementation review. This analysis determines if the cost savings or efficiency improvements are in the expected range, what problems arose during the implementation that should be avoided during future projects, and what issues are still unresolved from the current implementation. This last point is particularly important, for many managers do not follow through completely on all the stray implementation issues which inevitably arise after a new system is put in place. Only by carefully listing these issues and working through them will the employees using the new system be completely satisfied with how a best practice has been installed.

An issue that arises during all phases of a project implementation is communications. Since there may be a wide range of activities going on, many of them dependent upon each other, it is important that the status of all project steps be continually communicated to the entire project team, as well as to all affected employees. By doing so, a project manager can avoid such gaffes as having one task proceed without knowing that, due to changes elsewhere in the project, the entire task has been rendered unnecessary. These communications should not just be limited to project plan updates, but should also include all meeting minutes in which changes are decided on, documented, and approved by team leaders. By paying attention to this important item at every step of an implementation, the entire process will be completed much more smoothly.

As described in this section, a successful best practice implementation nearly always includes a review of the current system, a cost-benefit analysis, responsible use of new technology, system testing, training, and a post-implementation review, with a generous dash of communications at every step.

WHY BEST PRACTICES FAIL

There is a lengthy list of reasons why a best practice installation may not succeed, as noted in the following bullet points. The various reasons for failure can be grouped into a relatively small cluster of primary reasons. The first is lack of planning, which can include inadequate budgeting for time, money, or personnel. Another is the lack of cooperation by other entities, such as the programming staff or other departments that will be impacted by any changes. The final, and most important, problem is that there is little or no effort to prepare the organization for change. This last item tends to build up over time as more and more best practices are implemented, eventually resulting in the total resistance by the organization to any further change. At its root, this problem involves a fundamental lack of communication, especially to those people who are most impacted by change. When a single implementation is completed without totally informing employees of the change, this may be tolerated, but a continuous stream of them will encourage a revolt. In alphabetical order, the various causes of failure are noted as follows:

- *Alterations to packaged software.* A very common cause of failure is that a best practice requires changes to a software package provided by a software supplier; after the changes are made, the company finds that the newest release of the software contains features that it must have and so it updates the software—wiping out the programming changes which were made to accommodate the best practice. This problem can also arise even if there is only a custom interface between the packaged software and some other application needed for a best practice, because a software upgrade may alter the data accessed through the interface. Thus, alterations to packaged software are doomed to failure unless there is absolutely no way that the company will ever update the software package.

- *Custom programming.* A major cause of implementation failure is that the programming required to make it a reality either does not have the requested specifications, costs more than expected, arrives too late, is unreliable—or all of the above! Since many best practices are closely linked to the latest advances in technology, this is an increasingly common cause of failure. To keep from being a victim of programming problems, one should never attempt to implement the most "bleeding-edge" technology, because it is the most subject to failure. Instead, wait for some other company to work out all of the bugs and make it a reliable concept, and then proceed with the implementation. Also, it is useful to interview other people who have gone through a complete installation to see what tips they can give that will result in a smoother implementation. Finally, one should always interview any other employees who have had programming work done for them by the in-house staff. If the results of these previous efforts were not acceptable, it may be better to look outside of the company for more competent programming assistance.

- *Inadequate preparation of the organization.* Communication is the key to a successful implementation. Alternatively, no communication keeps an organization from understanding what is happening; this increases the rumors about a project, builds resistance to it, and reduces the level of cooperation that people are likely to give to it. Avoiding this issue requires a considerable amount of up-front communication about the intentions and likely impact of any project, with that communication targeted not just at the impacted managers, but also at all impacted employees, and to some extent even the corporation or department as a whole.

- *Intransigent personnel.* A major cause of failure is the employee who either refuses to use a best practice or who actively tries to sabotage it. This type of person may have a vested interest in using the old system, does not like change in general, or has a personality clash with someone on the implementation team. In any of these cases, the person must be won over through good communication (especially if the employee is in a controlling position) or removed to a position which has no impact on the project. If neither of these actions are successful, the project will almost certainly fail.

- *Lack of control points.* One of the best ways to maintain control over any project is to set up regular review meetings, as well as additional meetings to review the situation when pre-set milestone targets are reached. These meetings are designed to see how a project is progressing, to discuss any problems which have occurred or are anticipated, and to determine how current or potential problems can be avoided best. Without the benefit of these regular meetings, it is much more likely that unexpected problems will arise, or that existing ones will be exacerbated.

- *Lack of funding.* A project can be canceled either because it has a significant cost overrun that exceeds the original funding request, or because it was initiated without any funding request in the first place. Either approach results in failure. Besides the obvious platitude of "don't go over budget," the best way to avoid this problem is to build a cushion into the original funding request that should see the project through, barring any unusually large extra expenditures.

- *Lack of planning.* A critical aspect of any project is the planning that goes into it. If there is no plan, there is no way to determine the cost, number of employees, or time requirements, nor is there any formal review of the inherent project risks. Without this formal planning process, a project is very likely to hit a snag or be stopped cold at some point prior to its timely completion. On the contrary, using proper planning results in a smooth implementation process that builds a good reputation for the project manager and thereby leads to more funding for additional projects.

- *Lack of post-implementation review.* Though it is not a criterion for the successful implementation of any single project, a missing post-implementation review can be the key to success for later projects. For example, if such a review reveals that a project was completed in spite of the inadequate project planning skills of a specific manager, it might be best to use a different person in the future for new projects, thereby increasing their chances of success.

- *Lack of success in earlier efforts.* If a manager builds a reputation for not successfully completing best practices projects, it becomes increasingly difficult to complete new ones. The problem is that no one believes that a new effort will succeed and so there is little commitment to doing it. Also, upper management is much less willing to allocate funds to a manager who has not developed a proven track record for successful implementations. The best way out of this jam is to assign a different manager to an implementation project, one with a proven track record of success.

- *Lack of testing.* A major problem for the implementation of especially large and complex projects, especially those involving programming, is that they are rushed into production without a thorough testing process to discover and correct all bugs which might interfere with or freeze the orderly conduct of work in the areas they are designed to improve. There is nothing more dangerous than to install a wonderful new system in a critical area of the company, only to see that critical function fail completely due to a problem that could have been discovered in a proper testing program. It is always worthwhile to build some extra time into a project budget for an adequate amount of testing.

- *Lack of top management support.* If a project requires a large amount of funding or the cooperation of multiple departments, it is critical to have the complete support of the top management team. If not, any required funding may not be allocated, while there is also a strong possibility that any objecting departments will be able to sidetrack it easily. This is an especially common problem when the project has no clear project sponsor at all—without a senior level manager to drive it, a project will sputter along and eventually fade away without coming anywhere near completion.

- *Relying on other departments.* As soon as another department's cooperation becomes a necessary component of a best practice installation, the chances of success drop markedly. The odds become even smaller if multiple departments are involved. The main reason is that there is now an extra manager involved, who may not have the commitment of the accounting manager to make the implementation a success. In addition, the staff of the other department may influence their manager not to help out, while there may also be a problem with the other department not having a sufficient amount of funding to complete its share of the work. For example, an accounting department can benefit greatly at period-end if the warehouse is using cycle-counting to keep inventory accuracy levels high, since there is no need for a physical inventory count. However, if the warehouse does not have the extra staff available to count inventory, the work will not be done, no matter how badly the accounting staff wants to implement this best practice.

- *Too many changes in a short time.* An organization will rebel against too much change if it is clustered into a short time. The reason is that change is unsettling, especially when it involves a large part of people's job descriptions, so that nearly everything they do is altered. This can result in direct employee resistance to further change, sabotaging new projects, a work slowdown, or (quite likely) the departure of the most disgruntled workers. This problem is best solved by planning for lapses between implementation projects to let the employees settle down. The best way to accomplish this lag between changes without really slowing down the overall schedule of implementation is to shift projects around in the accounting department, so that no functional area is on the receiving end of two consecutive projects.

The primary reason for listing all of these causes of failure is not to discourage the reader from ever attempting a best practice installation. On the contrary, this allows one to prepare for and avoid all roadblocks on the path to ultimate implementation success.

THE IMPACT OF BEST PRACTICES ON EMPLOYEES

The impact of best practices on employees is significant. In the short run, there is an overwhelming feeling of discontent, because any kind of change makes employees nervous about what the impact will be on their jobs. Admittedly, a primary purpose of using best practices is to reduce the payroll expense in the accounting department, or at least to handle an increased workload with the same number of employees. Consequently, employees have a reason to be concerned.

There are several ways to deal with employee concerns. One is to create a standard policy of rolling all displaced employees onto a project team that will be used to implement even more best practices. This approach tends to attract the best employees to the project team, but also has the disadvantage of eventually displacing so many employees that there are too many people staffing the implementation team. The opposite approach is to be up-front about projected changes to employee jobs and to give a generous amount of both notice and severance pay to those people who will be displaced. Given the realities of paying extra money to departing employees and the need for well-staffed implementation teams, the recommended approach is somewhere in the middle—to retain a few of the best employees to run new projects, which reduces the amount of severance that must be paid out to departing employees.

The other problem, which is more of a long-run issue, is communications. Even after the initial round of lay-offs, there will be a continued emphasis on constantly improving the accounting department's processes. These changes cannot take place in a vacuum. Instead, the implementation team must carefully research the costs and benefits of each prospective best practice, discuss the issue with those employees who are most knowledgeable about how any changes will impact the organization as a whole, and rely to a considerable extent on their advice in regard to whether there should be any implementation at all, and if so, how the best practice should be modified to fit the organization's particular circumstances. Only by making the maximum use of employees' knowledge and by paying close attention to their opinions and fears can an implementation team continually succeed in installing a series of best practices.

Thus, communications is the key—both in handling employee departures in the short term, while the accounting department is reducing its staffing levels to match greater levels of efficiency, and in the long run, when employee cooperation is crucial to continued success.

SUMMARY

This chapter has given an overview of the situations in which best practices implementations are most likely to succeed, what factors are most important to the success or failure of an implementation, and how to successfully create and follow through on an implementation project. By following the recommendations made in this chapter, not only those regarding how to implement, but also those regarding what *not* to do, a manager will have a much higher chance of success. With this information in hand, one can now confidently peruse the remaining chapters, which are full of best practices. The reader will be able to select those practices having the best chance of a successful implementation, based on the specific circumstances pertaining to each manager, such as the funding, time available, and any obstacles, such as entrenched employees or a corporate intransigence pertaining to new projects.

Chapter 3

Accounts Payable Best Practices

The accounts payable function is the most labor-intensive of all the accounting functions and is therefore an excellent source of labor savings if the correct best practices can be implemented. The basic process in most companies is to receive three types of information from three sources—an invoice from the supplier, a purchase order from the purchasing department, and a proof of receipt from the receiving department. The accounts payable staff then matches all three documents to ensure that a prospective payment is authorized and that the underlying goods have been received, and then pays the bill. The process is labor-intensive partially because there is such a large amount of matching to do, but also because the three documents almost never match. Either the purchase order quantities or prices do not match what the supplier is charging, or else the amount received does not match the quantities on the other two documents. Because of these inaccuracies, the amount of labor required to issue a payment can be extraordinarily high.

The best practices in this chapter fall into a few main categories, most of them designed to reduce the matching work. One category attempts to consolidate the number of invoices arriving from suppliers, thereby shrinking the paperwork from this source—typical best practices in this area are using procurement cards and shrinking the number of suppliers. Another category tries to reduce or eliminate the number of receiving documents. Typical best practices in this area are substituting occasional audits for ongoing matching of receiving documents, as well as directly entering receipts into the computer system. Finally, another category reduces the number of purchase orders that must be matched. Typical best practices in this area include using blanket purchase orders and automating three-way matching. Other solutions to the matching problem involve going away from the traditional matching process entirely, by using payments based solely on proof of receipt. It is not possible to use all of these best practices together, since some are mutually exclusive—one must be careful in choosing the correct best practices.

Lastly, a number of best practices focus on the overall accounts payable process, attempting to either shrink or automate the number of steps required before a company issues payment to a supplier. Examples of best practices in this area include using a signature stamp and switching to wire transfers.

The number of best practices in the accounts payable area indicates that this function is ripe for improvements. However, some best practices require a large investment of money or time, as noted in the chart in the next section, so the person doing the improving should verify that resources are available before embarking on an implementation.

IMPLEMENTATION ISSUES FOR ACCOUNTS PAYABLE BEST PRACTICES

This section notes a number of issues related to the implementation of each best practice. The reader should peruse Exhibit 3.1 to ensure that the effort required to install a best practice is in agreement with the available constraints. For example, automating expense reporting is listed as being difficult to implement, requiring a long implementation period, and being moderately expensive (all because of the programming required). If the reader has a large staff of traveling employees who constantly submit expense reports, this may be a viable option, despite the projected implementation barriers. However, if only a few expense reports are submitted, then perhaps this is a best practice that should be passed over in favor of more practical opportunities.

Exhibit 3.1 lists all of the best practices in this chapter in alphabetical order. Next to the best practices are ratings for the ease of implementation. Any items requiring the support of multiple departments or which require extensive programming are considered to be difficult implementations. Conversely, projects that can be completed within a department (and especially with very few employees) are considered to be easy. The next column shows the duration of implementation, which can be an issue for anyone looking for quick results. Once again, any large programming projects are assumed to have long implementation durations. Finally, the last column estimates the cost to completely install each best practice—it is impossible to give a dollar estimate, since it will vary by the size of company, so the range used is from "cheap" to "expensive."

One should be careful to select only "quick hits" from Exhibit 3.1. Though these best practices are certainly worth the effort of installing, it is important to remember that some of the most difficult items on the list can have the largest payback. Accordingly, it is best to review the list in detail and assemble a set of best practices that provide for a combination of quick and easy victories, while also allowing for solid, long-term improvements that will impact the accounts payable function's levels of efficiency and effectiveness.

AUDIT EXPENSE REPORTS

A labor-intensive task for the accounts payable employees involves carefully reviewing every line item on employee expense reports, comparing everything to the company policy for allowable travel or entertainment expenses, and then con-

Exhibit 3.1.   Implementation Issues for Best Practices

Description	Ease of Implementation	Duration of Implementation	Cost of Implementation
Audit Expense Reports	Easy	Short	Cheap
Automate Expense Reporting	Difficult	Long	Medium
Automate Payments for Repetitive Invoicing	Easy	Short	Cheap
Automate Three-Way Matching	Difficult	Medium	Expensive
Automate Value-Added Tax Analysis	Moderate	Medium	Medium
Centralize the Accounts Payable Function	Difficult	Long	Expensive
Create Direct Purchase Interfaces to Suppliers	Moderate	Medium	Medium
Create On-Line Purchasing Catalog	Difficult	Long	Medium
Digitize Accounts Payable Documents	Moderate	Medium	Medium
Directly Enter Receipts into Computer	Moderate	Medium	Medium
Eliminate Manual Checks	Easy	Short	Cheap
Fax Transmission of Accounts Payable Documents	Easy	Short	Cheap
Have Suppliers Include Their Supplier Numbers on Invoices	Easy	Medium	Cheap
Internet-Based Monitoring of Credit Card Purchases	Moderate	Medium	Medium
Issue Standard Account Code List	Easy	Short	Cheap
Link Corporate Travel Policies to an Automated Expense Reporting System	Difficult	Long	Expensive
Link Supplier Requests to the Accounts Payable Database	Moderate	Medium	Expensive
Outsource the Accounts Payable Function	Difficult	Medium	Cheap
Pay Based on Receiving Approval Only	Moderate	Medium	Expensive
Receive Billings through Electronic Data Interchange	Difficult	Long	Expensive
Reduce Required Approvals	Easy	Short	Cheap
Request That Suppliers Enter All Invoices through a Web Site	Moderate	Medium	Medium

Exhibit 3.1. *(Continued)*

Description	Ease of Implementation	Duration of Implementation	Cost of Implementation
Shift Incoming Billings to an EDI Data-Entry Supplier	Short	Medium	Medium
Shrink the Supplier Base	Difficult	Long	Medium
Substitute Petty Cash for Checks	Easy	Short	Cheap
Substitute Wire Transfers for Checks	Moderate	Medium	Cheap
Transmit Expense Reports by E-Mail	Difficult	Medium	Expensive
Use Blanket Purchase Orders	Moderate	Medium	Cheap
Use Procurement Cards	Easy	Short	Cheap
Use Signature Stamp	Easy	Short	Cheap

tacting employees regarding inconsistencies prior to issuing a check. For a large company with many traveling employees, this can be an extraordinarily labor-intensive task. Furthermore, most employees create accurate expense reports, so the labor expended by the accounts payable staff is rarely equal to the cost savings all the review work generates. To make the situation more unbearable for employees, the expense reviews take so long to complete that there can be a serious delay before an employee receives payment for a check—especially if the expense report is rejected due to reporting failures by the employee, resulting in the expense report moving back and forth several times between the employee and the accounting department before it is paid. When there is so much document travel time, it is also common for the expense report to be "lost in the shuffle," meaning that the employee may have to create the expense report all over again and resubmit it. All of these factors result in an inefficient process in the accounting department and lots of angry employees who are waiting for reimbursement.

The solution to this problem is to replace a total review of all expense reports with an occasional audit. This approach involves taking a sample of many employees' expense reports every few months and comparing the reported amounts to the company travel and entertainment policy to see if there are any exceptions. If the exceptions are significant, it may be necessary to follow up with additional reviews of the expense reports of the same employees to investigate possible abuse. The audit usually results in a list of common expense reporting problems, as well as the names of employees who are abusing the expense reporting system. There are several solutions to ongoing expense reporting problems:

- *Employee education.* It may be necessary to periodically issue the company policy on travel and entertainment, with follow-up calls to specific abusers to reinforce the policy. This advance work keeps problems from showing up on expense reports.

*   *Flag employees for continual audits.* If some employees simply cannot create a correct expense report, they can be listed for ongoing audits to ensure that every report they create is reviewed for accuracy.

*   *Flag employees for complete reviews by the accounts payable staff.* Some employees may be so bad at issuing proper expense reports that their reports must be totally reviewed prior to reimbursement. These problem employees can be flagged during the audits.

The audit work is usually carried out by the internal audit department, rather than the accounts payable personnel, since the internal auditors are heavily experienced in this sort of review work.

When using this best practice, there can be a concern that employee reporting abuses will go unnoticed until an auditor finds a problem after the fact. This is true. However, when the audit staff selects expense reports for review, it should stratify the sample of reports so that there is a preponderance of very expensive expense reports in the sample, which means that any potentially exorbitant abuses will have a greater chance of being discovered. Though these discoveries will be after the fact, when employees have already been paid, the company can still seek reimbursement, especially if the employees are still on the payroll, so that adjustments can be taken from their paychecks. On the other hand, if employees have already left the company, any overpayments probably cannot be reimbursed.

In short, replacing a total review of all expense reports with an occasional audit can significantly reduce the workload of the accounts payable staff, though there is some risk that employee reporting abuses will result in large overpayments prior to discovery.

AUTOMATE EXPENSE REPORTING

One of the tasks of the accounts payable staff is to check carefully all of the expenses reported in an employee's expense report to ensure that all expenses are valid and have the correct supporting documentation. This can be a major task if there are many expense reports. This will be the case if a company is a large one or has a large proportion of personnel who travel, which is common if a company is in the consulting or sales fields. Luckily, some companies have found a way to get around all of this review work.

A best practice that nearly eliminates the expense report review work of the accounts payable staff is to create a "smart" computer program that walks an employee through the expense reporting process, flagging problem expenses as soon as they are entered, and requiring back-up receipts for only selected items. The system is highly customized, since the review rules will vary by company. For example, one company may have a policy of requiring backup for all meals, whereas another company may automatically hand out a *per diem* meals payment and will not care about meals receipts. Such variations in expense reporting policies will inevitably result in an automated expense reporting system that is closely tailored to each company's needs; such a system should probably be programmed in-house, which is a very expensive undertaking. Due to the high level of expense, this best practice will only pay for itself if it offsets a great deal of accounts payable work, so there should be a very large number of expense reports being submitted before anyone tries to implement the concept. These software packages are quite expensive. A package that is hosted on the Internet, with a dedicated line to the customer, can cost as little as $35,000, while a full-blown installation at a large company could cost as much as $500,000.

The logical flow of automated expense reporting is noted in the following bullet points. The key issue here is that all employees must have direct access to the program, so it can respond to their expense entries as soon as they make them. This requires on-line access by anyone who will use the program, which means that every user must not only have access to a computer or terminal, but probably also have a modem for dial-in access. One must consider these hardware costs as well as the previously noted software costs before implementing this best practice. The processing steps are as follows:

- The user accesses an on-line expense reporting form that is linked to the central expense reporting software and database.
- The user enters expenses by date and category.
- The software reviews all expenses as entered and flags those that are not allowable. It rejects these and notifies the user, along with an explanation.
- The software reviews all remaining expenses and decides which items require a back-up receipt.
- The user prints out a transmittal form that details all required receipts and that also contains a unique transmittal number that is linked to the expense report that was just entered into the computer.
- Upon completion by the user, the electronic expense report is routed by e-mail to the user's supervisor, which electronically approves or rejects the report. If rejected, the supervisor can note the problem on the expense report, which is then routed back to the user for re-submission.
- The user attaches all receipts to the transmittal form and mails it to the accounts payable department.
- When the accounts payable department receives the transmittal form and receipts, it verifies that all receipts are included and that the expense report has been approved by the supervisor, and then approves the entire package.

- Upon approval by the accounts payable staff, the expense report is immediately paid by wire transfer to the bank account of the user.
- The transmittal form and receipts are filed.

These detailed steps are shown in graphical form in Exhibit 3.2. Though there appear to be more steps in the automated process than there are in a traditional process, the extra steps are automatic or much simpler. The overall result is far less processing time, as well as a significant reduction in the time needed before an employee is paid.

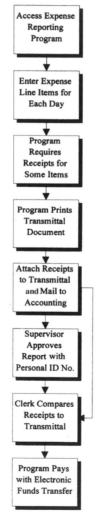

Exhibit 3.2.   The Automated Expense Reporting Process

The solution just noted is for an automated employee expense reporting system that is entirely custom programmed. However, many organizations do not process a sufficient number of employee expense reports to justify the cost of all the programming time that is required to create the system. For these organizations, a good alternative is to purchase one of the automated expense reporting software packages that are now available. These packages are entirely self-contained and do an effective job of processing employee expense reports, but they do not provide direct linkages to the rest of a company's accounting system. For this, a custom-designed interface module is still required. Examples of such packages are made by Captura Software (*www.captura.com*), Concur Technologies (*www.concur.com*), and Extensity, Inc. (*www.extensity.com*).

AUTOMATE PAYMENTS FOR REPETITIVE INVOICING

The typical company has a small proportion of invoices which arrive at regular intervals and are for the same amount, month after month. Examples of such payments are rent invoices or lease payments. These payments usually go through the typical accounts payable matching process, including searches for approval documents, before they are paid. However, it is possible to utilize their repetitive nature to create a more efficient sub-process within the accounts payable area.

The simple best practice that streamlines repetitive supplier invoices is to create a payment schedule to bypass the approval process and automatically issue a check in a pre-specified amount and on a pre-specified date. This can be done by creating a table of repetitive payments in the accounting computer system, but there is no reason why the programming expense cannot be avoided by just listing the payments on a piece of paper and posting it in the accounts payable area. In either case, there is no need to look for approvals, so there is less labor required of the accounts payable staff. However, there are two problems. First, the repetitive payment schedule must note the termination date of each payment, so that checks are not inadvertently issued after the final payment date. These payments can be time-consuming when the supplier returns them, if the company even notices the overpayment at all. Second, the repetitive payments may change from time to time, so the schedule must note both the dates when payment amounts change and the amounts of the changes. For example, rental payments frequently contain pre-set escalation clauses, which must be recognized by the repetitive payment schedule.

Automating repetitive payments that occur in the same amounts and on the same dates is a good way to remove the approval step from the accounts payable process, though this improvement typically only covers a small percentage of the total workload of the accounts payable staff.

AUTOMATE THREE-WAY MATCHING

The three-way matching process is a manual one at most companies; that is, a clerk matches a supplier invoice to a company purchase order and a receiving document in order to ensure that the correct quantities (and costs) ordered are the same ones received and billed. This is a painfully slow and inefficient process, given the large number of documents involved, as well as the startling number of exceptions that nearly always arise.

There are two ways to solve the problem. One is to dispense with three-way matching entirely, which requires considerable re-engineering of the accounts payable process, as well as retraining of the receiving staff and even of suppliers. It is described in detail in the "Pay Based on Receiving Approval Only" section. Though the most elegant solution, it also requires the most work to implement.

The second solution requires some software changes that may already be available in the existing software package with minimal changes to employee procedures, while still resulting in efficiency improvements (though not on the scale of the first solution). This best practice involves keeping the matching process in its current form, but using the computer system to perform the matching work. In order to automate three-way matching, all three documents must be entered into the computer system. This is easy for purchase orders, since most companies already enter purchase orders directly into the computer in order to track purchase orders through the manufacturing system. The next easiest document to enter is the receiving document, which can be either a bill of lading or a packing slip. To do so, there should be a computer terminal at the receiving dock that is linked to the main accounting database so that all information entered at the dock is centrally stored. Finally, the supplier invoice must be entered into the computer system—line by line. It is common enough to enter the supplier's invoice number and dollar amount into the computer system, but automated matching requires the complete entry of all line items, quantities, and costs into the system, which can be a considerable chore. Once this information is in the accounting database, the computer system automatically matches the three documents (usually using the purchase order number as the index), compares all line items, and presents a summary of the matched documents to the accounting staff, showing any variances between the matched documents. The accounting staff can then scan the information and decide if the variances require further analysis, or if they can be paid as is. This best practice automates an existing manual process without a large number of changes.

When deciding to use this best practice, it is useful to compare the savings from eliminating manual matching to the added cost of keying all the documents into the central database. There may also be an expense associated with installing the matching software in the system, though it is usually an integral part of the more advanced accounting packages. Low-end accounting packages do not normally contain the automated matching feature.

AUTOMATE VALUE-ADDED TAX ANALYSIS

Any company that does business on an international scale has probably been charged a value-added tax through its supplier invoices. A value-added tax (VAT) is incrementally levied on almost all business transactions in more than 130 countries. From the perspective of U.S. companies, the primary areas in which the VAT is used are the European Union and Canada. It is possible to file a reclamation application with those governments from whom products or services were purchased that contained the VAT tax, so that a refund can eventually be garnered. The trouble is that, for most companies, this involves a painstaking process of searching through all international receipts, identifying those that contain the VAT, summarizing them, and filing the appropriate claim form. Fortunately, there is now software available that identifies target expenses with a high probability of recoverable VAT charges, and summarizes the data for use in applying for refunds.

Corporate VAT Management Company sells a software product called auto VAT, which focuses on the recovery of foreign value-added taxes. It parses and analyzes in-house data sources to identify, summarize, and report on expenses for which VAT can be reclaimed. The company also sells process re-engineering services that focus on shifting and aggregating the flow of VAT-related data in a company toward those who need it for processing VAT refund applications. More information can be obtained about this best practice at the company's web site, *www.corporatevat.com.*

CENTRALIZE THE ACCOUNTS PAYABLE FUNCTION

A company with many subsidiaries or locations usually has a separate accounts payable function located in each facility. This can be inefficient for several reasons. First, the accounting staff at each location requires a supervisor, so the sum total of supervisors at all the locations can be substantial. Second, there can be problems with suppliers sending invoices to the wrong locations. This is a particular problem when the subsidiaries all have the same or similar names, since it is difficult for a supplier to figure out which location is the correct one to which a bill should be sent. The problem is exacerbated if a supplier ships to several company locations and then must issue a separate invoice to each location, since it is confusing to issue billings when not only the company names are identical, but also the goods shipped to all of them. Third, the many accounts payable departments all require training and auditing to ensure that they all process payments in the same manner. If a company does not do this, it is likely that discounts will not be taken or that payments will be made without proper authorization. Finally, there is a lack of control when the accounts payable function is widely distributed. Local management can interfere with the payable process to make payments to themselves or to entities they control, while still giving the appearance of good local controls. All of these problems can be either eliminated or mitigated by using a central accounts payable facility.

This facility does not have to be near any other company locations. It pays all supplier invoices, using a single computer system and a single accounting database, and operating under the control of a small, unified group of managers. It has multiple advantages. First, there are far fewer managers, since there is only one group of people to control. Second, there are no problems with supplier invoices and related information disappearing, because all invoices are sent to the one processing location. If a supplier incorrectly sends paperwork to the wrong location, all facilities know where it must be forwarded to, so the documents always arrive at the correct point (though they may take a roundabout route to get there). Third, all accounts payable activities can be easily monitored and corrected, since the auditing personnel only have to review one facility. Finally, there is better control over the process, since the accounts payable function is divorced from local control; there is no way for a local manager to influence payments. All of these advantages have a single result—lower cost, primarily through an overall reduction in the number of personnel. It has been proven many times that a single, centralized accounts payable function is considerably cheaper than a dispersed function.

Despite all these advantages, some companies balk at centralizing because of protests by local managers. They claim that some payments must be made locally, because some payments are cash-on-delivery, in cash, or require such short payment intervals that the central facility cannot respond in time. They are correct. However, this is such a small proportion of the bills at most facilities that a local plant can get by with a few checks per month, which are drawn on a separate bank account in which the company keeps a very small cash reserve. By limiting the size of local payments, a company can limit its exposure to any unwarranted local payments. By meeting local management demands partway, a company can still centralize the bulk of its payments while continuing to allow some local flexibility. This is a very good best practice to implement if a company has multiple locations.

CREATE DIRECT PURCHASE INTERFACES TO SUPPLIERS

A common practice when purchasing is to issue a separate purchase order to a supplier whenever a company wants to buy additional items. One solution to this problem is to consolidate all the purchase orders into a single large one that covers a long time period, which is called a blanket purchase order. This best practice is described elsewhere in this chapter in the "Use Blanket Purchase Orders" section. Though an excellent approach, it is sometimes possible to eliminate the purchase order entirely by using a direct purchase interface to a supplier.

This best practice involves creating a computer or fax linkage to a supplier, so that employees can order supplies directly from the supplier. By doing so, the purchasing staff does not have to become involved in any purchases and the accounts payable staff does not have to match any purchase orders to supplier invoices, thereby saving time in two departments. Though a clear efficiency improvement, this approach must be used with care because it eliminates some control over purchases. Accordingly, it is usually only used for the purchase of small-dollar items that are bought on a repetitive basis. Good examples of suppliers who might be used for this approach are office or maintenance supply vendors. In these cases, a company can create a standard form that only includes certain products. Employees are allowed to fill out the form with any quantity they want (within reason) and fax or mail it to the supplier, who uses it as authorization to send goods to the company. A more advanced version of this format is to set up the form on e-mail or on an electronic form directly linked to a supplier's customer orders database, for instant electronic transmission to the supplier. This later approach is faster and may allow a supplier to directly input an order into its computer system, eliminating keypunching errors. By using a pre-set form for ordering, a company can effectively curtail purchases to a few pre-selected items that do not require further control.

The accounting staff will know in advance that any billings from the suppliers to whom employees send orders directly do not require purchase order matching, and so it will expend less effort on paperwork prior to releasing a payment—just match the supplier's invoice to receiving documents to prove that the billed items were really received. Though this is not an approach that can be applied to all purchases, given the inherent lack of control, it can be used in a few cases, resulting in increased accounts payable processing efficiency.

CREATE ON-LINE PURCHASING CATALOG

The typical purchasing process involves the creation of a purchase requisition by whomever needs to buy something; this is used by the purchasing staff to search for the lowest price offered by a supplier, at which point a purchase order is issued to the appropriate supplier. The accounting department then has to match the receiving documentation to the purchase order and supplier invoice before generating a payment. This cumbersome process is being dismantled in many instances through the use of an on-line purchasing catalog.

When a user buys through an on-line catalog, he or she scrolls through a list of standard products that have been compiled by the purchasing staff, and selects the appropriate item. This automatically places an order on an electronic purchase order, on which is noted the number of the blanket purchase order that has already been negotiated with the supplier from whom the item is being bought. The computer system then sends either an electronic or paper-based order to the supplier, who fills the order. Upon receipt, the receiving department checks off the item in the on-line system, which flags the accounting system to make a payment to the supplier.

This on-line catalog approach has the exceptional benefit of enormously reducing the workload of the purchasing and accounting staffs, to the point where they are simply monitoring the flow of transactions, rather than directly creating them. It also channels the flow of purchases through a small set of pre-approved suppliers, so there is little chance that a new supplier will be foisted on the purchasing staff by an employee. However, there are also downsides to this approach. The required software is a major programming project that will be quite expensive to create. Also, the time required to set up blanket purchase orders with a number of suppliers will be very time consuming, requiring a long lead time to complete the project. Finally, it cannot be used for inventory purchases, since these are driven by production requirements rather than employee needs. Nonetheless, a large corporation can experience a dramatic decline in the amount of manual procurement transactions by implementing an on-line purchasing catalog.

DIGITIZE ACCOUNTS PAYABLE DOCUMENTS

When accounting files are sent to the archives at the end of the year, the portion taken up by the accounts payable documents usually exceeds that of all other documents combined. For some companies with voluminous accounts payable files, it is a major expense to remove all the paperwork, box it up and identify it, and ship it off to a warehouse, from which it must be recalled occasionally for various tasks. Digitizing the documents is a means of avoiding the expense of archiving.

Digitizing a document means that it is laid on a scanner which converts the document image into an electronic image stored in the computer database which can be recalled by anyone with access to the database. To digitize a document, there should be a high-speed scanner available that is linked to a computer network. Documents are fed into the scanner and assigned one or more index numbers or codes, so that it will be easy to recall the correct documents from storage. For example, a document can be indexed by its purchase order number, date, or supplier number. A combination of several indexes is the best approach, since one can still recall a document, even if one does not remember the first index number. The document images are usually stored on an optical disk since it can hold enormous amounts of storage space (and digitized documents take up a lot of computer storage space). There will probably be many optical disks to provide a sufficient amount of storage, so the disks are usually stored in a "jukebox," which gives the user access to all the data on all the storage disks. Users can then call up the images from any terminal that is linked to the network where the information is stored.

There are additional advantages to using digitization of documents. Besides the reduced archiving costs, it is also possible to nearly eliminate the time needed to access documents. With a traditional archiving system, older documents must be requested from a warehousing facility that may require several days to deliver. Even in-house documents may require several minutes to an hour to locate. If customer service is important and that service is linked to providing rapid access to data, then digitizing documents allows a company to instantly satisfy customer requests for documents by searching the computer files for them, no matter how old the documents may be. Another advantage to using digitization is that it avoids having to take out and replace files. Whenever someone removes a file and later returns it, there is a risk that the file will be misplaced. Every time a file is misplaced, it will be time consuming to find it again. By accessing documents through a computer network, there is no need to take out or replace the document—it is always sitting in the same storage location in the computer, and cannot be lost. Yet another advantage is that multiple users can access the same file at the same time. Since it is a digital image, there is no reason why the computer cannot potentially distribute a copy of the digital document to everyone who asks for it, even if they all do so at the same time. A final advantage to digitization is that it can be used to send an electronic file to a manager requesting an electronic approval before a payment will be made. This approach keeps the digital document from being lost during the approval process (a common enough problem when paper documents are used for approvals), while instantly moving a digital approval through the computer network, which also speeds up the transfer of approval information. In short, there are a variety of good reasons for digitizing accounts payable documents, besides the most common one of eliminating archiving costs.

Though this best practice may seem like an ideal way to avoid lost files, reduce archiving costs, shrink document search times, and allow for remote payment approvals, there is one problem with it that bars most small companies from installing it. The main issue is cost. The price of a high-speed scanner, computer, and optical storage jukebox can easily exceed the cost savings from all the advantages of this approach. The most cost-effective situations for digital storage are when there is either a very high storage cost that can be eliminated (especially common in high-rent accounting facilities where storage space is at a premium) or the volume of transactions is so high that there is no practical alternative to storing, filing, and moving all the paperwork. Consequently, digitizing accounts payable documents is normally limited to larger companies or those with expensive storage facilities.

DIRECTLY ENTER RECEIPTS INTO COMPUTER

One portion of the accounts payable matching process is to physically match some evidence of receipt, usually a packing slip or bill of lading, to a supplier invoice, thereby proving that the goods being paid for were actually received. The receiving documentation usually wends its way to the accounts payable staff over a period of several days, and may be lost on the way. Once it arrives, the information may not agree with the quantities being billed by the supplier. Consequently, the matching of receiving documentation tends to be either delayed, missing, or cause for extra reconciliation work by the accounting staff.

There are several solutions to the receiving paperwork problem. Two are outlined in other sections of this chapter. One is using fully automated matching of all accounts payable documents, which requires the input of all paperwork into the computer—receiving information, the supplier invoice, and the purchase order—so that the computer can automatically match the documents. This requires complicated software that not all computer systems may have available. It is described further in the "Automate Three-Way Matching" section. Another solution is to have the receiving staff approve purchase orders for payment based on what has just been received. This is a more radical approach that is extremely efficient, but which requires a complete redesign of the accounts payable process. This section describes a less monumental change that can usually be implemented by most accounting systems.

The alternative approach is to enter receipts directly into the computer system, rather than forwarding receiving documents to the accounting department for manual matching to the supplier invoice. This approach has the advantage of instant communication of receipts to the accounting staff, since an entry into the accounting database at the receiving dock will be instantly transmitted to the accounting staff. The accounting software can then compare received amounts to the purchase order (which is usually entered into the computer already). All that is left for the accounting staff to do at this point is to enter the purchase order number listed on the supplier's invoice into the computer to see what quantity has been received and how much has not yet been paid. By taking this approach, the bulk of the accounts payable matching process is eliminated.

Before implementing this best practice, there are a few issues to review. One is that the receiving staff must be properly trained in how to enter receipts into the computer. If they are not, receipts information will be inaccurate, probably resulting in the accounts payable staff going back to manual matching, since it is the only way to ensure that invoices are accurately paid. Another issue is ensuring that the existing accounting software allows the receiving personnel to enter receipts information. This is a standard feature on most accounting software packages. However, some software packages do not use the information once it is entered, so it is important to see if the software will match receipts to purchase orders, showing any variances that may arise. If these issues can be overcome, then it is reasonable for companies of any size or complexity to implement the direct entry of receiving information into the computer at the receiving dock.

ELIMINATE MANUAL CHECKS

The accounts payable process can be streamlined through the use of many best practices that are listed in this chapter; however, a common recurring problem is those payments that go around the entire pre-planned payable process. These are the inevitable payments that are sudden and unplanned, and which must be handled immediately. Examples are payments for pizza deliveries, flowers for bereaved employees, or cash on delivery payments. In all of these cases, the accounting staff must drop what it is doing, create a manual check, get it signed, and enter the information on the check into the computer system. To make matters worse, due to the rush basis of the payment, it is common for the accounting person to forget to make the entry into the computer system, which throws off the bank reconciliation work at the end of the month, which creates still more work to track down and fix the problem. In short, issuing manual checks significantly worsens the efficiency of the accounts payable staff.

One can use two methods to reduce the number of manual checks. The first method is to cut off the inflow of check requests, while the second is (paradoxically) to automate the cutting of manual checks. The first approach is a hard one, since it requires tallying the manual checks that were cut each month and following up with the check requesters to see if there might be a more orderly manner of making requests in the future, thereby allowing more checks to be issued through the normal accounts payable process. Unfortunately, this practice requires so much time communicating with the check requesters that the lost time will overtake the resulting time savings by the accounting staff from writing fewer manual checks. The second, and better, approach, is to pre-set a printer with check stock, so that anyone can request a check at any time and an accounting person can immediately sit down at a computer terminal, enter the check information, and have it print out at once. This approach has the unique benefit of avoiding any trouble with not re-entering information into the computer system, since it is being entered there in the first place (which avoids any future problems with the bank reconciliation). It tends to take slightly longer to create a check in this manner, but the overall time savings are greater.

If one adopts this approach, it is important to consider the cost of the printer. As it is generally a more expensive tractor feed model, this approach is probably not cost-effective unless there are a substantial number of manual checks being created.

FAX TRANSMISSION OF ACCOUNTS PAYABLE DOCUMENTS

A centralized accounts payable department may have some difficulty receiving documents from outlying locations or suppliers in time to take early payment discounts. For example, a supplier invoice may be sent to the wrong location, from which it must be mailed to the accounts payable location, or a bill of lading must be forwarded. In either case, the time delay involved may be so long that there is no way to take an early payment discount.

The best way to avoid this problem is to find an alternative method for transmitting documents (with all due respect to the Postal Service). Though one approach is to enter all information directly into the accounting database from any location (see the "Directly Enter Receipts into Computer" section earlier in this chapter), many companies cannot afford an enterprise-wide computer system that makes such an approach feasible. A simpler approach is to fax all documents to the accounts payable facility. To do so, there should be a separate fax machine that only handles incoming accounts payable documents; by setting aside a machine for this purpose, it guarantees that the fax machine will not be tied up by outgoing fax transmissions. Also, since it is only used for one purpose, it is unlikely that incoming faxes will be mistakenly taken to other departments. To make this system work even better, the accounting manager should look into getting a fax re-routing capability that sends incoming faxes to an electronic mailbox if the fax machine is busy, with transmission occurring as soon as the fax machine is available to receive new incoming transmissions. This service is inexpensive and ensures that all documents sent are received.

There are few disadvantages to this best practice. It requires a separate phone line for the fax machine, a fax re-routing capability that is nothing more than a voice mailbox for faxes, and a fax machine. None of these requirements are expensive. Also, there is a slight risk that some faxes will not be sent correctly or lost in transmission. In these cases, it may be possible to generate a custom report from the accounting software that lists all missing documents needed to process various accounts payable transactions. The accounting staff can use this report to fax out requests to subsidiaries for missing documents, so that anything that was lost on the first transmission attempt can be sent again. On the whole, this is an easy best practice to implement for those organizations that use centralized processing of accounts payable for multiple company locations.

HAVE SUPPLIERS INCLUDE THEIR SUPPLIER NUMBERS ON INVOICES

The typical vendor database includes listings for thousands of suppliers. Every time an invoice arrives from a supplier, the accounts payable staff must scroll through the list to determine the vendor code for each one. If there are similar names for different suppliers, or multiple locations for the same one, it is quite likely that the resulting check payments will go astray, leading to lots of extra time to sort through who should have been paid. This basic problem can be partially resolved by having suppliers include the supplier number, as created by the company's accounting system, on their invoices. The easiest way to do so is to mail out a change-of-address form to all suppliers, listing the same company address, but also noting as part of the address an "accounts payable code" that includes the supplier number. Suppliers will gladly add this line to the mailing address to which they send their invoices, since they think it is a routing code that will expedite payment to them (which, in a way, it will). Some follow-up may be necessary to ensure that all suppliers adopt this extra address line. Even if not all of the suppliers elect to make the change, there will still be an increase in efficiency caused by those that have done so.

There are two problems with this approach. One is that the change of address mailing cannot be a bulk mailing of the same letter, since each letter must include the supplier code that is unique to each recipient. This will call for a mail merge software application that can create a separate and unique letter for each recipient. The other problem is that new suppliers (i.e., those arriving *after* the bulk mailing) must be given a supplier code at the time they are first set up on the system. This may require a special phone call to the supplier's accounts payable department to ensure that the code is added to their address file, or else a periodic mailing to all new suppliers that specifies their supplier codes.

INTERNET-BASED MONITORING OF CREDIT CARD PURCHASES

Have you ever been surprised at the end of the month when an employee's company-issued credit card statement arrives in the mail, containing an inordinate number of charges? How about having to scramble to increase the credit limit on an employee's credit card? These problems can be avoided through the use of a credit card that is issued and monitored by a company that maintains a credit card monitoring operation on the Internet. For example, this service is provided by Pocketcard.com. For an annual fee of $20 and an additional charge of $.25 per transaction, this web site allows a company to issue Visa cards to its employees, as well as monitor their use of those cards as soon as they use them. In addition, the controller can adjust their maximum credit levels on the spot.

This service has the unique advantage of allowing for very tight monitoring of employee purchases. In reality, very few companies will want to call up this web site to check on employee purchases every day, but it can be of great use in cases where a company is suspicious of employee spending patterns, and needs to keep a close eye on specific individuals. The better feature is the ability to adjust spending levels with a few keystrokes, which is much more efficient than calling the credit card provider and pleading with a service representative for a credit limit increase. In addition, the use of credit cards allows a company to avoid the use of petty cash, since employees can use the cards to access cash from automated teller machines. The only downside to this best practice is the relatively large service fee that is charged for each employee transaction.

ISSUE STANDARD ACCOUNT CODE LIST

Accounts payable can be a difficult area in which to replace employees while still experiencing high levels of productivity. The problem is caused by the time a new person needs to learn the accounts to which invoices should be coded. Even when experienced accounts payable clerks are hired, they still must memorize the account codes, which will slow them down considerably. Even an experienced, long-term employee may occasionally misdirect a supplier invoice to the wrong account, so some solution is necessary to resolve the issue.

The easiest way to resolve the problem is to reduce the chart of accounts (which can be a very lengthy document) down to a single page of key accounts to which invoices are to be coded. Most invoices can be applied to a very small number of accounts, so this is usually a very viable option. When the shortened list is posted at each accounts payable clerk's desk, it becomes a simple reference tool for finding the correct account, which improves productivity while reducing the error rate.

A more sophisticated way to resolve the problem is to encode the accounting software with an account number for each supplier. Under this method, the clerk does not have to worry about the account to which anything should be coded because the computer already contains the information. However, there are two problems with this approach. One is that some software packages do not contain this information and expensive programming is necessary to install it. The second problem is that the account code may change, depending on what the supplier is billing. Given the trend toward supplier consolidation, it is increasingly likely that a company will go to one supplier for a wide range of products and services, so that several account codes may apply to a single supplier.

A simple list of approved account codes is an easy way to improve the productivity and reduce the error rate of the accounts payable staff, especially that of new employees.

LINK CORPORATE TRAVEL POLICIES TO AN AUTOMATED EXPENSE REPORTING SYSTEM

The typical set of travel policies used by a company is quite detailed—thou shalt not charge to the company the cost of movies, clothing, first-class upgrades, and so on. However, the overburdened accounts payable staff has little time to review expense reports for these items, much less to then create variance reports and send them out to the violating employees and their supervisors. An additional problem is that corporate travel policies change with some regularity, which makes it difficult for the accounts payable staff to even know which policies are still valid. A further problem arises when a company reimburses its employees based on the per diem rates listed in the Federal Travel Regulation. This document is used by the federal government to determine a reasonable cost of living at each of over a hundred cities throughout the country; given the frequency of change in these numbers (at least quarterly), it becomes very labor-intensive to determine what payments to make to employees. However, these problems can be eliminated by converting the travel policies into rules that can be used by a computer to automatically spot problems with expense reports that have been submitted through an automated expense reporting system.

For example, input from a corporate travel card into an automated expense reporting system can tell if an airfare is for a first-class seat, which may be prohibited by company travel policy. If the first-class purchase can be set up as a flagged field, then the computer system can automatically spot this issue and either note it on a report or (more proactively) send an e-mail to the appropriate person that makes note of the issue. Examples of other rule violations are to verify that the correct airline was used (since there may be a bulk-purchase agreement in place) and that restaurant bills were actually incurred during the period spanned by a business trip (rather than before or after, which would be suspicious). However, this sort of early-warning system can be quite expensive to create. There are no standard software packages that perform this task, so the programming staff must be called on to convert policies into rules that can be understood by the computer system, and then set up an interface between the rules database and the expense report database that will spot rule violations. In short, this can be an expensive option to install, and so should only be considered if there is a clear likelihood that there will be significant resulting cost savings.

LINK SUPPLIER REQUESTS TO THE ACCOUNTS PAYABLE DATABASE

A significant task for an accounts payable person, especially one working for a company that pays its bills late, is to answer payment queries from suppliers. They want to know when their invoices were paid, the amount of the payments, and the check numbers that were issued. For a company that is seriously delinquent in its payments, this can be a full-time job for the accounting staff, which is also a clear loss of productive time.

A recent innovation that largely eliminates verbal responses to suppliers is to have suppliers call a phone number that links them to a keypad-activated inquiry system that will answer their most common questions. For example, they can enter the company's purchase order number, their invoice number, or the supplier's name; the system will then respond with the specific payments made, the date on which the check was cut, and the check number. The system can even be extended to list the date on which payments are scheduled to be made.

However, there are some issues to consider before installing an automated supplier response system. One issue is that this is a very recent innovation and most suppliers will not be used to it—they want to talk to a person and will deluge the company's operator with this opinion. To quell this type of response, the system should include an option to exit the automated system and contact a person. This allows the more technologically versed suppliers to use the automated system, while other users can still talk to a person. This option is also necessary for those cases where there are unusual circumstances. For example, a company may not be paying due to a lack of receiving documentation, or because the quantity billed was incorrect; it is better to discuss these problems with a person instead of a computer, since special actions may need to be taken to resolve the situation. The other problem is the cost of the installation. It requires an interface computer that links to the main accounting computer system, as well as modem access and software to translate supplier requests into inquiries that the accounting database can answer. These costs can be considerable, especially when there are expected to be many callers and many requests for information. The price range typically starts at $20,000 for the smallest installations and can be many times higher for large systems. Nonetheless, this is a good approach for companies that feel they can bring about a major efficiency improvement by routing suppliers straight to the accounts payable database for information.

An alternative to having suppliers access accounts payable information through a phone connection is to do so through an Internet site. This approach is somewhat more flexible than a voice-activated system that is generally limited to a few simple status messages. Instead, a web page can itemize the exact status of each payable item, assign a code to it that explains the reasons for any delays, and notes the name of the contact person in the accounts payable department who is responsible for processing the supplier invoice. It can also list any missing information that is delaying payment, such as a purchase order number or bank account number for the supplier, which can be entered by the supplier directly into the web site, and which will be automatically loaded into the accounting database to assist in the completion of processing. The web page may even list the name of the person who is responsible for approving the invoice, as well as this person's contact information. A company may not want to add this last piece of information, since it can greatly increase the volume of phone calls to these people, who will in turn bother the accounts payable staff about payment—something that it is trying to avoid through the use of this web site.

OUTSOURCE THE ACCOUNTS PAYABLE FUNCTION

Many controllers do not want to waste time managing such a mundane function as accounts payable. It does not directly contribute to the mission of any company, nor does it impact customer service. In short, it is a baseline clerical function that merely takes up management time with no particular payback. By offloading this function to a supplier who specializes in accounts payable processing, a controller can reduce the management time devoted to this functional area and allocate more time to other more profitable company functions.

Besides reduced management time, it can also be less expensive to outsource to a qualified supplier. A well-run supplier has an excellent knowledge of accounts payable best practices and uses that knowledge to drastically cut the processing effort needed. This is an especially attractive option for those companies that are in difficult financial circumstances, who would prefer to pay just a per-transaction fee, rather than an entire staff. This essentially converts a large fixed cost to a variable cost that will not be incurred if there are no transactions to process.

Outsourcing accounts payable usually means that the entire company staff devoted to this work will be shifted to the supplier who is taking over the work, though it is also possible that the supplier will not need these people, or will "cherry-pick" only the most qualified. If the latter is the case, then the controller should meet with the staff to honestly appraise their future prospects with the supplier, or to provide outplacement counseling. The supplier should also be available at these meetings to answer any employee questions, as well as to enroll employees in supplier benefit plans and to convert them to the supplier's payroll system.

Besides the staff conversion, the controller must also determine how to manage the supplier. This is not a case of handing the work to the supplier and then paying the supplier's bills—on the contrary, some oversight will always be necessary to handle any problems that may arise, such as complaints from suppliers who are not being paid, verifications that discounts are being taken, and approvals of all payments prior to payment. These activities are most commonly handled at the level of an assistant controller, though the controller may manage the supplier directly if the transaction volume is minimal. In all cases, some continuing oversight by the remaining accounting staff is necessary.

One should also consider the degree and form of ongoing interaction with the supplier necessary to ensure that accounts payable are processed correctly. For example, if a company has a fully integrated accounting and manufacturing software package, it will be impossible for the supplier to process accounts payable on its own accounting software, because these transactions must be completed on the company's software package. The best way to resolve this problem is to give the supplier remote access to the company's computer system, so that it can process accounts payable as though it were an on-site service. However, this arrangement will require an extra expenditure to train the supplier's employees in how to use the system. Another option is to have the supplier perform only the most mundane accounts payable tasks, such as matching documents, and leave any data entry or check-cutting work to the in-house staff. This option eliminates the worst drudge work from the function, while still allowing for greater control over it. Yet another variation is to allow the supplier to cut checks in payment of accounts payable, though this loses some company control over cash flows. The best way to resolve the problem is to have company management approve check runs before they are printed and mailed. Clearly, there are a variety of approaches to the extent to which the accounts payable function can be outsourced.

PAY BASED ON RECEIVING APPROVAL ONLY

The accounts payable process is one of the most convoluted of all the processes that a company can adopt, irrespective of the department. First, it requires the collection of information from multiple departments—purchase orders from the purchasing department, invoices from suppliers, and receiving documents from the receiving department. The process then involves matching these documents, which almost always contain exceptions, and then tracking down someone either to approve exceptions or at least to sign the checks, which must then be mailed to suppliers. The key to success in this area is to thoroughly re-engineer the entire process by eliminating the paperwork, the multiple sources of information, and the additional approvals. The only best practice that truly addresses the underlying problems of the accounts payable process is paying based on receipt.

To pay based on receipt, one must first do away with the concept of having an accounts payable staff that performs the traditional matching process. Instead, the receiving staff checks to see if there is a purchase order at the time of receipt. If there is, the computer system automatically pays the supplier. Sounds simple? It is not. A company must have several features installed before the concept will function properly. The main issue is having a computer terminal at the receiving dock. When a supplier shipment arrives, a receiving person takes the purchase order number and quantity received from the shipping documentation and punches it into the computer. The computer system will check against an on-line database of open purchase orders to see if the shipment was authorized. If so, the system will automatically schedule a payment to the supplier based on the purchase order price, which can be sent by wire transfer. If the purchase order number is not in the database, or if there is no purchase order number at all, the shipment is rejected at the receiving dock. Note that the accounts payable staff takes no part whatsoever in this process—everything has been shifted to a simple step at the receiving location. The process is shown graphically in Exhibit 3.3.

Before laying off the entire accounts payable staff and acquiring such a system, there are several problems to overcome. They are as follows:

- *Train suppliers.* Every supplier who sends anything to a company must be trained to include the purchase order number, the company's part number, and the quantity shipped on the shipping documentation, so this information can be punched into the computer at the receiving location. The information can be encoded as bar codes to make the data-entry task easier for the receiving employees. Training a supplier may be difficult, especially if the company only purchases a small quantity of goods from the supplier. To make it worthwhile for the supplier to go to this extra effort, it may be necessary to concentrate purchases with a smaller number of suppliers to give each one a significant volume of orders.

- *Alter the accounting system.* The traditional accounting software is not designed to allow approvals at the receiving dock. Accordingly, a company will have to reprogram the system to allow the re-engineered process to be performed. This can be an exceptionally major undertaking, especially if the software is constantly being upgraded by the supplier—every upgrade will wipe out any custom programming that the company may have created.

- *Prepare for miscellaneous payments.* The accounts payable department will not really go away because there will always be stray supplier invoices of various kinds arriving for payment that cannot possibly go through the receiving dock, such as subscription payments, utility bills, and repair invoices. Accordingly, the old payments system must still be maintained, though at a greatly reduced level, to handle these items.

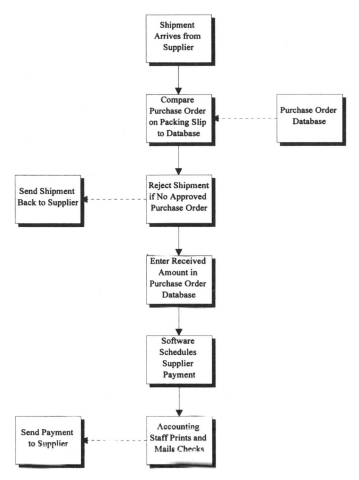

Exhibit 3.3. The Process Flow for Payment Based on Receiving Approval

- *Pay without a supplier invoice.* One of the key aspects of the re-engineered process is paying based on the information in the purchase order, rather than the information in the supplier's invoice. To do so, one must have a database of all the tax rates that every supplier would charge, so that the company's computer system can automatically include these taxes in the invoice payments. Also, there will sometimes be discrepancies between the purchase order prices and quantities paid, versus those expected by suppliers, so an accounts payable staff must be kept on hand to correspond with suppliers to reconcile these issues.

The above bullet points reveal that there are a wide array of problems that must first be overcome before the dramatic improvements of this new process can be realized. However, for a company that has a large accounts payable staff, this can be a highly rewarding system to install, for the savings realized can be the elimination of the majority of the accounts payable department.

RECEIVE BILLINGS THROUGH ELECTRONIC DATA INTERCHANGE

Many of the larger companies, especially those in the retailing industry, have been using electronic data interchange (EDI) for some time. This section describes what EDI is, how it works, why more companies should use it, and why so many do not.

EDI involves the transfer of electronic documents between companies. These documents are sent in strictly defined formats, of which there are over a hundred, one for each type of standard company transaction, including a supplier billing. These formats tend to be very large and complex because they are designed for use by multiple industries; most companies only need to fill out a small portion of each EDI message. Once completed, an EDI message is transmitted to the recipient. This can be done directly, but it usually goes to a third-party provider who maintains a mainframe computer that receives messages from a number of subscribing companies. The message recipient dials into its electronic mailbox at the third-party's mainframe (usually several times a day) to pick up any EDI messages. The recipient then enters each EDI message into its own system for further processing. The reader may notice that a company could achieve the same rapid transfer of information by sending a fax with the same information. This is true, but if properly installed, EDI allows for a greater degree of automation by linking directly into a company's computer system. For example, a paper-based fax must be re-keyed into the recipient's computer system, whereas an EDI message is in a standardized electronic format and so can be run through an automatic conversion program that enters the data into the recipient's computer system with no manual data-entry work at all. This feature gives EDI a distinct advantage over a fax transmission.

Larger companies use EDI most frequently because it allows them to automatically process large quantities of transactions with no manual data-entry work, which can be important when there are hundreds of thousands of transactions flowing through the system. When data is entered by hand, there is a potential for errors in the keypunching, which probably means that there will be hundreds or thousands of man-made errors to correct in these larger companies, just given the volumes of data that must be entered. Thus, EDI allows them to not only avoid the expense of data entry, but also the expense of tracking down and fixing data-entry errors.

If EDI makes a company so efficient, why are only the largest companies using it? The answer is simple—it is expensive to implement and only the largest transaction volumes will offset the cost of the initial setup. For example, if a company wants to receive all of its accounts payable billings by EDI, it must first contact each supplier and persuade it to send EDI transmissions, set up procedures between the two companies for doing so, and then test the system before "going live." In addition, the true labor savings will only be realized if the incoming EDI messages are automatically entered into the recipient's computer system, which calls for the customized programming of an automated interface between the EDI system and the recipient's computer system—this can be an expensive undertaking. Most suppliers will not want to participate in this system unless there are significant transaction volumes between them and the company—why go to the trouble for a small customer? In short, EDI is not catching on in smaller companies because of the expense and effort of installing the system, plus the difficulty of forcing suppliers to participate. Though larger companies may convince their direct trading partners to use EDI, this best practice will only spread through the ranks of smaller companies with the greatest difficulty.

REDUCE REQUIRED APPROVALS

The accounts payable process is typically a long one. Part of the problem is that many accounting systems require a manager's signature (or those of several managers!) on a supplier invoice before it can be paid. Though it is reasonable to have such a requirement if there is no purchase order for the invoice, many systems require the signature even if there is already a purchase order (which is, in effect, a form of prior approval). Also most accounting systems require a manager's signature on unapproved invoices, no matter how small the invoice may be. The result of these common approval procedures is that the accounts payable staff delivers invoices to managers for signatures and then waits until the documents are returned before proceeding further with the payment process. If the manager is not available to sign an invoice, then it sits; if the manager loses the invoice (a common occurrence), the invoice is never paid, resulting in an angry supplier who must send a fresh copy of the invoice for a second pass through the dangerous shoals of the company's approval process. This is a clearly inefficient process, both lengthy and likely to annoy suppliers. What can be done?

A superb best practice for any company to implement is to limit approvals to a single event or document and, wherever possible, to limit this approval to a period prior to the receipt of the supplier invoice. For example, an authorized signature on a purchase order should be sufficient overall approval to pay an invoice. After all, if the signature was good enough to authorize the initial purchase of the item or service, shouldn't the same signature be sufficient approval for the payment of the supplier's bill? In addition, by shifting the approval to the purchase order, we avoid having the accounts payable staff track down someone after the supplier's invoice has been received, which effectively chops time from the overall accounts payable process. Another variation is to use a signature on the purchase requisition, which comes before the purchase order. As long as either document is signed by an authorized person and sent to the accounts payable staff in advance, it does not matter which document is used as authorization. The key is to use a single authorization, before the supplier sends an invoice.

One reason why so many companies require multiple approvals, both at the time of purchasing and at the time of payment, is that they do not have a sufficient degree of control over the authorization process. For example, there may not be any real check of authorization signatures when purchase requisitions are converted into purchase orders, nor might there be any required signature when purchase orders are issued to suppliers. In addition, the signature stamp used to sign checks may not be properly controlled. In all these cases, if there were tight control over the authorization used, there would only be a need for a single authorization. For example, there should be an audit of all purchase orders to ensure that every one of them has been signed, that every signature is by an authorized person, and that the person signing is authorized to purchase what was ordered. This level of control requires continual internal audits to ensure that the control point is working, as well as continual follow-up and training of employees so that they know precisely how the control system is supposed to work. Only by instituting this degree of control over authorizations can a company reduce the number of approvals to a minimum.

Using tight control over approvals that are given early in the accounts payable process results in a shorter processing cycle and fewer delays.

REQUEST THAT SUPPLIERS ENTER ALL INVOICES THROUGH A WEB SITE

A company may be experiencing some difficulty in persuading its suppliers to switch over to the transmission of invoices by EDI, which would allow it to automatically process all incoming invoices without any data re-keying. A typical complaint when this request is made is that special EDI software must be purchased and stored in a separate computer, while someone must be trained, not only in how to use the software, but also in how to re-format the invoicing data into the format used by the EDI transaction. This problem can be partially avoided by having suppliers access a web site where they can conduct the data entry.

By having suppliers enter data into a web site instead of through an EDI transaction, they can avoid the need for any special software that is stored on an in-house computer. A web site merely requires Internet access, which is commonly available through most computers. Once the data has been entered at the web site, a company can shift the data to an automated EDI transaction processing program that will convert the data into an EDI format and transmit it to the company's accounting system. Thus, suppliers can use either EDI or web-based data entry to send invoices to a company, which will process them both in EDI format.

There are some costs associated with this best practice. One is that the company may have to use special discounts or early payments to convince suppliers to use the web site, rather than simply mailing in their invoices. Also, the web site must be constructed and maintained, while other software must be created that converts the incoming transactions into EDI format and then ports the resulting data to the accounting system for further processing. Consequently, this can be a relatively expensive option to implement, and so may only be useful for those organizations experiencing a large volume of transactions.

SHIFT INCOMING BILLINGS TO AN EDI DATA-ENTRY SUPPLIER

A company may have the best intentions for improving its accounts payable process, but cannot shift to a fully automated system because its suppliers refuse to send invoices in EDI format. Consequently, the company has no opportunity to automatically shift incoming EDI messages into the accounts payable system, automatically process them, and automatically send out an automated clearinghouse payment. In short, the company is stuck with a manual data entry front end to the accounts payable process. This is a particular problem when a company is so small that its suppliers see no reason to shift over to EDI transactions just for its benefit. This issue can be surmounted by sending the incoming invoices to an EDI supplier that is willing to keypunch the invoices into an EDI format.

To do so, a company can either have suppliers mail all invoices to a lockbox that is accessed by the EDI supplier, or else it can re-mail the invoices to the EDI supplier. This supplier (really just a "body shop" that keypunches data) will re-enter the invoice information into an EDI format and transmit it to the company, which can then process the invoices in a highly automated manner. Though this may seem like an expensive way to handle invoice processing, it will allow an accounts payable department to eliminate virtually all of its data entry positions. The disadvantages to this approach are a slight increase in costs over what it would take to process the invoices in-house, as well as a time delay while the invoices are re-mailed to the supplier (which may have an impact on the timing of payments back to suppliers).

SHRINK THE SUPPLIER BASE

Part of the job of the accounts payable staff is maintaining a complete and accurate database of suppliers, which typically includes address and payment information. If data is entered incorrectly, the accounting staff is usually notified by a supplier that has not received a payment (because it was sent to the wrong address), has been paid the wrong amount (because of an incorrect early payment discount rate), or has been paid at the wrong time (because of an incorrect due date). This type of problem is inevitable in even the best-run company and will require some time to research and fix. However, the problem is greatly exacerbated in a company that has many suppliers, because there are so many chances for the supplier information to be incorrect. Another problem with having many suppliers is that there is typically little control over adding new suppliers (after all, that is how there came to be so many suppliers in the first place!). The accounting staff must deal constantly with adding new data to the supplier database, consolidating supplier records that have been entered multiple times, and (especially) making a multitude of small payments to a plethora of suppliers. Wouldn't it be so much easier if there were just fewer suppliers?

This is a best practice—reducing the number of suppliers. It is much easier to maintain accurate data in a relatively small number of supplier records, while there are few new suppliers to add to the database. In addition, the volume of purchases from the smaller number of suppliers tends to be larger, so there are typically fewer, larger invoices that can be keypunched into the accounting database more easily and paid with fewer, larger checks. Essentially, shrinking the supplier database reduces a variety of data-entry tasks.

Unfortunately, shrinking the number of suppliers is not easy. The first problem is that the accounting staff must convince the purchasing staff to adopt a supplier reduction strategy, which the purchasing staff may not be so eager to pursue, especially if it prefers the strategy of sourcing parts from multiple suppliers. In addition, company employees may be in the habit of buying from any supplier they want, which can require a considerable amount of re-training before they are willing to buy from a much shorter list of approved suppliers. The effort required to reduce the number of suppliers is frequently far in excess of the productivity gains realized by the accounts payable staff, so most controllers do not pursue this best practice unless there is already either an active supplier reduction campaign in place in the company, or else the head of the purchasing department appears to be amenable to the idea. Even then, a supplier reduction strategy does not take place overnight. On the contrary, it can take years to effect a massive cutback in the supplier base. Accordingly, this strategy should only be adopted when there is multi-departmental support for the idea as well as a long implementation timeline.

SUBSTITUTE PETTY CASH FOR CHECKS

Cutting and issuing a check is a lengthy, multi-step process. One must match a supplier invoice to a purchase order and receiving document, enter the invoice into the computer, wait for the due date, and then print the check, have it signed, and mail it to the supplier. For small payments where the supplier shows up at the company offices, there is a simpler way.

It is much easier to pay a supplier from the petty cash box. This approach eliminates the entire process needed to cut a check. However, there are some severe limitations on the use of petty cash that limit its effectiveness to a small number of situations. First, since the intention is to bypass the usual checks and balances of the accounts payable process, it must only apply to those payments that are so small that no one cares if the system is bypassed. In most companies, the amount that can be paid with minimal controls is usually below $100. For amounts larger than this, the usual check paying process is probably better, since it requires tighter control over payment approvals. Another problem is that it makes little sense to stuff money into an envelope and mail it to the supplier, since the money can be intercepted and removed at many points along the way, resulting in no payment. Consequently, it is better to hand the money directly to a supplier representative, who should be on the company premises to sign for the money. By limiting the use of petty cash to small amounts and on-site payments, we have effectively reduced this option to a small percentage of the total amount that most companies pay out. Nonetheless, it is a simple and effective approach that will result in some decrease in the volume of transactions flowing through the typical accounts payable system.

Some control is needed if petty cash is used as a regular form of payment. One key item is to require a signed receipt for all moneys handed out, preferably with an accompanying invoice from the supplier. This provides sufficient evidence of why an expense was incurred and covers the company if the supplier claims that it was never paid. Also, there should be a monthly reconciliation of the petty-cash box to ensure that all expenditures and replenishments are accounted for. It is particularly important when there is a high volume of payments going out of the petty-cash box, since there is a potential for thousands of dollars to disappear over time if there is not a constant reconciliation. Finally, given the high volume of usage, it is important to give control of the petty-cash box to a single person who will accept responsibility for the money. When accompanied by storage in a locked container, these measures present an effective set of controls over continual petty-cash disbursements.

SUBSTITUTE WIRE TRANSFERS FOR CHECKS

It is possible to save some of the labor associated with check payments by converting to wire transfers, though one must be aware of the changes in costs that will result.

Paying with a wire transfer involves entering each supplier's identifying bank number and account number into a computer database, which the accounting software then uses to compile a listing of wire transfer payments instead of check payments. It is common for someone to review this list of wire transfers before it is sent to a bank (in case there are obvious errors in the amounts to be paid), at which point the information is electronically transmitted to a bank, which immediately deducts the money from the company's bank account and transfers it to the accounts of the recipients. This process completely avoids all of the check-cutting steps outlined at the beginning of this chapter.

However, there are other steps and costs associated with using wire transfers that one must be aware of before using them. First, it is no longer possible to take advantage of the mail float that goes with check payments (the time interval before the recipient actually receives the check and cashes it), so a company will lose some interest income. This problem can be avoided by delaying the wire transfer payments to match the payment delay associated with mail float. Another issue is the cost of each wire transfer. A company will be charged a fee by its bank for every wire transfer it handles. The fee may go down if there is a large amount of wire transfer volume, but the cost will still probably exceed the mailing cost of sending a supplier a check. However, if a company maintains a large cash balance at the bank, it is possible that the bank will reduce or eliminate these costs in exchange for keeping the cash invested at the bank. The last problem with wire transfers is the one that keeps many companies from using this best practice—the wire transfer does not contain any information about what is being paid, so a company must still mail a remittance advice that lists each item. This means that a company must still mail something to the supplier, so it loses any prospect of savings in this area. However, with the advent of the Internet, it is possible for a company to send remittance advises to its suppliers by e-mail, avoiding having to mail this information. Linking an e-mail remittance advice to a wire transfer is not yet available on any accounting software packages, so a company would have to customize its accounting software with special programming to make this happen. Consequently, one must factor in the cost of the programming when deciding to use e-mail transmissions.

Given the large number of issues surrounding the use of wire transfers, it is clear that a company considering its use should carefully weigh all the costs and benefits before implementing this best practice. Because of the large number of issues associated with it, usually only larger companies with lots of check volume are tempted to install it.

TRANSMIT EXPENSE REPORTS BY E-MAIL

In an earlier section in this chapter, "Automate Expense Reporting," there was a discussion of how a company can install an automated system to walk users through the process of submitting an expense report. Though it is so automated that there is only a minimal need for any human intervention, it is also a system that is usually created with custom programming. This is very expensive and probably not worth the effort for companies without a sufficient volume of expense reporting. This section describes a "poor man's automated expense report" for those companies that cannot afford a more sophisticated system.

The "poor man's approach" involves using the existing e-mail system to transmit expense reports to the accounts payable department. This approach does not automatically route the expense report to a supervisor for electronic approval—either the person submitting the report or the accounts payable staff must do this. Also, most e-mail systems do not allow for electronic approvals, so this step may not be possible, in which case the only options are to route a paper copy to a supervisor (which defeats the purpose of using e-mail) or to avoid the approval step and just audit reports after the fact to ensure that they would have been approved. Also, an e-mail transmission does not allow for an interactive review of all expenses as they are entered, so the electronic form being used to create the expense report should contain a text section that describes all travel and entertainment expense reporting rules. Each person submitting an expense report must read these rules to determine which expenses to report and which back-up materials to submit. In addition, each person transmitting an expense report must mail in all receipts that go with the expense report, without the transmittal document that would be used with a more advanced expense reporting system. Finally, payments are made by check, with entries being made manually into the accounts payable system, rather than automatically with wire transfers. Thus, this simplified system may not allow for supervisory approval, does not interactively review all expenses, does not issue a transmittal document, and does not automatically issue a payment. On the other hand, it is much easier and cheaper to implement than a full-blown automated expense-reporting system.

As an example of how this simplified reporting system works, the accounts payable department periodically issues a spreadsheet to all employees (by e-mail), set up in an expense-reporting format. It shows where expenses are to be listed, and contains the key reporting rules within the body of the spreadsheet. When a user completes the spreadsheet with actual data, the file is attached to an e-mail addressed to the accounts payable department. All receipts are sent to the department by mail, along with a paper copy of the expense report. The accounting staff receives the e-mail, prints out the expense report, and then enters the data immediately into the accounts payable database for payment. The staff has the option of either issuing payment right away or waiting until the receipts are received. Later, the internal auditing staff can review a selection of expense reports to see if all reporting rules were followed.

This approach does not allow for as much control over expense reporting as a fully interactive system, but it does allow most companies to quickly install a partially automated system that improves the efficiency of the accounts payable staff—usually in just a few days or weeks.

USE BLANKET PURCHASE ORDERS

One of the most time-consuming parts of the accounts payable process is matching supplier invoices to purchase orders to ensure that all payments have been authorized. This task is a difficult one if there are a multitude of supplier purchase orders. In the typical company, there are hundreds if not thousands of open purchase orders at any time; it is standard practice to issue a separate purchase order every time an item is purchased. However, by shrinking the number of purchase orders to be matched, we can reduce the workload of the accounts payable staff.

A best practice that vastly reduces the number of purchase orders is blanket purchase orders. These are long-term purchase orders, typically extending for a one-year time period, which cover all of the expected purchases from a supplier for that entire time period. By using blanket purchase orders, the accounts payable staff can continually match to the same purchase orders for the entire year, reducing the number of purchase orders that must be kept on hand.

This best practice is a simple one to implement from the accounting perspective. There is no change in the way the accounting staff stores or matches blanket purchase orders. It will continue to staple the purchase order to the invoice and move it on for further processing. The only difference is that because the amounts on the blanket purchase orders are so large, they will hardly ever be equaled by a single supplier delivery. The accounting clerk must instead make a facsimile of each purchase order and staple the copy to the supplier invoice. This is a minor change and will be easily accepted by the accounting staff when they see that, in exchange, the volume of purchase orders has dropped significantly.

Though this seems like a best practice that should be implemented at once due to the obvious benefits, one should consider the problem of working with an extra department to ensure that the new system works. The problem with a blanket purchase order is that it cannot be implemented without the cooperation of the purchasing staff and the suppliers. Since there are many more entities involved in this implementation, it is no surprise that relatively few companies have implemented this best practice. To ensure that blanket purchase orders are used, one must discuss the benefits of the system with the purchasing manager (who will see a significant decline in paperwork as a result of using blanket purchase orders). The purchasing manager *must* buy into the concept because this is the person who must in turn sell the concept to suppliers. Another problem is that a typical company has so many suppliers that it takes a substantial amount of time to implement blanket purchase order agreements with all of them. Instead, it is frequently easier to either pare down the number of suppliers or just implement blanket purchase orders with the 20 percent of suppliers with whom a company typically does 80 percent of its business. Either approach will allow a company to enter into blanket purchase orders with suppliers that will substantially reduce the total number of blanket purchase orders.

USE PROCUREMENT CARDS

Consider the number of work steps required to process a payment to a supplier: receiving paperwork, sorting and matching it, entering data into a computer, routing invoices through the organization for approvals, expediting those invoices that have early-payment discounts, creating month-end accruals, setting up files on new suppliers in the computer and the filing system, processing checks, obtaining check signatures, mailing payments, and filing away check copies. Now consider how many purchases are so small that the cost of all these activities exceeds the cost of the purchase. In many instances, one-quarter or more of all payment transactions fall into this category.

The answer to this problem is not to find a more efficient way to process the supplier invoices, but to change the way in which these items or services are purchased. Instead of using a purchase order or check to purchase something, one should instead use a procurement card. A procurement card, also known as a purchasing card, is simply a credit card that has a few extra features. The card is issued to those people who make frequent purchases, with instructions to keep on making the same purchases, but to do so with the card. This eliminates the multitude of supplier invoices by consolidating them all into a single monthly credit card statement.

As there is always a risk of having a user purchase extraneous items with a credit card, including cash advances or excessively expensive purchases, the procurement card adds a few features to control precisely what is purchased. For example, it can have a limitation on the total daily amount purchased, the total amount purchased per transaction, or the total purchased per month. It may also limit purchases to a specific store, or to only those stores that fall into a specific Std Industry Code (SIC code) category, such as a plumbing supply store and nothing else. These built-in controls effectively reduce the risk that procurement cards will be misused.

Once the credit card statement arrives, it may be too jumbled, with hundreds of purchases, to determine the expense accounts to which all the items are to be charged. To help matters, a company can specify how the credit card statement is to be sorted by the credit card processing company; it can list expenses by the location of each purchase, by SIC code, or by dollar amount, as well as by date. It is even possible to receive an electronic transmission of the credit card statement so that a company can do its own sorting of expenses. The purchasing limitations and expense statement changes are the key differences between a regular credit card and a procurement card.

Another feature provided by those entities that offer procurement cards is "Level II" data; this includes a supplier's minority supplier status, incorporated status, and its tax identification number. Another option to look into when reviewing the procurement card option is the existence of "Level III" reporting, which includes such line-item details as quantities, product codes, product descriptions, and freight and duty costs—in short, the bulk of the information needed to maintain a detailed knowledge of exactly what is being bought with a company's procurement cards. Most major national suppliers of credit cards can supply Level II or Level III data.

The American Express Corporate Card has now expanded the range of uses to which its procurement can be put by allowing for the inclusion of many recurring business expenses, such as long-distance phone bills, Internet services, monthly parking, wireless phone bills, and office security systems. By having suppliers send their bills to American Express, the accounts payable staff can consolidate the quantity of check payments that it must make to a single payment. American Express also provides a "Summary of Account" that itemizes all of the business expenses for which payments are being made—which provides sufficient proof for account auditing purposes.

There are two ways to set up invoices to run through this procurement card. The first approach is to refer to American Express's list of existing companies that are willing to provide this service (which can be obtained from American Express). The list includes such organizations as AirTouch Cellular, GTE Wireless, SkyTel Communications, MCI Worldcom, Sprint, America Online, Brinks Home Security, *Fortune* magazine, and the *Boston Globe.* If the company wants to add a supplier to this list, it can contact American Express, which will call the supplier to request a rebilling to it.

One issue with this service is that the company must notify its suppliers if its American Express card number changes, since they will continue to send their billings to the old number until otherwise notified. Also, it may take a number of months to line up a sufficient number of suppliers to see a significant reduction in the number of checks issued by the accounts payable department.

An alternative service is offered by Mastercard, through its Air Travel Card Mastercard. This procurement card splits airfare charges from all other charges made to the card, and bills them directly to the company. This makes it easier for the accounting department to segregate and analyze corporate air travel costs.

Though this best practice may appear to be nirvana to many organizations, the following issues must be carefully considered in order to ensure that the program operates properly:

- *Card misuse.* When procurement cards are handed out to a large number of employees, there is always the risk that someone will abuse the privilege and use up valuable company funds on incorrect or excessive purchases. There are several ways to either prevent this problem or to reduce its impact. One approach is to only hand out the procurement cards to the purchasing staff, who can use them to pay for items for which they would otherwise issue a purchase order; however, this does not address the large quantity of very small purchases that other employees may make, so a better approach is a gradual rollout of procurement cards to those employees who have shown a continuing pattern of making small purchases. Also, the characteristics of the procurement card itself can be altered, either by limiting the dollar amount of purchases per transaction, per time period, or even per department. One can also restrict the number of usages per day. An additional method for avoiding employee misuse of procurement cards is to have them sign an agreement that describes the sanctions that will be imposed when the cards are misused, which may include termination. Some mix of these solutions can mitigate the risk of procurement card abuse.

- *Spending on special items.* The use of a procurement card can actually interfere with existing internal procedures for the purchase of such items, rendering those systems less efficient. For example, an automated materials planning system for the inventory can issue purchase orders to suppliers with no manual intervention; adding inventory items to this situation that were purchased through a different methodology can interfere with the integrity of the database, requiring more manual reconciliation of inventory quantities. Thus, procurement cards are not always a good idea when buying inventory items. Also, capital purchases typically have to go through a detailed review and approval process before they are acquired; since a procurement card offers an easy way to buy smaller capital items, it represents a simple way to bypass the approval process. Thus, they are not a good choice for capital purchases.

- *Dealing with users of the old system.* Some employees will not take to the new procurement card approach, if only because they are used to the old system. This can cause headaches for both the purchasing and accounting departments, since they must deal with both the old system and the new one in combination. It may be impossible to completely eliminate the old purchase order system in some cases (if only because of company politics), so a good alternative is to charge to those departments using the old system the fully burdened cost of each transaction that does not use a procurement card. Since this burdened cost, which includes the cost of all the processing steps noted at the beginning of this section, can easily exceed $100 per transaction, it becomes a very effective way to shift usage toward the procurement card solution.

- *Summarizing general ledger accounts.* The summary statements that are received from the credit card processor will not contain as many expense line items as are probably already contained within a company's general ledger (which tends to slice-and-dice expenses down into many categories). For example, the card statements may only categorize by shop supplies, office supplies, and shipping supplies. If so, then it is best to alter the general ledger accounts to match the categories being reported through the procurement cards. This may also require changes to the budgeting system, which probably mirrors the accounts used in the general ledger.

- *Purchases from unapproved suppliers.* A company may have negotiated favorable prices from a few select suppliers in exchange for making all of its purchases for certain items from them. It is a simple matter to ensure that purchases are made through these suppliers when the purchasing department is placed in direct control of the buying process. However, once purchases are put in the hands of anyone with a procurement card, it is much less likely that the same level of discipline will occur. Instead, purchases will be made from a much larger group of suppliers. Though not an easy issue to control, the holders of procurement cards can at least be issued a "preferred supplier yellow pages," which lists those suppliers from whom they should be buying. Their adherence to this list can be tracked by comparing actual purchases to the yellow pages list and giving them feedback about the issue.

- *Paying sales and use taxes.* Occasionally, a state sales tax auditor will arrive on a company's doorstep, demanding to see documentation that proves it has paid a sales tax on all items purchased. This is not easy to do when procurement cards are used, not only because there may be a multitude of poorly organized supplier receipts, but also because the sales tax noted on a credit card payment slip only shows the grand total sales tax paid, rather than the sales tax for each item purchased; this is an important issue, for some items are exempt from taxation, which will result in a total sales tax that appears to be too low in comparison to the total dollar amount of items purchased. One way to alleviate this problem is to obtain sales tax exemption certificates from all states with whom a company does business; employees then present the sales tax exemption number whenever they make purchases, so that there is no doubt at all—no sales taxes have been paid. Then the accounting staff can calculate the grand total for the use tax (which is the same thing as the sales tax, except that the purchaser pays it to the state, rather than to the seller) to pay, and forward this to the appropriate taxing authority. An alternative is to "double bag" tax payments, which means that the company pays the full use tax on all procurement card purchases, without bothering to spend the time figuring out what sales taxes have already been paid. This is a safe approach from a tax audit perspective, and may not involve much additional cost if the total of all procurement card purchases is small. Yet another alternative is the reverse—to ignore the entire sales tax issue, and only confront it when audited; this decision is usually based on the level of risk tolerance of the controller or chief financial officer.

Though the problems noted here must be addressed, one must understand the significance of the advantages of using procurement cards in order to see why the problems are minor in relation to the possible benefits. Here are the main attractions of this best practice:

- *Fewer accounting transactions.* Some of the accounts payable staff may be redirected to other tasks, because the number of transactions will drop considerably.

- *Fewer invoice reviews and signatures.* Managers no longer have to review a considerable number of invoices for payment approval, nor do they have to sign so many checks addressed to suppliers.

- *No cash advances.* Whenever an employee asks for a cash advance, the accounting staff must create a manual check for that person, record it in the accounting records, and ensure that it is paid back by the employee. This can be a very time-consuming process in proportion to the generally meager advances given to employees. A credit card can avoid this entire process, because employees can go to an automated teller machine and withdraw cash, which will appear in the next monthly card statement from the issuing bank—no check issuances required. Of course, this benefit only applies if those employees needing cash advances are the same ones with access to a procurement card.

- *Fewer petty-cash transactions.* If employees have procurement cards, they will no longer feel compelled to buy items with their own cash, and then ask for a reimbursement from the company's petty-cash fund.

- *Fewer purchasing transactions.* A whole range of purchasing activities are reduced in volume, including contacting suppliers for quotes, creating and mailing purchase orders, resolving invoicing differences, and closing out orders.
- *Reduced supplier list.* The number of active vendors in the purchasing database can be greatly reduced, which allows the buying staff to focus on better relations with the remaining ones on the list.
- *Reduced mailroom volume.* Even the mailroom will experience a drop in volume, since there will be far fewer incoming supplier invoices and outgoing company checks.

A procurement card is easy to implement (just hand it out to employees), though one should keep a significant difficulty in mind. The banks that issue credit cards must expend extra labor to set up a procurement card for a company, since each one must be custom-designed. Consequently, they prefer to issue procurement cards only to those companies that can show a significant volume of credit card business—usually at least one million dollars per year. This volume limitation makes it difficult for a smaller company to use procurement cards. This problem can be partially avoided by using a group of supplier-specific credit cards. For example, a company can sign up for a credit card with its office supply store, another with its building materials store, and another with its electrical supplies store. This results in a somewhat larger number of credit card statements per month, but they are already sorted by supplier, so they are essentially a "poor man's procurement card."

USE SIGNATURE STAMP

One of the most common delay points in the accounts payable process is when an accounting clerk must go in search of someone to sign checks. If there is only one person who is so authorized, and who is not always available, it can keep any checks from being issued at all. The situation grows worse when multiple signatures are required for larger checks. On top of these delays, it is also common for the check-signers to require backup documents for each check being signed, which requires a considerable extra effort by the accounting staff, not only to clip the correct documents to each check, but also to unclip the documents after the checks are signed and file them away in the appropriate files (which also increases the risk that the documents will be filed in the wrong place). This is an exceptional waste of time, since it does not add a whit of value to the process.

The solution to the multitude of inefficiencies related to check-signing is to get rid of the check-signers completely. Instead of assuming that there must be a complete review of all checks prior to signing, one must get management used to the idea of installing approvals earlier in the process, needing no approval at the point of signing. Once management is comfortable with this idea, it is a simple matter of complying with bank regulations, which require a signature on each stamp—this is now a matter of finding the easiest way to stamp checks, rather than an approval process. Check-stamping can be accomplished most simply by creating a signature stamp from the signature of an authorized check-signer, which requires that someone stamp all checks by hand. A more efficient, though more complicated approach is to digitize an authorized signature and incorporate it into the check printing program, so that the signature is automatically affixed to each check with no manual intervention.

The only problem with a signature stamp is that it can be misused to sign unauthorized checks or legal documents. This problem can be avoided by locking it up in the company safe and severely limiting access to the safe. It may also be necessary to lock up check stock, thereby making it doubly difficult for anyone to issue an unauthorized signed check.

By using a signature stamp, one can eliminate the time wasted to find a check-signer, while also avoiding the work required to attach back-up documents to checks and then file away these documents subsequent to review. This is one of the easiest best practices to implement and should be one of the first ones that a controller should institute.

TOTAL IMPACT OF BEST PRACTICES ON THE ACCOUNTS PAYABLE FUNCTION

The preceding list of accounts payable best practices is too voluminous and over-lapping for a company to install all of them—in fact, there is no need to. If a small number of the most radical changes are implemented, such as using the receiving personnel to approve payments to suppliers, many of the other practices are rendered ineffective. Accordingly, this section does not attempt to describe the impact of all the best practices. Instead, it assumes that all of the changes requiring considerable re-engineering *are* implemented, since they have the most impact on the efficiency and effectiveness of the department. This leaves a much smaller number of additional best practices to be tacked on to make a truly world-class accounts payable function.

As just noted, the most important and far-reaching item to install is approval of payment at the receiving dock by the receiving staff. This best practice negates a number of incremental improvements to the accounts payable function, such as automated three-way matching and digitizing accounts payable documents. Once that improvement is made, the remaining best practices for the new accounts payable functions are primarily those that deal with special payment situations that will not be routed through the receiving dock. For example, expense reports and repetitive payments should be automated. The number of payments can also be reduced by using procurement cards to consolidate the number of billings received, while blanket purchase orders are useful for shrinking the number of purchase orders in the system. Another piece of automation is the use of wire transfers, which avoids the time-consuming process of creating, signing, and

Exhibit 3.4.   An Accounts Payable Function That Uses Best Practices

mailing checks. Suppliers can also be linked directly to the accounts payable database to see if payments have been made, which avoids any regular need for the suppliers to talk to the staff. When taken together, the accounts payable function is transformed into a small group of highly computer-literate employees who monitor ongoing automated transactions to ensure that all processing is proceeding in accordance with expectations. There is very little paper-processing, nor is there much need to correspond with suppliers. This is the accounts payable function of the future. The combination of these best practices is noted in Exhibit 3.4.

Though the system advocated in this exhibit is certainly the most efficient one of all the combinations of best practices presented in this section, it is important to note that it is not for everyone. It requires substantial implementation time and cost; accordingly, it may not be practicable for smaller companies that are operating on a limited budget. In these cases, other combinations of best practices can be used to create a system that is somewhat less efficient, but at a much lower cost.

SUMMARY

This chapter itemized a number of best practices that can be used to vastly streamline the accounts payable function, one of the most labor-intensive accounting functions. Of all the functional areas, this is the one that can yield the most impressive productivity gains with the use of best practices.

One can select a series of small and simple changes, such as using signature stamps and auditing expense reports, to make incremental improvements in the accounts payable process. However, this is an area where massive gains are possible if a controller is willing to completely restructure the traditional accounts payable processing approach. To this end, the most important best practice listed in this chapter is that of paying upon receiving approval—the receiving staff authorizes payment simply by looking up all items received in an on-line database of open purchase orders. No further work is required by the accounts payable staff, resulting in a major reduction in the accounting workload. However, this approach requires new computer systems, as well as a complete retraining of the receiving staff regarding its role in paying suppliers. Only through such paradigm shifts can an accounting department achieve sensational productivity improvements in the area of accounts payable.

Chapter 4

Billing Best Practices

This chapter covers the best practices that can be used to create a more efficient billing operation. The best practices fall into three main categories. One group covers the need for more accurate information that is used to create an invoice. These items focus on the stream of information going from the shipping department to the invoicing staff, with a particular emphasis on rooting out any missing or incorrect information. The next group of best practices covers the efficiency of the invoicing operation itself, eliminating month-end statements and using a smaller number of multi-part invoice forms. The final group focuses on changing the method of invoice delivery to the customer, such as using electronic data interchange or allowing the delivery person to create the invoice at the point of delivery. When taken as a whole, these best practices result in an invoicing operation that is remarkably error-free, issues invoices as soon as products are shipped, and ensures that customers receive invoices almost at once.

IMPLEMENTATION ISSUES FOR BILLING BEST PRACTICES

The best practices in this chapter comprise a broad mix of issues that are easily put in place, and others that are much more challenging to implement, depending on a company's specific circumstances. This section contains a table (Exhibit 4.1) that notes, in general terms, the difficulty of implementation for all of the best practices noted in this chapter. The table lists the best practices in alphabetical order and then describes the ease, duration, and cost of implementation for each one. The most difficult ones are those that require extra computer programming to achieve, as well as those that require the cooperative efforts of other departments. The easiest ones can generally be achieved within the accounting department and with no additional capital or personnel costs of note. The implementation issues for billing best practices are as follows.

Though six of the best practices noted in Exhibit 4.1 are described as easy implementations, one should not fall into the trap of only implementing those items. The reason is that some of the most difficult implementation jobs result in the greatest improvements in the performance of the billing function. Accordingly, it is best to alternate easy implementations with more difficult ones so that there is a constant stream of successes, some of which represent significant advances in efficiency. Also, by including an occasional "quick-hit" implementa-

Exhibit 4.1.   Implementation Issues for Billings Best Practices

Description	Ease of Implementation	Duration of Implementation	Cost of Implementation
Add Carrier Route Codes to Billing Addresses	Moderate	Medium	Medium
Automatically Check Errors during Invoice Data Entry	Difficult	Long	Medium
Computerize the Shipping Log	Moderate	Medium	Medium
Delivery Person Creates the Invoice	Difficult	Long	Expensive
Delivery Person Delivers the Invoice	Easy	Short	Inexpensive
Early Billing of Recurring Invoices	Easy	Short	Inexpensive
Eliminate Month-End Statements	Easy	Short	Inexpensive
Issue Electronic Invoices through the Internet	Moderate	Medium	Medium
Issue Single, Summarized Invoices Each Period	Moderate	Medium	Medium
Offer Customers Secure Internet Payment Options	Easy	Short	Inexpensive
Print Seperate Invoices for Each Line Item	Easy	Short	Inexpensive
Reduce Number of Parts in Multi-Part Invoices	Easy	Short	Inexpensive
Replace Inter-Company Invoicing with Operating Transactions	Easy	Medium	Inexpensive
Track Exceptions between the Shipping Log and Invoice Register	Easy	Medium	Inexpensive
Transmit Transactions via Electronic Data Interchange	Difficult	Long	Expensive
Use Automated Bank Account Deductions	Easy	Short	Inexpensive

tion, a controller can point toward a continuing stream of successes, which is useful when trying to obtain funds for more best practices-related projects.

The remainder of this chapter describes the best practices that were touched on in Exhibit 4.1. Each description includes the benefits and problems associated with each best practice, as well as any implementation problems to be aware of. The descriptions should be sufficient for the reader to form a knowledgeable opinion regarding the need to implement one or more of these best practices, depending on the specific operations of the reader's organization.

ADD CARRIER ROUTE CODES TO BILLING ADDRESSES

For those organizations that issue large quantities of small-dollar invoices, the cost of mailing is a substantial portion of the total cost of doing business. For these organizations, a lower-cost approach to mailing an invoice must be found. One alternative is to include a carrier route code in the address field for each customer. This information is used by the postal service to more easily sort incoming mail pieces by carrier route. In exchange for this information, the postal service allows a small reduction in the cost of each item mailed. At the time of this writing, the difference between the standard price for an automated letter-size mailing and one that includes the carrier route code is about three cents (for the most recent rates, go to *www.usps.com*). This difference is sufficiently large that a billing manager who processes thousands of invoices per year should certainly consider it as a potential way to save costs.

To implement this best practice, one must obtain the route codes from the postal service on either a monthly or bi-monthly basis. It is available on tape, CD-ROM, cartridge, or hard copy. The company's customer address files must be updated with the latest carrier route information, as specified in the postal service's Domestic Mail Manual. To determine the exact format of the file, one can download a sample file from the postal service's web site. These steps obviously require some effort on a continuing basis, so one must carefully determine the cost-benefit associated with this best practice before implementing it. Realistically, only a very large mailing operation will save money through this approach.

AUTOMATICALLY CHECK ERRORS DURING INVOICE DATA ENTRY

Errors during the data-entry phase of creating an invoice can result in a variety of downstream problems. For example, an incorrect billing address on an invoice means that the customer will never receive it, which means that the collections staff must send a new invoice copy. Also, if the quantity, product description, or price is entered incorrectly, the customer may have a good reason for not paying the bill. If this happens, the collections staff will have to get involved to work out the reason for non-payment and negotiate extra payments (if possible) by customers. All of these problems are exceptions and require very large amounts of time to research and fix.

A very useful best practice is to prevent as many data-entry problems in advance as possible by using computerized data-checking methods. For example, a field for zip codes can only accept five-digit or nine-digit numbers, which prevents the entry of numbers of an unusual length. The field can also be tied to a file of all cities and states, so that entering a zip code automatically fills in the city and state fields. Also, prices of unusual length can be automatically rejected, or prices can be automatically called up from a file that is linked to a product number. Similarly, product descriptions can be automatically entered if the product number is entered. An example of a "smart" data-entry system is one that flags part numbers that are being entered for an existing customer for the first time. The computer can check the part number entered against a file of items previously ordered by a customer and see if there is a chance that the part being ordered might not be the correct one. There can also be required fields that must have a valid entry or else the invoice cannot be processed; a good example is the customer purchase order number field, required by many customers, or else they will not pay the invoice. By including these automatic error-checking and expert systems into the data-entry software, it is possible to reduce the number of data-entry errors.

The main problem with creating automatic error-checking is that it can be a significant programming project. There may be a dozen different error-checking protocols linked to the invoice data-entry screen, and each one is a separate programming project. Also, if a company purchased its software from a third party, it is common for the company to periodically install software updates issued by the supplier, which would wipe out any programming changes made in the interim. Accordingly, it is best to apply these error-checking routines only to custom-programmed accounting systems. An alternative is to use error-checking as a criterion for the purchase of new packaged software, if a company is in the market for a new accounting system. In either of these two cases, having automatic error-checking is a worthy addition to an accounting system.

COMPUTERIZE THE SHIPPING LOG

For a company with no computer linkage to the shipping dock, the typical sequence of events that leads up to the creation of an invoice is that copies of the packing slip and the initial customer order form are manually delivered to the accounting department from the shipping dock; then the accounting staff uses this information to create an invoice. Unfortunately, this manual transfer of information can sometimes lead to missing documents, which means that the accounting department does not create an invoice and sales are lost. In addition, this system can be a slow one—if the shipping department is a long way away from the accounting department, perhaps in a different city, it may be several days before the invoice can be created, which increases the time period before a customer will receive the invoice and pay it. Finally, there is a problem with data entry, because the accounting staff must manually re-enter some or all of the customer information before creating an invoice (depending on the amount of data already entered into the computer system by the order entry department). Any additional data entry brings up the risk of incorrect information being entered on an invoice, which may result in collection problems, especially if the data-entry error related to an incorrect shipment quantity.

The solution to this problem is to provide for the direct entry of shipping information by the shipping staff at the shipping location. By doing so, there is no longer any time delay in issuing invoices, nor is there a risk that the accounting staff will incorrectly enter shipping information into an invoice. There is still a risk that the shipping staff will incorrectly enter information, but this is less likely, since they are the ones who shipped the product and they are most familiar with shipping quantities and other related information. For this system to function properly, there must be a computer terminal in the shipping area that is directly linked to the accounting database. In addition, the shipping staff must be properly trained in how to enter a shipment into the computer. There should also be a continuing internal audit review of the accuracy of the data entered at this location, to ensure that the procedure is continuing to be handled correctly. Finally, the accounting software should have a data input screen that allows the shipping staff to enter shipping information. These tend to be minor problems at most companies, since there is usually a computer terminal already in or near the shipping area, and most accounting packages are already set up to handle the direct entry of shipping information; some even do so automatically as soon as the shipping staff creates a bill of lading or packing slip through the computer system. In short, unless there are very antiquated systems on hand or a poorly trained or unreliable shipping staff, it is not normally a very difficult issue to have the shipping employees directly enter shipping information into the accounting system, which can then be used to immediately create and issue invoices.

DELIVERY PERSON CREATES THE INVOICE

Many companies have difficulty with their customers when the company bills for the quantity that it believes it shipped to the customer, but the customer argues that it received a different quantity and only pays for the amount it believes it has received. This problem results in the invoicing staff having to issue credits after the fact, in order to reconcile the amount of cash received from its customers to the amounts that were billed to them. The amount of work required in these cases to match the amounts billed to the amounts paid is usually greatly in excess of the dollar amounts involved and has a profound impact on the efficiency of the billing staff.

New technology makes it possible for some companies to completely bypass this problem. If a company has its own delivery staff, it can equip them with portable computers and printers and have them issue invoices at the point of receipt, using the quantities counted by the customer as the appropriate amount to invoice. A flowchart of the procedure is shown in Exhibit 4.2. To begin, the shipping staff determines the amount to be shipped to a customer and enters this amount into the main accounting database. The amount in a specific truckload is downloaded into the portable computer of the delivery person, who then brings the truckload of goods to the customer. The customer counts the amount received. The delivery person calls up the amount of the delivery on the screen of the portable computer, enters the quantities that the customer agrees has been received, and prints out and delivers an invoice (which may be on a diskette if the

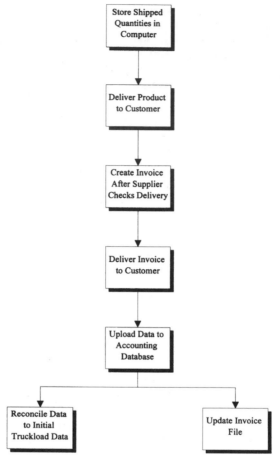

Exhibit 4.2.   Off-Site Invoice Creation

customer has a compatible computer system that can receive invoice data in this fashion). The delivery person then returns to the company and uploads all invoicing information from the portable computer to the main accounting database, which records the invoices and notes any variances between the amounts shipped and the amounts received by customers (which will be investigated if the variances are significant). It is also possible to upload information at the customer site, either by dialing up the accounting database through a local phone connection or by using cellular phone access. This process is capable of eliminating problems caused by customer disputes over delivered quantities, resulting in less work for the accounting staff.

    Though a technologically elegant solution, this best practice is one that applies to only a small number of companies that meet some very specific criteria. First, a company must make deliveries with its own staff; a third-party delivery service will not perform the on-site invoicing function. Next, this solution requires a good knowledge of computer systems to implement. There must be not only a qualified and knowledgeable in-house computer system department, but also one that has the budget to create such a system. Also, this is an expensive solution to implement (if only because every driver must be furnished with a computer and printer), so there must be a clear trade-off between the implementation and capital cost of the system and benefits from reduced accounting staff labor. These criteria tend to point toward only larger companies that make frequent deliveries to a large number of customers. Smaller firms will not find that this is a cost-effective practice to install and use.

DELIVERY PERSON DELIVERS THE INVOICE

A company may not have the wherewithal to create invoices at the point of delivery, as described in the preceding section. However, it may still be possible to have the delivery person hand-carry the invoice at the time of delivery to the customer's accounts payable department. By doing so, a company can compress the mail time that would otherwise be required to get an invoice to a customer and also ensure that the invoice is delivered directly into the hands of the person who is responsible for paying it. Thus, direct delivery of an invoice carries with it the advantages of reducing the total transaction time, while also ensuring that the invoice is not lost in transit.

However, having the delivery person deliver the invoice only works in a small number of situations. The key element is that a company must make deliveries with its own personnel; if not, a third-party delivery person will not hand-carry an invoice, which makes this best practice impossible to implement. Also, there must be a close linkage between the accounting department and the shipping dock, so that invoices are prepared slightly in advance of shipment and sent to the delivery person at the time of shipment. In addition, a customer may not allow delivery personnel to have access to the accounting department, resulting in the delivery of the invoice to the customer's front desk, which may result in a delayed or incorrect delivery to the accounting department. Finally, there may be a problem with creating invoices slightly in advance of shipment—what if the invoice is created but the shipment never leaves the dock? The invoice must then be credited out of the computer system, which adds an unneeded step to the invoicing process. Consequently, given the number of problems with this best practice, it is best used in only a few situations, where a company has its own delivery staff and the accounting department can efficiently produce accurate invoices either in advance of, or at the time of, shipment.

Though there seem to be many obstacles to this best practice, there is one scenario under which it can work very well. If the shipping dock has a computer terminal and printer, it may be possible to create an invoice at the dock as soon as a delivery is ready for shipment. This alternative keeps the accounting staff from having to be involved in the invoicing process at all, and also keeps invoices from being produced by mistake when a delivery is not actually ready for shipment. This alternative requires a modification to the accounting system, so that invoices can be produced singly, rather than in batches, which is the customary mode of invoice creation. The shipping staff also must be given permission to create invoices in the computer system, and must be thoroughly trained in how to do so. If these problems can be overcome, an incremental increase in the level of technology used at the shipping dock can make this best practice a viable alternative.

EARLY BILLING OF RECURRING INVOICES

There are many situations in which a company knows the exact amount of a customer billing, well before the date on which the invoice is to be sent. For example, a subscription is for the pre-set amount, as is a contractual obligation, such as a rent payment. In these cases, it makes sense to create the invoice and deliver it to the customer one or two weeks in advance of the date when it is actually due. By doing so, the invoice has more time to be routed through the receiving organization, passing through the mailroom, accounting staff, authorized signatory, and back to the accounts payable staff for payment. This makes it much more likely that the invoice will be paid on time, which improves cash flow and reduces a company's investment in accounts receivable.

The main difficulty with advance billings is that the date of the invoice should be shifted forward to the accounting period in which the invoice is supposed to be billed. Otherwise, the revenue will be recognized too early, which distorts the financial statements. Shifting the accounting period forward is not difficult for most accounting software systems, but the controller must remember to shift back to the current period after the invoice processing has been completed; otherwise, all other current transactions that are subsequently entered will be recorded in the next accounting period, rather than the current one.

ELIMINATE MONTH-END STATEMENTS

The employees who are in charge of printing and issuing invoices each day have another document that they print and issue each month, the month-end statement. This is a listing of all open invoices that customers have not yet paid. Though it seems like a good idea to tell customers what they still owe, the reality of the situation is that most customers throw away their statements without reading them. The reason is that the person receiving a statement, the accounts payable clerk, does not have time to research strange invoices that appear on a supplier's statement, nor is it likely that this person will call the supplier to request a copy of a missing invoice. Instead, it is easier to wait for a contact from the supplier, asking about a specific invoice. By waiting, the onus of doing some work falls on the supplier instead of the accounts payable person, which is a preferable shifting of the workload from the latter person to the former.

The simple approach to eliminating this problem is to stop printing statements. By doing so, one can avoid not only the time and effort of printing the statements, but also eliminate the cost of the special form used to print the statements, as well as the cost of stuffing them in envelopes and mailing them. Though it is possible that the collections staff may complain that this collection tool is being taken away from them, it is at best a poor method for bringing in errant accounts receivable, and does little to reduce the workload of the collections personnel. Thus, eliminating the periodic issuance of statements to customers is an easy way to shift the accounting staff away from a non-value-added activity, which gives them time to pursue other more meaningful activities.

ISSUE ELECTRONIC INVOICES THROUGH THE INTERNET

The traditional invoicing process is extraordinarily wasteful in terms of the effort and time that goes into creating and issuing an invoice. It must be created and inserted into an invoice printing batch, which in turn requires the use of a customized invoice with prepositioned fields and logos, plus a review of the printed invoices, stuffing into envelopes, affixing postage, and mailing. Even then, there is a risk that the invoice will be lost in the mail, either due to a problem at the post office, or because the recipient's address has changed. Further, there are delays at the receiving company, while the mailroom sorts through the mail and delivers it internally (sometimes to the wrong person).

Some of these problems can be avoided through the use of e-mailed billings that are delivered through the Internet. There are several ways to do this. The least recommended approach is to post the invoices on a company's own web site. This means that customers can access the company's credit card payment system at the same time they access their invoices, which results in accounts receivable that are collected with inordinate speed. However, this approach requires customers to access the company's web site in order to find their invoices, which they are not likely to do (especially because this will result in their immediate use of funds to pay for the invoice). In addition, this requires an interface between the accounting database and the web site, so that invoices are posted regularly to the web site. Further, there may be a need to create user identification numbers and passwords, so that they can access their invoices (otherwise they would be viewable by *all* visitors to the web site). Also, if customers forget their access codes, there must be an internal customer service function that can assist them with this information, and this involves additional personnel costs to maintain.

A better approach is to "push" electronic invoices to customers by e-mail. This requires the collection of an e-mail address from each customer at the time an order is taken (or verification of an existing one when a re-order occurs). This address is then attached to an electronic invoice form that is generated instead of a paper-based invoice, and issued to the customer over the Internet. It is then available to the customer a few moments later, allowing for immediate payment (possibly) or at least a quick perusal of the invoice and a return of information to the company regarding any problems discovered by the customer. This approach greatly reduces the time required to get invoicing information to the customer.

There are several problems with Internet invoicing that one must be aware of. First, some customers change their e-mail addresses with some regularity, so that there is a chance that invoices will be sent to an old address, and therefore never accessed. Also, there is some risk that customers will accidentally erase an incoming electronic invoice without reviewing it. Furthermore, this approach leaves no paper record of the invoice at the company, just a computer record; this is a problem for those organizations where the collections effort is primarily based on paper files, rather than ready access to the accounting database.

Another issue is creating the software that will in turn create an invoice (either text-based or using the industry-standard Portable Document Format (PDF) promulgated by Adobe Systems), and then send it to an e-mail address. This can be a significant programming effort if done internally, and runs the additional risk of being wiped out if the attached packaged accounting software is upgraded, which may destroy or alter some of the software linkages to which the custom software is attached. Fortunately, a number of accounting software providers are now adding this feature to their accounting systems, so that internal programming can be avoided.

Some of the problems with e-mailed invoices can be addressed through the careful analysis of which customers reliably pay their invoices by this means, and (more importantly) which do not. If there is a consistent problem with payment by some customers, then they can be flagged in the accounting database, and a traditional paper-based invoice can be created for them. Alternatively, the same invoices can be continually re-issued every week or two by e-mail. This is a zero-cost option, since there are no mailing or printing costs. When using this approach, the entire file of unpaid invoices can be re-issued electronically to customers. However, to avoid multiple payments for the same invoices, it may be useful to alter the format of these secondary issuances, so that they are clearly labeled as reminder invoices. An alternative format is to cluster all unpaid invoices for each customer into an electronic statement of unpaid invoices, which can be issued at regular intervals.

The use of direct e-mails to customers is particularly enticing, not from an accounting perspective, but from a marketing view. A complete list of customer e-mail addresses allows one to send sales, marketing, and customer service information to a company's entire mailing list at the touch of a button, and with no associated distribution cost whatsoever.

A final variation on the use of electronic invoices through the Internet is the use of a consolidator. This is an entity that maintains a web site that allows a company's customers to access not only their billings, but those of their other suppliers, too. This approach has the distinct advantage of allowing customers to pay a number of different bills at the same time, without switching to a number of different web sites in order to do so. Examples of these consolidators are Check-free, Transpoint, Speedpay, Derivion, and Microvault.

A company that wishes to have its invoices posted on a consolidator web site must create a data file that reformats the invoice information into the format needed by the consolidator, and then send this file (over the Internet) to the consolidator, which then posts the information. Customers then access their invoices in a summary format, which are clustered together for all of their suppliers, and either accept or reject them for payment; if there is a problem, customers can access greater levels of detail for each invoice, and usually access an e-mail account that will be sent to the company's customer service department.

The cost of this service varies considerably by consolidator, with some charging the customer, some the company, and some charging both. It is best to refer to the fee schedule of each one to determine the precise amounts. The fees charged to a company are not excessive, and should not get in the way of adopting this option.

The main problem with using a consolidator is that not all customers will want to use the one that the company prefers to send its invoicing information to, since they may have already set up payment plans with many of their other suppliers through different consolidators. Accordingly, a company may find itself issuing invoice files to a large number of consolidators, which presents additional work for the person reformatting the invoice file.

The most common of these electronic invoicing options is bill posting on a company's own web site, since it is the simplest of all options. However, with the growing use of invoice consolidators by customers, the issuance of invoices through this medium, in addition to their posting on a company-owned web site, is a reasonable alternative. These are not mutually exclusive options.

ISSUE SINGLE, SUMMARIZED INVOICES EACH PERIOD

Some companies make a business out of selling small quantities of products in small batches, which necessitates a very large quantity of invoices. For example, a company that sells nails in batches of an ounce per sale will issue sixteen more invoices than one that sells nails in batches of no less than one pound. If the cost of issuing an invoice is as little as one dollar (and it is usually much more), then the price at which the nails were sold will probably be far less than the cost of issuing the associated invoices. Clearly, companies that must issue enormous numbers of invoices in this manner will find that their administrative costs are excessive.

A way out of this dilemma is to group all sales for a specified time period, such as a month, and then issue a single invoice that covers all of the sales during that period. This approach, which is used by W.W. Grainger for many of its customers, is similar to the invoicing method used by credit card companies, which congregate all sales for a full month and then issue a single billing. By using this best practice, a company can eliminate a very large proportion of its total invoice volume.

There are some issues to consider before using this best practice. One is that this approach is obviously most suitable for companies that issue large quantities of low-dollar invoices. Conversely, it is *not* a reasonable approach if invoice volume is low and dollar volumes are high. If a billing is for a large amount of money, it makes little sense to wait until the end of the month to issue an invoice, since this only delays the time period before the customer will pay for it. Another issue is that the existing accounting software may not support this feature. If not, a company must go through the added expense of custom-programming to group a series of shipments or sales into a single invoice. Another problem may be customers—they are accustomed to receiving a single invoice for each shipment, with a separate purchase order authorizing each invoice, and they will not know what to do when a single, summary-level invoice arrives in the mail. The best way to resolve this problem is to make it an option for customers to accept summary-level invoices, rather than unexpectedly springing it on them with no warning and requiring their use of it. By taking the time to explain the reason for the single invoice and how it can benefit customers, too (with less paperwork for them to sort through), the customer acceptance rate should be quite high. The final problem with this method is that it takes longer to bring cash in to pay for shipped goods, since some shipments may be sent out at the beginning of a month, but not billed until the end of the month. To avoid this problem, a company can impose a shorter due date in which customers must pay, but customers rarely receive this well. Instead, it is best to carefully analyze the interest cost of the large amount of committed working capital to the reduced cost of invoicing; if there is a clear benefit despite the added cost, then this best practice should be implemented. For many billing departments, it should be implemented sooner rather than later.

In short, issuing a single invoice to customers each period makes a great deal of sense for those companies that ship many small-dollar orders. Companies that deal with large-dollar orders should probably leave this best practice alone, since there is an added working capital cost associated with its use.

OFFER CUSTOMERS SECURE INTERNET PAYMENT OPTIONS

Many prospective customers are not interested in shopping at a company's Internet store, because they are concerned that their credit card information will either be intercepted at the point when they transmit it to the store, or else that it will be kept on file by the company, where it may be illegally accessed at any time in the future. As long as credit cards are viewed as the primary form of payment on the Internet, these shoppers will find other channels for buying products and services. However, a company called IPin has arrived at an alternative way to process payments that may attract these additional shoppers.

A company that wants to offer its customers the alternative of being able to pay without the transmission of credit card information can use IPin's service. This service, which is located at *www.ipin.com,* allows customers to store their credit card information in a highly secure environment at that web site in exchange for an IPin identification number, which they can use as a form of payment at selected web sites (which must set up operating agreements with IPin to use its software to process customer transactions). This approach has the advantage of keeping customer-specific credit card information off the Internet. Also, for those customers who are truly paranoid about leaving their credit card information in the hands of *anyone,* including IPin, it also offers the option of linking customer payments through their IPin identification numbers to the billing statements of selected Internet service providers, or the monthly invoices of a customer's phone company or wireless phone company.

This last option also yields the unique benefit of allowing a company to charge its customers for micro-purchases (those purchases of just a few cents), which can be summarized and billed directly to customers. This avoids the use of credit cards, which charge minimum fees (usually twenty cents) for purchases, while also allowing companies access to a new form of revenue—perhaps fees for access to small amounts of data that were previously given away for free.

PRINT SEPARATE INVOICES FOR EACH LINE ITEM

When an accounting department issues an invoice that contains a large number of line items, it is more likely that the recipient would have an issue with one or more of the line items, and will hold payment on the entire invoice while those line items are resolved. Though this may not be a significant issue when an invoice is relatively small, it is a large issue indeed when the invoice has a large dollar total, and holding the entire invoice will have a serious impact on the amount of accounts receivable outstanding.

One way to avoid this problem is to split apart large invoices into separate ones, with each invoice containing just one line item. By doing so, it is more likely that some invoices will be paid at once, while other ones over which there are issues will be delayed. This can have a significant positive impact on a company's investment in accounts receivable.

The only complaint that arises from this approach is that customers can be buried under quite a large pile of invoices. This can be ameliorated by clustering all of the invoices in a single envelope, rather than sending a dozen separately mailed invoices on the same day. Also, it may be prudent to cluster small-dollar line items on the same invoice, since this will cut down on the number of invoices issued, while not having a significant impact on the overall receivable balance if these invoices are put on hold.

REDUCE NUMBER OF PARTS IN MULTI-PART INVOICES

Some invoices have the thickness of a small magazine when they are printed because they have so many parts. The top copy usually goes to the customer (or even the top two copies), while another one goes into a file that is sorted alphabetically, another goes into a file for invoices that is sorted by invoice number, and another copy may go to a different department, such as customer service, so that they will have an additional copy on hand in case a customer calls with a question. This plethora of invoice copies causes several problems. One is that the printer is much more likely to jam if the number of invoice copies running through it is too thick. Another much more serious problem is that each of those copies must be filed away. The alphabetical copy is probably a necessary one, since all of the shipping documentation is attached to it, but there is no excuse for filing invoices in numerical order; they can be found just as easily by calling them up in the computer. A final problem is that multi-part forms are more expensive.

The best practice that avoids this problem is to reduce the number of invoice copies. Only one copy should go to the customer, and one copy should be retained. That is two copies, not the four or five that some companies use. By reducing the number of copies, there is much less chance that the printer will jam and the cost of the invoices can be substantially reduced. The biggest cost saving, however, is of the filing time that has been eliminated, which can be many hours per month, depending on the volume of invoices that are created periodically.

The biggest objection to reducing the number of invoice copies is from those parts of the company that are accustomed to using the extra invoice copies. This group is rarely the accounting department, which must do the work of filing the extra copies, but rather other departments that have an occasional need to look at them. The best way to overcome these objections is to educate the dissenters in advance regarding the required filing time needed to keep extra copies, so they understand that the cost of additional filing does not match the benefit of their occasional need for the invoices. Another option is to give these people read-only access to invoices in the accounting computer system, so that they can call up invoice information on their computers, rather than manually looking for it in an invoice binder. The combination of these two approaches usually eliminates any opposition to reducing the number of invoice copies, allowing the accounting staff to achieve extra efficiencies with this best practice.

REPLACE INTER-COMPANY INVOICING
WITH OPERATING TRANSACTIONS

Those companies with subsidiaries will find some difficulty at the end of the fiscal year, because they must back out all sales between subsidiaries, which are not, according to accounting rules, true sales. The most common way to record product shipments between locations is to issue an invoice to another subsidiary, which pays it as though it is from an independently owned organization. At the end of the year, the accounting staff must then determine the margin on all sales to subsidiaries (which can be a lengthy undertaking) and create a journal entry to reverse out the margin. This is clearly not a value-added activity, and reducing it to the minimum gives the accounting staff more time to deal with other, more productive issues.

A best practice that multiple-subsidiary companies can use is to avoid using invoices when shipping between company-owned facilities. Instead, there are two ways to record the transactions. The first and easiest approach is to record any inventory transfers as a simple movement of inventory between warehouse locations in the computer system. This approach is only possible if a company uses a single enterprise-wide database of information to control activities in all company locations. If such a system is in place, a shipping clerk can simply record a delivery as being moved from one warehouse to another, or as being in transit to another warehouse, where it will be recorded as having been received as soon as it arrives at that location. The other possibility is to accumulate all material transfers in a log and create a journal entry at the end of each reporting period (or sooner, such as daily) to record inventory as having been shifted to a different company location. This second approach requires more manual labor and is more subject to error than the first approach, but can be used even if there is no enterprise-wide computer system for all locations. In either case, there is no need to create an invoice, nor does the accounting staff have to worry about backing out the profit on sales to company subsidiaries.

TRACK EXCEPTIONS BETWEEN THE SHIPPING LOG AND INVOICE REGISTER

If a company relies on the manual transfer of shipping information from the shipping dock to the accounting department, it is likely that some shipments are never billed, resulting in a permanent loss of revenue. This situation arises because information can be lost on its way from the shipping dock; it can be mixed with other paperwork, put into the wrong bin, given to the wrong person, or any number of other variations. In even the best-run companies, there is a strong chance that, from time to time, a shipment will not be invoiced. If the shipment in question is a high-dollar one, the cost of the missing transaction can be considerable and may make it worthwhile to take steps to remedy the situation.

Fortunately, the solution is not a very expensive one. To avoid any missing invoices, one must continually compare the shipping log maintained by the shipping department with the invoice register that is maintained by the accounting department. Any shipment that is listed on the shipping log, but which has not been invoiced, must be investigated at once. There may be good reasons for a shipment that is not invoiced, such as the delivery of a free sample, but the investigation must still be completed in order to ensure that there are no problems. If a problem is uncovered, it is not enough to just issue the missing invoice. One must also determine the reason why the paperwork for the shipment never reached the accounting department and fix the underlying problem. Only by taking this extra step can a company keep from having a continual problem with its invoicing. Any company that uses a manual transfer of information between these two departments should always track exceptions between the shipping log and invoice register.

It is also possible to avoid the entire problem by having the shipping department record all shipments directly into the accounting database, which is described in this chapter in the section, "Computerize the Shipping Log." By using this approach, there is no manual transfer of information, so there is no exception tracking to perform. It is also possible to have the shipping department not only enter shipments into the computer, but also print out invoices in the shipping department for delivery with the shipments. This approach is also described in this chapter, in the section "Delivery Person Creates the Invoice." However, if the shipping area does not have the level of computerization or training to use either of these more advanced best practices, a periodic comparison of the shipping log to the invoice register is mandatory, in order to avoid not billing customers for shipments to them.

TRANSMIT TRANSACTIONS VIA ELECTRONIC DATA INTERCHANGE

Sending an invoice to a customer requires some labor, cost, and time, but does not guarantee that the invoice will be paid. For example, someone must print out an invoice, separate out the copy that goes to the customer, stuff it in an envelope and mail it, which may then take several days to reach the customer, be routed through its mailroom, reach the accounts payable department, and be entered into the customer's computer system (where the data may be scrambled due to key-punching errors). The invoice may even be lost at the customer site and never entered into its computer system for payment at all.

To avoid all of these issues, a company can use electronic data interchange (EDI). Under this approach, a company's computer system automatically issues an electronic invoice that is set up in a standard format (as defined by an international standard-setting organization) and transmits it to a third-party mainframe computer, where it is left in an electronic mailbox. The customer's computer automatically polls this mailbox several times a day and extracts the electronic invoice format. Once received, the format is automatically translated into the invoice format used by the recipient's computer and stored in the accounting system's database for payment. At no time does anyone have to manually handle the data, which eliminates the risk of lost or erroneous invoicing data. This is an excellent approach for those companies that can afford to invest in setting up EDI with their customers, since it fully automates a number of invoicing steps, resulting in a high degree of efficiency and reliability.

There are several problems with EDI that keep most smaller companies from using it, especially if they have many low-volume customer accounts. The main problem is that it takes some time and persuasion to get a customer to agree to use EDI as the basis for receiving invoices. This may take several trips to each customer, including time to send trial transmissions to the customer's computer to ensure that the system works properly. To do this with a large number of low-volume customers is not cost-effective, so the practice is generally confined to companies with high-volume customers, involving a great many invoices, so that the investment by both parties pays off fairly quickly. The other problem is that the most efficient EDI systems require some automation. A standard EDI system requires one to manually enter all transactions, as well as manually extracting them from the EDI mailbox and keypunching them into the receiving computer. To fully automate the system, a company must have its software engineers program an interface between the accounting computer system and the EDI system, which can be an expensive undertaking. Without the interface, an EDI system is really nothing more than a fancy fax machine. Thus, installing a fully operational EDI system is usually limited to transactions with high-volume customers and requires a considerable programming expense to achieve full automation.

USE AUTOMATED BANK ACCOUNT DEDUCTIONS

In some industries, the invoices sent to customers are exactly the same every month. This is common in service industries, where there are standard contracts that provide the same services for the same price, and do so for long periods of time. Examples of such cases are parking lots or health clubs, both of which put their customers on long-term contracts to pay fixed monthly amounts. In these cases, a company issues invoices for the same amount every month to all of its customers. The customers then pay the same amount every month and the accounts receivable staff enters the same amounts into the accounting software as having been received.

When the same amount is due every month, a company can use automatic deductions from the bank accounts of customers. This approach eliminates the need to run any invoices, since the customers do not need them to make a payment. There are also no collection problems, since everything is automatic. Thus, this approach can completely eliminate the invoicing and collection steps from the accounting department.

Before implementing automatic deductions, one must first review the obstacles that stand in the way of a successful project. One issue is that some invoices will still be needed if a company elects to "grandfather" its existing customers, so that they do not have to pay through bank deductions. Another problem is that invoices are also required for the first month or two of business with a new customer, because it usually takes some time before the automatic deduction is set up and operating smoothly. A regular invoice may also be necessary for a new customer because the first month of service may be for only part of the month (e.g., if the customer starts at the middle of the month, rather than at the beginning), which is easier to bill through an invoice than a deduction. Another issue is if the customer's bank account is canceled. Though these appear to be a significant number of issues, they are still a small minority of the total number of transactions processed. Generally speaking, if a company has a large base of customers for whom there are consistent and identical billings, a very effective best practice is to convert those customers to automatic bank deductions.

TOTAL IMPACT OF BEST PRACTICES ON THE BILLINGS FUNCTION

This section describes a set of best practices that, when integrated into the billings function, results in significant efficiency improvements. The best practices presented here are a subset of the complete list presented earlier in this chapter, in Exhibit 4.1. This listing, as noted in Exhibit 4.3, eliminates several best practices that are mutually exclusive. For example, if a company uses a computerized shipping log to create invoices, there is no need to use another best practice, such as tracking variances between invoices created and the paper-based shipping log. When these types of conflicts arise, only the most advanced best practice is assumed to be used. As a result, the best practices shown in Exhibit 4.3 note that a company should always directly link its shipping dock with the accounting database by having all shipments automatically invoiced as soon as the shipping staff puts a delivery on an outbound truck. The printed invoice should use a minimum number of copies, avoiding several downstream steps to file them. The invoicing function should also avoid the use of month-end statements. Finally, a company has a variety of invoice-delivery options to choose from, ranging from EDI transmissions to point-of-delivery invoicing, or even the complete elimination of invoices by using direct cash withdrawals from customer bank accounts. The exact invoicing method or combination of methods chosen will depend upon the special circumstances and requirements of each company.

If some of the best practices noted in Exhibit 4.3 cannot be completed for any reason, some lesser combination of best practices will still result in efficiency improvements, though not to as large a degree as would be possible if the entire set of improvements were implemented.

SUMMARY

This chapter focused on improving the speed and accuracy of invoice preparation and delivery. There are several ways to achieve these goals. One is to increase the accuracy of invoicing information reaching the accounting department, which calls for changes in the shipping department, as well as the method for transferring shipping information to the accounting department.

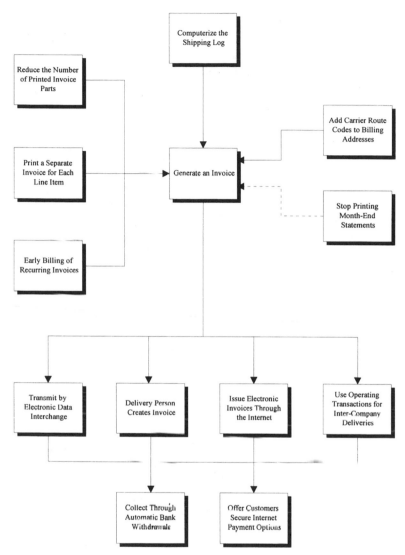

Exhibit 4.3. Impact of Best Practices on the Billings Function

Another set of methods involve how invoices are transmitted to customers. New technologies allow us to do so electronically or at the point of delivery, so that customers receive more accurate invoices more quickly than ever before. Finally, invoices can be completely eliminated in a limited number of cases, resulting in direct cash transfers from customer bank accounts to the company. When used together, these best practices result in a significant improvement in the efficiency of the billing function.

Chapter 5

Budgeting Best Practices

Many companies find the budgeting process to be an excruciatingly slow and painful process, requiring many months of continual effort before a reasonable budget document is completed. Once it is done, they wonder why the company went to all the effort, since no one makes a strong effort to follow it. This chapter addresses both problems. There are fifteen best practices that focus on creating and implementing a budget model, ranging from defining capacity levels and step-costing points to using activity-based budgeting. These are designed not only to make the budgeting process simpler, but also to result in a better budget that closely reflects management's expectations regarding operations in the upcoming budget period. In addition, there are several best practices that can improve a company's usage of the budget, so that it is closely integrated into daily operations.

This chapter begins with an overview of implementation issues for all of the best practices, followed by a discussion of individual best practices, each one being presented in a separate section. The chapter finishes with a review of how these best practices will change a company's budgeting operations.

IMPLEMENTATION ISSUES FOR BUDGETING BEST PRACTICES

With few exceptions, improvements to the budgeting system are easy to implement and can be done rapidly, with a minimum of fuss. The difficulty of implementation is noted in Exhibit 5.1. The reason is that most changes are to the budgeting model and procedures, neither of which are under the control of anyone but the accounting department, and neither of which need, unlike humans, some explanation and cooperation. Accordingly, one can assume a rapid implementation process that can mostly be completed during the current budget cycle, resulting in immediate and rapid improvement in the entire process.

There are only two best practices requiring a considerable amount of implementation effort. One is linking the budget to the purchase order system, since this usually requires some custom programming. The other one is switching to an activity-based budget model, since this approach requires a complete re-vamping of the budget model, as well as a new chart of accounts to reflect the changes. Of the two, the activity-based budgeting model is certainly the more difficult to complete. Also, on-line budget updating and video conferencing have a moderate associated

Exhibit 5.1. Implementation Issues for Budgeting Best Practices

Description	Ease of Implementation	Duration of Implementation	Cost of Implementation
Automatically Link the Budget to Purchase Orders	Difficult	Long	Expensive
Budget by Groups of Staff Positions	Easy	Short	Inexpensive
Clearly Define All Assumptions	Easy	Short	Inexpensive
Clearly Define All Capacity Levels	Easy	Short	Inexpensive
Create a Summarized Budget Model for Use by Upper Management	Easy	Short	Inexpensive
Establish Project Ranking Criteria	Easy	Short	Inexpensive
Establish the Upper Limit of Available Funding	Easy	Short	Inexpensive
Identify Step-Costing Change Points	Easy	Short	Inexpensive
Include a Working Capital Analysis	Easy	Short	Inexpensive
Issue a Budget Procedure and Timetable	Easy	Short	Inexpensive
Link to Performance Measurements and Rewards	Easy	Short	Inexpensive
Reduce the Number of Accounts	Easy	Long	Inexpensive
Simplify the Budget Model	Easy	Short	Inexpensive
Store Budget Information in a Central Database	Easy	Medium	Inexpensive
Use Activity-Based Budgeting	Difficult	Long	Inexpensive
Use Flex Budgeting	Moderate	Medium	Inexpensive
Use On-Line Budget Updating	Moderate	Medium	Moderate
Use Video Conferencing for Budget Updating	Moderate	Medium	Moderate

expense, since they require modem access (in the first case) and video conferencing equipment (in the later case). With these exceptions, one can expect best practice implementations in this area to be an easy chore, resulting in quick improvements.

AUTOMATICALLY LINK THE BUDGET TO PURCHASE ORDERS

A budget is not of much use if it is not tightly linked to company operations. It is common for a company to spend an inordinate amount of time constructing a fine budget and then to struggle with how to force the company to live by it. When this happens, the people who participated in creating the budget wonder why they spent time on it and will certainly be less willing to do so in the future. In this instance, the budget is seen as a mere formality.

To avoid the problem, one can link the budget to purchase orders. Under this method, the budget is loaded into the purchasing database used by the purchasing staff to create purchase orders. Whenever they enter a new purchase order into the computer system, they must include the account number to which the expense is charged; the system then compares the total year-to-date or period-to-date expense for this item to the budgeted amount and either issues a warning for an over-budget expenditure or rejects it. By using this best practice, one can be assured of keeping expenditures within budgeted levels.

However, there are some issues to deal with when using this system. One is that there may be necessary reasons for making an expenditure, such as an emergency purchase of some kind that must be made in order to keep the facility running. In this case, it may be useful to allow a manager to override the system with a special password. Also, some managers may be caught unawares toward the end of the year—if they have spend an inordinate amount earlier in the year, they will have no funding available at all for the last few weeks or months of the year. In this situation, it is best to forewarn managers over the course of the year by issuing a simple report, such as the one shown in Exhibit 5.2, that lists each expense item, the year-to-date amount spent, the full-year budget, and the amount left to spend. This information allows managers to know the exact amount available for their use and generally avoids problems with people running out of money at the end of the year.

Exhibit 5.2.   Budget versus Actual Report

Description	Spent Year-to-Date	Full Year Budget	Budget Remaining
Auto	$ 42,000	80,000	38,000
Building Repairs	100,100	150,000	49,900
Insurance	53,000	55,000	2,000
Interest Expense	12,000	24,000	12,000
Maintenance	39,000	41,000	2,000
Office Supplies	5,000	7,000	2,000
Telephones	14,000	20,000	6,000
Travel	18,500	19,000	500
Utilities	21,000	30,000	9,000

BUDGET BY GROUPS OF STAFF POSITIONS

The payroll portion of the budget model can be an excessively long one because every person in the company is listed on it. In particular, many accountants have difficulty avoiding a complete listing of *all* people who are not categorized as direct labor. As a result, this portion of the budget becomes an unwieldy cluster of information, requiring a long time to read as well as a considerable amount of updating work to keep track of everyone's pay levels.

A simple best practice is to summarize these positions by title, ensuring that there are far fewer line items, so the budget becomes much easier to update and review. To do so, one must summarize the pay levels of everyone with the same job title and post the average pay rate in the model. For those people who object that they can no longer determine who is summarized into which category, one can either issue a separate list that identifies the title of each person in the company or else insert the initials of all the people with each job title next to the summary-level description in the budget (a difficult proposition when there are many people with the same title!). The only real problem is in those companies where there is no record of the job titles of employees. In this case, it may be sufficient to summarize all payroll for each department into a single line item in the budget, with an average pay rate for the entire group; this approach completely avoids the problem of determining pay by title. Any of these variations will result in a simplified payroll section of the budget, while still retaining a high degree of accuracy.

CLEARLY DEFINE ALL ASSUMPTIONS

When the budget model is first presented to senior management, the person doing the presenting is deluged with questions about what assumptions are used in the model. Examples of assumptions that can cause problems are tax rate percentages, sales growth rates (especially by product line, since some of those lines may be exceedingly mature), capacity levels (see the next section), cost-of-goods-sold margins, commission rates, and medical insurance rates per person. Upper management wants to make sure that all assumptions are reasonable before they spend a great deal of their time reviewing the presented information. If there are specious assumptions, they will probably kick the budget back and demand changes before they will agree to look at it.

The best way around this problem is to list all key assumptions either right at the top of the budget model or else in clearly noted spots on each page. It is also helpful to note how these assumptions have changed from previous years, either by providing this information in a commentary or by showing prior year information in an extra column in the budget. By providing this information as clearly as possible, there will be fewer questions for the budgeting team to answer.

An even better approach is to tie as many of these assumptions into the budget model as possible, so that a change to an assumption will result in an immediate ripple effect through the budget. For example, changing a tax rate assumption will immediately alter the tax expense in the budget, while altering the medical expense per person will have a similar impact on personnel costs. Linking assumptions to the budget allows one to make nearly instantaneous changes to a budget with minimal effort.

CLEARLY DEFINE ALL CAPACITY LEVELS

When creating a budget that contains major increases in revenues, a common problem is failing to reflect this change in the rest of the budget, resulting in an inadequate amount of manpower, machinery, or facilities to handle the added growth. For example, a planned increase in revenue requires a corresponding increase in the number of sales staff who are responsible for bringing in the sales, not to mention a time lag before the new sales personnel can be reasonably expected to acquire new sales. Similarly, new sales at a production facility may result in machine utilization levels that are too high to maintain—has anyone thought of adding machinery purchases to the budget? This problem can be turned around and dealt with from the point of view of planned expense reductions, too—if the percentage of direct labor is budgeted to decline due to the use of automation, has anyone included the cost of the automation in the budget, and has a suitable time lag been built into the plan to account for the ramp-up time needed to implement the automation? Some of these problems are present in all but the best budget models.

The best practice that resolves this issue is the definition of capacity levels in the budget model. This can take the form of a table in the budget, such as the one shown in Exhibit 5.3. This example notes the capacity levels for manpower, such as a specific number of shipments per warehouse worker, sales per salesperson, and new product releases per engineer. It is very important to list these capacity levels for previous years in the same table, providing a frame of reference that tells the reader if the assumed capacity levels in this year's budget are attainable. It may also be possible to include another comparison column in the table that shows the capacity levels of competitors or of best practice companies against which the company has benchmarked its activities. By using this informational layout, one can easily tell if more or less resources are needed to attain the revenue and expense goals in a budget.

CREATE A SUMMARIZED BUDGET MODEL FOR USE
BY UPPER MANAGEMENT

The full budget model used by the accounting staff is a large one, with separate pages for the balance sheet, income statement, cash flow, capital expenditures, and each department, not to mention additional subsets of this information for

Exhibit 5.3.   Capacity Assumptions Table

Employee Description	Capacity/Person in 2003	Capacity/Person in 2002
Computer Help Desk	1 per 250 Computer Users	1 per 238 Computer Users
Engineer	1 per 5 Engineering Change Requests/Month	1 per 4.8 Engineering Change Requests/Month
Machine Operator	1 per 2 Presses	1 per 1.7 Presses
Salesperson	1 per $1,200,000 Sales	1 per $1,174,000 Sales
Shipper	1 per 12 Truck Ships/Day	1 per 9 Truck Ships/Day

each subsidiary. The full budget for a small company should run about twenty pages, while one for a multi-location corporation can easily run into the hundreds of pages. This presents a problem for senior management when it wants to conduct "what if" analysis work with the budget. For example, the president of the company may want to know what would happen to profits if there were one percent less direct labor, or if materials costs changed due to an increase in inflation. Given the size of the model, a senior manager's only way to get this information is to request that a budget analyst access the budget model, make the changes, and send the results back. This can take days for one request to be completed, which is a problem when the manager may want to model dozens of changes. Waiting for the results of all possible variations on the manager's requests may require months. During the budget period, there is not enough time to process all of these modeling requests, which leads to delays in completing the budget and frustration on the part of senior management.

The best practice that eliminates this problem is to create a small, summarized version of the full budget model for use by the senior management team. By doing so, these managers can play with all possible "what if" variations on the budget on their own computers, without waiting for someone in the accounting department to process these changes for them, saving a very large amount of time. To create such a budget model, it is extremely important to interview senior managers to see what kinds of variables they will want to alter. These will not vary much from year to year, unless there are drastic changes in the business, so once the variables are identified, they can be listed in the front of the model for easy access by the managers. For example, the variables can include the direct labor and materials percentages, the inflation rate, average pay raise, average employee benefit percentage, seasonality percentage for revenues, changes in revenues, and the tax and interest rates. The remainder of the budget should be shrunken down to the point where there is only a single expense line item for each department and the smallest possible number of revenue line items. The goal should be to keep the summarized budget model down to just a couple of pages. Also, to keep the data in this model fresh, one can either give it a direct computer link to the main budget model, automatically extracting the most current data from the real budget, or else manually extract the information and re-type it into the manager's budget model (which is a much easier proposition, and avoids any special programming). Creating this model may take a few extra weeks, but will be greatly appreciated by senior management.

The only problem with this budget model is that senior managers may not know how to use it or the computer on which it runs. If so, training is necessary, which may be difficult to fit into a manager's busy daily schedule. A good alternative is to train each manager's executive assistant, who can process any changes to the budget model that the manager wishes to make.

ESTABLISH PROJECT RANKING CRITERIA

When it comes time for the annual budget process, the accounting staff is usually inundated with a flood of requests for funding capital projects. These are sometimes pet projects, others are for repairs or replacements, and still others are entirely new business propositions. The trouble is that a great deal of time is spent in sorting through them all to see which ones are viable. Further, after the remaining ones are put in the budget, capital constraints typically lead to some of them being thrown back out. As a result, capital projects can be a bottleneck during the formation of the budget.

The best practice that reduces this bottleneck is to establish project ranking criteria in advance and distribute this information to anyone who may be submitting a capital request. These criteria should itemize how funds will be allocated. For example, any project with a return on capital that exceeds a target level is a top priority; next in line may be any project needed to bring a company in line with government regulations, and so on. Once they see the criteria, budget participants may voluntarily eliminate some of their own requests. In addition, if the capital expenditure request form accompanies the ranking criteria, applicants can fill out all the information the accounting staff needs to sort through the various projects, making the accountant's jobs much easier. This method not only eliminates some of the least probable capital projects up front, but also does a better job of categorizing those that are left.

ESTABLISH THE UPPER LIMIT OF AVAILABLE FUNDING

Too many budgeting processes take an inordinate amount of time to complete because management goes through too many iterations while deciding on how much money it has to spend. For example, the initial budget model may include funding for a new facility, an acquisition, or a distribution to stockholders. However, once management determines that the amount of available funding is not sufficient, it must recast the budget in order to arrive at a much smaller total expenditure. This plays havoc with the accounting staff, who must coordinate all the budgeting changes, modify the model, and reissue it.

The answer to this issue is to determine the amount of available funding as early in the process as possible. For example, the amount of fixed assets, inventory, and accounts receivable currently on hand can be extrapolated into the next year to determine the total amount of borrowing base that is likely to be available for borrowing purposes. Also, one can inquire of senior management if there is any likelihood of making a public offering of shares or of making a bond placement in the near future; this option is most unlikely for smaller companies, while larger ones may be constrained by established policies regarding the suitable debt-to-equity ratio that management is not allowed to exceed. Finally, the company may spin off cash from continuing operations; a review of current margin levels and cash flows can be used to determine the level of funds originating from this source. When all of these sources are put together, management usually finds that there is far less money available than they had wished for, which keeps them from developing overblown budgets that cannot possibly succeed.

The only issue with this approach is that some managers like to produce budgets that represent flights of fancy and do not appreciate having the extra information regarding funding, since it brings them back to reality rather abruptly. When these unique personalities are in management, it is best to use a great deal of tact when presenting funding information. A good variation that works in this situation is to present a range of funding amounts, along with the percentage chance of having each amount available, plus the likely interest rate that the company will have to pay in order to obtain the funds. By showing a probable interest rate, management will then understand that extra tiers of funding will only be available at a greater cost, since its credit risk rises as it borrows more money. This form of presentation is an effective way to increase management's understanding of funding availability.

IDENTIFY STEP-COSTING CHANGE POINTS

A typical problem for anyone constructing a budget is to determine when step-costing points occur. A step-cost is a block of additional expenses that must be added when a certain level of activity is reached. For example, machinery can only operate at a reasonable capacity level, perhaps 75 percent, before another machine must be added to cope with more work, even if that workload will only fill the machine at a very low level of capacity. The same principle applies to adding personnel or building space. In all cases, there is a considerable added expense that must be incurred in one large block. If the expense is sufficiently large, it can play havoc with the total level of expenses. Or, in the case of a really large capital purchase, it may leave no room for other capital purchases for the next year. Accordingly, it is necessary to keep close track of step-cost change points.

The best way to determine when an increase in step-costs will occur is to create a table of activity measures that directly relates to each step-cost. For example, a new shipping person is needed for every 135 pallets of product shipped per day. By relating sales for the next year to the number of pallet loads of shipments, one can reasonably predict when an additional shipper is needed. Similarly, if a piece of production machinery will support $1 million of sales, it is an easy matter to extrapolate this relationship based on expected sales to determine when additional machine purchases must be made. However, keep in mind that step-costs can be delayed by using new work methods, which can alter these relationships. For example, an automated shrink-wrapping machine can substantially increase the number of pallets that a single shipper can handle in a day, while a good preventive maintenance routine can reduce the amount of machine downtime, thereby increasing utilization rates and delaying the need for more production equipment. When these changes are added to the budget, it becomes necessary to change the relationship between the activity levels and step-costs, possibly with the relationships varying over the course of the budgeted period, as more work methods are implemented.

Thus, identifying step-costing change points is necessary to understand when new costs will be added to a budget, but one must also account for alterations in the relationship between the underlying activity measures that cause the step-costs to occur.

INCLUDE A WORKING CAPITAL ANALYSIS

All too many companies have found that their budgets are entirely unworkable because they have not accounted for the added cash required for working capital. This is a particular problem for those organizations forecasting extremely high rates of growth. They do not realize that they must have funds in advance to pay for the staff and materials required to produce products, as well as to fund the considerable increases in accounts receivable that will occur. Because of this, a company finds that its sales take off, as per the budget, while cash reserves rapidly dry up, resulting in a cash-starved organization that must scramble to find more cash to keep it growing. More times than not, a promising start is hamstrung because of lack of anticipation of working capital needs.

Clearly, the budget must account for working capital. There should be an extra page devoted to it in the budget, or it can be included in the cash flow page. In either case, the budget should make an assumption regarding the amount of inventory, accounts payable, and accounts receivable that will occur as sales go up; for example, there may be inventory turns of twelve per year, accounts receivable turns of nine, and accounts payable turns of ten. These turnover figures must then be built into the working capital formulas to determine how much extra cash will be needed as sales increase. An alternative approach is to assume that all working capital changes will be cleared in one month; for example, accounts payable will be paid in precisely one month, and accounts receivable paid by customers in the same period. This simpler approach is the one most commonly found in budgets, though it is not quite as accurate as the first method. The importance of accurate working capital forecasting cannot be overstated, especially for a cash-strapped company.

ISSUE A BUDGET PROCEDURE AND TIMETABLE

The typical budget dies a lingering death. It is not issued on time, nor is the first issuance likely to be the last one. Instead, there are a multitude of last-minute changes that force the budget process to continue into the next year. As a result, the budget may not be usable as a basis of comparison for new year results for several months.

The best solution to this problem is to issue a tightly structured budget procedure to the organization, along with an accompanying timetable, that specifies when all activities will occur, who will complete them, and when a deliverable is due back at the budget manager's office. By laying out the process in this manner and following up closely on all due dates, it is possible to issue a complete budget on time, every time. A good budget procedure should include the following steps, at a minimum:

- *Benchmarking comparison.* Though rarely used in a budget, it is extremely useful to conduct a benchmarking comparison of corporate performance against those of "best in class" companies, and to provide this information with the budget packages that go out to all departments, so that they can set expectations for improvements in their areas. This task can be completed well in advance of the regular budget process.

- *Revenue budget.* The first part of the budget process is always a determination by the sales staff of what they think they can sell in the upcoming year. Without this information, the remainder of the budget is impossible to construct. This portion must be completed and returned before any other steps can be completed.

- *Materials budget.* The purchasing department uses the revenue budget to determine its purchasing volumes, which is necessary for forecasting materials costs based on purchase volumes.

- *Automation budget.* The industrial engineering staff must determine what automation it plans to add to the production floor in order to eliminate direct labor and improve efficiencies. The timing of when these changes will be completed has a major impact on when to budget changes in labor and efficiencies into the forthcoming budget.

- *Personnel budget.* There must be a separate budget that outlines all the staff positions needed, their average pay rates, and the associated payroll burden.

This number will vary based on the revenue volumes that were previously determined, not to mention any automation projects.

- *Capital budget.* The automation budget will feed into the capital budget, since these projects usually require a considerable amount of funding. There may be other capital projects that do not run through the engineering department, such as for office equipment, so this budget is not normally completed until all departments have submitted their budgets.

- *Departmental budget.* Each department must note its expected expenditures, as well as personnel requirements.

- *Cash flow budget.* After all the previous budgets are returned, the accounting staff loads them into the budget model, which determines any resulting profits or losses, working capital changes, and capital requirements, all of which feed into the cash flow budget.

- *Funding and investments budget.* The cash flow budget feeds into the funding and investments budget. This one is used by the chief financial officer, who determines either the sources and cost of funds (if cash is needed) or where it is to be invested and the expected returns from doing so (if there will be a cash surplus). The results of this budget will also feed back into the interest expense and investment income line items elsewhere in the budget.

- *Employee performance budget.* Finally, after the budget is completed, the human resources manager uses it to create an employee performance budget that links pay levels and bonus payments to the performance levels noted elsewhere in the budget, such as completing automation projects or attaining budgeted sales levels.

Also, some companies may want to include an acquisitions budget, which is closely linked to the funding and investments budget, since this activity will have a major impact on cash flows.

The above list of budget modules makes it obvious that the budget process flows in a very specific sequence, with one part of the budget being used as a basis for the next part. The budget procedure and timetable must be built around this budget flow; specific dates of completion for one piece of the budget tie into the start date of the next part of the budget that requires information from the first part. It is wise to include a buffer of a few days between the completion date of one part and the start of the next, so that inevitable completion troubles can still be ironed out, leaving sufficient time to complete the overall budget by the targeted date. Do not be surprised if the timetable is not accurate in the first year it is used, since it is difficult to estimate completion times. Just be sure to note actual completion dates in the first year and adjust the timetable accordingly in the following year. Only by constant adjustment over a long period of time will the budget procedure and timetable become fine-tuned tools for the efficient and orderly completion of the budget.

LINK TO PERFORMANCE MEASUREMENTS AND REWARDS

A continuing frustration for senior managers is to see an immense amount of time being put into the formation of the annual budget, only to have employees completely ignore it over the ensuring year. Some wonder why they bother with the budget at all. A common result is little or no management support of the annual budgeting process.

The best practice that resolves this problem is a tight linkage between the budget and employee reward systems. By doing so, employees are forced to peruse the budget continually to ensure that their actual performance matches the standard laid down by senior management at the start of the year—if not, then their next pay raise and bonus may not arrive, or be much smaller than expected. At worst, they may find themselves looking for employment elsewhere. To make this best practice work, the human resources staff should be brought in at the end of the budgeting process to devise a set of reward mechanisms that directly link employee pay to attaining the budget. For example, if a revenue budget requires sales of $1 million per salesperson, there should be a hefty bonus for the sales staff associated with attaining that goal. Similarly, if an automation project is scheduled for completion in July, at a cost of $500,000 and an immediate reduction of eleven direct labor personnel, the engineering manager should be tied to a bonus that is paid out only if all of these budgeted items are attained. This should be a very clear-cut document that is an integral part of the budget, one that is reviewed by senior management for reasonableness. Further, this linkage should be carefully reviewed with all concerned managers several times during the year to ensure that there is no question about how much they will be paid and the basis upon which all pay calculations are based. This is an excellent management tool for ensuring that the budget will be followed and attained.

The only problem with this best practice is when senior management puts unrealistic expectations into the budget, such as assuming that sales can be doubled without a corresponding increase in the sales staff. When this happens, managers will ignore the budget once again, since they know in advance that there is no conceivable way they can meet their assigned tasks. Setting attainable targets is key to making this best practice work correctly.

REDUCE THE NUMBER OF ACCOUNTS

Some budget models are astoundingly complex because there are so many account line items in which to record budgeting information. This is nearly always the fault of the controller, who has allowed the chart of accounts to grow to an excessive degree. Once there are too many accounts in the general ledger, it becomes obligatory to budget for the contents of each one. This presents the dual problems of adding new lines to the budget every year, and of forcing managers to do extra analysis to determine the budgeted amounts for the upcoming year.

The simple, though long-term, approach is to eliminate as many accounts as possible from the chart of accounts. This takes a long time, since one must be careful to shift account balances to surviving accounts, verify that inactivated accounts are not used for some special purpose, and that there will be no impact on the resulting financial reports. Given the intricacies of eliminating accounts, it is usually best to do so in small groups of just a few per month, with an overall reduction in the number of accounts taking as long as a year to complete. Once this is done, it is a simple matter to eliminate the same accounts from the budget.

Another approach that is not only quicker, but also bypasses the need for a lengthy reduction in the chart of accounts, is to eliminate the accounts in the budget model, but to keep them in the actual chart of accounts. This option will result in no budget in the upcoming budget period for those accounts that have been excluded from the budget model, so it is only useful for those accounts with very small balances. Thus, this is only good for a few accounts and is not as definitive a solution as eliminating accounts from the chart of accounts for good.

SIMPLIFY THE BUDGET MODEL

A company that has used the same budgeting model for many years will find that it gradually becomes more complicated. This is because there are incremental changes each year—a new analysis page here, extra departments there, perhaps some assumptions as well. Though the changes seem minimal if looked at for just one year, the accumulation over many years makes the model very cumbersome, difficult to understand, and prone to error. For example, if formulas are added to the budget that require inputting the final balance sheet numbers from the previous year, it is possible that no one will remember this when the next budgeting cycle arrives in the following year, especially if the person who made the change in the previous year is no longer with the company, or if the change was not documented anywhere. As the number of these changes pile up over the years, it becomes increasingly difficult to complete the budget on time. The person managing the budget model becomes increasingly indispensable, for no one else knows how to use it.

To avoid these problems, it is necessary to regularly simplify the budget model. This does not mean that the simplification can be done once and then dropped. On the contrary, the standard budget procedure should begin with a review of the model from the previous year to ensure that all budget line items and calculations are thoroughly documented and understandable, and that they are still needed. There should also be a step that specifically requires the budget manager to review the need for extra line items and formulas, with an eye to eliminating as much as possible from the budget model every year. Though it may not be possible to completely streamline the budget model in one year, a continuing effort in this area will yield excellent results as long as the review is continual.

Though the main focus of this best practice is to reduce the complexity of the budget model, it is sometimes sufficient to ensure that the model is adequately documented. Some businesses really become more complex over time and therefore require more detailed budget models. This is particularly true of companies on a fast growth track, especially if they are growing by acquisition and must account for the operations of many new businesses. In these cases, the budget manager should review the model at the end of each budget cycle to see what has been added to the model this year, and verify that complete and thoroughly understandable descriptions have been included in the budget procedure that note the reasons for the changes, how they work, and the resulting impact on the entire budget model. This step may be all that is needed for some companies.

STORE BUDGET INFORMATION IN A CENTRAL DATABASE

Too often, a budget manager assembles all of the information needed to create the annual budget, has done so with days to spare, and yet somehow cannot release the budget on time. The reason is that the budget pieces are just that—in pieces—and cannot be easily put together, requiring a great deal of labor to re-key it all into a central budget model. The information is especially difficult to assemble if department heads have added new line items for new types of expenses, or deleted or merged existing ones. When this happens, someone must contact the department managers to request a clarification, sometimes resulting in last-minute changes to the underlying budget model that may introduce errors into the budget formulas, resulting in incorrect cost or revenue summarizations. When there are many departments or subsidiaries, it is possible for all these issues to add up to more time to assemble the data than it took for the rest of the company to complete its part of the budget!

The solution to this problem is to centralize the budget into a single database. Department managers are issued templates for the budget that are derivatives of this database and they must fill in the blanks provided—no exceptions allowed. When these budget forms are turned in to the budget manager, it is a simple matter to quickly peruse them and determine which revenue or expense line items have been left blank and which additions have been made that do not fit into the standard template; managers can be contacted at once and asked to revise their budgets to fit the existing model. It may even be possible to give managers direct access to the budget model through modems or the internal company computer network (see the "Use On-Line Budget Updating" section in this chapter), so that managers are forced to enter information into the existing budget model. This approach is a quick and easy way to greatly reduce the back-end work by the accounting department to assemble incoming budget information.

The only problem with this best practice is that sometimes there will be new company activities that cannot be easily shoehorned into the existing budget model. This is an especially common circumstance when a company acquires another corporation that operates in an entirely different industry. For example, the expenses in a freight-hauling company will vary significantly from those of a mail-order business. In these cases, the budget model obviously must be changed. The best way to do so is to have the budget manager be informed of decisions by senior management to acquire or start up businesses, so that the manager can make changes to the budget model in advance, which eliminates the need for any last-minute changes to the model.

USE ACTIVITY-BASED BUDGETING

For many organizations, the existing budgeting system simply does not yield adequate results. Management can fiddle with the numbers all it wants, but working within the existing structure of revenues by product line and expenses by department is so rigid that there is little room for improving operating results. Only by using outlandish assumptions, such as inordinate price increases or cost reductions, can any reasonable profit improvement be attained. As the new budget year progresses and everyone realizes that those absurd assumptions are, in fact, not attainable, some of the blame is put on the budgeting process, resulting in a loss of credibility. This problem is especially common in old, established industries, where competition is high and low profits are the norm.

Activity-based budgeting is the best solution for companies in this quandary. To use it, the existing budget model must either be scrapped or used alongside a new model, which pools all costs into cost centers, assigns these costs to activities, and charges the activities to products and customers. By using this new approach, one can see much more clearly the products on which a company really makes (or does not make) money, and margins on all customers, based on the services they demand from the company. With this better information, management can target cost reductions in those areas where there is little return on the money invested, while targeting expense increases if there is a corresponding increase in margin. This is a very large topic that requires a separate book to fully comprehend. For more information, read *Driving Value Using Activity Based Budgeting,* by James Brimson and John Antos (John Wiley & Sons, 1999).

The biggest problem with activity-based budgeting is that it requires an entirely new budget model, as well as a new chart of accounts in which to store the budget information. Both of these changes are significant and require months (and sometimes years) of careful planning and implementation. The reason for all the planning is that all accounting information systems are designed to feed information into the existing chart of accounts, so these systems must be modified to accumulate data in the manner required for the activity-based budgeting system instead. One way to get around this problem and activate the new system much more quickly is to keep the old budgeting model and continue to account for it through the chart of accounts in the traditional manner, manually maintaining the new budgeting model to one side and reporting on actual results with a separate system. Though certainly more labor-intensive, this approach can be implemented at once and requires very little change in the existing accounting systems.

USE FLEX BUDGETING

Perhaps the single most tedious part of updating a budget is altering the myriad of expense line items every time someone makes a change to the estimated revenue level. Revenue is far and away the most commonly tweaked number in a budget, so the underlying expenses have to be recast to be in proportion to the changed revenue levels a multitude of times. This is a major chore not only for the accounting staff maintaining the budget, but also for those managers who must be contacted about changes to the expense levels they had previously authorized.

A recasting of the budget model will largely eliminate this problem. Instead of making changes to the expense line item for every expense in the budget, it is much easier to set up each one as either a flexible expense account or one that is fixed within a broad range of revenue levels. If it is fixed, there is no need for change, unless there is an enormous alteration in budgeted revenue levels. However, many other expenses will vary directly with revenue; in these cases, it is possible to revise the budget formulas so that they are listed as percentages of the monthly revenue level. By making these formula alterations, it becomes an easy matter to adjust revenue and see a swath of expense changes ripple through the budget model—with no manual intervention whatsoever. This best practice can reduce budget maintenance work to a fraction of the amount formerly needed.

Though the flex budget discussion has centered on tying expenses to specific revenue levels, it is also possible, and probably more accurate, to tie some expenses to other levels of activity. For example, telephone usage or office expenses should be linked more properly to the number of budgeted employees, while utility costs can be tied either to square footage used or the number of machines in operation. Thus, one can link expenses to a number of activity measures in a flex budget.

USE ON-LINE BUDGET UPDATING

One of the largest problems for a budget manager in a large company is bringing together the budget information arriving from a multitude of outlying company locations. For example, a location may send budget updates on paper or a floppy disk, either of which requires the manual translation of this information into the budget model by the budget manager's staff. If there are many locations reporting budget information, this can result in a flood of work for several days. Also, the person re-entering the budget information may make a typing error, thereby altering a budgeted amount from what a subsidiary intended, or may misconstrue the submitted data and list a budget number in the wrong account. In either case, the budget must be reviewed by the subsidiary and a request made to adjust the error, which takes still more time and effort.

An excellent best practice that entirely eliminates this problem is to give subsidiaries direct access to the budget model via modems. They can then dial up the budget model, enter it themselves, make any necessary changes, and review the results. By doing so, all errors are made, and must be corrected, by the subsidiaries, taking this chore away from the central accounting group.

There are two problems with this best practice. One is that all subsidiaries must go through the effort of acquiring modems, as well as direct phone line access to those modems, in order to acquire on-line access to the budget model. However, in these days of universal Internet access, it is a rare company that does not already have modem access. The second item is more critical; anyone from any subsidiary can now have access to the entire budget model, with the ability to delete it, alter information for other parts of the company, or just observe the numbers budgeted for other divisions or departments, which can be confidential. To avoid this problem, it may be necessary to split the budget into different files, one for each subsidiary, and then give password access only to the portion of the budget assigned to each subsidiary. Another option is to keep the budget model in one piece, but to restrict access by passwords to just those account codes that apply to each subsidiary. The first option allows a company to use an electronic spreadsheet to contain the model, but the latter approach requires that it be stored in a database with better password protection than is typically available for an electronic spreadsheet. A company can pick either option based on its overall need for securing budget information.

USE VIDEO CONFERENCING FOR BUDGET UPDATING

Companies with many locations have the added budgeting cost of bringing together managers from outlying locations, sometimes for a number of meetings. Given the high price of travel and lodging, this can be a significant expense. Further, the activities in which those people are normally engaged will stop while they are traveling to and from budget meetings, so there is an added degree of waste.

Technology can be used to eliminate these costs. The latest innovation is to use video conferencing to hold meetings, thereby avoiding all travel costs and only taking up people's time for the duration of an actual meeting. The range of options for a video conferencing system runs from a company-owned video production room that has projection screens and television cameras, down to a small device that mounts on top of one's computer, allowing for transmission of the image of whomever is sitting in front of the computer. The larger and more complex option is recommended for the budgeting chore, since it has the added features of allowing for the video transmission of documents to other sites, much better video quality, and the option to have simultaneous conferences with up to two other locations.

The main problem with using a quality video conferencing system is that it can cost $100,000 per location, though this cost is rapidly coming down. The smallest video units only cost about $100, though the video quality is quite poor. One must choose the system that fits a company's ability to pay (which may be high if there are other applications to which such a system can be put, such as for the transmission of engineering meetings). It is also possible to rent video conferencing centers, which may be considerably less expensive than purchasing one. This is an especially good option if there are few other uses to which a company-owned video conferencing center can be put. In addition, there must be very tight scheduling of meetings, requiring everyone is on-line at the same time. Otherwise, some very expensive equipment will be tied up while waiting for someone to arrive at their conferencing site. The underlying problem is system cost, so a careful analysis of all expenses is necessary before buying a video conferencing system.

TOTAL IMPACT OF BEST PRACTICES ON THE BUDGETING FUNCTION

All of the best practices discussed in this chapter are noted in Exhibit 5.4, where they are clustered around the three main budgeting activities—creating the budget model, implementing it, and using it. Most of the best practices impact the creation of the budget model, either by increasing its simplicity or by improving the information that goes into it. For example, reducing the number of accounts and budgeting by groups of staff positions reduces the size of the model, while using activity-based budgeting improves the resulting information. Other best practices improve the ability of the company to quickly and effectively input data into the budget model or to discuss changes to it, either through video conferencing, a budget procedure, or on-line budget updating. Finally, several methods are available for closely linking the resulting budget model to company operations, so that most activities cannot be completed without some interaction with budget information. What all of these changes amount to is a highly efficient budgeting process that can be completed in less time than the previous budgeting system, while providing much better information to the management team.

SUMMARY

This chapter focused primarily on those best practices that improve a budget model's ease of use as well as the quality of the information it produces. These are the very issues most managers complain about, since many budget models take an eternity to produce and are not that accurate when released. Since the

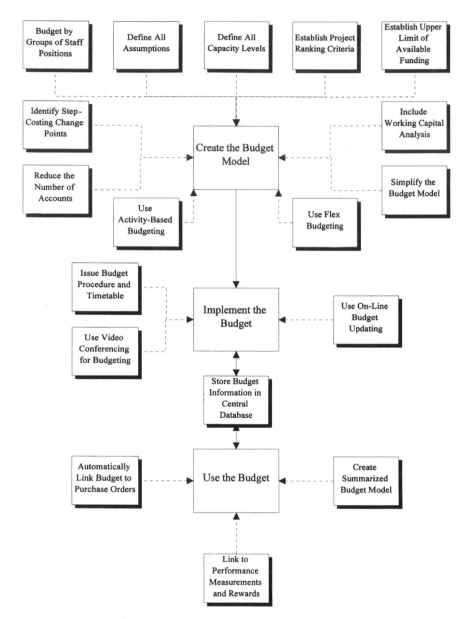

Exhibit 5.4.   Impact of Best Practices on the Budgeting Function

bulk of the changes in this area are easy and inexpensive to implement, there is no reason why an active and enterprising accounting manager cannot swiftly replace the old budgeting system with one that is easy to use and results in excellent budgeting information.

There was a lesser focus on best practices that enhance one's use of the budget once it has been produced. Since the budget is an excellent control tool, the best of these practices is one that ties the budget directly to the purchase order system, so that purchase orders can be automatically compared to the remaining available budget and rejected by the computer if there are no budgeted funds remaining. Another best practice links employee performance to the budget, while another creates a summarized budget model for further financial modeling work by members of management. These are effective ways to maximize the budget once it has been produced.

Chapter 6

Cash Management Best Practices

This chapter covers the best practices that can be used to create a more efficient cash management function. Though this area falls into the finance function at many larger companies, it is typically under the authority of the controller in a smaller company, and so is covered in this book.

The best practices in this chapter are primarily concerned with creating an orderly flow of cash into and out of a company's coffers, leaving no cash in the system that is not being properly utilized to the fullest extent. This method frees up the largest possible amount for investment purposes. The vast majority of these best practices should be clustered together, since they are complementary, working most effectively if they are all used at once.

This chapter begins with a discussion of the implementation problems associated with each best practice and then moves on to cover the advantages and disadvantages of using each one. The final section discusses how to use most of these best practices as a group to achieve a cash management system with a high degree of efficiency.

IMPLEMENTATION ISSUES FOR CASH MANAGEMENT BEST PRACTICES

All of the best practices covered in this chapter are noted in alphabetical order in Exhibit 6.1, which shows the relative ease of implementation for each item. In nearly all cases, cash management implementations are quite inexpensive and can be completed in a short time. The reason for these easy set-ups is that there is no custom programming involved, and no need to involve other departments. Without these two problem areas, it becomes an easy matter to install a whole range of best practices in short order. To make the situation even easier, a company's bank is usually eager to help install most of these items, because most of them involve creating close banking ties, which keeps a company from realistically being able to move its banking business elsewhere. A bank can also charge fees for many of these services, which gives it an added incentive to help out. Thus, cash management is an area in which a controller can enjoy great success in improving operations.

Exhibit 6.1. Implementation Issues for Cash Management Best Practices

Description	Ease of Implementation	Duration of Implementation	Cost of Implementation
Area-Concentration Banking	Moderate	Medium	Inexpensive
Consolidate Bank Accounts	Moderate	Medium	Inexpensive
Controlled Disbursements	Moderate	Short	Inexpensive
Electronic Funds Transfer	Easy	Short	Inexpensive
Lockbox Collections	Moderate	Medium	Medium
On-Line Access to Bank Account Information	Easy	Short	Inexpensive
Positive Pay System	Moderate	Medium	Medium
Proliferate Petty-Cash Boxes	Moderate	Medium	Medium
Utilize an Investment Policy	Easy	Short	Inexpensive
Zero-Balance Accounts	Moderate	Short	Inexpensive

Though all of the best practices noted in Exhibit 6.1 are covered in some detail later in this chapter, it is useful to see how the most important ones fit together into a coherent set of cash management practices. Accordingly, there is a flow-chart in Exhibit 6.2 that shows how lockboxes and area-concentration banking can be used to accumulate cash from customers and forward it into a central bank account, from which cash is distributed only as needed to a payroll zero-balance account (for payments to employees) and a controlled disbursements account (for payments to suppliers). By using this approach, cash can be quickly sent to the main bank account and doled out only when company checks are cashed, which allows the cash management staff to transfer all remaining funds to an investment account where it can earn interest, rather than lying idle in any number of corporate checking accounts.

AREA-CONCENTRATION BANKING

Perhaps the greatest cash management problem, especially for a company with many locations, is what to do with a multitude of bank accounts. When trying to find a way to invest excess funds most efficiently, it is necessary to call all banks with which a company has an account, check on the balance in each account, determine how much of that amount can be safely extracted for investments without increasing the risk of having a presented check bounce due to a lack of funds, shift the excess funds to a central account, and finally invest it in an interest-bearing account of some kind. To conduct this much work every day may take up all

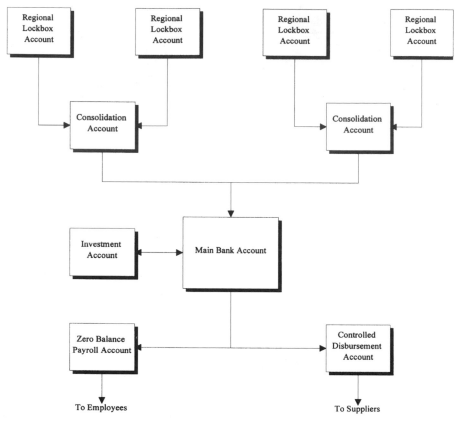

Exhibit 6.2.   Bank Account Structure Using Best Practices

of the time of several people, depending on the number and location of accounts. A tedious chore indeed, and one that may take up the largest proportion of the cash management staff's time.

The best way to avoid all of this work is to create an area-concentration banking system. This best practice automatically shifts funds from outlying bank accounts into regional accounts, from which the cash management staff can invest funds more easily. Under this arrangement, a company's bank is asked to automatically clear out the excess funds in an account every day, forwarding the money to a single account for each bank. Most banks will not automatically forward money to an account at a different bank, so the money tends to stop at an account within the geographical region covered by the bank. This still reduces the number of accounts sufficiently to make it much easier for the cash management staff to determine the amount of cash available. To avoid the problem of not being able to automatically transfer cash between banks, some companies are transferring all of their business to those large banks that have established a national presence, so that a complete automatic centralization of all funds can be achieved, no matter where in the country an account may be located. To make this concept work properly, it is necessary to set up all outlying bank accounts as lockboxes, only meant to receive cash (see the "Lockbox Collections" section in this chapter), with all disbursements coming out of a single, centralized account, to which funds are only doled out as needed. By using this approach, a cash management staff can eliminate the majority of its clerical work.

An area-concentration banking system is an excellent way to efficiently consolidate a company's cash holdings, but there are some problems with it. One is that it may require the complete revision of the existing banking system, no longer using a number of smaller banks which may not offer this service, in favor of a single national bank that does. In addition, as the bank will charge a fee for each cash transfer, there must be a minimum volume of cash moving through the system each day to make this arrangement a cost-effective one. Finally, this method assumes that disbursements are from one location, so that no extra funds must be distributed to outlying bank accounts that are needed to cover outstanding checks. It can sometimes be quite difficult to revise the existing system of bank accounts, especially due to the pressure by local managers who want to retain their existing accounts, in order for the company to establish the most efficient area-concentration banking layout.

Though the attainment of an area-concentration banking system may require a significant amount of time, it is a best practice of particular help to those companies with a national presence, a multitude of bank accounts, and a significant amount of cash flow.

CONSOLIDATE BANK ACCOUNTS

A time-consuming chore at the beginning of each month is to complete reconciliations between the bank statements for all the company's bank accounts and the book balances it maintains for each of those accounts. For example, a retail store operation may have a separate bank account for each of hundreds of locations, each of which must be reconciled. Also, if it is the controller's policy to wait for all bank accounts to be reconciled before issuing financial statements, this can be the primary bottleneck operation that keeps financial statements from being issued in a timely manner. Finally, having many bank accounts raises the possibility that cash will linger in all of those accounts, resulting in less total cash being available for investment purposes. To use the previous example, if there are 100 retail stores and each has a bank account in which is deposited $5,000 (a decidedly modest sum for a single location), then $500,000 has been rendered unavailable for investment. Thus, having a multitude of bank accounts leads to a variety of downstream problems which can seriously impact the efficiency of some portions of the accounting department, while also reducing the amount of cash readily available for investment purposes.

The best way to resolve the multi-account problem is to merge as many of them together as possible. To use the previous example, rather than give a bank account to each store, it may be possible to issue a fixed number of checks to each location, all of which will be drawn upon the company's central bank account. This reduces the number of bank accounts from 100 to one. If anyone feels that there is a danger of someone fraudulently cashing a large check on the main bank account, this problem can be resolved by mandating a maximum amount for each check, above which the bank will not honor the check. By limiting the amount per check and the number of checks, this control effectively resolves any risk of a major fraud loss by consolidating all bank accounts. This is also an effective approach when acquiring another company, since its bank accounts can be merged into the existing account. In both cases, reducing the number of accounts also makes it much easier to track the cash balances in each account. Thus, account consolidation is an effective approach for improving accounting efficiency as well as the management of cash flows.

There are some problems to consider before consolidating bank accounts. One is that there may be automatic withdrawals taken out of an account. If the account is closed down and merged into a different account, the automatic withdrawal will be terminated, resulting in an unhappy supplier who is no longer receiving any money. To avoid this problem, the transactions impacting each account must be reviewed to ensure that all automatic withdrawals are being shifted to the consolidated account. Also, there are legal reasons for keeping some accounts separate, such as a cafeteria plan account, into which employee deductions are deposited and from which a plan administrator withdraws funds. Finally, consolidating too many bank accounts may result in a very difficult bank reconciliation chore. Sometimes it is easier to keep a small number of separate accounts, just to make the reconciliation process somewhat easier to untangle and resolve. However, with the exception of these few cases, it is generally possible to reduce the number of a company's bank accounts to a bare minimum, resulting in greater efficiency and more cash available for investment.

CONTROLLED DISBURSEMENTS

The person who is in charge of managing corporate cash flows is always trying to find ways to retain cash legitimately for as long as possible to invest it, thereby earning interest for a company. There are unethical ways of doing so, such as not paying suppliers even when previously agreed-upon pay dates have been surpassed. However, these activities can destroy a company's reputation with its suppliers and even impact its credit rating.

A legitimate way to retain cash for an extra day or two is to use controlled disbursements. This best practice is based on the principle of mail float, which means that one can print and immediately mail a check to pay for an invoice on its due date and the supplier can receive and cash it, but the check will not clear for a day or two longer than was previously the case, resulting in extra time during which a company still has control over its funds. For example, a company in Denver can issue checks that are made payable to a bank in Aspen, Colorado, which, due to its isolated location, requires an extra day for checks to clear. When checks are presented to the Aspen location for payment, a daily batch of cash required to cover the payments is forwarded to the company's primary bank. The company can access this cash requirement information every day and forward just enough money to the controlled disbursement account to cover cash requirements for that day. These extra steps give a company the capability to keep virtually all of its excess cash in investments, extracting only the bare minimum each day to cover immediate cash requirements. Thus, controlled disbursements not only allow a company to retain its cash longer, but also to use the new off-site bank account as a zero-balance account. Both of these actions can significantly increase the amount of a company's operating funds on hand.

Though a sound best practice to use, there are a few issues involved with a controlled-disbursements account to consider. One is that the amount of additional float made available through this method is gradually shrinking, as the Federal Reserve Bank gradually eliminates those pockets of inefficient-check clearing throughout the country. This may require a company to periodically change the location of the bank that it uses as its check-clearing point. Eventually, the longest additional float time to be gained by this method will probably be limited to a single day. Also, the concept is one of the most expensive bank services. Consequently, the cost must be carefully calculated and offset against projected benefits to ensure that it is a worthwhile implementation project.

Given the cost of controlled disbursements, this is a best practice that is best used by a company with a significant volume of cash flow, which ensures that the incremental benefits of retaining a large amount of cash for an extra day or two will adequately offset the cost of this service.

ELECTRONIC FUNDS TRANSFER

The cash management staff is sometimes called upon to make money transfers that are either very large, complex, or on a rush basis. A good example of this situation is a letter of credit (LOC), commonly used for international transactions. The paperwork needed to initiate an LOC is exceedingly lengthy and is usually wrong on the first try, requiring some additional iterations before it is correct. Another example is a large payment that must go to a supplier at once, possibly to avert a loss of credit standing. This may require a hand-carried local delivery or an overnight express delivery to the supplier. In any of these cases, the cash management staff will take an inordinate proportion of its time to process the movement of funds. There must be an easier way.

There is, and it is the wire transfer. This transaction is handled through a company's bank, which can shift money out of the company's bank account in moments and route it to the supplier's account, even if it is located at another bank. There is little paperwork and no hand-carrying of checks. To function properly, a company needs the recipient's bank account number and bank routing number. The person sending the funds (who must be authorized to do so, with this authorization on file at the bank) then faxes the transfer information to the bank and waits for the transfer to take place. To make the process even more efficient, one can have fax forms already prepared for the most common wire transfer destinations, with all of the bank account information already filled in. A more advanced set-up used by larger companies is to have all the wire transfer information stored in the computer system, so that wire transfer information can be sent electronically to the bank. Yet another version is to send wire transfers by accessing the bank's database on-line and performing all the work yourself. With all of these options for sending money to suppliers, there is bound to be an approach that meets the particular needs and resources of any company.

Despite the obvious nature of this best practice, it is surprising how rarely it is used. By maintaining a database of recipient bank information, however, this can become a simple matter that can be converted into a routine procedure, improving the efficiency of the cash management function.

LOCKBOX COLLECTIONS

There are a number of problems associated with receiving all customer payments at a company location. For example, checks can be lost or delayed in the mail room, given to the wrong accounting person for further processing, or delayed in transit from the company to the bank. It is also necessary for the mail room staff to log in all received checks, which are later compared to the deposit slip sent out by the accounting staff to ensure that all received checks have been deposited— this is a non-value-added step, though it is necessary to provide some control over received checks. All these steps are needed if checks are received and processed directly by a company.

The answer is to have the bank receive the checks instead. To do so, a company's bank sets up a lockbox, which is essentially a separate mailbox to which deposits are sent by customers. The bank opens all mail arriving at the lockbox, deposits all checks at once, copies the checks, and forwards all check copies and anything else contained in customer remittances to the company. This approach has the advantage of accelerating the flow of cash into a company's bank account, since the lockbox system typically reduces the mail float customers enjoy by at least a day, while also eliminating all of the transaction-processing time that a company would also need during its internal cash-processing steps. The system can be enhanced further by creating lockboxes at a number of locations throughout the country, with locations very close to a company's largest customers. Customers will then send their funds to the nearest lockbox, which further reduces the mail float and increases the speed with which funds arrive in a company's coffers. If there are multiple lockboxes, a company should periodically compare the locations of its lockboxes to those of its customers, to ensure that the constantly changing mix of customers does not call for an alteration in the locations of some lockboxes to bring the overall mail float-time down to the lowest possible level. In short, there are some exceptional advantages to using lockboxes.

There are only two problems with lockboxes, one involving fees and the other being a one-time problem with implementation. A bank will charge both a fixed and variable-rate fee for the use of a lockbox. There is a small, fixed monthly fee for the lockbox, plus a charge of a few cents for every processed check. For a company with a very small number of incoming checks, these costs may make it uneconomical to maintain a lockbox. Also, the work required to convince customers to change the company's pay-to address can be considerable. Every customer must be contacted, usually by mail, to inform them of the new lockbox address to which they must now send their payments. If they do not comply (a common occurrence), someone must make a reminder call. If there are many customers, this can be a major task to complete and may not be worthwhile if the sales to each customer are extremely small—the cost of contacting them may exceed the profit from annual sales to them. Thus, a company with a small number of customers or many low-volume customers may not find it cost-effective to use a lockbox.

An additional issue is the number of lockboxes that should be used. A company cannot maintain an infinite number of them, since each one has a fixed cost that can add up. Instead, a common approach is to periodically hire a consultant, sometimes provided by a bank, who analyzes the locations and average sales to all customers, calculates the average mail float for each one, and offsets this information with the cost of putting lockboxes in specific locations. The result of this analysis will be a cost-benefit calculation that trades off excessive mail float against the cost of additional lockboxes to arrive at the most profitable mix of lockbox locations.

A final issue is what to do with the residual checks that will continue to arrive at a company. Despite its best efforts, some customers will ignore all lockbox addresses and continue to send their checks directly to a company. When this happens, the controller can either process the checks as usual, using all the traditional control points, or simply have the mailroom staff put all the checks into an envelope and mail them to the lockbox. The later approach is frequently the best because it allows a company to completely avoid all cash deposit procedures. The only case where the traditional cash-processing approach may still have to be followed is when a company is in extreme need of cash and can deposit the funds more quickly by walking them to the nearest bank branch to deposit immediately. Otherwise, all checks should be routed through the lockbox.

Consequently, one or more lockboxes can be a highly effective way to avoid the cumbersome check deposit procedure, while also accelerating the speed of incoming cash flows. In only a minority of situations will a lockbox not be a cost-effective alternative.

ON-LINE ACCESS TO BANK ACCOUNT INFORMATION

It is a common occurrence for an accounting department to find that because of a few missed transactions during the month, its book balance of cash is substantially different than its actual balance, as reported by the bank in the bank statement that arrives a few days after the end of the month. This can cause great difficulty if the book balance is so far off that the company is unintentionally keeping less than the minimum amount of cash in its bank accounts to cover checks presented by suppliers for payment. This can result in bounced checks and additional bank fees. Also, if a company conducts a large part of its business with wire transfers (incoming or outgoing), it has no way of knowing when transfers have arrived or left the bank until the bank statement arrives. In particular, if an incoming wire transfer does not arrive as expected, a company will not know that it should be making collection calls until the bank statement arrives, resulting in poor cash flow. In short, using only a monthly bank statement to verify account balances can severely handicap a company's cash management operations.

A simple best practice that eliminates all of these problems is to use on-line access to bank account information. To do so, a company must install a modem in an accounting computer, link it to an outside phone line, and use it to dial up its bank's database of daily cash transactions. By doing so, it is not only possible to see what checks have cleared and what deposit amounts have arrived, but also (in the more sophisticated banking systems) to transfer money between accounts and to send out wire transfers. In addition, by tracking cash inflows and outflows each day, it is possible to keep the book balance so accurate that the bank reconciliation is usually much easier to complete each month. This amount of up-to-date information, when closely monitored each day, allows a company to continually update its cash management records, resulting in better management of cash balances and tighter control over the collections process.

The only problems with on-line bank information are cost and availability. There is usually a fixed monthly fee charged by a bank to access its database, plus additional fees if extra services are used. These fees are usually outweighed by the benefits of having the additional information. The other issue is that some smaller banks do not have an on-line access system. In this situation, if there is a great need for the information, it may be better to switch to a bank that does provide on-line access (which includes nearly all regional banks).

On-line access to bank information is a fundamental best practice that allows a company to maintain tight control and knowledge of its cash flows.

POSITIVE PAY SYSTEM

Some organizations have a problem with check fraud, whereby checks are presented to the bank for payment that either were not issued by the company, or were issued for a lesser amount than is noted on the presented checks. Though not normally a large problem, some companies can lose a considerable amount of money to fraudulent activities by this means.

A few banks now allow a company to use a program called "positive pay," which virtually eliminates check fraud. This best practice works by having a company send to the bank a daily list of all checks issued, which is usually stored in a specific data storage format that the bank can use to update its files of authorized checks it is allowed to cash. All presented checks are compared to this master list, with both the check number and amount being reviewed. If there is a discrepancy, the check is rejected. By using this method, check fraud can be completely eliminated.

This best practice is being used only by a small number of companies, for several reasons. One is that few banks currently offer the system (and usually only large ones). Another problem is its cost. Even if a participating bank is willing to provide the service for free, there is still a cost for the company because it must pay to store check data on a tape and have it sent to the bank, usually using an expensive overnight or same-day delivery service. Finally, a major problem is that a company must make sure that all checks are included in the information it sends to the bank, or else some checks may be rejected for payment—this can be a major problem if manual checks are not immediately loaded into the accounting database. Consequently, positive pay is only useful in a minority of situations.

PROLIFERATE PETTY-CASH BOXES

One of the greatest nuisances for the accounts payable staff is when it receives a constant stream of requests from all over the company for manual checks in very small amounts, usually for small daily transactions that cannot possibly be anticipated, such as flowers for an employee who is in the hospital or fees for an emergency building repair. When these manual checks are cut, it is a common occurrence to forget to log them into the computer system, resulting in a difficult bank reconciliation process for an accounting clerk, as well as cash balances that are lower than expected—both problems that impact the orderly management of cash. One way to offset this problem is to give departments their own checking accounts or even a set of checks that are drawn on the main checking account. The first option requires additional bank reconciliations, and both options will probably result in even more checks not initially recorded in the computer system. In short, the need for small amounts of cash can add up to a moderate headache for the cash management staff.

A good way to avoid this problem is to set up a number of small petty-cash boxes in those areas of the company where cash requests are the most common. A person in each department is responsible for the cash in each box, trained in how to record cash receipts and expenditures, and allowed to handle all cash transactions from that point forward. To ensure that there is proper control, the internal audit staff may reconcile the balances in each petty-cash box from time to time. By using this approach, the demand for manual checks will be significantly reduced, improving the accuracy of the cash book balance while also making the bank reconciliation process a much easier one. The only problem with this method is that there is some risk of theft from the petty-cash boxes, but this risk is a minor one, given the small amount of cash kept in the boxes. On the whole, this is a good best practice to use in situations where a company is having difficulty in precisely determining its cash balances.

UTILIZE AN INVESTMENT POLICY

Sometimes a controller or treasurer implements all of the cash management best practices and experiences a singular increase in cash flows, only to have no idea of what to do with the money. Though it is always tempting to invest the money in some high-yield investment, there may be associated problems with risk or liquidity that make such investment inappropriate. In fact, an improper investment that results in losses or no chance of short-term liquidity to meet immediate needs may even cost the investment officer his job. Consequently, this is an area in which a best practice is needed, not to improve efficiency or profits, but to contain risk.

An appropriate best practice for every company is an investment policy. This is used to define the level of risk a company is willing to tolerate and defines the exact types of investment vehicles to be used (or not used). Such a policy should cover the level of allowable *liquidity*. For example, the policy may state that all investments must be capable of total liquidation upon notification, or that some proportion of investments must be in this class of liquidity. For example, the policy could state that 75 percent of all investments must be capable of immediate liquidation (which rules out real estate holdings!), or that any investments over a base level of $50 million can be invested in less liquid instruments. Generally speaking, the policy should severely restrict the use of any investments which cannot be liquidated within 90 days, since this gives a company maximum use of the money in case of special opportunities (such as an acquisition) or emergencies (such as a natural disaster destroying a facility). Such careful delineation of investment liquidity will leave a small number of investments that an investment officer can safely use.

The other main policy criterion is *risk*. Many companies have decided that they are not in the business of making investments and so they avoid all risk, even though they may be losing a significant amount of investment income by putting all excess cash in U.S. government securities. Other companies take the opposite tack and attempt to derive a significant proportion of their profits from investment income. No matter which direction a company takes, it is necessary to delineate which kinds of investments can be used, thereby keeping the investment officer focused on a specific set of investment options. The policy may go into such detail as to define exact types of securities to be used.

Once the investment policy is in place, the investment officer can use it to standardize the procedure for daily investing activities. For example, if only one type of investment is authorized (a common situation), then a clerk can be authorized to increase or decrease the investment amount each day, using a standard investment form for transmission to the investing organization (e.g., a bank or brokerage house). With this approach, investing becomes a simple and mechanical activity that requires little further management attention.

An investment officer should strongly encourage the creation and use of an investment policy, for it keeps the officer from being held liable in the event of a sudden loss of investments, while also acting as the foundation for a day-to-day investment procedure.

ZERO-BALANCE ACCOUNTS

Whenever a company cuts a check to a supplier, it must deposit enough cash in its checking account to cover payment on the check. If it does not do so, then the bank may not honor the check when it is presented for payment, or it may advance payment but charge a fee for doing so. In either case, the penalties are considerable for not having sufficient cash on hand to cover company obligations. Many companies run the risk of not having sufficient funds on hand because they want to earn interest on their money for as long as possible (most checking accounts do not pay interest, or very little). Accordingly, the typical organization assigns someone the task of monitoring the rate at which checks are being cashed, guesses when checks will be cashed, and uses all sorts of time-consuming averaging methods to make a reasonable guess as to how much money should be left in the account each day. Not only is this an expensive way to manage cash, but sometimes those guesses are wrong, resulting in bounced checks or additional bank fees.

The zero-balance account is a better way. As its name implies, the zero-balance account requires no balance. Instead, when checks are presented to the bank for payment, the bank automatically transfers money from another company account, in the exact amount required to cover the check. This approach allows a company to eliminate the amount of funds stored in various bank accounts, which results in the storage of all funds in just one account, where it is easier to track and invest. There is also no problem with forgetting to manually transfer funds into the zero-balance account because all transactions are handled automatically. There is no risk of not having cash available to pay for a check, unless there are no funds in the account from which money is automatically being drawn. A common use of the zero-balance account is for payroll checks. A variation on this type of account is the controlled disbursement account (see the "Controlled Disbursements" section earlier in this chapter), which is most commonly used for accounts payable checks. By using either or both of these types of accounts, a company can consolidate its funds into a central holding account, where it is both more visible and easily transferred out to various investment vehicles.

There are few problems with having a zero-balance account. One is that the bank will charge a small monthly fee for maintaining the account, but this amount is easily offset by the interest earned on money that would otherwise have been sitting in the account. In addition, some very small companies with limited banking needs do not bother with a zero-balance account because they do not like the notion of having extra complexity in their banking procedures. These small organizations prefer to handle all banking transactions through a single bank account, which is certainly an acceptable approach when there is a limited volume of cash flow in and out of a company. With the exception of these two cases, however, most companies will find that having a zero-balance account is an excellent way to centralize their funds in a single location.

TOTAL IMPACT OF BEST PRACTICES ON THE CASH MANAGEMENT FUNCTION

An accounting department is well advised to implement nearly all of the best practices advocated in this chapter, for most of them work well together to centralize funds for easier investment, while accelerating the flow of incoming cash and slowing its outflow. The layout of the recommended best practices are shown in the flowchart in Exhibit 6.3. That flowchart shows that most cash management best practices are concentrated in just two areas—the inflow of cash from customers and its outflow to suppliers. To make these best practices work most efficiently, it is best to implement them fully in either of these two main areas in order to achieve the most efficient flow of cash. For example, the subcategory of cash inflows should be completely implemented, which means installing both the lockbox and area-concentration banking best practices, prior to moving on to the other subcategory of cash outflows. If one were to take a more scattershot approach to implementing these best practices, the efficiency of the overall process would be severely degraded. For example, implementing the lockboxes without area-concentration banking would run the risk of having received funds sit idle in various bank accounts around the country, since the area-concentration banking practice, which automatically moves the funds into a central account, has not yet been implemented.

If it is not possible, for whatever reason, to implement a cluster of these best practices, then it is best to first implement those with either the greatest cost-benefit, or else the one that will result in the greatest increase in operational efficiency. Under this scenario, the best practices with the greatest cost-benefit impact would be either controlled disbursements or lockboxes, since both approaches result in the retention of cash for a longer period, which gives a company more days to invest it. Alternatively, if efficiency is the main implementation criterion, then a controller should strongly consider a combination of area-concentration banking

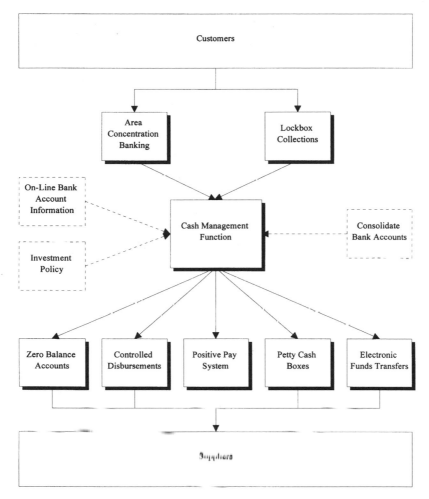

Exhibit 6.3.   Impact of Best Practices on the Cash Management Function

and reducing the number of bank accounts—both practices result in much less work for the accounting staff in tracking where cash is located in a company's bank accounts. However, rather than focusing on a few best practices, it is best to implement a complete cash management system; the resulting impact on cash flows and profitability is worth the effort.

SUMMARY

This chapter is unusual in that none of the best practices presented are mutually exclusive, nor are any of them especially difficult to implement, and they can be created at low cost, in most cases. As a result, this is a prime area for an accounting manager to explore in order to achieve the highest possible level of cash management efficiency. Best of all, efficiency in this area directly equates to having more cash available for investments, which has a direct impact on company profits—one of the few functions covered in this book in which corporate management can see an immediate and measurable impact as a result of implementing best practices.

Given the high visibility of implementing cash management best practices, it is important to install as many of them as possible. In particular, there should be a set of lockboxes in place that will reduce the mail float from customers, as well as consolidation accounts that accumulate funds from the lockbox accounts and move them to the central bank account. There should also be zero-balance accounts to handle cashed payroll checks and a controlled-disbursement account for paying suppliers. If this array of bank accounts is in place and is properly managed, there should be a noticeable increase in the average amount of funds on hand that can be profitably invested.

Chapter 7

Collections Best Practices

One of the worst jobs in any company is collecting on overdue accounts receivable. The person who must do the collecting never knows if an invoice has gone unpaid due to the company's fault or the customer's. There may be a very valid problem caused by the company that is making the customer wait on payment of the invoice, such as a damaged product shipment, a billing for the incorrect amount, or pricing that does not match the customer's purchase order amount. In these cases, the collections person apologizes to the customer for the company's sins and then tries to correct the internal problems responsible for the collection trouble. In other cases, the collections problem may be caused by the customer, who either cannot pay or who is deliberately stretching the payment period past the agreed-upon date. In these cases, the collections person must diplomatically bring pressure to bear on the customer, which is a difficult skill. No matter what the reason for an invoice being overdue, the collections person must ascertain the correct reason for the problem and fix it.

This chapter provides many best practices that allow a collections staff to reduce the error rate of invoices being sent to customers, while also providing new tools to force customers to pay by the due dates listed on company invoices. In addition, there are several best practices here that can enhance the operational efficiency of the collections staff. In short, this chapter makes the collections task easier, while reducing the amount of overdue accounts receivable at the same time.

IMPLEMENTATION ISSUES FOR COLLECTIONS BEST PRACTICES

There are a surprisingly large number of best practices that can be applied to collections. Some are located in other functions, such as sales and credit, that have a direct impact on the collections function, while others are more directly associated with the activities of the collections department. Most of these best practices are relatively easy to implement, as noted in Exhibit 7.1. The exhibit notes the ease of implementation of each best practice, as well as the estimated time and cost of implementation. In most cases, it is a relatively simple matter to complete an implementation, with the exception of those items that require custom computer programming, or which involve the participation of another department. In these two cases, either the risk of a lengthy programming project or the refusal of

Exhibit 7.1. Implementation Issues for Collections Best Practices

Description	Ease of Implementation	Duration of Implementation	Cost of Implementation
Access to Customer Assets Database	Moderate	Medium	Medium
Access to Customer Orders Database	Easy	Short	Inexpensive
Automatic Bankruptcy Notification	Easy	Short	Inexpensive
Automatic Fax of Overdue Invoices	Difficult	Long	Expensive
Automatic Issuance of Dunning Letters	Moderate	Medium	Medium
Collection Call Database	Moderate	Long	Medium
Collection Call Stratification	Easy	Short	Inexpensive
Customer Order Exception Tracking	Moderate	Medium	Medium
Grant Percentage Discounts for Early Payment	Easy	Short	Expensive
Immediate Review of Unapplied Cash	Easy	Short	Inexpensive
Linkage to Comprehensive Collections Software Package	Difficult	Medium	Expensive
Lockbox Collections	Moderate	Medium	Inexpensive
Outsource Collections	Easy	Short	Expensive
Pre-Approved Customer Credit	Moderate	Medium	Inexpensive
Pricing Structure Simplification	Difficult	Long	Medium
Standardized Credit Level Determination System	Easy	Short	Inexpensive
Write Off Small Balances with No Approval	Easy	Short	Medium

another department to cooperate can jeopardize a successful implementation. An example of the first problem is automatically faxing overdue invoices to customers, while a good example of the second problem is persuading the sales department to adopt a simplified pricing structure. However, with the exception of these two problem areas, one will find that improving the collections function with the best practices contained in this chapter is a relatively easy endeavor.

ACCESS TO CUSTOMER ASSETS DATABASE

If a collections person finds that a customer will not pay, the usual recourse is to reduce or eliminate the customer's credit limit and to use threats—dunning letters and phone calls. These instruments are frequently not sufficient to force a customer to pay. However, what a collections person does not always realize is that there may be some other customer assets on the premises that the company can refuse to ship back to the customer until payment is made. When these assets are grouped into a database of customer assets, the collections staff has a much better chance of collecting on accounts receivable.

A customer assets database lists several items the customer owns, but which are located on the company premises. One common customer asset is consigned inventory. This is stock the customer has sent to the company either for resale or for inclusion in a finished product the company is making for the customer. Another customer asset is an engineering drawing or related set of product specifications. Yet another is a mold, which the customer has paid for, and which a company uses in the plastics industry to create a product for the customer. All of these are valuable customer assets, which a company can hold hostage until all accounts receivable are paid.

The best way to keep this customer assets information in one place is to store it in the inventory database. The reason is that the inventory database is already set up in most accounting systems and includes location codes, so that it is an easy matter to determine where each asset is located. Most important in using this database, a collections person can designate a customer in the accounting system as one to whom nothing can be shipped (with a shipping hold flag of some kind), which effectively keeps the shipping department from sending the asset to the customer— it cannot print out shipping documentation or remove the asset from the inventory database. This is an extremely effective way to keep customer assets in-house, rather than inadvertently sent back to a customer who refuses to pay its bills.

The only problem with this best practice is making sure that customer assets are recorded in the assets database when they initially arrive at the company. Otherwise, there is no record of their existence, making it impossible to use these assets as leverage for the collections staff. The best answer to this problem is to force all receipts through the receiving department, whose responsibility is to record all receipts in the inventory database. The internal auditing staff can review the receiving log to verify that this action has been completed. The only customer asset that may not be recorded in this manner is a set of engineering drawings, which enters the company site through the engineering department, rather than the receiving dock. The only way to record this information is by fostering close cooperation with the engineering manager, who must realize the need for tracking all customer assets. These steps will result in tight control over customer assets, and a better chance of collecting overdue accounts receivable by the collections staff.

ACCESS TO CUSTOMER ORDERS DATABASE

The previous section noted the need for compiling a listing of customer assets which can be used to apply leverage to customers to collect on overdue accounts.

The same approach applies to customer orders. If a customer has a large open order with a company, it is likely that the customer will be quite responsive to pressure to pay for open invoices when those orders are put on hold. Consequently, an excellent best practice to implement is to give the collections staff current knowledge of all open orders.

Implementation of this practice is an easy one for most companies; just give password access to the existing customer orders database to the collections staff. This access can be read-only, so that there is no danger of a staff person inadvertently changing key information in a customer order. An additional issue is that someone must be responsible for flagging customers as "do not ship" in the customer orders database. This is a necessary step since orders will inadvertently pass through the system if there is not a solid block in the computer on shipments to a delinquent customer. However, many companies are uncomfortable with allowing the collections staff to have free access to altering the shipment status of customers, since they may use it so much that customers are irritated. Consequently, it may be better to allow this access only to a supervisor, such as an assistant controller, who can review a proposed order-hold request with the sales staff to see what the impact will be on customer relations before actually imposing a hold on a customer order.

In summary, giving the collections staff access to the open orders database for customers results in better leverage over delinquent customers by threatening to freeze existing orders unless payment is made. The use of this database should be tempered by a consideration for long-term relations with customers; it should only be used if there is a clear collections problem that cannot be resolved in some other way.

AUTOMATIC BANKRUPTCY NOTIFICATION

It is an easy matter for a collections department to be completely blindsided by a sudden drop in the credit rating of a customer, possibly resulting in bankruptcy and the loss of all accounts receivable to that customer. Though a company can track payment histories over time, talk to other suppliers of a customer, or periodically purchase credit records from a credit analysis group, all of these options require a continual planned effort. Many collections departments do not have the time to complete these extra tasks, even though the cost of being blindsided can be very high. They just take the chance that customers will continue to be financially stable.

Rather than undergo the embarrassment of losing an account receivable through the sudden decline of a customer, it is better to arrange for automatic notification of any significant changes to the credit standing of a customer. To do this, a company can contract with a major credit rating agency, such as Dun & Bradstreet. This organization will immediately fax a notification of any changes to the status of a customer, such as a change in its credit rating which may signal a decline in the customer's ability to pay its bills. With this information in hand, a credit manager can take immediate steps to shrink a customer's credit limit and put extra emphasis on collection efforts for all outstanding accounts receivable, thereby avoiding problems later on, when a customer may sink into bankruptcy.

The only problem with advance notification of a customer's credit standing is that the credit agency will charge a fee for its work. However, the price of the notification, usually in the range of $25 to $40, is minor compared to the potential loss of existing accounts receivable. The only case where a company would not want to have advance notification set up is for customers who rarely make orders and usually of a small size when they do; in this case, a small credit limit is adequate protection against any major bad debt losses.

AUTOMATIC FAX OF OVERDUE INVOICES

The most common request that a collections person receives from a customer is to send a copy of an invoice that the customer cannot find. To do so, the collections person must either access the accounting computer system to print out a copy of the invoice, or go to the customer's file to find it. Then the collections person must create a cover letter and fax the cover letter and invoice to the customer. In addition, the fax may not go through, in which case the collections person must repeat this process after learning from the customer that the fax never arrived. This process is typically the longest of all collections tasks—a collection call may only take a few minutes, but faxing an invoice can take several times that amount.

Few companies have found a way around the faxing problem. Those that have done so use the most advanced of all best practices in the collections area—automatically extracting an invoice record from the accounting database and faxing it to the customer—all at the touch of a button. To do so, a company must link the invoice file in the accounting database to another file that contains the name and fax number of the recipient, combine these two files to create a cover letter and invoice, and route the two records to a fax server for automatic transmission, one that will keep transmitting until the fax goes through, and then notify the sender of successful or failed transmissions. The advantages of this approach are obvious: immediate turnaround time, no need for the collections person to move to complete a fax, and automatic notification if there is a problem in completing a fax. For a company with a large collections staff, this represents a monumental improvement in efficiency.

The trouble with setting up an automatic invoice-faxing system is that one must put together several functions which are not normally combined. This almost certainly calls for customized programming and may have a risk that the system will periodically fail, due to the complex interlinking of different systems. To give a picture of the complexity of this system, the front end of the system must include an input screen for the collections person that allows entry of the customer's contact name and fax number, as well as any accompanying text that should go on the cover letter to accompany the faxed invoice. On the same screen, one should be able to enter an invoice number so that the software automatically searches the invoice file and selects the correct invoice. There may be an additional step at this point, where the system presents a text image of the invoice so that the collections person can verify that the correct invoice is about to be transmitted. Next, both the invoice text and the information that goes on the cover letter must be converted to a digital image that can be transmitted by fax. After that, the images are transmitted to a server that is a stand-alone fax transmission device. The server will repeatedly fax out the images to the recipient for a fixed number of attempts. If the transmission is not successful, the fax server will notify the sender via an e-mail message (which requires a pre-existing e-mail system); conversely, it should also send a message indicating a successful transmission.

Obviously, it is a difficult task to combine the accounting database with fax server and an e-mail system and expect it all to work properly at all times. Common problems are that information will not be successfully transmitted between the various components of the system, resulting in no fax transmission, or that the e-mail notification system does not work, resulting in no messages to the collections staff, who have no idea if their faxes are being sent or not. Consequently, most companies with small collections staff do not deem it worth the effort to attempt such an installation. Only the largest corporations, with correspondingly large collections staffs, attempt to install this best practice.

AUTOMATIC ISSUANCE OF DUNNING LETTERS

Some companies have so many small accounts to collect that they cannot possibly take the time to call all of them to resolve payment disputes. This is an especially common problem for very small accounts receivable, where the cost of a contact call may exceed the amount of revenue outstanding. In other cases, there is some difficulty in contacting customers by phone, usually because all collection calls are automatically routed to the voice mail of the accounts payable departments. In these cases, a different form of communication is needed.

The best way to contact either unresponsive customers or accounts with very small overdue balances is the dunning letter. This is a letter that lists the overdue amount, the invoice number, and date, and requests payment. There are normally several degrees of severity in the tone of the dunning letter; the initial one has a respectful tone, assuming that there has been some mistake resulting in non-payment. There is a gradual increase in severity. The final letter is the most threatening and usually requires immediate payment within a specific number of days or else the account will be turned over to a collection agency, the customer will be converted to cash-on-delivery for all future sales, or some similar dire warning. As it is impossible to craft a separate dunning letter for every customer situation (given the cost of doing so), a collections department must create a standard set of dunning letters that can be used for all customers. Though an informal way of communicating, a form letter still gets the point across to the customer. There is also a standard time interval between the issuance of each in a series of dunning letters—perhaps two weeks past the initial invoice due date before the first letter is sent, with additional letters being sent every two weeks thereafter. This use of a series of dunning letters, issued at standard intervals, is an effective and low-cost way to communicate with customers for whom it is not cost effective or otherwise possible to communicate.

There are various degrees of automation that can be applied to the use of dunning letters. The easiest approach is to have a standard pre-printed letter, easily copied and mailed to a customer. The next level of automation is to store standard letters in a computer network, where all collections personnel can access them and make small modifications to match the customers to whom they are being sent. Though simple, both of these approaches suffer from the same complaint—there is no way to automatically issue dunning letters at set intervals. Instead, one must rely on the collections staff to remember to send out the letters. A more automated approach that takes into account the time interval since the last letter is merging the dunning letters into the accounting software. To do so, some custom programming is required. The programming must automatically access a text file as soon as an invoice reaches a certain number of days past due and issue a dunning letter. A different text file must be accessed as the number of days past due increases, since more strident letters must be sent as the invoices become older. The letters can then be printed and mailed out each day in a batch. Though this last method provides the tightest control over the standard issuance of the correct kinds of dunning letters, it is more complicated to set up, so it is generally best to calculate the programming cost of making such a significant enhancement before proceeding.

The automatic issuance of dunning letters is a cost-effective method for establishing a continual communication with customers regarding overdue invoices. It is particularly suitable to those situations where it is impossible to create personal relationships with customers through more expensive collection calls.

COLLECTION CALL DATABASE

A poorly organized collections group is one that does not know which customers to call, what customers said during previous calls, and how frequently contacts should be made in the future. The result of this level of disorganization is overdue payments being ignored for long periods, other customers being contacted so frequently that customers become annoyed, and continually duplicated efforts. To a large extent, these problems can be overcome by using a collection call database.

A typical collection call database is a simple one recorded on paper, or a complex one that is integrated into a company's accounting software package. In either case, the basic concept is the same—keep a record of all contacts with the customer, as well as when to contact the customer next and what other actions to take. The first part of the database, the key contact listing, should contain the following information:

- Customer name
- Key contact name
- Secondary contact name
- Internal salesperson's name with account responsibility
- Phone numbers of all contacts
- Fax numbers of all contacts

The contact log comprises the second part of the database and should contain:

- Date of contact
- Name of person contacted
- Topics discussed
- Action items

The information noted above is easily kept in a notebook if there is a single collections person, but may require a more complex, centralized database if there are many collections personnel. In the latter case, a supervisor may need to monitor collections activities for all employees and can do this more easily if the data is stored in a single location. However, a notebook-based database can be set up in a few hours with minimal effort, whereas a computerized database, especially one that is closely linked to the accounting records for each account receivable, may be a major undertaking. The reason for the added effort (and expense) is that it may be necessary to custom-program extra text fields into the accounting software so that notations can be kept alongside the record for each invoice; this is a surprisingly difficult endeavor, given the number of changes that must be made to the underlying database. The most difficult situation of all is if a company uses a software package that is regularly updated by a software supplier. Any changes made to the software (such as adding text fields) will be destroyed as soon as the next upgrade is installed, since the upgrade will wipe out all changes made in the interim.

A good midway approach for avoiding these difficulties with a computerized database is to use a separate tracking system not linked to the accounting software. Such software packages are commonly used by the sales department to track contacts with customers and can be easily modified to work for a collections department. They can be modified for use by multiple employees, resulting in a central database of contact information easily perused by a collections manager. An example of such a software package is Act! The only problem with this approach is that there is no linkage between the customer contact information contained in the accounting software (e.g., names and addresses) and the same information in the tracking software. This contact information must be re-loaded manually from the accounting software into the tracking software. Likewise, any change to the contact information in the tracking software must be manually updated in the accounting system. Despite its limitations, maintaining a separate tracking system in the computer is an inexpensive way to maintain a centralized contact database.

COLLECTION CALL STRATIFICATION

The typical list of overdue invoices is so long that the existing collections staff cannot possibly contact all customers about all invoices on a sufficiently frequent basis. This problem results in many invoices not being collected for an inordinately long time. Additional problems that require time-consuming research may include an incorrect product price, missing shipping documentation, or a claim that the quantity billed is incorrect. Consequently, collection problems linger longer than they should, resulting in slow collections and sub-standard cash flow.

A good approach for improving the speed of cash collection is to utilize collection call stratification. The concept behind this approach is to split up, or stratify, all of the overdue receivables and concentrate the bulk of the collections staff's time on the very largest invoices. By doing so, a company can realize improved cash flow by collecting the largest dollar amounts sooner. The downside of this method is that smaller invoices will receive less attention and therefore take longer to collect, but this is a reasonable shortcoming if the overall cash flow from using stratified collections is improved. To implement it, one should perform a Pareto analysis of a typical accounts receivable listing and determine the cutoff point above which 20 percent of all invoices will constitute 80 percent of the total revenue. For example, a cutoff point of $1,000 means that any invoice of more than $1,000 is in the group of invoices that represents the bulk of a company's revenue. When it is necessary to contact customers for collections work, a much higher number of customer contacts can be assigned for the invoices over $1,000. For example, a collections staff can be required to contact customers about all high-dollar invoices once every three days, whereas low-dollar contacts can be limited to once every two weeks. By allocating the time of the collections staff in this manner, it is possible to collect overdue invoices more rapidly.

The stratification approach can also be expanded to include other members of a company. If there is an extremely large invoice that must be collected at once, the collections staff can be authorized to request the services of other departments, such as the sales staff, in making the collection. This approach needs to be limited to large-dollar invoices, since the sales staff does not want to be making collection calls all day. However, using the stratification approach, it is reasonable to request their assistance in collecting the largest invoices. This approach is very effective for accelerating the collection of large overdue accounts.

CUSTOMER ORDER EXCEPTION TRACKING

Many of the problems that result in collections work begin much earlier, from the time an order is entered into the system to the time it is produced, shipped, and invoiced. This interval is not one that the collections staff has any direct control over (unless the collections manager happens to run the entire company!), which means that problems upstream from the collections department will nonetheless have a direct and continuing impact on the quantity and type of problems that the collections staff must handle.

A good best practice for rooting out problems before they become collection issues is to set up a reporting system to track exceptions for customer orders as they move through all of a company's various processes. By keeping close tabs on these reports, the manager of the collection function can tell when there will probably be collection difficulties. By determining problems with specific customer orders in advance, the collections manager can work with the managers of other departments (mostly by suggestion) to correct problems before orders are shipped. A crucial factor in the success of this best practice is the interpersonal skill of the collections manager, who must bring customer order exceptions to the attention of other managers in such a way that they will not reactive negatively, but rather work with the presented information to make prompt corrections to their systems.

Another use of the reports is to recognize which orders are likely to result in collection problems and to use this information to start making collection calls earlier than normal, so that any customer problems can be discovered, addressed, and resolved before the associated accounts receivable become inordinately old. By using the exception reports to manage accounts receivable more closely, it is possible to maintain a high accounts receivable turnover ratio, which frees up working capital for other purposes.

The number of reports used to track customer order exceptions will vary dramatically, depending on the types of systems already in place, the services or products offered to customers, and the type of industry. This range of options makes a complete list of all exception reports impossible to present, but the following list is a representative sample of the types of information that a collections manager should consider using as the foundation of a comprehensive order exception tracking system:

- Customer orders with non-standard prices
- Customer orders for which the delivery date has exceeded the requested date
- Customer orders for which the quantity on hand is less than the amount ordered

- Customer orders for which the scheduled production is later than the requested delivery date
- Customer orders for which partial deliveries have been sent
- Customer orders requiring special-order parts
- Customer orders requiring a special form of transportation
- Customer orders requiring a special form of packaging

All of these exception reports focus on non-standard customer orders, or orders for which there is some kind of shortfall. They are a very effective tool for honing in on those orders for which there will probably be customer complaints, which may result in collection problems.

The ability of a collections manager to create all these reports will depend on the type of computer database used to collect data about customer orders. If the database does not cover all of the items noted in the previous list of reports, it will be very difficult to create the reports, unless it is cost effective to do so manually. Also, there should be a good report-writing tool or a willing programming staff to assist in the creation of these reports. If these factors are in place, a collections department can benefit greatly from an advance knowledge of which customer orders are likely to result in collection problems.

GRANT PERCENTAGE DISCOUNTS FOR EARLY PAYMENT

Some companies have large customers who pay late all the time. These customers are important to the company and the customers abuse the one-sidedness of the relationship by stretching out their payments. In these cases, a company has little leverage, for it will lose a significant volume of sales if it cuts off the errant customers or cuts back on their credit limits.

In these cases, a company may have no choice other than to grant an early payment discount to customers in order to bring in cash sooner. This approach is especially effective if a company is in immediate need of cash. Also, accounts receivable that are outstanding for a long time period will require a number of collection actions, whereas one that is paid immediately will not require any; thus, the use of an early payment discount reduces the cost of collections.

The discount is easy one to implement. A company usually prints the discount on its invoices so that customers will see the discount the next time an invoice is mailed to them. However, most customers already have payment terms included in their payment databases and a sudden change in terms may not be noticed. Accordingly, it may be necessary to call the customers' accounts payable staffs to notify them of the change. An alternative approach is to offer the discount only to a few key customers who represent a high volume of sales or who are constant late-payers. By reducing the number of customers who take discounts, a company can make more selective use of this tool.

There are three problems with using an early payment discount. One is the cost. To entice a customer into an early payment, the discount rate must be fairly high. A common discount rate is two percent, which translates into a significant expense if used by all customers. Another problem is that it is somewhat more difficult to apply cash against accounts receivable if a discount is taken. Depending on the facility of the accounting software, an accounting clerk may have to go to the extreme of manually calculating the discount amount taken and charging off the difference to a special discounts account. Finally, a discount can be abused. If a customer is already stretching its payments, it may take the discount rate without shrinking its payment interval to the prescribed number of days. This can lead to endless arguments over whether or not the discount should have been taken, which the customer will win if it makes up a large enough percentage of a company's sales.

Granting early payment discounts can significantly reduce the amount of a company's overdue accounts receivable, but this is at the high cost of the discount, which can be abused by some customers. Accordingly, this best practice should be used with care to improve the payment performance of selected customers.

IMMEDIATE REVIEW OF UNAPPLIED CASH

It is a common occurrence for a collections person to call a customer about an overdue invoice, only to be told that the check was already sent. Upon further investigation, the collections staff finds that, for a variety of reasons, the offending check has been sitting in an accounting clerk's "in" box for several weeks, waiting to be applied to an invoice in the accounts receivable aging. Common reasons for not performing this cash application include not having enough time, not understanding what the check is intended to pay, or because there are unexplained line items on a payment, such as credits, that require further investigation before the check can be applied.

None of the reasons for not applying cash are valid, given the consequences of wasting the time of the collections staff. Only two solutions need to be installed to ensure that cash is applied at once. First, cash application is always the highest priority of whomever is responsible for cash applications, thereby avoiding all arguments regarding other items taking priority, or not having enough time to complete the task. Second, all cash must be applied, even if it is only to an "unapplied cash" category in the accounts receivable register for those items that cannot be traced immediately to an open invoice. In these cases, simply having the total of unapplied cash for a customer clearly shown in the aged accounts receivable listing is a clear sign that the customer is correct—it has paid for an invoice and now the collections person knows how to apply the cash that was already received. Applying cash to accounts receivable as soon as it is received is critical to ensuring that the collections staff has complete information about customer payments before calling a customer.

Ensuring that cash is applied on time is a key internal auditing task. Without periodic review by a designated auditor, the person in charge of cash applications may become lazy and delay some application work. To avoid this problem, audits must be regularly scheduled and should verify not only that all cash is applied in a timely manner, but that the amount of cash received each day matches the amount applied. If these controls are rigidly followed, it becomes an easy matter to enforce this most fundamental of best practices.

LINKAGE TO COMPREHENSIVE COLLECTIONS SOFTWARE PACKAGE

Many of the other system-related best practices noted in this chapter are based on the assumption that a company wants to incrementally create separate applications that are directly linked to an existing accounting computer system. If so, a fair amount of programming work will be required to arrive at a complete in-house solution. This can be both expensive and time consuming. For those who prefer to install a complete solution on a more rapid time schedule, it is also possible to purchase a software package that incorporates many of the system-related best practices for collections.

An example of this new breed of software is GetPAID, which can be reviewed at the *www.getpaid.com* web site. This product is linked to a company's legacy accounting systems (specifically, the open accounts receivable and customer files) by customized interfaces, so that there is either a continual or batched flow of information into it. A key feature it offers is the assignment of each customer to a specific collections person, so that each person can call up a subset of the overdue invoices for which he or she is responsible. Within this subset, the software will also categorize accounts in different sort sequences, such as placing those at the top that have missed their promised payment dates. Also, the software will present on a single screen all of the contact information related to each customer, including the promises made by customers, open issues, and contact information. The system will also allow the user to enter information for a fax, and then route it directly to the recipient, without requiring the collections person to ever leave his chair. It can also be linked to an auto-dialer, so that the collections staff spends less time attempting to establish connections with overdue customers. To further increase the efficiency of the collections staff, it will even determine the time zone in which each customer is located, and prioritize the recommended list of calls, so that only those customers in time zones that are currently in the midst of standard business hours will be called.

The GetPAID system does not just store collections data—it can also export it to other systems, where it can be altered for other uses or reformatted for management reporting purposes (though the package contains its own reporting features, as well). Some of the standard reports include a time-series report on performance of individual collection personnel, as well as the same information for each customer. It can also create reports that are tailored by recipient—for example, all of the collection problems for a specific salesperson's customers can be lumped into one report and sent to that salesperson for remedial action. The software can also export data files into Excel or Access.

There are several cost issues to consider when installing this type of software—not only of the software itself, but also for staff training time, installation by consultants, and on-going maintenance costs. Offsetting these problems is a much shorter time period before a company will have an advanced collections software system fully operational. The record time period for a GetPAID installation is just five days, though a more typical installation speed is sixty days. For those companies with a serious collections problem, and who need help right away, a comprehensive collections software package may be the answer.

LOCKBOX COLLECTIONS

Customers sometimes have difficulty in sending their payments to the correct address; they send them to the attention of someone they know at a company, such as a salesman, or they send it to the wrong company location. Sometimes, even if they send a payment to the correct company location, the mailroom personnel mistakenly direct the payment to the wrong department, where it languishes for a few days until it is re-routed to the correct person. Finally, even if the payment goes to the correct person in the correct department, that person may not be available for a few days, perhaps due to sickness or vacation. In all of these instances, there is a delay in cashing checks and, more importantly from a collections standpoint, there is a delay in applying checks to open accounts receivable. When this delay occurs, the collections staff may make unnecessary phone calls to customers who have already paid, which is a waste of time. How can we eliminate this problem?

The easiest method for consolidating all incoming payments is to have them sent to a lockbox, a mailbox that is maintained by a company's bank. The bank opens all incoming envelopes, cashes all checks contained therein, and then forwards copies of the checks to a single individual at the company. The advantage of this approach is that if all customers are properly notified of the address, all checks will unerringly go to one location, where they are consolidated into a single packet and forwarded to the cash application person at the company. By sending a single packet of each day's receipts to a single person, it is much easier to ensure that the packet is routed to the correct person for immediate application. However, there are two disadvantages that must be considered. One is that there is a one-day delay in routing checks through a lockbox, which translates into a one-day delay in applying the cash. The other problem is that all customers must be notified of the change to the lockbox address, which usually requires several follow-up contacts with a few customers who continue to send their payments to the wrong address. Despite these restrictions, a collections staff that suffers from mislaid check payments should seriously consider switching to a lockbox solution.

OUTSOURCE COLLECTIONS

Some companies have a very difficult time creating an effective collections department. Perhaps the management of the function is poor, or the staff is not well trained, or it does not have sufficient sway over other departments, such as sales, to garner support in changing underlying systems in a way that will reduce the amount of accounts receivable to collect. Whatever the reason or combination of reasons may be, there are times when the function simply does not work. A variation on this situation is when a collections staff is so overwhelmed with work that it cannot pay a sufficient amount of attention to the most difficult collection items. This is a much more common problem. In either case, the solution may be to go outside the company for help.

The best practice that solves this problem is to outsource the entire function, or some portion of it. When doing so, a company sends its accounts receivable aging report to a collections agency, which contacts all customers with overdue invoices that have reached a pre-specified age—perhaps sixty days old, or whatever the agreement with the supplier may specify. The supplier is then responsible for bringing in the funds. In exchange, the collections agency either requires a percentage of each collected invoice (typically one-third) as payment for its services, or it charges an hourly rate for its efforts. It is almost always less expensive to pay an hourly fee for collection services, rather than a percentage of the amounts collected, though going with an hourly approach gives the supplier less incentive to collect on old invoices. To counteract the reduced level of incentive, it is useful to continually measure the collection effectiveness of the supplier, and switch to a new supplier if only a low percentage of invoices is being collected. This can be an effective approach for quickly bringing a trained group of collection professionals to bear on an existing collections problem.

Before deciding on the outsourcing route, one must consider a variety of important issues that make this a solution for only a minority of situations. The first problem is cost. It is always cheaper to keep the collections function in-house because the fees charged by any supplier must include a profit, which automatically makes its services more expensive. This is a particularly important problem if the payment method is a percentage of the invoices collected, since the percentage can be considerable. Another problem is that this approach does not allow one to use most of the other best practices that are discussed in this chapter—by moving the entire function elsewhere, there is no longer any reason to improve the department's efficiency. Only a few best practices, those that involve other departments, such as the sales and credit departments, are still available for implementation. Finally, and most importantly, outsourcing the collections function puts the emphasis of the department squarely on collecting money, rather than on the equally important issue of correcting the underlying problems that are causing customers to not pay their bills on time. A collections supplier has absolutely no incentive to inform a company of why customers are not paying because by doing so, it is giving a company information that will reduce the number of overdue invoices, and reduce the amount of its business. For example, if a customer does not pay its bills because a company repeatedly misprices the products it is selling, the collections agency will not inform the company of its error because then the invoices will be fixed and there will be fewer invoices to collect. All of these issues are major ones, requiring considerable deliberation before a company decides to outsource its collections function. Typically, this best practice should only be used in situations where a company wants to outsource the collection of a few of its most difficult collection problems. In most other cases, it is infinitely less expensive to go in search of a qualified manager who can bring the collections department up to a peak level of efficiency.

PRE-APPROVED CUSTOMER CREDIT

The collections staff suffers severely from credit that is granted after the sales force makes a sale to a customer. The typical situation is that a salesperson finds a new customer and makes an inordinately large sale to it; the salesperson then badgers the credit department to grant a large credit limit to the customer since there is a large commission on the line. The credit staff yields to this pressure and allows more credit than the supplier's credit history warrants, resulting in a difficult collection job for the collections staff. The answer to this quandary lies in fixing the credit-granting process well before the collections staff even knows the new customer exists.

An outstanding best practice for those companies that want to avoid bad debt situations is to work closely with the sales staff to create a "hit list" of new customer prospects before any sales effort is made to contact them. The credit staff then reviews existing credit information about these customers, which is easily gleaned from credit reporting agencies, and calculates the credit levels that it is comfortable granting. These credit levels are given to the sales staff, which now knows the upper limits of what it is allowed to sell to each customer. This approach greatly reduces the pressure that salespeople are wont to bring on the credit staff for higher credit limits. A major by-product of this process is that the collections staff no longer has to deal with inordinately high accounts receivable with customers who have no way of paying on time.

The only problem with this approach is that a great deal of intra-departmental discipline is needed. The sales manager, in particular, must be able to carefully plan in advance for upcoming sales campaigns and control the sales staff in following sales targets. In addition, this person must see the importance of setting up credit levels in advance and must be able to work closely with the credit department in granting appropriate credit levels. If this type of person is not running the sales department, it will be difficult to enforce this best practice.

Thus, planning carefully to grant appropriate levels of credit to customers before the sales force contacts them is an excellent way to reduce the number of customers the collections staff must contact.

PRICING STRUCTURE SIMPLIFICATION

A common problem for the collections staff is when it tries to collect on an invoice that contains a pricing error. This problem most commonly arises when the order entry staff has a complicated set of rules to follow when deriving pricing. For example, rather than using a single price for each product, there may be a different price for various volume levels a customer orders—perhaps one dollar per unit if 1,000 units are ordered and two dollars if only 500 units are ordered. The situation can become even more complicated if there are special deals in place, such as an extra 10 percent discount if an order is placed within a special time period, such as the last week of the month. When all of these variations are included in the pricing structure (and some companies have even more complicated systems), it is a wonder that the order entry staff ever manages to issue a correct product price! A special circumstance under which pricing becomes nearly impossible to calculate is when the order entry department of an acquired company is merged with that of the buying company, leaving the order entry people with the pricing systems of the purchased company, as well as that of its own. This situation can quickly result in bedlam. The inevitable result is that customers will frequently disagree with the pricing on the invoices they receive and will not pay for them without a long period of dissension regarding the correct price. Alternatively, they will pay the price they think is the correct one, resulting in arguments over the remainder. In either case, the collections staff must become involved.

The best practice that resolves this situation is a simplification of the pricing structure. The easiest pricing structure to target is one that allows only one price to any customer for each product, with no special discounts of any kind. By using this system, not only does the collections staff have a much easier time, but so does the order entry staff—there is no need for them to make complicated calculations to arrive at a product price. However, there are two main implementation barriers to this approach: the sales staff and customers. The sales staff may be used to using a blizzard of promotional discounts to move product and may also have a long tradition of using volume discounts as a tool for shipping greater volume. Similarly, customers may be used to the same situation, especially those who benefit from the current tangle of pricing deals. To work through these barriers, it is critical for the controller to clearly communicate to senior management the reasons why a complicated pricing structure causes problems for the collections and order entry staffs. The end result is usually a political tug-of-war between the sales manager and controller; whoever wins is the one with the most political muscle in the organization.

Thus, simplifying the pricing structure is one of the most obvious ways to reduce the difficulty of collections, but it can be very difficult to implement because of resistance from the sales staff. One must build a clear case in favor of pricing simplification and present it well before the concept can become a reality.

STANDARDIZED CREDIT LEVEL DETERMINATION SYSTEM

A common complaint of the collection staff is that there does not appear to be any reasoning behind the credit levels that are granted customers, resulting in inordinately high credit levels for some customers who cannot begin to re-pay their debt. This results in considerable effort for the collections staff to bring in cash from these customers, as well as pleas to the credit department to lower credit to levels that have some reasonable chance of being repaid. This condition is caused by the approach of many credit departments to granting credit, which is that they grant the highest possible credit level to meet the latest order received from a customer. This approach is advocated heavily by the salesperson who stands to receive a substantial commission if the sale is approved. Consequently, granting credit based on the size of a customer's order rather than its ability to pay leads to considerable additional collections work.

To solve the problem of an uncertain credit-granting standard, we must create a procedure for granting credit that uses a single set of rules which are not to be violated, no matter how much pressure the sales staff applies to expand credit levels. The exact procedure will vary by credit department and the experience of the credit manager. As an example, a credit person can obtain a credit report for a prospective customer and use this as a source of baseline information for deriving a credit level. A credit report is an excellent basis upon which to create a standard credit level, for the information contained in it is collected in a similar manner for all companies, resulting in a standardized and highly comparable basis of information. Such a credit report should include a listing of the high, low, and median credit levels granted to a customer by other companies, giving a credit manager the range of credit that other companies have determined is appropriate. However, just using the range of credit levels is not normally sufficient, since one must also consider the number of extra days beyond terms that a customer takes to pay its customers. This information is a good indicator of creditworthiness and is also contained in a credit report. A good example of how the "payment" information can be included in the calculation of a credit level is to take the median credit level other companies granted as a starting point and then subtract 5 percent of this amount for every day that a customer pays its suppliers later than standard payment terms. For example, if the median credit level is $10,000 and a customer pays an average of ten days late, 50 percent of the median credit level is taken away, resulting in a credit level for the customer of $5,000. The exact system a company uses will be highly dependent on its willingness to incur credit losses and expend extra effort on collections. A company willing to obtain more marginal sales will adopt the highest credit level shown in the credit report and not discount the impact of late payments at all, whereas a risk-averse company may be inclined to use the lowest reported credit level and further discount it heavily for the impact of any late payments by the potential customer.

The range of standard procedures for granting credit levels is infinite. The main point is to have one consistent basis for creating reasonable customer credit levels, which gives the collections staff far less work to collect on sales that exceed the ability of a customer to pay. The procedure presented in this section involves using the information shown on a credit report, but other sources of information can also be used.

WRITE OFF SMALL BALANCES WITH NO APPROVAL

The typical procedure for writing off a bad debt is for a collections person to write up a bad debt approval form, including an explanation of why an account receivable is not collectible, which the controller must then review and sign. The form is filed away, possibly for future review by auditors. This can be a time-consuming process, but a necessary one if the amount of the bad debt is large. However, some bad debts are so small that the cost of completing the associated paperwork exceeds the bad debt. In short, the control point costs more than the savings for small write-offs.

The obvious solution is to eliminate approvals for small amounts that are overdue. A company can determine the appropriate amount for the upper limit of items that can be written off; an easy way to make this determination is to calculate the cost of the collections staff's time, as well as that of incidental costs, such as phone calls. Any account receivable that is equal to or less than this cost should be written off. The timing of the write-off, once again, depends on the particular circumstances of each company. Some may feel that it is best to wait until the end of the year before writing off an invoice, while others promptly clear them out of the accounts receivable aging as soon as they are 90 days old. Whatever the exact criteria may be, it is important for management to stay out of the process once the underlying guidelines have been set. By staying away, management is telling the collections staff that it trusts employees to make these decisions on their own, while also giving managers more time to deal with other issues. If managers feel that they must check on the write-offs, they can let an internal audit team review the situation from time to time.

By avoiding the approval process for writing off small accounts receivable, the collections staff avoids unnecessary paperwork while managers eliminate a waste of their time.

TOTAL IMPACT OF BEST PRACTICES
ON THE COLLECTIONS FUNCTION

This section covers a group of collections best practices that, when used together, will result in a very efficient collections department. The group does not include all of the best practices covered in this chapter, for a small number are mutually exclusive. In particular, outsourcing the collections function does not allow one to implement many of the other best practices. Accordingly, it is assumed that collections work is kept in-house, so a number of other improvements can be implemented.

The recommended best practices are laid out in Exhibit 7.2 in order of the typical transaction flow that results in a completed collection activity. It begins

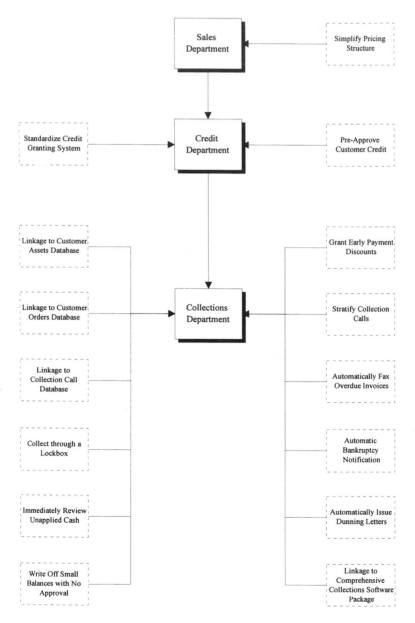

Exhibit 7.2. Impact of Best Practices on the Collection Function

with the sales department, which can reduce the amount of customer confusion by simplifying the product pricing structure. We then move on to the credit department, which can pre-approve customer credit and standardize the credit-granting system, both of which result in consistent and reasonable customer credit levels, keeping the collections staff from having to collect on excessive sales amounts to customers who are not capable of paying. Finally, we reach the collections department, where there are many best practices that can make the collections task more efficient: lockbox collections, immediate cash application, unapproved write-offs of small balances, early payment discounts, stratified collections, and automatic faxing of overdue invoices and dunning letters, as well as automatic bankruptcy notifications. One can supplement these activities with three databases (e.g., customer assets, customer orders, and collection calls) to assist in making more effective collection calls. Nearly all of these changes can be completed in a relatively short time, with only a few requiring significant investments. Consequently, the activities shown in Exhibit 7.2 can all be implemented in most companies, resulting in a profound difference in the level of efficiency of the collections department.

SUMMARY

The job of collecting accounts receivable is a hard and thankless one. The person who performs well in this position is the one who finds out why a customer pays late and then works with other departments in the company to ensure that the customer has fewer reasons for doing so in the future. This approach is embodied by many of the best practices that were presented in this chapter, such as simplifying the pricing structure, examining customer orders to see if there are any shipment problems, and granting credit levels in advance, eliminating any last minute pressure to grant an inappropriate level of credit that the customer can abuse. It is also important for a good collections person to keep accounts receivable from becoming overdue in the first place. Some of the best practices in this chapter address this issue, such as granting early payment discount terms and immediately applying all cash as soon as it is received. Another part of the collections job is to perform collection calls as efficiently as possible; this task is addressed by other best practices, such as using automated faxes of overdue invoices and dunning letters, as well as a collection call database. Finally, the collections staff must use all possible pressure points to collect from customers, which it can do with the use of such best practices as collection call stratification and a database of customer assets. When all of these tools are properly utilized, a collections staff can not only perform its job more efficiently, but can reduce significantly the amount of overdue accounts receivable at the same time.

Chapter 8

Commissions Best Practices

The application of best practices to commissions hardly seems to be worth a separate chapter; however, there are a surprisingly large number of actions that can streamline the calculation of commissions and their payment to sales personnel. This chapter contains ten best practices, which are discussed in alphabetical order.

The main factor to keep in mind is that these best practices are designed to improve the operations of the accounting department only. Though none of them will worsen the systems in the sales department, the other area that is directly impacted, they may have an opposite impact on the morale of that department. For example, one best practice is to replace convoluted commission structures with a simplified model. Though this will obviously lead to easier commission calculations by the accounting staff, it may also have the negative impact of reducing the sales incentive for those salespeople who are no longer receiving quite such a good compensation package. Accordingly, before installing any of the following best practices, it is a good idea to first gain the approval of the sales manager to any changes that will directly or indirectly impact the sales department.

IMPLEMENTATION ISSUES FOR COMMISSIONS BEST PRACTICES

This section illustrates the relative degree of implementation difficulty for commission best practices, as displayed in Exhibit 8.1.

The level of implementation difficulty in this area is quite polarized because of one major issue—some of the recommended changes require the complete cooperation of the sales manager, who will probably actively resist at least a few of them. Accordingly, the ease and duration of implementation for these best practices is rated as difficult and long, though they are actually quite simple if the agreement of the sales manager can somehow be obtained in advance. An example of this problem is simplifying the commission structure.

Those best practices that can be completed by the accounting staff without any outside approval are rated as both easy, short, and inexpensive installations. An example of such a best practice is paying commissions through the traditional

Exhibit 8.1.   Implementation Issues for Commissions Best Practices

Description	Ease of Implementation	Duration of Implementation	Cost of Implementation
Automatically Calculate Commissions in the Computer System	Moderate	Medium	Expensive
Calculate Final Commissions from Actual Data	Difficult	Long	Inexpensive
Construct a Standard Commission Terms Table	Easy	Short	Inexpensive
Include Commission Payments in Payroll Payments	Easy	Short	Inexpensive
Lengthen the Interval between Commission Payments	Difficult	Long	Inexpensive
Only Pay Commissions from Cash Received	Difficult	Long	Inexpensive
Periodically Audit Commissions Paid	Easy	Short	Moderate
Periodically Issue a Summary of Commission Rates	Easy	Short	Inexpensive
Post Commission Payments on the Company Intranet	Moderate	Medium	Moderate
Show Potential Commissions on Cash Register	Difficult	Long	Expensive
Simplify the Commission Structure	Difficult	Long	Inexpensive

payroll system. The only exceptions to the easy internal accounting changes are two items that may require some expensive programming assistance. Thus, the range of implementation difficulty is extraordinarily wide in this functional area.

AUTOMATICALLY CALCULATE COMMISSIONS IN THE COMPUTER SYSTEM

For many commission clerks, the days when commissions are calculated are not pleasant. Every invoice from the previous month must be assembled and reviewed, with notations on each one regarding which salesperson is paid a commission, the extent of any split commissions, and their amounts. Further, given the volume of invoices and the complexity of calculations, there is almost certainly an error every month, so the sales staff will be sure to pay a visit as soon as the commission checks are released in order to complain about their payments. This results in additional changes to the payments, making them very difficult to audit, in case the controller or the internal audit manager wants to verify that commissions are being calculated correctly. The manual nature of the work makes it both tedious and highly prone to error.

The answer is to automate as much of it as possible by having the computer system do the calculating. This way, the commission clerk only has to scan through the list of invoices assigned to each salesperson and verify that each has the correct salesperson's name listed on it and the correct commission rate charged to it. To make this system work, there must be a provision in the accounting software to record salesperson names and commission rates against invoices, a very common feature on even the most inexpensive systems—though if it does not exist, an expensive piece of programming work must be completed before this best practice can be implemented. Then the accounting staff must alter its invoicing procedure so that it enters a salesperson's name, initials, or identifying number in the invoicing record for every new invoice. It is very helpful if the data-entry screen is altered to *require* this field to be entered, in order to avoid any missing commissions. Once this procedure is altered, it is an easy matter to run a commissions report at the end of the reporting period and then pay commission checks from it. This is a simple and effective way to eliminate the manual labor and errors associated with the calculation of commissions.

The main problem with using automated commission calculations is that it does not work if the commission system is a complex one. For example, the typical computer system only allows for a single commission rate and salesperson to be assigned to each invoice. However, many companies have highly varied and detailed commission systems, where the commission rates vary based on a variety of factors and many invoices have split commissions assigned to several sales staff. In these cases, only custom programming or a return to manual commission calculations will be possible, unless someone can convince the sales manager to adopt a simplified commission structure. This is rarely possible since the sales manager is the one who probably created the complicated system and has no intention of seeing it dismantled.

CALCULATE FINAL COMMISSIONS FROM ACTUAL DATA

A common arrangement for departing salespeople is that they are paid immediately for the commissions they have not yet received, but which they should receive in the next commission payment. Unfortunately, the amount of this commission payment is frequently a guess, since some sales have not yet been completed and orders have not even been received for other spotential sales on which a salesperson may have been working for many months. Accordingly, there is usually a complicated formula in the typical salesperson's hiring agreement that pays out a full commission on completed sales, a partial one on orders just received, and perhaps even a small allowance on expected sales for which final orders have not yet been received. The work required to complete this formula is highly labor-intensive and frequently inaccurate, especially if an allowance is paid for sales which may not yet have occurred (and which may never occur).

A better approach is to restructure the initial sales agreement to state that commissions will be paid at the regular times after employee termination until all sales have been recorded. The duration of these payments may be several months, which means that the salesperson must wait some time to receive full compensation, but the accounting staff benefits from not having to waste time on a separate, and highly laborious, termination calculation. Instead, it takes no notice of whether or not a salesperson is still working for the company and just calculates and pays out commissions in accordance with regular procedures.

There are three problems with this approach. One is that if the commission calculation is made automatically in the computer system, sales will probably be assigned to a new salesperson as soon as the old one has left, requiring some manual tracking of exactly who is entitled to payment on which sale during the transition period. The second problem is that if a salesperson is fired, most state laws require immediate compensation within a day or so of termination. Though the initial sales agreement can be modified to cover this contingency, one should first check to see if the applicable state law will override the sales agreement. Finally, this type of pay-out usually requires a change to the initial employee contract with each salesperson; the existing sales staff may have a problem with this new arrangement since they will not receive payment so quickly if they leave the company. A company can take the chance of irritating the existing sales staff by unilaterally changing the agreements, but may want to try the more politically correct approach of grandfathering the existing staff and only apply the new agreement to new sales employees. In short, delaying the final commission payment runs the risk of mixing up payments between old and new salespeople, may be contrary to state laws, and may only be applicable to new employees. Despite these issues, it is still a good idea to implement this best practice, even though it may be several years before it applies to all of the sales staff.

CONSTRUCT A STANDARD COMMISSION TERMS TABLE

As salespeople may make the majority of their incomes from commissions, they have a great deal of interest in the exact rates paid on various kinds of sales. This can lead to many visits to the commissions clerk to complain about perceived problems with the rates paid on various invoices. Not only can this be a stressful visit on the part of the commissions clerk, who will be on the receiving end of some very forceful arguments, but it is also a waste of time, since that person has other work to do besides listening to the arguments of the sales staff.

A reasonable approach that greatly reduces sales staff complaints is a commission terms table. It should specify the exact commission arrangement with each salesperson so that there is absolutely no way to misconstrue the reimbursement arrangement. Once this is set up, it can be distributed to the sales staff, who can refer to it instead of the commissions clerk. There will be the inevitable rash of complaints for the first few days after the table is issued since the sales staff will want clarification on a few key points, possibly requiring a re-issuance of the table. However, once the table has been reviewed a few times, the number of complaints should rapidly dwindle. The only problem with this approach is that listing the commission deals of all the sales staff side-by-side on a single document will lead to a great deal of analysis and arguing by those sales personnel who think they are not receiving as good a commission arrangement. The best way to avoid this problem is to separate the table into pieces so each salesperson only sees that piece of it that applies to the individual. By following this approach, the number of inquiries and commission adjustments that the accounting staff must deal with will rapidly decline.

INCLUDE COMMISSION PAYMENTS IN PAYROLL PAYMENTS

If a company has a significant number of sales personnel, the chore of issuing commission payments to them can be a significant one. The taxes must be compiled for each check and deducted from the gross pay, the checks must be cut or a wire transfer made, and, for those employees who are out of town, there may be other special arrangements to get the money to them. Depending on the number of checks, this can interfere with the smooth functioning of the accounting department.

A simple but effective way to avoid this problem is to roll commission payments into the regular payroll processing system. By doing so, the payroll calculation chore is completely eliminated, once the gross commission amounts are approved and sent to the payroll staff for processing. The system will calculate taxes automatically, issue checks or direct deposits, or mail to employees, depending on the distribution method the regular payroll system uses. This completely eliminates a major chore.

There are two problems with this best practice. One is that the commission payment date may not coincide with the payroll processing date, which necessitates a change in the commission payment date. For example, if the commission is always paid on the fifteenth day of the month, but the payroll is on a biweekly schedule, the actual pay date will certainly not fall on the fifteenth day of every month. To fix this issue, the commission payment date in the example could be set to the first payroll date following the fifteenth of the month. The other problem is that by combining a salesperson's regular paycheck with the commission payment, the combined total will put the employee into a higher pay bracket, resulting in more taxes being deducted (never a popular outcome). This issue can be resolved either by setting employee deduction rates lower, or by separating the payments into two separate checks in the payroll system in order to drop the payee into a lower apparent tax bracket (though most payroll systems do not have this feature). As long as these issues are taken into account, merging commissions into the payroll system is a very effective way for the accounting staff to avoid cutting separate commission checks.

LENGTHEN THE INTERVAL BETWEEN COMMISSION PAYMENTS

Some commissions are paid as frequently as once a week, though monthly payments are the norm in most industries. If there are many employees receiving commission payments, this level of frequency results in a multitude of commission calculations and check payments over the course of a year.

It may be possible in some instances to lengthen the interval between commission payments, reducing the amount of commission calculation and paycheck preparation work for the accounting department. This best practice is only useful in a minority of situations, however, because the commissions of many sales personnel constitute a large proportion of their pay and they cannot afford to wait a long time to receive it. However, there are some instances where salespeople receive only a very small proportion of their pay in the form of commissions. In this situation, it makes little sense to calculate a commission for a very small amount of money and is better to only do it at a longer interval, perhaps quarterly or annually. Though it can be used only in a few cases, this best practice is worth considering.

ONLY PAY COMMISSIONS FROM CASH RECEIVED

A major problem for the collections staff is salespeople who indiscriminately sell any amount of product or service to customers, regardless of the ability of those customers to pay. When this happens, the salesperson is focusing only on the commission that will result from the sale and not on the excessive work required of the collections staff to bring in the payment from the supplier, not to mention the much higher bad debt allowance needed to offset uncollectible accounts.

The best practice that avoids this difficulty is to change the commission system so that salespeople are paid a commission only on the cash received from customers. This change will instantly turn the entire sales force into a secondary collection agency, since they will be very interested in bringing in cash on time. They will also be more concerned about the creditworthiness of their customers, since they will spend less time selling to customers who have little realistic chance of paying.

There are a few problems that make this a tough best practice to adopt. First, as it requires salespeople to wait longer before they are paid a commission, they are markedly unwilling to change to this new system. Second, the amount they are paid will be somewhat smaller than what they are used to receiving, since inevitably there will be a few accounts receivable that will never be collected. Third, because of the first two issues, some of the sales staff will feel slighted and will probably leave the company to find another organization with a more favorable commission arrangement. Accordingly, the sales manager may not support a change to this kind of commission structure.

A problem directly related to the accounting systems (and not the intransigence of the sales department!) is that since commissions are now paid based on cash received, there must be a cash report to show the amounts of cash received from each customer in a given time period, in order to calculate commissions from this information. Alternatively, if commissions are based on cash received from specific invoices, the report must reflect this information. Most accounting systems already contain this report; if not, it must be programmed into the system.

PERIODICALLY AUDIT COMMISSIONS PAID

Given the complexity of some commission structures, it comes as no surprise that the sales staff is not always paid the correct commission amount. This is particularly true of transition periods, where payment rates change or new salespeople take over different sales territories. When this happens, there is confusion regarding the correct commission rates to pay on certain invoices, or who is paid for each one. The usual result is that there are some overpayments that go uncorrected; the sales staff will closely peruse commission payments to make sure that *under*payments do not occur, so this is rarely a problem. In addition, there is a chance that overpayments are made on a regular basis, since any continuing overpayment is unlikely to be reported by the salesperson on the receiving end of this largesse.

The best way to review commissions for this problem is to schedule a periodic internal audit of the commission calculations. This review can take the form of a detailed analysis of a sampling of commission payments or a much simpler overall review of the percentage of commissions paid out, with a more detailed review if the percentage looks excessively high. Any problems discovered through this process can result in some retraining of the commissions clerk, an adjustment in the commission rates paid, or a reduction in the future payments to the sales staff until any overpayments have been fully deducted from their pay. This approach requires some time on the part of the internal audit staff, but does not need to be conducted very frequently and so is not an expensive proposition. An occasional review is usually sufficient to find and correct any problems with commission overpayments.

PERIODICALLY ISSUE A SUMMARY OF COMMISSION RATES

Even companies with a simplified and easily understandable commission structure will sometimes have difficulty communicating this information to the sales staffs. The problem is that the information is not readily available for sales personnel to see, and so they are always breeding rumors about commission alterations impacting their income. This causes a continuing morale problem, frequently resulting in needless inquiries to the accounting department.

The simple solution to this problem is to periodically issue a summary of commission rates. If management is comfortable with revealing the entire commission structure for all personnel, it can issue a commission table to the entire sales force. If not, it can issue a salesperson-specific commission listing. The table should be issued no less frequently than annually. A good way to present the commission information to a salesperson is to include it in the annual review, allowing each salesperson time to review it and ask questions about it. Also, the commissions table should be reissued and discussed with the sales force *every time* there is a change in the table, which keeps the accounting staff from having to explain the changes after the fact when the sales staff calls to inquire about the alterations. In short, up-front communications with the sales staff is a good way to keep the accounting department from having to answer inquiries about the commission information.

POST COMMISSION PAYMENTS ON THE COMPANY INTRANET

A sales staff whose pay structure is heavily skewed in favor of commission payments, rather than salaries, will probably hound the accounting staff at month-end to see what their commission payments will be. This comes at the time of the month when the accounting staff is trying to close the accounting books, and so increases its workload at the worst possible time of the month. However, by creating a linkage between the accounting database and a company's Internet site, it is now possible to shift this information directly to the web page where the sales staff can view it at any time, and without involving the valuable time of the accounting staff.

There are two ways to post the commission information. One is to wait until all commission-related calculations have been completed at month-end, and then either manually dump the data into an HTML (HyperText Markup Language) format for posting to a web page, or else run a batch program that does so automatically. Either approach will give the sales staff a complete set of information about their commissions. However, this approach still requires some manual effort at month-end (even if only for a few minutes while a batch program runs).

An alternative approach is to create a direct interface between the accounting database and the web page, so that commissions are updated constantly, including grand totals for each commission payment period. By using this approach, the accounting staff has virtually no work to do in conveying information to the sales staff. In addition, sales personnel can check their commissions at any time of the month, and call the accounting staff with their concerns right away—this is a great improvement, since problems can be spotted and fixed at once, rather than waiting until the crucial month-end closing period to correct them.

No matter which method is used for posting commission information, a password system will be needed, since this is highly personal payroll-related information. There should be a reminder program built into the system, so that the sales staff is forced to alter its passwords on a regular basis, thereby reducing the risk of outside access to this information.

SHOW POTENTIAL COMMISSIONS ON CASH REGISTER

The sales manager can have difficulty in motivating the sales staff to sell those products with the highest margins. This is a particularly galling issue when there are so many products on hand it is almost impossible to educate the staff about margins on each one. Consequently, the sales staff sells whatever customers ask for, rather than attempting to steer them in the direction of more profitable products, resulting in less-than-optimal corporate profitability.

A rarely used best practice is to itemize the commission rates salespeople earn on individual products right on the cash register. When combined with a listing of the commissions on a range of related products, the sales staff can quickly scan the data, identify those that will make them the most money, and steer customers toward them. Since the products with the highest commissions will presumably have the highest margins, this practice should result in higher company margins. The tool can also be used to emphasize sales on products the company is discontinuing and wishes to clear out of stock. Thus, by bring detailed information to the sales staff which is also tied to sales incentives, a company can increase its margins while also better managing its mix of on-hand products.

One problem with listing commissions on cash registers is that this approach is only useable in a retail environment where salespeople ring up sales on the spot. It would not be functional at all, for example, if a salesperson conducts multiple sales calls on the road, though the concept can be modified by loading commission rates by product into a laptop computer, which the salesperson can consult during sales calls. Given the cost of a computer, however, this can be an expensive option. Another issue is that the commission database will be a very complicated one, especially if commissions on products are changed frequently, necessitating a listing of commissions by both product and date. This can be a major programming job, requiring significant computer resources. Finally, the cash registers must include video display terminals of a sufficient size to show multiple products and their commissions—if such terminals do not exist, all retail locations using the system must be re-equipped with them, a significant extra expense. If these problems can be overcome, however, the posting of product commissions on cash registers can lead to a major improvement in corporate profitability.

SIMPLIFY THE COMMISSION STRUCTURE

The banc of the accounting department is an overly complex commission structure. When there are a multitude of commission rates, shared rates, special bonuses, and retroactive booster clauses, the commission calculation chore is mind-numbing, and highly subject to error, which causes further analysis to fix. An example of such a system, based on an actual corporation, is for a company-wide standard commission rate, but with special increased commission rates for certain counties considered especially difficult regions in which to sell, except for sales to certain customers, who are the responsibility of the in-house sales staff, who receive a different commission rate. In addition, the commission rate is retroactively increased if later quarterly sales targets are met, and are retroactively increased a *second* time if the full-year sales goal is reached, with an extra bonus payment if the full-year goal is exceeded by a set percentage. Needless to say, this company went through an endless cycle of commission payment adjustments, some of which were disputed for months afterwards. Also, this company had great difficulty retaining a commissions clerk in the accounting department.

The best practice that resolves this problem is a simplification of the overall commission structure. For example, the previous example can be reduced to a single across-the-board commission rate, with quarterly and annual bonuses if milestone targets are reached. Though an obvious solution and one that can greatly reduce the work of the accounting staff, it is only implemented with the greatest difficulty because the sales manager must approve the new system, and rarely does so. The reason is that the sales manager probably created the convoluted commissions system in the first place and feels that it is a good one for motivating the sales staff. In this situation, the matter may have to go to a higher authority for approval, though this irritates the sales manager. A better and more politically correct variation is to persuade the sales manager to adopt a midway solution that leaves both parties partially satisfied and still able to work with each other on additional projects. In the long run, as new people move into the sales manager position, there may still be opportunities to more completely simplify the commission structure.

TOTAL IMPACT OF BEST PRACTICES ON THE COMMISSIONS FUNCTION

This section describes the overall impact of best practices on the commissions function. The best practices noted in this chapter have an impact on three major accounting activities, as noted graphically in Exhibit 8.2. They impact the motivation of sales personnel, the calculation of commissions, and their payment. The vast majority of these best practices are centered on the calculation of commissions, since this step requires the most work from the accounting department. All of the best practices associated with commission calculations can be implemented together—none are mutually exclusive. Though the permission of the sales manager is required for several of these items, the end result—standardized commissions that are regularly audited, automatically calculated, and only paid

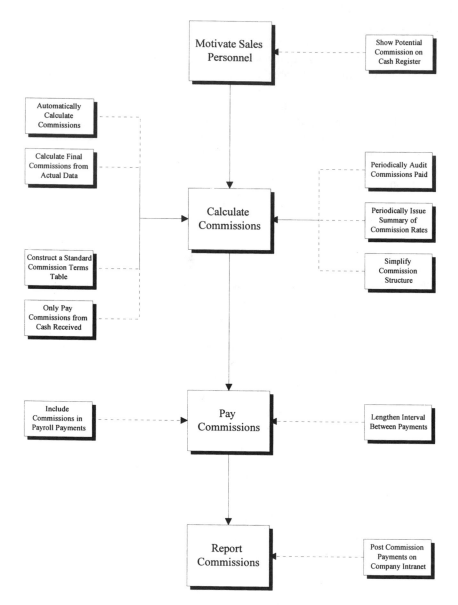

Exhibit 8.2. Impact of Best Practices on the Commissions Function

from actual cash receipts—reduces the work of the accounting staff to a remarkable degree. Those best practices affecting the payment of commissions have a
much smaller impact on accounting efficiency, while the one item affecting the
motivation of the sales staff does nothing to improve the accounting department.

Accordingly, the bulk of management attention in this area should go to improving the efficiency of calculating commissions.

SUMMARY

This chapter concentrated primarily on ways to reduce the time, effort, and number of errors in the calculation of commissions, with a reduced emphasis on better ways to pay commissions once they have been calculated. They are mostly easy best practices to implement. However, as noted several times in this chapter, several of them will directly affect the sales staff and so require the approval of the sales manager before they can be implemented. Since some of these changes will not be popular with the salespeople, do not be surprised if that approval is not forthcoming. If so, an occasional review of unapproved best practices may eventually find a more malleable sales manager in place, with a different result. Thus, if at first you don't succeed, try, try again.

Chapter 9

Costing Best Practices

This chapter is concerned with those best practices impacting the cost of products and the valuation of inventory. They are grouped into three main areas: information accuracy, cost reports, and costing systems. The first category, information accuracy, covers several best practices that review the accuracy of key information driving the costing of inventory: bills of material, labor routings, and units of measure. The second category, cost reports, is covered by the largest number of best practices. These are concerned with modifying or even eliminating the current cost-reporting systems in favor of a tighter focus on direct costs, materials, costs trends, and obsolete inventory. The final category, costing systems, addresses the two costing systems that should at least supplement, if not replace, traditional costing systems: activity-based costing and target costing. When the complete set of best practices advocated in this chapter has been implemented, a company will find that it has a much better grasp of its key product costs and how to control them.

IMPLEMENTATION ISSUES FOR COSTING BEST PRACTICES

This section covers the general level of implementation difficulty for each of the best practices discussed later in this chapter. Each best practice is noted in alphabetical order in Exhibit 9.1, along with a rating of the ease, duration, and cost of implementation for each one. Generally speaking, these are easy best practices to install because most of them can be completed with no more approval than the controller's, they have a short implementation duration, and they are quite inexpensive to install and operate. The main exceptions are target costing and activity-based costing, which require a major commitment of time and staff and also the approval of other department managers, depending on their levels of involvement in the implementations. However, despite the level of installation difficulty for these two best practices, they both have the largest positive impact of all the improvements noted in this chapter and thus are well worth the effort.

There are also several cost-reporting changes advocated in this chapter. Though the reports are not hard to alter or replace, it can be quite another matter to convince the report recipients that they are now receiving better information, especially if they are old-line managers who have received the same cost reports

Exhibit 9.1. Implementation Issues for Costing Best Practices

Description	Ease of Implementation	Duration of Implementation	Cost of Implementation
Audit Bills of Material	Easy	Short	Inexpensive
Audit Labor Routings	Easy	Short	Inexpensive
Eliminate High-Leverage Overhead Allocation Bases	Moderate	Short	Inexpensive
Eliminate Labor Variance Reporting	Easy	Short	Inexpensive
Follow a Schedule of Inventory Obsolescence Reviews	Moderate	Easy	Inexpensive
Implement Activity-Based Costing	Difficult	Long	Medium
Implement Target Costing	Difficult	Medium	Medium
Limit Access to Unit of Measure Changes	Easy	Short	Inexpensive
Review Cost Trends	Easy	Short	Inexpensive
Review Material Scrap Levels	Easy	Short	Inexpensive
Revise Traditional Cost Accounting Reports	Moderate	Medium	Expensive

for decades. Consequently, the time required to insert a new cost report into a company's standard reporting package can take much longer than one would normally expect.

AUDIT BILLS OF MATERIAL

When the accounting department issues financial statements, one of the largest expenses listed on it is the material cost (at least in a manufacturing environment). Unless it conducts a monthly physical inventory count, the accounting staff must rely on the word of the logistics department in assuming that the month-end inventory listed on the books is the correct amount. If it is not, the financial statements can be off by a significant amount. The core document used by the logistics department that drives the accuracy of the inventory is the bill of materials. This is a listing of the components that go into a product. If it is incorrect, the parts assumed to be in a product will be incorrect, which means that products costs will be wrong, too. This problem has the largest impact in a backflushing environment, where the bills of material determine how many materials are used to produce a product. Thus, the accuracy of the bills of material have a major impact on the accuracy of the financial statements.

The best practice that improves the situation is following an ongoing program of auditing bills of material. By doing so, errors are flushed out of the bills, resulting in better inventory quantity data, which in turn results in more accurate financial statements. The best way to implement bill audits is to tie them to the production schedule, so that any products scheduled to be manufactured in the near future are reviewed the most frequently. This focuses attention on those bills with the highest usage, though it is still necessary to review the bills of less frequently used products from time to time. The review can be conducted by the engineering staff, the production scheduler, the warehouse staff, and the production staff. The reason for using so many people is that they all have input into the process. The engineering staff has the best overall knowledge of the product, while the production scheduler is the most aware of production shortages caused by problems with the bills, and the warehouse staff sees components returned to the warehouse that were listed in the bills but not actually used; the production staff must assemble products and knows from practical experience which bills are inaccurate. Thus, a variety of people (preferably all of them) can influence the bill of material review process.

Measuring a bill of material includes several steps. One is to ensure that the correct part quantities are listed. Another is to verify that parts should be included in the product at all. Yet another is that the correct sub-assemblies roll up into the final product. If any of these items are incorrect, a bill of material should be listed as incorrect in total. For a large bill with many components, this means that it will almost certainly be listed as incorrect when it is first reviewed, with rapid improvement as corrections are made. The target that a company should shoot for when reviewing bills of material is a minimum accuracy level of 98 percent. At this level, any errors will have a minimal impact on accuracy, cost of the inventory, and cost of goods sold. Thus, it is not uncommon for a company to record an initial overall bill of material accuracy of zero.

If a controller can effectively work with the engineering, production, and logistics staffs to create a reliable bill of material review system, the result is a much more accurate costing system.

AUDIT LABOR ROUTINGS

The labor a company charges to each of its products is derived from a labor routing, which is an engineering estimate of the labor hours required to produce a product. Unfortunately, an inaccuracy in the labor-routing information has a major impact on a company's profitability for two reasons. One is that the labor hours assigned to a product will be incorrect, resulting in an incorrect product cost. By itself, this is not usually a major problem, because the labor cost is not a large component of the total product cost. However, the second reason is the real problem—since the labor rate is frequently used as the primary basis upon which overhead is allocated to products, a shift in the labor rate can result in a massive change in the allocated overhead cost, which may be much larger than the underlying labor cost. Thus, an inaccurate labor routing can have a large impact on the reported cost of a product.

The best practice that addresses this problem is auditing labor routings. By doing so, one can gradually review all labor records and verify their accuracy, thereby avoiding any mis-costing of products. To do so, one must enlist the help of the engineering manager, who must assign a staff person to review this information on a regular basis and make changes as needed. The accounting department can assist in the effort by comparing the labor routings of similar products to see if there are any discrepancies and bring them to the attention of the engineering department for resolution. Also, it can review computer records (if they exist) to see when labor routings have been changed and verify the alterations with the engineering staff. Finally, the accounting staff can work with the production planning department to see if the assumed production-run quantities noted in the labor routings match actual production quantities. This last item is a critical one, for the assumed per-unit labor quantity will go down as the run length increases, due to the improved learning curve that comes with longer production runs, as well as the larger number of production units over which the labor set-up time can be spread. Some unscrupulous businesspeople will assume very short production runs in order to increase the assumed labor rates in their labor routings, resulting in the capitalization of much higher labor and overhead costs in the inventory records. Thus, a continual review and comparison of labor-routing records by the accounting staff is a necessary component of this auditing process.

ELIMINATE HIGH-LEVERAGE OVERHEAD ALLOCATION BASES

There is nothing more damaging to a company than to make a management decision based on inaccurate information. Though the accounting department is devoted to presenting the best possible information to senior management at all times, there is one area in which it continues to provide inaccurate data: overhead costs. This is an increasingly large proportion of the costs of many companies, and it is critical to allocate it to various activities and products properly. To be blunt, most accountants do a very poor job of allocating these costs, resulting in cost reports that show inordinately high or low overhead costs being assigned to various items. When a manager acts upon this information, the decision may be a wrong one because the overhead cost component of the information was wrong. The reason why overhead costing information is incorrect in so many instances is a faulty allocation base. For example, the most common allocation base is to assign overhead costs to a product based on the amount of labor cost used to build it. The trouble is that labor is an increasingly small component of total labor costs, resulting in large overhead amounts being allocated based on tiny labor costs. The ratio of overhead to labor costs can reach absurd levels, such as 10 dollars for every one dollar of labor. When there are large differences between the proportion of overhead to the allocation base, even a slight change in the allocation base will result in a large swing in the overhead costs. Thus, minute month-to-month differences in the allocation base can falsely alter product costs by significant amounts.

The best practice that resolves this problem is to find new allocation bases that are not so highly leveraged. By doing so, there is less chance of having unusual cost swings based on small alterations in the allocation base. A good rule of thumb is to keep the ratio of allocation base to overhead cost no higher than one to one and preferably much less. This way, small changes in the allocation base will result in similarly small changes in the overhead cost. If the allocation base is not monetary, use an allocation base that is so large that any large changes are unlikely. For example, if square footage is used as the allocation base, the chance that the amount of square footage will suddenly change by an inordinate amount is quite small. In either case, the goal of reducing wide swings in overhead costs has been achieved.

This is a simple best practice to implement, usually requiring a modest investment in investigation time in order to find new allocation bases to replace the existing ones, as well as a few days of work to set up the allocation formulas. Since there is little or no programming required and the approval of other departments is unnecessary, there is no reason why this implementation cannot succeed in short order.

This best practice addresses the problem of keeping overhead costs from changing significantly. Another best practice reviews the problem from a different angle, which is linking overhead costs to specific activities as tightly as possible, resulting in a more informed allocation of costs to those activities which drive the costs. For more information on this approach to overhead allocation, see the "Implement Activity-Based Costing" section in this chapter.

ELIMINATE LABOR VARIANCE REPORTING

The cost components of work-in-process and inventory goods will inevitably include some labor. However, the proportion of labor in the total cost mix has dropped markedly over the years, with material and overhead costs now predominating. Nonetheless, the costing reports the accounting staff has traditionally generated are mostly concerned with labor. Examples of these reports are those detailing overtime, comparing actual to standard labor rates or usage, and labor efficiency. By comparison, the reports concerned with the materials expense typically cover only scrap rates and purchase price variances, while many companies have no reporting for overhead costs at all. Hence, most accounting departments are misallocating their time in reporting on the smallest component of product costs.

The best practice that addresses this problem is one of the easiest to implement—simply stop reporting on labor variances. The accounting staff will have more time to spend on reports concerning costs which make up a larger proportion of product costs. The problem with this best practice is the remarkable uproar it frequently incites, especially on the part of traditional production managers who were raised on the concept of tight control over labor costs. Thus, the best way to implement this item is to carefully educate the production staff on the following points:

- *Direct labor is really a fixed cost.* In many manufacturing situations, the direct labor staff cannot be sent home the moment there is no work left to do. Instead, a company must think about retaining them since they are trained and more efficient than other people who might be brought in off the street. Accordingly, it makes a great deal of sense to guarantee regular working hours to the direct labor staff (within reason). By doing so, it becomes apparent that direct labor is not a variable cost at all and requires much less detailed investigation and reporting work for the accounting staff.

- *Other reports are more valuable.* If the accounting department only has enough resources to issue a fixed number of reports, there is a good argument for eliminating the least useful ones (labor reporting) in favor of ones involving more costs, such as materials and overhead. One can reinforce this argument by formulating trial report layouts for new reports which will replace the labor reports.

- *Target costing is the real area of concern.* Many studies have shown that costs are not that variable once a product design is released to the factory floor. Instead, the primary area in which costs can truly be impacted is during the product design (see the "Implement Target Costing" section in this chapter). A strong argument in this area, especially if combined with visits to other companies which have installed target costing, will go a long way toward convincing management on this point.

If production management can be convinced that these three points are accurate, it becomes much easier to eliminate labor variance reporting, either completely or in part.

The only situation in which this best practice should not be implemented is one where labor costs still make up the majority of product costs (an increasingly rare situation) and where those costs are variable. If labor costs are highly fixed in nature, there is not much point in continuing to issue reports showing that the costs have not changed from period to period.

FOLLOW A SCHEDULE OF INVENTORY OBSOLESCENCE REVIEWS

A great many companies find that the proportion of their inventory that is obsolete is much higher than expected. This is a major problem at the end of the fiscal year, when this type of inventory is supposed to be investigated and written off, usually in conjunction with the auditor's review or the physical inventory (or both). If this write-off has not occurred in previous years, the cumulative amount can be quite startling. This may result in the departure of the controller, on the grounds that he should have known about the problem.

The best practice that resolves this problem is adopting and sticking to a schedule of regular obsolete-inventory reviews. This is an unpopular task with many employees because they must pore over usage reports and wander through the warehouse to see what inventory is not needed and then follow up on disposal problems. However, these people do not realize the major benefits of having a periodic obsolete-inventory review. One is that it clears space out of the warehouse, which may even allow for a reduction in the space this department needs, resulting in a possible reduction in the overall square footage that a corporation requires. Also, spotting obsolete inventory as early as possible allows a company to realize the best salvage value for it, which will inevitably decline over time (unless a company is dealing in antiques!). Further, a close review of the reason why an inventory item is in stock and obsolete may lead to discoveries concerning how parts are ordered and used; changing these practices may lead to a reduction in obsolete inventory in the future. Thus, there are a number of excellent reasons for maintaining an ongoing obsolete-inventory review system.

The composition of the obsolete-inventory review committee is very important. There should be an accountant who can summarize the costs of obsolescence, while an engineering representative is in the best position to determine if a part can be used elsewhere. Also, someone from the purchasing department can tell if there is any resale value. Consequently, a cross-departmental committee is needed to properly review obsolete inventory.

The main contribution of the accounting department to this review is a periodic report that itemizes those parts most likely to be obsolete. This information can take the following forms:

- *Last usage date.* Many computer systems record the last date on which a specific part number was removed from the warehouse for production or sale. If so, it is an easy matter to use a report writer to extract and sort this information, resulting in a report that lists all inventory, starting with those products with the oldest "last used" date.

- *No "where used" in the system.* If a computer system includes a bill of materials, there is a strong likelihood that it also generates a "where used" report, which lists all of the bills of material for which an inventory item is used. If there is no "where used" listed on the report, it is likely that a part is no longer needed. This report is most effective if bills of material are removed from the computer system as soon as products are withdrawn from the market; this more clearly reveals those inventory items that are no longer needed. This approach can also be used to determine which inventory *is going to be* obsolete, based on the anticipated withdrawal of *existing* products from the market.

- *Comparison to previous-year physical inventory tags.* Many companies still conduct a physical inventory at the end of their fiscal years. When this is done, a tag is usually taped to each inventory item. Later, a member of the accounting staff can walk through the warehouse and mark down all inventory items with an inventory tag still attached to them. This is a simple visual approach for finding old inventory.

- *Acknowledged obsolete inventory still in the system.* Even the best inventory review committee will sometimes let obsolete inventory fall through the cracks and remain in both the warehouse and the inventory database. The accounting staff should keep track of all acknowledged obsolete inventory and continue to notify management of those items that have not yet been removed.

Any or all of these reports can be used to gain a knowledge of likely candidates for obsolete-inventory status. This information is the mandatory first step in the process of keeping the inventory up-to-date. Consequently, the accounting staff plays a major role in this process.

IMPLEMENT ACTIVITY-BASED COSTING

The vast majority of companies only accumulate and report on costs by department and product. The first method is tied to responsibility accounting, whereby the costs of the specific department are tied to the performance bonus of its manager. The second method assumes that the cost of overhead—mostly made up of those departmental costs noted in the first method—is assigned to products based on the amount of labor they accumulate. The problem with this approach is that the two methods should be combined so that *all* company costs, to the greatest extent possible, are tied to the actual cost required to produce a product. Without this information, a company is doomed to make incorrect decisions related to the correct pricing of products, or even if they should be continued or discontinued. The same problem applies to determining the cost or profit associated with each customer. Again, a company can work incorrectly to increase its business with a "high maintenance" customer that results in much lower overall profits, while abandoning other customers who are really much more profitable. Poor costing methodologies are at the bottom of many bad corporate decisions.

The solution to this problem is a system called activity-based costing. Under this approach, a company summarizes all of its costs into a number of cost pools, then allocates the expenses in those pools to a variety of activities, using a large number of allocation measures. It becomes much easier to accurately assign the costs of these activities to various products and customers, based on their usage of the activities. Though this may seem like nothing more than an elaborate allocation of overhead, it is actually a carefully constructed methodology for determining the true cost of a company's products and services. Along with target costing, it is the most significant advance in costing methodologies in the last few decades, eminently worth the effort of putting in place.

However, installing an activity-based costing system is not that easy. The cost pools must be constructed, allocation measures determined, and new systems created to store, calculate, and report all of this information. In addition, the cooperation of other departments is necessary to ensure that new allocation measures are properly and consistently calculated. Finally, management must be apprised of the content of the new reports that will come out of this system and how they can be used. Given the considerable cost, time, and training required to ensure that this system becomes fully operational and accepted by management, it is no surprise that many such installations have not been completed, and even completed ones do not enjoy the full support of upper management. Thus, it is not so strange that activity-based costing is the best cost-accounting tool available and yet does not enjoy universal popularity or usage.

From the perspective of the accounting department, installing this system is a difficult chore. Depending on the size of the company, one or more staff people should be allocated to the project full-time for many months. In addition, the existing accounting software almost certainly does not track activity-based costs; a secondary software package must be purchased that takes information from the general ledger, as well as allocation bases from a variety of locations, summarizes data into cost pools, allocates it to activities, and charges costs to products. Also, given the newness of this approach and the lack of instruction about it at the college level, the services of a consultant may be worth the added cost. Further, a considerable amount of management time must go into planning and controlling the work effort, so that it is completed on time without exceeding the budgeted expenditure level.

IMPLEMENT TARGET COSTING

A cost-accounting staff can create the best costing reports in the world, constantly update this information, and hound the production, engineering, and purchasing staffs incessantly to improve the situation, and find little change in product costs. The reason is that most product costs are locked in when the product is *designed.* For example, a poor microwave oven design will lead to production inefficiencies because the product was not designed for ease of manufacturability. Similarly, if the oven was not designed to be sufficiently sturdy, there will be a number of customer returns, resulting in added engineering and manufacturing costs to fix the problem. Further, the oven may contain non-standard parts which are both difficult and expensive to obtain, and which may not allow for the use of existing parts used with other products. Thus, cost accounting is focusing on the wrong target—product costs during production, instead of product costs during the design stage.

The best practice that addresses this issue is called target costing. Under this concept, the existing market is reviewed and a target price is determined at which a certain set of product specifications will probably sell quite well. A design team is then brought together and assigned the task of creating a product with those specifications and a maximum cost. The maximum cost figure allows a company to sell for the previously determined price while still making an acceptable profit. If it is impossible to produce the product for the maximum assigned cost, the project is abandoned. This approach is in contrast to the more traditional method of designing a product, determining how much it costs when the project is finished, and then adding on a profit percentage to arrive at a selling price.

The obvious advantage of target costing is that a company has total control over product costs before any product reaches the production floor. It is easy to determine which products should be produced and which ones abandoned, thereby keeping losing or marginally profitable products out of a company's product mix. From the accounting department's perspective, its costing work shifts away from tracking production costs and into tracking costs during the design phase. This means that a cost accountant should be re-assigned from the first activity to the latter so that there is a daily review of the range of costs into which target costs are likely to fall. By shifting the direction of the accounting department's costing analysis, one can report on the activities which truly have the greatest impact on product costs.

LIMIT ACCESS TO UNIT OF MEASURE CHANGES

The unit of measure field, an innocuous field in the computer system, can have a major impact on the accuracy of product costs. When the quantity in a bill of material or inventory record is created, it has a unit of measure listed next to it. For example, one inch of tape on a bill of materials will have a quantity of one and a unit of measure of "IN," or "inch." However, if the unit of measure is changed to "RL," or "roll," without a corresponding reduction in the amount of tape listed in the quantity field, the amount of tape picked for production will increase from one inch to an entire roll. The same problem applies to the inventory, where a change to the unit of measure field without a corresponding change in the quantity field will result in a potentially massive change in the amount of inventory on the books. This seemingly minor issue can result in a major change in the cost of goods sold.

The best practice that resolves this problem is limiting access to the unit of measure field in the computer system, preferably to one person or position. By doing so, all changes must be reviewed by one person, who will presumably be trained well enough to realize the relationship between units of measure and quantities. If access by multiple people cannot be avoided, then a less-reliable variation is to require approval by a manager before making a change. However, as someone can make a change without approval, this system is too easy to bypass. A third variation is to carefully review changes in the unit of measure fields after the fact, perhaps with an occasional internal audit, but this approach only finds problems after they have already been made; the best solution is always to keep the problem from occurring in the first place.

An excellent alternative is to set up the computer system so that multiple units of measure are allowed. To use the previous example, the roll of tape can be listed as both one roll or 1,760 inches in the same inventory or bill of material record; this approach eliminates anyone's need to change the unit of measure field, since all possible variations are already described. Unfortunately, only the more advanced accounting and manufacturing software packages contain this feature; it is not normally available unless a company is willing to invest in some complicated and expensive programming.

REVIEW COST TRENDS

The typical cost accounting report shows the current cost of each product, perhaps in relation to a standard cost that was put in place when the product was first created. Though this report does give management a snapshot of how existing costs relate to standards, there is no way to see if the cost was gradually increased or decreased from the pre-set standard cost, if the actual cost was ever close to the standard cost, or if there have been sudden changes in costs which are probably related either to step-costs in the overhead category (such as adding a new facility) or to material cost changes. Given the lack of information, management has no way of knowing if the current costing situation reflects a deterioration in costs or an improvement.

The best practice that eliminates this problem is to switch to reporting based on cost trends. An example is shown in Exhibit 9.2. As noted in the exhibit, the report starts with a base cost established with actual cost data when the product was first released to production. Then the series of columns in the middle of the report show the historical total cost of each product, based on any time period that is most appropriate (quarterly costs are shown in the exhibit). Then the projected target cost that the company is striving for is noted to the far right of the report, with a final column noting the percentage difference in cost between the most recent cost and the target cost, along with the date by which the company is expecting to achieve the target cost. This format allows management to easily determine where costing problems are developing, or if there are potential problems with reaching a targeted cost by the due date. This approach gives management a much more potent tool to use in tracking product costs.

Supplemental information can enhance the information shown on the cost trend chart. For example, it can include a column showing either unit or dollar volume for each item, allowing management to quickly determine where it should invest the bulk of its time in fixing problems—on those products that have a large dollar impact on total revenues, as opposed to those that may have large

Exhibit 9.2.   Sample Cost Trend Analysis

Product Description	Base Cost	Actual Cost 3/31/01	Actual Cost 6/30/01	Actual Cost 9/30/01	Target Cost	Variance from Target	Target Date
Pail	$4.00	$4.12	$4.15	$4.29	$3.98	8%	03/31/02
Bucket	3.92	3.92	3.90	3.88	3.75	3%	03/31/02
Trowel	1.57	1.65	1.72	1.67	1.57	6%	03/31/02
Spade	8.07	9.48	10.93	10.93	8.07	35%	06/30/02
Shovel	8.08	9.49	10.94	10.94	8.08	35%	06/30/02
Hose	15.01	14.98	14.95	14.90	14.90	0%	06/30/02
Sprinkler	23.19	28.01	28.77	27.75	23.00	21%	06/30/02

cost variances but which have only a negligible profitability impact. It may also be useful to include the price and margin in the table, though this can be difficult to determine if pricing varies significantly by customer, perhaps due to variations on the volumes sold to each one. Another reporting possibility is to issue a subsidiary-level report that breaks down product costs into multiple components, so management can determine which costs are deviating from expected values. If this option is used, there should be matching target costs for each component, so management can compare actual to expected costs in all categories and see where there are problems. Finally, if there are many variations on a standard product design, the report may become too lengthy and unwieldy to be easily readable. For example, this can happen when the same product is issued in ten different colors, resulting in a report with ten line items—one for each product variation. In this instance, it is useful to cluster product groups together into a single line item for each group, resulting in a much shorter and more readable report. All or some of these reporting variations can give management a better idea of the cost trends to which their products are subject.

REVIEW MATERIAL SCRAP LEVELS

There are a number of ways to tell if a production process is not operating as efficiently as it could. For example, labor hours are higher than expected, material usage exceeds the standard, or delivery times are chronically late. However, the accounting department does not do well in reporting on late deliveries, since this does not involve the database of financial information that the accounting staff normally accesses. Also, the direct labor pool tends to be relatively fixed in the short term, and so is surprisingly difficult to reduce. Thus, accounting reports showing excessive labor may not result in an immediate impact on this area.

However, reporting on material scrap rates is well worth the effort. The reason is that a high scrap rate is the primary indicator of a host of potential problems in the production process. For example, scrap can be caused by poor operator training, bad machine maintenance, an excessive level of work-in-process inventory, and design flaws. By using material scrap as the prime indicator of problems in the production process, management can further refine the reasons for it, target those problems, and eliminate them.

The problem for the accounting department is how to issue a valid material scrap rate report. If the report is inaccurate, management will not believe the numbers and will not use the information to improve the production process. It is vital to derive the most accurate information possible from the evidence at hand. There are a variety of scrap reporting methods available, noted in the following bullet points:

- *Weigh the scrap.* The simplest method for determining the amount of scrap is to put it in a pile and weigh it. This is a practical approach if a company can recycle the bulk of its scrap and therefore keeps it in recycling bins. One can then weigh the bins and multiply the weight by the average cost of the scrap to determine a total scrap cost.

- *Summarize receipts from scrap purchasers.* An even easier approach is to let the scrap purchaser weigh the scrap bin and use this information to derive the total cost of the scrap.

- *Compare standard to actual material usage.* The approach that results in the most detailed information about exactly which material has been scrapped is a comparison of standard material quantities to actual usage. This requires accurate bills of material, production records, and inventory counts; without them, a comparison of these records will not result in an accurate determination of scrap costs.

- *Create a floor reporting system.* This is the approach used the most by those companies with poor production records. If they cannot use the preceding option due to the existence of inaccurate bills of material, production records, or inventory records, they must require the production staff to manually track the scrap they are generating. This approach tends to under-report scrap, since production personnel do not like to report on the inefficiencies of their own department. Also, the scrap reporting by the manufacturing personnel can be voluminous and may require extra staff to summarize and analyze. Thus, this approach is prone to inaccuracy and high reporting costs.

Of the previous scrap reporting methods, some are not accurate enough to provide more than a rough guess at the exact items that were scrapped; these include weighing the scrap or perusing the receipts from scrap purchasers. The other two reporting systems reveal the most useful information because they detail the exact items that were scrapped. Of the two, comparing actual to standard usage is the easiest to implement, since it requires no additional reporting by the manufacturing personnel; however, the standards must be accurate, or the basis of comparison will not function properly. If the standards (e.g., bills of material, production records, and inventory records) are not accurate, one is faced with the problem of either correcting the underlying information or implementing the final reporting option, which is creating a shop floor reporting system for tracking actual material scrap rates. The exact reporting method used will depend on the level of reporting detail needed, as well as the accuracy of a company's production database.

REVISE TRADITIONAL COST ACCOUNTING REPORTS

Though many of the other best practices advocated in this chapter involve doing away with or replacing the existing set of cost accounting reports, there are instances in which they can be modified sufficiently to still be of great use. This section deals with a number of small changes that can greatly enhance these reports. Though it would be best to install all of these upgrades, even using just one or two of them would bring about an incremental improvement in costing information. The changes are as follows:

- *Assemble products into reporting groups.* Too often, a cost report presents a list of hundreds of products, sorted by product number. Though there may be plenty of valid information in such a report, there is no easy way for a busy executive to determine where it is. Instead, it should be grouped into relevant categories, such as clustering all product variations into a single summary number or clustering product sales by customer. These clusters should always contain subtotals so managers can take in the total cost impact of each group at a glance.

- *Give rapid feedback.* There is no point in compiling a perfect cost analysis if it is done months after a product is produced. Instead, a good cost report should be issued as soon as possible after a product is completed, allowing management to make changes to improve costs the next time the product is made. The best case of all is when a cost report is issued to management while a product is still being made (and preferably near the beginning of a production run) so immediate alterations will result in a rapid cost reduction.

- *Only report on exceptions.* Some companies have such enormously long cost reports that there is no way to glance through them and spot the problem situations. To resolve this issue, reports should be issued that only show exceptions. For example, a report may only show those products with negative cost variances of at least 10 percent. By doing so, a voluminous report can be reduced to a short memo revealing those items requiring immediate attention.

- *Report on costs by customer.* All too many cost reports only focus on product costs, not the total costs of dealing with each customer. By widening the focus of a traditional cost report to include this extra information, one can reveal some startling information, especially if a customer who was previously thought to be highly profitable is eating up an outsized proportion of a company's resources in such areas as purchasing, warehousing, and order entry.

- *Use direct costing.* Many costing reports only show product margins after overhead is included in the total costing mix. However, if the overhead allocation is not valid, management has no way of knowing what margins really are and usually ends up ignoring the cost reports entirely. An easy way to avoid this problem is to insert an extra pair of columns in the cost report, in which are inserted the dollar margin after direct costs (i.e., price minus labor and materials) and the direct cost margin percentage. Though this variation leaves no room for any overhead cost at all, it does result in a good analysis of direct costs.

These best practices focus on assembling information into a format that is easy to read, relevant, and does not require the reader to wade through vast amounts of data, and presents information as rapidly as possible. By installing them, one can make the existing cost reports much more relevant to the decisions that management must make every day.

TOTAL IMPACT OF BEST PRACTICES ON THE COSTING FUNCTION

This section describes the impact of all the best practices described in this chapter on the costing function. They address three main areas within the costing function, as noted in Exhibit 9.3. Auditing various sources of costing information will improve its accuracy. Eliminating old costing reports and replacing them with ones that focus on scrap levels, obsolescence, cost trends, and direct costs will have a major impact on the quality of information presented to the rest of the organization. Finally, implementing activity-based costing and target costing systems will drastically improve the types of cost information that management can use to make costing-related decisions.

Of all these best practices, it is difficult to pick out the one or two that must be implemented before all others, due to their impact. The reason is that these best practices are highly interrelated. For example, an activity-based costing system provides valuable new information, but no one will see it if the new data is shoehorned into the same old cost accounting reports. Similarly, new costing reports are vital but will still contain inaccurate information unless the underlying data is improved through regular audits. Thus, it is necessary to install these best practices as a group in order to obtain the maximum impact of quality information presented in a new and informative format.

If all of these best practices are installed, the primary impact on the organization will be costing information much better than what was previously available to management. However, the reports will not have an impact on the organization unless they are acted upon. This calls for a very active role for the controller, who must peruse the new information, devise action plans based on it, and aggressively market both the reports and his conclusions to management on a continu-

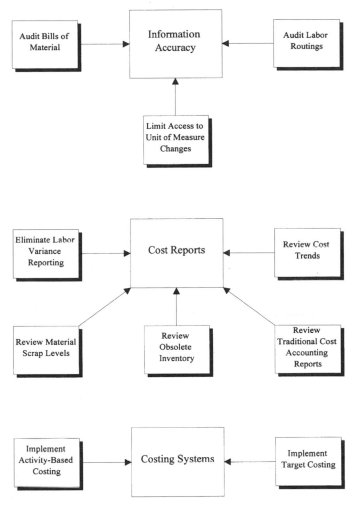

Exhibit 9.3. Impact of Best Practices on the Costing Function

ing basis. Without this proactive approach, senior managers will receive the new reports and not realize that they are holding a powerful new tool in their hands. Thus, the controller is the key to the rapid acceptance and use of the new costing data that will result from the best practices advocated in this chapter.

SUMMARY

This chapter described a number of best practices that impact inventory costing. Some involve auditing those underlying documents with the greatest impact on profitability, such as bills of material and labor routings. Others alter or replace existing cost reports, resulting in better visibility of costing problems. Finally, target costing and activity-based costing systems can be installed, giving much control over costs (in the first case) and vastly more accurate information about costs (in the later case). These are generally easy implementations, with the exception of the two new costing systems, but implementing the reports will require the approval and acceptance of those members of management who will read them. If properly implemented, all of these changes will result in much better knowledge of costs, which, if acted upon, can make the difference between profits and losses.

Chapter 10

Filing Best Practices

This chapter covers the best practices that can be used to create a more efficient filing system for an accounting department. Though this may seem like such an easy topic that it does not warrant its own chapter, there are actually many steps that a progressive accounting staff can take to greatly enhance the efficiency of its filing work.

This chapter does not focus on doing a better job of filing documents. On the contrary, filing is a totally non–value-added activity, so the focus here is on finding ways to completely avoid filing. This can be done through a variety of approaches, including an increased use of electronic documents, standard procedures for destroying old documents, and keeping paper from being used in the first place. All of these document prevention techniques are designed to keep paper from ever reaching the filing staff, thereby allowing a company to reduce the clerical work associated with filing while also reducing the amount of space needed to store documents. These major benefits deserve a separate chapter, no matter how minor the subject matter may at first appear to be.

IMPLEMENTATION ISSUES FOR FILING BEST PRACTICES

This section discusses the relative ease or severity of implementation of the best practices to be covered later in this chapter. Each best practice is noted in alphabetical order in Exhibit 10.1. For each best practice, there are columns that note the ease, duration, and cost of implementation. These are relative measures and will vary considerably depending on the circumstances in each company. In general, the overall level of implementation is considered to be easiest if they are entirely within the control of the accounting department, such as for adopting a document-destruction policy. However, if they involve the cooperation of another department, or if they require special computer programming to implement, which is the case for many of the best practices related to storing data on a computer, then the implementation is assumed to be much more difficult to complete.

The two most expensive best practices are document-imaging and extending the time period before computer records are purged from primary computer storage. The reason for this assessment is data storage—document-imaging requires extremely large amounts of storage, usually involving a compact disc jukebox

Exhibit 10.1.   Implementation Issues for Filing Best Practices Description

Description	Ease of Implementation	Duration of Implementation	Cost of Implementation
Add Digital Signatures to Electronic Documents	Moderate	Short	Inexpensive
Adopt a Document-Destruction Policy	Easy	Short	Inexpensive
Archive Canceled Checks on CD-ROM	Easy	Short	Inexpensive
Archive Computer Files	Easy	Short	Medium
Document Imaging	Difficult	Long	Expensive
Eliminate Attaching Back-Up Materials to Checks for Signing	Easy	Short	Inexpensive
Eliminate Reports	Moderate	Medium	Inexpensive
Eliminate Stored Paper Documents If Already in Computer	Moderate	Medium	Inexpensive
Extend Time Period before Computer Records Are Purged	Moderate	Medium	Expensive
Extend Use of Existing Computer Database	Difficult	Long	Expensive
Improve Computer System Reliability	Moderate	Medium	Medium
Move Records Off-Site	Moderate	Medium	Medium
Reduce Number of Form Copies To File	Moderate	Medium	Inexpensive

with storage levels in the very high gigabyte range, as does increasing primary storage to extend the time period over which records are kept in the computer system. In both cases, one should carefully research costs with the assistance of the computer department before taking any additional implementation steps.

The remainder of this chapter covers the best practices for the filing function in alphabetical order, as presented in Exhibit 10.1.

ADD DIGITAL SIGNATURES TO ELECTRONIC DOCUMENTS

One of the primary difficulties with converting paper-based forms to electronic ones is that many documents require a signature to be affixed to them. This results in an electronic form being printed out, signed, and then either scanned back into a digital format, or else used from that point forward as a paper document. As a result, the multitude of benefits associated with digital documents— minimal storage costs, infinite replication, ease of search, and so on—are lost. This problem has recently been corrected through the passage of a new federal law in June 2000 that legalizes the use of digital signatures.

It is still unclear how the courts will rule on the multitude of variations that can arise in relation to the type of digital signature used. At this time, it is quite possible that a character-based name on a message will be sufficient, though encrypted digital signatures that are much more difficult to duplicate will likely become the norm.

As more companies take advantage of this new law, we will see efficiency improvements in all of the following areas:

- *Customer orders.* A customer order typically requires a signature by a corporate manager, which is then hand-carried, mailed, or faxed to the receiving company. Digital signatures can cut much of the delivery time out of this process by sending orders by e-mail straight to the recipient, which will greatly speed up the order fulfillment process. In addition, it reduces the risk that an order will be lost (as is frequently the case when orders are faxed).

- *Human resources.* The human resources department is awash in documents that require signatures—W-4 forms, I-9 forms, 401(k) forms, benefit forms, and so on. By switching to digital signatures, a company could not only avoid much of the physical paper flow that is currently needed, but also reduce much of the face-to-face time between human resources staff and other employees that is now needed to complete paperwork. This could be replaced by a vastly greater degree of automation that would convert the human resources staff from paper processors to managers of the process.

- *Legal documents.* Many business agreements require the transfer of documents back and forth between the concerned parties, usually by expensive overnight delivery service, to ensure that signatures are appropriately affixed before the documents are finalized. This extra time period can be avoided by the use of e-mail documents.

- *Purchasing.* The purchasing staff can issue purchase orders to suppliers by e-mail, with full digital authorization, rather than having to laboriously print out a purchase order, find an authorized signer for it, and fax or mail it to a supplier. This improved process will greatly increase the speed and efficiency of the purchasing department.

The exact type of digital signatures used will become more apparent as the cost-effectiveness and security of various solutions become more apparent in the marketplace. At the moment, the market leaders include Entrust Technologies, Verisign, and Baltimore Technologies.

ADOPT A DOCUMENT-DESTRUCTION POLICY

Many companies keep on storing more documents year after year because they have no idea of when they are supposed to get rid of them. By default, they typically remain in a heap in the back corner of the most distant warehouse, eating up space that can be put to better uses. For companies that have been in operation for many years, this can become a considerable burden due to the many years paper has been allowed to accumulate, especially if management has a habit of purchasing expensive filing cabinets in which to store old records, rather than less expensive cardboard storage boxes.

An easy best practice to adopt is to work with a company's lawyers and certified public accountants (CPAs) to construct a document-destruction policy similar to the comprehensive one shown in Exhibit 10.2. The policy should take into account the document-retention requirements of all federal, state, and local regulatory agencies, always adopting the longest required retention period. Once this policy has been completed, the existing pile of paperwork can be sorted through with an eye to eliminating all items for which there is no legal reason to keep them. When conducting this elimination process, however, it is important to keep all documents for which there is no termination date whatsoever, such as corporate minute books, titles to automobiles, or project files for special machinery built for customers.

Once a document-destruction policy has been created to eliminate unnecessary paperwork, a common result is for a company to realize a significant savings in storage space as well as filing cabinets, both of which may be sold off or used for other more profitable purposes.

ARCHIVE CANCELED CHECKS ON CD-ROM

The filing and retrieval of canceled checks is a continuing problem for the accounting department. Typically, the canceled checks for one month are wrapped up, tagged with the date, and stored in a box that contains all of the checks for a given year. This works well, unless someone wants to find a check. Then a staff person must make a guess as to the month in which the check cleared, root through the storage box to find the checks that were canceled in that month, open the packet, and find the check. It may take several tries to even find the correct bundle of checks, since the date on which a check was printed and the date it was canceled may be several months apart, depending on the travels of the check in the interim. After the check has been found, the entire process shifts into reverse in order to restore all of the checks. After several such check retrievals, one can expect the quality of the check filing system to have been downgraded considerably. Several national banks have surmounted this problem by digitizing the checks.

The new approach is to scan the front and back of every check, digitize the images, and then store them on a CD-ROM, which is issued to the company that cut the checks on a periodic basis. Best of all, the CD-ROM comes with an index, so that one can retrieve checks based on the dollar amount, a range of amounts, the paid date, issue date, or check number. Given so many search criteria, it is quite difficult *not* to find a check copy, and to do so in a matter of moments. Also, there are no longer any check hard copies left on the premises, so storage issues

Exhibit 10.2 Detailed Document-Destruction Policy

Type of Record	Retention
Accident Reports/Claims (Settled)	7 Years
Accounts Payable Ledgers/Schedules	7 Years
Accounts Receivable Ledgers/Schedules	7 Years
Advertisement for a Job Opening	1 Year
Age Records	3 Years
Applications for Advertised Job Openings	1 Year
Bank Reconciliations	1 Year
Capital Stock Records	Permanent
Chart of Accounts	Permanent
Checks (Cancelled)	7 Years
Citizenship or Authorization to Work (I-9)	3 Years from Hire or 1 Year after Separation (Whichever Is Longer)
Contracts and Leases (Expired)	7 Years
Contracts and Leases in Effect	Permanent
Deeds, Mortgages, Bills of Sale	Permanent
Demotion Records	1 Year
Discrimination or Enforcement Charges	3 Years
Earnings per Week	3 Years
Employer Information Report	Keep Most Recent Report
Employment Contracts	3 Years
Financial Statements	Permanent
General Ledgers (Year-End)	Permanent
Hazardous Materials Exposure/Monitoring	30 Years
Hiring Records	1 Year from Date Record Made or Personnel Action Taken, Whichever Is Later
Insurance Policies (Expired)	3 Years
Insurance Records, Claims, Reports	Permanent
Insurance/Pension/Retirement Plans	1 Year after Termination
Internal Audit Reports	3 Years
Inventory Records	7 Years
Invoices to Customers	7 Years
Invoices from Suppliers	7 Years

(continues)

Exhibit 10.2 Continued

Type of Record	Retention
Lay-off Selection	1 Year
Material Safety Data Sheets	30 Years
Minute Books, Including Bylaws and Charter	Permanent
Notes Receivable Ledgers and Schedules	7 Years
Occupational Injuries	5 Years
Payroll Records—Pay Data	3 Years
Payroll Records—Employment Data	3 Years from Termination
Physical Inventory Tags	3 Years
Physical/Medical Examinations	Duration of Employment, plus 30 Years
Plant Cost Ledgers	7 Years
Polygraph Test	3 Years from Date of Test
Promotion Records/Notices	1 Year from Promotion
Property Appraisals	Permanent
Property Records	Permanent
Purchase Orders	7 Years
Receiving Sheets	1 Year
Sales and Purchase Records	3 Years
Sales Records	7 Years
Stock and Bond Certificates (Cancelled)	7 Years
Subsidiary Ledgers	7 Years
Tax Returns	Permanent
Termination Records	1 Year
Time Cards	3 Years
Time Worked Records	2 Years
Transfer Records	1 Year
Wage-Rate Tables	3 Years

are reduced. The only troubles with this best practice are that it is offered by only a few banks, and that an extra fee is charged for the service.

ARCHIVE COMPUTER FILES

Some companies have elected to use computer records as a direct replacement for their paper documents (see the group of best practices in Exhibit 10.4). When this happens, they have certainly eliminated the majority (if not all) of their filing work, but they have also put themselves at risk of losing electronic documents if they are not archiving computer records. In a typical organization, all records are purged from the computer system after one or two years, usually because maintaining a larger on-line database will require an inordinate amount of expensive storage space. However, purging these records runs counter to the document-destruction policies noted in the preceding section, "Adopt a Document-Destruction Policy," in which nearly all documents must be retained for longer than one or two years. Consequently, storing all documents on a computer system is not legally possible if the system is to be systematically purged of all records from time to time.

The answer to the purging problem is to archive data before it is purged. This means that the database must be transferred to some reliable storage medium, such as back-up tape or compact disc. By doing so, one can retrieve the back-up storage medium at some later date and review it for data, extracting any electronic document needed. Though this many seem like a simple matter of inserting an extra back-up tape into the daily computer back-up procedure and then putting the extra tape in permanent storage, there are some extra issues to consider. One is that back-up tapes are not especially reliable over many years. The data on them will degrade. A better storage medium is a compact disc (CD-ROM), though using it requires a company to purchase a special storage device that will write onto the CD-ROM. The other main problem is that the archived data may be in a format that will be unreadable a few years from now—after all, how many companies today have equipment that can read data stored on one of the old storage mediums from twenty years ago, such as paper tape or computer cards? The answer to this problem is a difficult one. It is possible to transfer all key electronic document images to microfilm or microfiche, or to store all data in the most "bombproof" of current data storage formats, American Standard Code for Information Interchange (ASCII). However, technological trends may shift away from using ASCII in the future, so storing in this format still has risks. Another option is to go back to all archived data and convert it to whatever the current data language may be whenever a company changes its systems, an expensive endeavor. As there is no clear answer to these storage problems, a company may need to store data in multiple file formats and carefully review the integrity of the data from time to time to ensure that it is still readable.

Carefully archiving all key computer files prior to purging them from the primary computer system is a fundamental best practice necessary for a fully digitized filing system to function properly.

DOCUMENT IMAGING

Many companies find themselves in the situation of constantly searching for files. Perhaps several departments need them at once and the files are constantly shifted back and forth, resulting in no one able to consistently locate them. Also, some employees are better than others at returning files when they are finished with them, while other companies just have a hard time obtaining a qualified group of staff people who can reliably file away documents in the right place. Whatever the case may be, it is a common problem and one that can seriously impact operations.

One answer to this quandary is to convert all paper documents into digital ones and store them in the central computer system so that, potentially, all employees can access them from all locations—and do so at the same time. Digital documents have the advantage of never being lost (with one caveat, noted later in this section), never being destroyed (as long as there are proper back-up routines taking place), and being available to anyone with the correct kind of access. These are formidable advantages and have caused many larger corporations to adopt this approach as the best way to avoid the majority of their filing problems.

To implement a document-imaging system, one must first obtain a document scanner with a sufficiently high throughput speed and resolution to allow scanning a multitude of documents, as well as scanning with a sufficient degree of clarity to obtain a quality digital image. This scanner must be linked to a high-capacity storage device, usually one using multiple compact discs that is called a "CD jukebox" and a file server containing the index file that tracks the location of all digital documents stored in the jukebox. A number of terminals are also necessary to link to this system, so that users may access digitized documents from as many company locations as necessary. A graphical view of this layout is shown in Exhibit 10.3.

There are some problems with digital document storage that make it useful in only selected cases. One is cost—the entire system, especially the storage

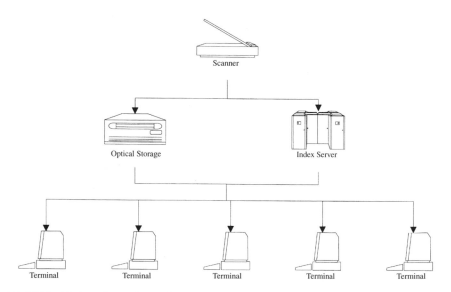

Exhibit 10.3.   Overview of the Document-Imaging Process

device, can easily bring the total cost into the six digit range, with high-end systems for large corporations exceeding a million dollars. Also, there is a considerable workload required to set up the system, for a large portion of a company's existing documents must be scanned into the system, as well as new documents generated every day. There is also an issue with legality, for it may be necessary to continue to retain some paper documents, given the murky nature of the law regarding the acceptability of digitized documents in a legal action. In addition, if a document is not properly indexed when it is first scanned into the system (i.e., given an access code that allows a user to more easily find it), it is possible that there will be great difficulty in later locating it in the computer; in effect, the document is lost in the storage device. Thus, there are a number of issues to be aware of before installing such a system. Generally speaking, the cost consideration alone will keep smaller companies from implementing this solution, unless they are in industries that require enormous amounts of paperwork, such as the legal or medical professions.

ELIMINATE ATTACHING BACK-UP MATERIALS TO CHECKS FOR SIGNING

A common cause for extra filing work is that many check-signers require back-up documentation to accompany all checks presented to them for signing. They want the extra information so they can tell exactly why a payment is being made. The extra paperwork typically includes the complete packet of accounts payable documents: the supplier's invoice, the company's purchase order, and receiving documentation. To fulfill the wishes of the check-signers, the filing staff must extract the accounts payable items from files, attach them to checks, wait for the checks to be signed, and then detach them from the checks and file them away again. All of this movement of paper also raises the risk that documents will be misfiled during the process of taking them out of files and then putting them back in. When this happens, an inordinate amount of time may be required to locate and refile the missing documents. These activities can take up a considerable proportion of the filing staff's time.

   The best practice that eliminates all of the above filing work is to stop attaching accounts payable backup information to checks about to be signed. Though this seems like a simple and obvious step, it can be a difficult one to convince the check-signers to agree with. By eliminating the back-up materials, the check-signers have no way of knowing what the company is paying for. The best way to deal with this complaint is to set up control points earlier in the accounts payable process, so that the check-signers are so comfortable with the level of control that goes into creating a check, they no longer care about what they are signing. Typically, the best control point is the purchase order. If no checks are cut without a purchase order in hand approved by the correct manager, there is no need for the additional control point of having one last review of the back-up documents by the check-signer. It can take some time for a good purchase order control system to be implemented; it is especially important that all exceptions be rooted out of the accounts payable system so that all payments are authorized by a purchase order. The check-signers may want proof of the efficacy of the new system before they relinquish the backup documentation, so the controller should work with the internal audit staff to schedule a review of the purchase order control system and make any changes that the auditors recommend, in order to ensure that the new control system works properly. If these changes can be made, there is no longer any need for back-up documentation for the check-signers, and a significant proportion of filing time can therefore be eliminated.

ELIMINATE REPORTS

Most companies are awash in reports. Typically, someone asks the accounting department to generate a report, which it does—and continues to do for the foreseeable future because no one has told it to stop doing so. The majority of these reports are really only needed once—perhaps to check on the profitability of a specific product line, or the cost of a service, or the usage of some equipment. Even though their usage is limited, the accounting department continues to churn them out and distribute them because the recipients are not aware of the cost of creating them. A further problem is the distribution of the reports. It is common for someone who does not realize the expense of distributing a report to have it sent to everyone in the company who might use it and to many who most certainly do not. Over time, the accumulation of, in many cases, hundreds of reports, and the enormous distribution lists creates a startlingly large filing burden. Not only are these reports stored, in case someone needs them, but they are distributed, and it is the job of the filing staff to do both things.

The solution to the reports problem is to reduce the number of reports as well as the number of recipients, but the method of implementing this best practice is worth some careful consideration. A common approach is to simply stop distributing reports and to see who complains. However, this is not a very astute political move by the controller, since an abrupt halt to reporting can irritate the heads of any departments who are receiving the information. Instead, it is better to use the following steps:

- *Issue a list of outstanding reports and distributions.* Sometimes it is sufficient to bring to the attention of other departments the extent of the report list that is being used. If issued along with a list of report recipients, as well as a plea from the controller to review the lists and cross out any reports and recipients that are no longer needed, it is usually possible to put a considerable dent in the accounting department's reporting and filing chore.
- *Notify recipients of the cost of reports.* If a simple notification of the number of reports does not result in any significant change, it may be necessary to

notify management of the total cost of creating and issuing those reports. If the cost is considerable, the management team may authorize the elimination of several additional reports.

- *Combine reports.* Once the report list has been pruned with the previous steps, it is time to interview the report recipients and see what information on each report is actually being used. It may then be possible to combine the data on several reports, resulting in fewer reports that are really needed. For many companies, these first three steps will bring about a sufficient reduction in the number of reports without having to proceed to the final two steps.

- *Charge recipients for reports.* If there are still a number of reports left to produce, it may be necessary to charge back the recipients for the cost of both creating and distributing the reports (with an extra charge for each additional person who is sent each report). Incurring an expense for information almost invariably will cause department managers to take a serious look at cutting back on their use of reports, which bodes well for the filing staff.

- *Post reports on the computer network.* This last option can be substituted for the previous step of charging for report usage. This one allows the filing staff to avoid all work by posting electronic reports on the computer network, where users can access it for themselves. This approach may not work for some reports that do not convert readily to a readable format for all computer terminals, nor is it available to those report recipients who do not have a computer or access to one. Still, given the recent surge in the use of corporate intranets, this may be the preferred approach of the future for the distribution of reports.

These steps, taken in the order presented, are usually sufficient to bring about a drastic reduction in the number of reports being used and issued, which has a correspondingly large and favorable impact on the quantity of filing work that can be eliminated.

ELIMINATE STORED PAPER DOCUMENTS IF ALREADY IN COMPUTER

Most companies store the bulk of their data in their computer systems and then periodically print it all out and file it away—even though all of the data still exists in the computer system. Though an argument can be made that employees are accustomed to handling paper documents more readily than digital ones, and that computer systems are too unreliable to constitute the sole repository of information, these are objections that can be overridden with the proper degree of training and system changes. In Exhibit 10.4, shown later in the "Total Impact of Best Practices on the Filing Function" section, there are a number of other best practices listed that will make a computer system essentially "bombproof," and therefore make it available for use during normal business hours with very few exceptions. Those best practices, which are described elsewhere in this chapter, are as follows:

* Archive computer files
* Avoid purging computer records
* Extend use of the computer database
* Improve computer system reliability
* Use document imaging

Once all or most of these best practices have been put in place, it is time to implement the one described in this section—to eliminate any paper documents already stored in the computer system. This is a step that must be completed with extreme care, for the computer system must be thoroughly proven to be fully operational and virtually incapable of failure before the paper files are removed from the corporate premises. The logical sequence of steps to follow for this implementation is to wait for a sufficient period of time to pass to verify that the computer system is thoroughly "bombproof"; then to shift all paper documents to an off-site location, so that they can still be called back in case of an emergency, and then, after a longer interval, to completely eliminate those documents except the ones required for legal purposes. This is a long implementation process that may require several years to complete, but it is essential that the elimination of paper documents does not interfere with the daily conduct of company business, which can fail or be severely impacted if the conversion to digital documents does not go as planned.

EXTEND TIME PERIOD BEFORE COMPUTER RECORDS ARE PURGED

An accounting department that relies on the data stored in its computer system to handle day-to-day transactions has a problem when those records are purged. The purging process usually occurs during the month-end or year-end closing process, typically destroying all transaction records that are more than one year old. When this happens, the accounting staff goes from having immediate access to all records via their computer terminals to having to retrieve paper documents, frequently from an off-site storage location. Clearly, this is a major reduction in the speed and efficiency of the department as it relates to the retrieval of data.

The reason why records are purged is that they take up a considerable amount of space in the hard drive storage of the computer system. By purging old records from time to time, it is possible to reduce storage requirements, which makes it unnecessary to purchase additional storage devices. The best practice advocated here is actually a set of variations on retaining some or all storage space, as noted below:

- *Delay purging old records.* The most comprehensive way to avoid additional filing work is to extend the period before which records will be deleted. For example, an automatic purge after one year can be shifted to a purge after two years. However, this policy will greatly expand a computer system's storage requirements, a serious consideration, especially when the purge period extends so far back in time that there is a diminishing return on the usefulness of the data in comparison to the cost of the extra computer storage. Though this is the most common version of the best practice currently in use, it should not extend storage too far back in time, given the high cost of doing so.

- *Only purge selected files.* Rather than purge all records, it may be possible to only purge those files containing specific types of records. For example, management may not feel that it is necessary to retain accounts payable records for more than one year, whereas it may want to retain sales records for a considerably longer period. Accordingly, the best approach in this case is to delete specific files regularly, while retaining others for longer periods. This is an effective way to retain data in the system while spending less money on computer storage. It is most effective when those files containing the largest numbers of records (and thus the ones that take up the most storage space) are deleted first, such as daily inventory transaction files.

- *Only purge obsolete records.* An approach that is even more selective than purging specific files is to purge only specific records. For example, management may decide to eliminate the records of all customers with whom the company has not done business for at least two years, while retaining the records of all current customers for five years. It is usually a simple matter to extract data from the database that clearly shows which customers can be deleted, along with all associated information. This method is more labor-intensive than doing a blanket purge with a single keystroke, but it retains the information that is most likely to be called into use.

- *Use slower access storage media.* Large corporations who can afford the expense may transfer older computer files to slower and less expensive tape back-up systems still linked to the primary computer storage system. By using this approach, they can allow fairly rapid access to data, even if it is several years old, by any employee with access to the computer system. However, since the slower storage devices are still much more expensive than simply purging data and leaving paper documents in a warehouse, this is typically an option that is only explored by companies with large computer system budgets.

Any of these alternatives will give the accounting staff better access to old records, which allows it to avoid the onerous task of manually picking through old files for needed records. When selecting one alternative over another, it is necessary to determine the need for various kinds of records, and to retain only those for which there is a reasonable expectation that some data retrieval will be needed.

EXTEND USE OF EXISTING COMPUTER DATABASE

Whenever the person responsible for filing makes the recommendation to have everyone access data directly through the computer system, rather than through documents, the response is usually that not everyone has access to the system. That is, some employees cannot access the correct files they need, they do not know how to access the information, or they do not have access to the computer network in order to do so. In most cases, this is not an idle complaint; these people really will not be able to function unless significant changes are made to the computer system.

This best practice is a mandatory one if on-line access to data is to take the place of paper documents. It involves several steps, which are needed to open up access to the computer system. This is not an item that can be completed in a haphazard manner, for it is too complicated to complete without using a rigid, step-by-step approach, which is as follows:

* *Determine who uses information.* Before opening up computer access to employees, it is necessary to determine who needs the access. For example, it makes no sense to provide computer terminals to everyone in a company, only to discover that half of them do not have the slightest need for information. Accordingly, one should interview all employees to see what they need and determine where in the computer system that information can be found.

* *Calculate changes in access volumes.* If the new system will result in a massive increase in user access to the system, this should be calculated well in advance, so that the central computer system can be upgraded to handle the extra workload. Additional software licenses may also have to be purchased to cover the extra users.

* *Construct new interface screens.* Some of the data that is needed, as discovered in the first step, may not reside in one place in the computer system and may require the construction of new screens in the computer that bring all of the necessary data together for easier use. This can be a laborious step with a large programming budget. It is also next to impossible to complete if a company uses a packaged software system that is regularly updated by the supplier, since each update will probably wipe out any custom programming.

* *Determine type of access.* Once all of the data has been clustered into the appropriate groups for employee use, it is very important to determine who gets to change the information. If some employees will not be allowed to, they must be given read-only access rights in the computer system; these rights may vary by screen, and should be set up well in advance, so that this task does not interfere with later implementation steps.

* *Add terminals.* There may be a need for extra terminals so that all employees have easy access to the system. This may require stringing additional cable or

the addition of leased phone lines from other locations for off-site access. It is also important to ensure that there are enough printers provided to meet the needs of the additional users.

• *Train employees.* The last step before going live with the new system is to train employees in how to use the computer system. This training should be custom-tailored to the exact needs of each group that will be accessing different information in the system, and the employees should train on the terminals, so that they know exactly what to do. They should also be given one-page summaries that show them how to access the information they need.

The above steps can take quite a long time to complete and will require a significant budget, so it is important to verify in advance that there is a reasonable payback to the company from implementing it—either through reduced filing costs or by improving the efficiency of the corporation as a whole.

IMPROVE COMPUTER SYSTEM RELIABILITY

Many of the recommendations in this chapter are based on the assumption that paper-based documents can be eliminated by calling up their electronic counterparts in a company's computer system. However, many controllers find that this assumption will not work, and it meets with great resistance throughout a company because the computer system has a bad reputation for not being functional at all times. If the system is down and there are no paper documents that are immediately available to serve as back-up information, a company can literally stop functioning at once. Since many departments know this, they resist all attempts to switch to a purely computer-based information system.

There are a number of steps that a company can take to improve the reliability of its computer systems. As many as possible of the following actions should be taken to improve system reliability. Though even one of them is helpful, the entire group will go a long way towards creating a "bombproof" system that employees will have confidence in. The best practices for improving system reliability are as follows:

• *Battery backups.* A computer system will experience power failures from time to time, as well as power spikes or brownouts. All of these problems result in computer system crashes, which corrupt data and keep the system down for long periods of time. This problem is an especially vexing one in a manufacturing environment, where power spikes may occur when large machinery is turned on in the same power grid as a company's computer system. The solution to this problem is a simple one—just install a battery backup, also known as an uninterruptible power supply (UPS) on all file servers or larger computers, as well as every personal computer, terminal, router, and hub—in short, everything attached to a computer network that requires electricity. By doing so, a computer system can be completely protected from all power fluctuations. Also, batteries will become worn out and fail over time, so it is critical to have a battery replacement schedule in place designed to replace batteries shortly before their scheduled failure dates.

- *Disk mirroring.* Some companies that cannot afford to have any system downtime at all will use two primary computers to record all transactions, rather than the more traditional single computer. Under this system, all transactions are recorded by two computers that are linked together and which mirror each other's functions. If one of these computers develops a problem, the other one takes over all processing and continues operating on its own so that users have no idea that there is a problem. The damaged computer can be repaired while the other unit continues to operate. Though this is a more expensive approach, it guarantees a very high level of system reliability.

- *Emergency planning and testing.* No matter how many precautions a company takes, it is likely that there will be system crashes from time to time. Rather than passively hope that these incidents do not occur, it is better to develop a formal plan for how to deal with them before they happen. By writing down the precise recovery steps to be followed, one can save a significant amount of time in fixing systems. This plan can also be used for practice; by scheduling periodic training sessions for recovering from system crashes, one can determine the weak points in the emergency plan, and fix them before a real emergency occurs. By using this approach, a company can keep system downtime to a minimum.

- *Re-do cabling.* Some employees have difficulty staying on-line with their central computer systems. This is caused by poorly constructed network cabling, which may in turn be caused by excessive cable lengths without repeaters, cables running near power sources (such as machinery), or the wrong types of cabling. In some cases, the best way to eliminate this problem is to completely re-do the cabling. This may require the installation of top-quality, high-capacity fiber optic cabling, as well as new hubs. Also, if there are links to distant locations, it may be necessary to convert from a dial-up modem access, which runs on standard copper cabling, to a high capacity T1 phone line, which is much more reliable, although also much more expensive to operate. By making these changes, a number of system reliability problems can be eliminated.

- *Scheduled downtime.* One of the most common employee complaints regarding system downtime is that maintenance occurs during regular business hours, rather than at other times. When maintenance, such as system backups, testing, or software upgrades, is going on, other users cannot access the system, which keeps them from performing their jobs. To avoid this problem, it is very important to cluster standard maintenance work together in a batch and run it automatically during low usage periods, such as late at night. Similarly, any other system work that may bring the computer system down must be carefully scheduled to match low transaction periods during the work week, such as just before or after the regular working hours, or during the lunch period. The best way to ensure that these times are properly scheduled is to create a work schedule for the computer department that identifies well in advance the periods when the system must be brought down so employees can be adequately prepared in advance for these periods, and so additional planning can be done to ensure that the downtime periods are kept to an absolute minimum.

- *System testing.* There is a saying that all systems have bugs in them—you just may not have found them yet. This is a major problem if a company implements a new system without proper testing. A rigid testing program will ensure that new systems have the appropriate back-up systems, will operate as promised, can handle large transaction volumes, and will handle unusual transactions. If a new system successfully passes all of these tests, then it can be put into service. If not, it must be fixed and tested again. Only by rigidly adhering to tough testing standards can a company provide reliable computer systems to its employees.

While all of the above system reliability improvements are being implemented, it is extremely important to publicize the progress of the work. If the improvements are undertaken quietly, employees may still be influenced by a long tradition of system problems and their opinions will not be changed for a long time. Instead, to bring employees to the point of accepting the computer system as their primary source of documents more quickly, it is necessary to publicize current system improvement projects, upcoming ones, and before-and-after measurements that clearly show the improvement in system reliability. Advertising system changes to employees is one of the best ways to get them behind a move to eliminate paper-based backup systems.

MOVE RECORDS OFF-SITE

A controller can have an exceedingly inefficient accounting operation for no other reason than the presence of an immense amount of records in the accounting area, which makes it difficult to find a sufficient amount of operating space and renders it difficult to find the most current information. Frequently, these records are kept near the accounting staff on the erroneous grounds that there will be times when they are needed and that it will be an exceptional hassle to recover them if they are stored elsewhere. This is a particularly difficult problem if the accounting staff has been in place for many years and is accustomed to having records kept close at hand.

The best practice to resolve clutter caused by too many records is to review the dates of the records and move the oldest items to a secondary location. The cut-off date for which records will be moved is usually for anything that is not in the current year of operations. There may be a few cases where additional records should be kept, such as records from the previous year that the auditors might request during their annual audit. However, in general, these records can be moved out with minimal impact on current operations.

The main objectors to this approach will be those staff members who have grown accustomed to keeping files close at hand, but this objection will usually recede over time, especially if a good index clearly identifies which storage box contains which records so that retrieving paperwork is an easy affair. The resulting benefits from the change will be a considerable increase in working space, less need for expensive office space, and fewer expensive filing cabinets. The best improvement of all is that it contributes to overall efficiency, for the amount of paperwork remaining will be so greatly reduced that it will be an easy matter to determine where the really crucial files are located, which reduces search time. Moving records off-site is an excellent method for reducing occupancy costs and clutter in the accounting area.

REDUCE NUMBER OF FORM COPIES TO FILE

Over time, it is a common occurrence for a company to continually add to the number of copies of printed documents. For example, an invoice that starts with two copies—one for the customer and one for the company—may later have another copy added so that invoices can be filed in numerical order and perhaps another copy so that the customer service department (or some other department) can have an extra copy. These additional documents are usually added without much thought to the consequences for the filing staff, which must put away all of those extra copies. Also, additional document copies result in more expensive documents (since there is more paper involved), as well as, in some cases, a much more heavy-duty printer that can punch through such a thick sheaf of documents (which can also bunch up quite easily, causing a printer jam). Thus, a large number of document copies results in a multitude of problems, not the least of which is a considerable increase in the workload of the filing staff.

The best practice that eliminates this problem is to reduce the number of copies. However, this is not a simple matter of ordering new documents with fewer parts. Both costs and politics can become an issue when implementing what appears to be, on the surface, a very simple matter. The main cost is that there may be many documents still in stock with extra copies. If so, it makes little sense to throw them all out. Instead, use them up, throwing away the extra copies that are generated, and then order new documents when the old ones are gone. The main problem is politics. If there is an extra copy being generated, it is a good bet that someone in the company asked for the extra copy and that person will not be happy when the copy is eliminated. If the person who wants the extra copy is a highly placed manager, it is unlikely that the change will go unnoticed or tolerated. Instead, if persuasion does not work, it is probable that implementation will be impossible until that person leaves the company or moves to a position having less influence over the decision. Also, before deciding to stop using a document copy, it is mandatory that the exact use of the copy be clarified with all users to ensure that there is not a problem if it is no longer printed.

Despite the number of possible problems, this is a best practice that can usually be implemented at least in part and will result in immediate gains for the filing staff in exchange for a moderate amount of implementation effort.

TOTAL IMPACT OF BEST PRACTICES ON THE FILING FUNCTION

This section groups together all of the best practices described in this chapter and shows how they can be applied in a typical corporate environment. As opposed to the best practices in most other chapters of this book, all of the filing best practices can be installed together, for they are not mutually exclusive. They tend to cluster into two categories: those that are concerned with the reduction of manual filing labor, and those that are intended to completely avoid filing by using a company's computer system as the primary data storage point. Though the computer system is obviously the more advanced and efficient method of storage, it takes a long time to convert a company entirely to that storage medium (if only because of employee resistance), so it is recommended that all of the best practices, including those for manual filing, be implemented.

As noted in Exhibit 10.4, there are six best practices that are associated with the manual filing function. Some involve cleaning up the work area by either moving old documents off-site or by using a document-destruction policy to entirely eliminate them. Other best practices eliminate documents before they ever have a chance to be filed, by such means as stopping the use of reports and reducing the number of form copies. The other main category of best practices assumes that there will be less need for filing work if documents are stored in a company's computer system. If so, the main focus is on increasing computer access to the largest possible number of employees, while also increasing the reliability of the computer system and storing the largest possible amount of information on it. By implementing the largest possible combination of these activities, one can, at a minimum, bring about a reduction in a company's filing workload, and may even be able to eliminate the majority of the work.

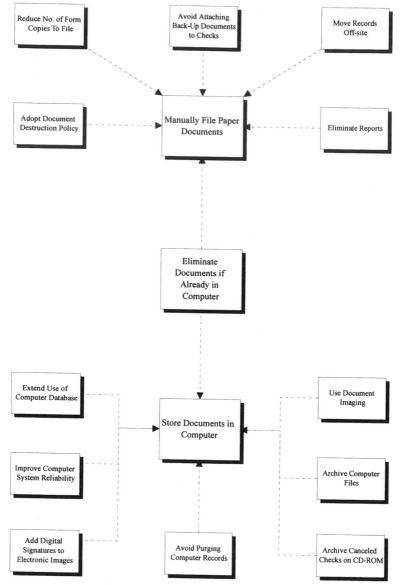

Exhibit 10.4.   Impact of Best Practices on the Filing Function

SUMMARY

This chapter covered two main categories of best practices for filing. One focused on ways to reduce the amount of filing work needed, on the assumption that some filing of paper documents must always be done. The second cluster of best practices covered how to use a computer system as the logical storage location for information, rather than a filing cabinet. This second alternative is the preferred approach, since it gives everyone with computer access the ability to call up a document without any risk of damaging or losing the information on the digitized document. However, there are a number of steps that a company must take to ensure that information is properly stored on its computer system and that the system is sufficiently operational during working hours to act as a proper substitute for a manual filing system. Thus, the best practices described in this chapter cover the two main filing alternatives—the filing cabinet and the computer system.

Chapter 11

Finance Best Practices

This book is primarily about improving the accounting function, not the finance function. However, this area is commonly integrated into the accounting department in smaller organizations, where the cost of a treasury staff cannot be justified. Thus, this area becomes part of the accounting function, and so a limited set of best practices are included here. They are primarily oriented toward treasury, risk management, and investor relations applications that can be located on the Internet. The reason for so many Internet-based best practices is that they can be readily accessed and used at a moderate cost, since there is no software to install on one's computer or large up-front costs to incur. These are important issues for the controllers of smaller companies, who can quickly browse through the web site addresses that are sprinkled throughout this chapter, and see what applications will be of the most use to them.

Only in one case is an expensive and time-consuming best practice listed—the use of a treasury workstation. It is really only cost effective for a larger company, but is included here because it does such a good job of integrating and improving on a number of rote treasury functions. It is highly recommended for those organizations that can afford it, but its substantial cost should be carefully reviewed before a decision is made.

This chapter begins with a short review of the level of implementation difficulty for each finance best practice, and then moves on to individual discussions of each one. There is no final section that describes how these items can be used in concert, since these functions operate just as well if implemented individually—there is little efficiency to be gained through overlapping finance best practices.

IMPLEMENTATION ISSUES FOR FINANCE BEST PRACTICES

This section notes in Exhibit 11.1 the level of implementation difficulty that one can expect when installing the finance-related best practices in this chapter. Exhibit 11.1 describes the ease, duration, and cost of implementation for each best practice. Since most of the best practices are Internet-based, there is no up-front acquisition cost, which keeps the cost of implementation squarely in the "inexpensive" category. However, many of these services are fee based or require extra fees for advanced services, so there will be incremental charges associated with their use.

The duration of implementation for these Internet-based applications is listed as "medium" in the exhibit, though a company can make them operational

Exhibit 11.1   Implementation Issues for Finance Best Practices

Description	Ease of Implementation	Duration of Implementation	Cost of Implementation
Access Bank Account Information on the Internet	Easy	Short	Inexpensive
Automatic 401(k) Plan Enrollment	Easy	Medium	Inexpensive
Avoid Delays in Check Posting	Easy	Short	Inexpensive
Centralize Foreign Exchange Management	Moderate	Medium	Inexpensive
Consolidate Insurance Policies	Moderate	Long	Inexpensive
Grant Employees Immediate 401(k) Eligibility	Moderate	Medium	Inexpensive
Install a Treasury Workstation	Difficult	Long	Expensive
Negotiate Faster Deposited Check Availability	Moderate	Short	Inexpensive
Optimize Cash Management Decisions through the Internet	Moderate	Medium	Inexpensive
Use Internet-Based Cash Flow Analysis Software	Moderate	Medium	Inexpensive
Use Internet-Based Options Pricing Services	Moderate	Medium	Inexpensive
Use Internet-Based Risk Measurement Services	Moderate	Medium	Inexpensive
Use Internet-Based Technical Analysis Services	Moderate	Medium	Inexpensive
Use Internet-Based Treasury Management Services	Moderate	Medium	Inexpensive
Use Web Broadcasting for Public Reporting	Moderate	Medium	Medium

in a relatively short time. The reason for the longer expected implementation duration is that one may find that a specific web site does not precisely match one's expectations, which may result in some shopping among related sites to find a better match. Alternatively, some missing functionality may have to be shifted in-house, which also requires more time to implement.

ACCESS BANK ACCOUNT INFORMATION ON THE INTERNET

If the accounting staff needs to know the current balance outstanding on a loan, savings, or checking account, the most common way to find out is to call the company's bank representative. This is a slow and sometimes inaccurate approach, since the representative may not be available or will misread the information appearing on the screen. More progressive companies have purchased software from their banks that allows them to dial into the bank database to view this information directly. While this is a reasonable approach, there is a cost associated with the modem and software, and there is also a time delay while the modem connects to the bank's database. Also, much of this software is relatively primitive and is character based, rather than graphics based.

An easier approach, and one which is rapidly supplanting the dial-up modem method, is to provide bank customers with direct access to their account information through a web site. This access is usually free, requires no special software besides an Internet browser, and can be accessed at once, if the user is connected to a direct-access Internet connection, such as a DSL, cable, or T1 phone line. The better web sites are also heavily engineered to be easy-to-read, with on-line, automated help text to walk the user through the screens. This is becoming such a powerful tool that users should consider switching their bank accounts to those financial institutions that offer this service.

AUTOMATIC 401(K) PLAN ENROLLMENT

In smaller organizations, the accounting department is tasked with the management of 401(k) plan additions, changes, and deletions. This is not an efficient process, for someone must arrange for a meeting with each employee who has now been working for the minimum amount of time, as specified in the plan documentation, explain the plan's features to them, wait for them to take the plan materials home for review, and (finally) enter the returned documents into the system of the 401(k) provider. This is a lengthy and time-consuming process.

An alternative is to automatically enroll employees in the 401(k) plan. This is also known as a "negative election," since an employee must make a decision *not* to be enrolled in the plan, rather than the reverse. This approach has the considerable advantage of reducing the paperwork needed to enter a person into the 401(k) plan, since it is done as part of the hiring process, alongside all other paperwork needed to set up a new employee.

There are only minor downsides to this best practice. With more employees in the plan, there will be somewhat higher fees charged by the 401(k) service provider (which are typically charged on a per-person basis). Also, there will still be some paperwork associated with those employees who *do* make a negative election. Finally, since the group of employees who tend to be added to the 401(k) plan through this method are at the lower end of the income stratum, it is more likely that they will want to take out loans against their invested funds, each of which calls for more paperwork.

AVOID DELAYS IN CHECK POSTING

When there is a sudden influx of checks, the accounting staff may require an extra day to post them all against the accounts receivable database. This delay can also occur when the payments being made are slightly different from the invoices that they are paying, which requires some delay while the differences are reconciled. Though these problems can create a real bottleneck in the accounting department, they also result in a lengthening of the time interval before the checks are deposited at the bank, which in turn results in lost investment income.

To avoid this problem, the accounting staff can photocopy checks as they arrive, so that postings can be done from the copies, rather than the original checks. This allows the deposit to be made at once, rather than later. The main problem with this approach is the danger that a check will not be copied, or that the copy will be lost, which results in a missing posting to the accounts receivable database. This problem leads to downstream collections and research problems involving backtracking to find the missing checks. This problem can be avoided through proper reconciliation procedures that match the total number of copied checks to the total number of actual checks, as well as the total amount posted to the total amount on the copied checks.

CENTRALIZE FOREIGN EXCHANGE MANAGEMENT

A company that has multiple divisions conducting business with other countries may be spending too much money hedging its foreign exchange risk. Each division will hedge its exposure without regard to the exchange positions of the other divisions, which may result in excess hedging costs. The reason for the excess costs is that one division may have a large *account receivable* that is payable in (for example) British Pounds, while another division may have a *payable* in British Pounds. Each one may pay to hedge the risk on Pounds, when in reality, from the perspective of the entire company, the receivable and payable positions of the two divisions offset each other. Only the difference between the two positions needs to be hedged, which is less expensive.

Another problem is that there are inter-company payments between subsidiaries located in different countries; these transactions should be netted to arrive at the minimum possible flow of foreign exchange.

To take advantage of these offsetting positions, a company needs to centralize its foreign exchange management in one place, so that a coordinated effort to net out all exchange risks can be created. This is not just a matter of moving all of the foreign exchange people from outlying locations into one building, but also (and much more importantly) a matter of channeling the flow of foreign exchange information from all divisions into a single location. This may call for customized interfaces from each division's accounting systems to the central database, or perhaps an extract of data from a centralized data warehouse (see Chapter 14). This function can also be outsourced to a bank that specializes in foreign exchange netting, such as CitiBank or Bank of America, though one should periodically comparison shop their foreign exchange rates to ensure that they are competitive. It can even be manually stored in an electronic spreadsheet, though this later approach requires some attention to the transfer of all inter-company payables and receivables to the person who is netting out the transactions; this involves setting a timetable that specifies a monthly settlement date, and then works backwards from that date to determine the deadlines by which all subsidiaries must report their payables and receivables. Once this information is gathered, it must then be merged to determine a company's net foreign exchange position at any given time. Once this information is available, a company will be able to achieve significant cost reductions in its hedging activities.

There are two other factors favoring the use of centralized foreign exchange management. One is that the reduced amount of currency being shifted between corporate subsidiaries results in a smaller amount of cash float within the organization (though this can be eliminated entirely with the use of wire transfers instead of checks). The other possibility is to use the netting of inter-company payables and receivables to make leading or lagging payments, which are effectively short-term loans that may assist in dealing with short-term cash flow problems at certain subsidiaries. However, these changes in the timing of payments can take on the appearance of inter-company loans, so expert international tax advice should be obtained before trying such an activity.

CONSOLIDATE INSURANCE POLICIES

Insurance policies are frequently added to a company's insurance portfolio in a piecemeal manner. Someone on the management team decides that some additional coverage is needed to mitigate a perceived risk, and so an additional policy is added—sometimes beginning at a different time of the year from the other policies already in existence, and perhaps with different insurance companies. This can be an expensive approach, for each insurer must factor in potential loss costs plus operating expenses and profit—on each policy it issues.

A better alternative is to aggregate the policies with a single insurer. By doing so, insurers can see that their administrative cost will be the same, despite the much higher volume of insurance, and so they can reduce their insurance prices. Also, there is little risk that claims will arise on every single policy held, so the overall risk to the insurer declines—which in turn can reduce prices yet again.

This option is best used by large companies with large-dollar insurance policies, since insurers will want their business badly enough to be willing to reduce prices based on the factors just noted.

GRANT EMPLOYEES IMMEDIATE 401(K) ELIGIBILITY

The most common way to enroll employees into a company's 401(k) pension plan is to make them wait either ninety days or a year from the date of hire. This calls for the maintenance of a list of dates for newly hired employees that must be watched to ascertain when someone become available for this benefit. Then they must be contacted, scheduled for a short lecture about how the plan works and how to invest in it. Then they complete paperwork to enroll, which is forwarded to the payroll department so that deductions can be made from their paychecks for advancement to the 401(k) plan administrator. All of the steps can more easily be compressed into the hiring process, as was just noted under the "Automatic 401(k) Plan Enrollment" section in this chapter. However, the issue can be taken one step further by not only completing all of the paperwork at the time of hire, but also by actually allowing *immediate* participation in the plan at the time of hire. This represents less a matter of improved efficiency than of giving new employees a fine new benefit, for they can begin investing funds at once, which may lead to a reduced level of employee turnover.

The main problem with this best practice is that new employees can impact a company's ability to pass pension plan non-discrimination tests, especially if the new hires are at low pay scales. If these new employees do not invest a reasonable proportion of their salaries in the 401(k) plan, this can force highly compensated employees to limit their plan contributions to less than the maximum amounts. Nonetheless, if there is a perception that immediate eligibility for the plan will improve the employee turnover rate, then this should be considered the overriding issue.

INSTALL A TREASURY WORKSTATION

The multitude of treasury based transactions can take up a large part of the finance staff's workday and is highly subject to error. These tasks involve management of a company's cash position, investment and debt portfolio, and risk analysis. The normal approach to these tasks is to track, summarize, and analyze them on an electronic spreadsheet, with manual input derived from all of the company's banks and investment firms on a daily basis. In addition, any changes that result from this analysis, such as the centralization or investment of cash, must be manually shifted to the general ledger. Given the highly manual nature of these tasks, this frequently results in errors that must be corrected through the bank reconciliation process. A treasury workstation can greatly reduce many of these work steps.

A treasury workstation is a combination of hardware and software that will manage cash, investments, debt issuance and tracking, as well as provide some risk analysis functions. It is an expensive item to purchase, typically ranging from $30,000 for a bare-bones installation to $300,000 for a fully configured one. The difference between these prices is the amount of functionality and bank interfaces added to the treasury workstation—if a buyer wants every possible feature and must share data with a large number of financial suppliers, then the cost will be much closer to the top of the range. Given these costs, this best practice is not cost effective for companies with sales volumes under $50 million. Also, because of the large number of interfaces needed to connect the workstation to other entities, the installation time can range from one to nine months.

Why spend so much money and installation time on a treasury workstation? Because it automates so much of the rote finance tasks. For example, if an employee enters an investment into the system, it will create a transaction for the settlement, one for the maturity, and another for the interest. It will then alter the cash forecast with this information, as well as create a wire transfer to send the money to an investing entity. Here are some of the other functions that it can perform:

- *Bank reconciliation.* It can do the bulk of a bank reconciliation, just leaving a few non-reconciling items to be resolved by an employee.
- *Cash forecasting.* It can determine all company cash inflows and outflows from multiple sources in order to derive a cash forecast.
- *Cash movement.* It can originate electronic funds transfers.
- *Debt tracking.* It can follow short-term debt with a link to a dealer-based commercial paper program.
- *Financial exposure.* It can identify and quantify financial exposure.
- *Foreign exchange.* It can determine a company's cash positions in any currency.
- *Investment tracking.* It can track and summarize a company's investment positions in money markets, mutual funds, short-term and fixed-income investments, equities, and options.
- *Risk analysis.* It allows an employee to use it as a giant calculator, performing "what if" analyses with yield-curve manipulation and scenario analysis.

Based on this lengthy list, it is evident that a large company can derive a sufficient benefit from a treasury workstation to offset its substantial cost. For more information about treasury workstations, contact any of the following workstation suppliers: SunGard Treasury Systems (*www.sungard.com*), Advanced Risk Management Solutions (*www.arms.com.sg*), Selkirk Financial (*www.selkirkfinancial.com*), or Integrity Treasury Solutions (*www.integra-t.com*).

NEGOTIATE FASTER DEPOSITED CHECK AVAILABILITY

One of the standard tricks used by banks to create a larger store of funds that they can invest is to delay the availability of money from deposited checks. One can see delays of as long as five days for some checks, and much longer periods for checks drawn on international banks, even though the checks may have cleared much sooner. As a general rule, if checks are not clearing the bank within two days, then it is time to either negotiate with the bank to reduce the amount of float it is taking, or else to switch to another bank that is willing to make money available within a shorter time frame.

This option is not a realistic one for smaller businesses, since they have minimal leverage with their banks. Also, some companies that deal with many out-of-state customers will experience a much slower actual check-clearing time than those whose customers are located within the same state—this simply reflects the mechanics of the check-clearing process, and cannot be accelerated below a minimum level.

OPTIMIZE CASH MANAGEMENT DECISIONS
THROUGH THE INTERNET

The accounting and finance staff is confronted with a daily quandary—what to do with any excess cash that is spun off by operations? Should it go into a simple money market account, or perhaps commercial paper? How long should the investment periods cover—one day, ten days, a few months? The people doing the daily investing rarely have enough time to make these determinations, and do not try to—they have generally settled into the use of a few tried-and-true investments that cover the same investment period. In short, the same investment strategy is used all the time, even if there is a better approach for making investments that will result in more interest income. There is a better way, and it can be found at *www.treasurypoint.com.*

This web site contains an analytical tool called the Optimizer that reviews a wide array of investment choices, using as inputs a company's current cash position, its short-term (up to ninety days) cash forecast, and a user-updated set of risk criteria. It then spends from five to fifteen minutes churning through thousands of possible investment variations, guided by a rules-based expert system, before arriving at an optimal set of investments that will yield the best possible return, given a user's investment criteria. The Optimizer makes no attempt at estimating short-term changes in interest rates; instead, it bases all calculations on current rates, thereby avoiding any risk due to incorrect estimations. These investment choices will vary daily based on the current interest rate structure of the market and changes in user cash positions, so the investing staff should access the site every day to glean new recommendations.

USE INTERNET-BASED CASH FLOW ANALYSIS SOFTWARE

Larger corporations will find that the task of consolidating and investing the cash flows from their multitude of subsidiaries is an extremely labor-intensive process, involving the collection of information from every company location about cash requirements and excess amounts, logging in related transactions, and managing the flow of cash from perhaps hundreds of accounts to centralized investment vehicles—and doing so every day. The labor associated with this work may remind one of the years-long work of a group of monks who write a book by hand.

A much easier approach is to use Internet-based software to more rapidly marshal the flow of information. An example of such software is provided by eTreasury (which is located at *www.etreasury.com*). Under this approach, a user organization signs up with eTreasury, which is paid on a subscription basis, and gives it the company's list of banks and bank accounts. The staff of eTreasury then takes two to three days to contact each bank and arrange for automated porting of the company's cash transactions to the eTreasury site, where they are combined and reconciled. This results in a daily cash position worksheet that the accounting and finance staffs can use to determine the correct borrowing or investing decisions for the day. Because of the great reduction in labor that would otherwise have been required to create the cash position worksheet, this also means that the information will be available much earlier in the day than would otherwise be the case, yielding more time in which to make the best cash management decisions.

In addition to this basic function, the site allows users at remote locations to enter special transactions, such as requests for wire transfers, directly into the site. This allows users at the corporate headquarters to see all cash-related transactions at the same time, while avoiding the use of manual entries of these transactions, which usually involve faxes of requested transactions from outlying locations, that are then keypunched into a central electronic spreadsheet.

This approach also carries with it the advantages associated with any application service provider (ASP), such as the avoidance of any investment in software or hardware, or the information technology staff that would otherwise be needed to maintain an internal installation. Furthermore, the responsibility for keeping the site up and running at all times falls on the supplier, rather than the accounting or treasury department. In addition, eTreasury will shortly have available a data file download that can be modified for automated porting to a company's general ledger, so that cash transactions can be integrated with internal accounting systems with a minimum of effort.

There are some disadvantages to using Internet-based treasury software. One problem is that access to it is predicated on the reliability of Internet access, which still does not match the reliability of internal networks. Also, these sites are designed for companies with a smaller range of banking relationships (in the case of eTreasury, information from four banks is the maximum allowable amount that will be automatically collected and presented); for those with a larger number of relationships, it is still necessary to purchase more expensive software and install it in-house (see "Install a Treasury Workstation" section in this chapter). However, despite these problems, the use of an Internet-based treasury site may be well worth the effort for those organizations that are currently spending a large amount of staff time consolidating banking information for investment and borrowing purposes.

USE INTERNET-BASED OPTIONS PRICING SERVICES

Any accounting or treasury staff that deals with options knows that this is a difficult area to analyze in terms of whether or not an options price is reasonable or excessive. One can now gain assistance in this effort by accessing the excellent *www.ivolatility.com* web site. This site compares the historical volatility of a stock to its estimated activity for the next few months, as determined through an examination of options purchased. If the forward-looking volatility is greater than the historical volatility, then the options on that stock may be overpriced. The site also includes daily charts and statistics about market performance, as well as linkages to news sources for each selected stock. There is a wealth of information in this site.

USE INTERNET-BASED RISK MEASUREMENT SERVICES

Anyone who invests in various types of equity on behalf of a company may, from time to time, have a queasy feeling that there is some degree of risk associated with those investments, but has no way of quantifying it without paying for the services of a finance expert. Also, it may be useful to report to senior management on the measured risk of the current basket of investments, if only to provide a defense in case there is a drop in their value at some point in the future. This valuable risk analysis tool is now available through the Internet at *www.riskgrades.com.*

This on-line service grades the risk of any equity that the user enters into the system, reviewing its equity, interest rate, currency, and commodity risk. This results in a "RiskGrade" that is an indicator of risk based on the volatility of returns. RiskGrades are determined by comparing the current estimated return volatility of an asset to the market-cap weighted average return volatility of a set of equity markets during normal market conditions. A RiskGrade of zero indicates price volatility of zero (as would be the case for pure cash holdings), with higher RiskGrade ratings indicating a higher degree of volatility. These RiskGrade scores can then be used to compare the risks of various assets or entire portfolios.

USE INTERNET-BASED TECHNICAL ANALYSIS SERVICES

Some investors believe that the future performance of a stock can be determined by a careful evaluation of how it has performed in the past. While others feel that this is akin to driving down a road by looking in the rearview mirror, it may still have some validity for reviewing historical trends and making investment decisions based on this information.

Technical analysis information can now be obtained on the Internet by accessing *www.techrules.com.* This site uses a simulation laboratory, in which prospective investors can enter either a single stock or a weighted portfolio, and determine their historical performance, including the impact of trading costs and profit re-investment. There is also a page that converts this information into a graphical representation of performance and variability. The site also includes direct access to a variety of brokers who can execute orders.

USE INTERNET-BASED TREASURY MANAGEMENT SERVICES

Smaller companies do not have ready access to information about the capital markets, or able to spend a considerable amount on monthly fees to maintain a Reuters or Bloomberg terminal that allows them access to up-to-the-minute financial information. Also, they must separately contact the providers of various financial instruments, such as options, forwards, swaps, single and cross-currency interest rate products, and money market deposits. This can result in a confusing and expensive jumble of activities. An alternative has been provided by the newly opened *CFOWeb.com* site.

This site is designed to give the user access to a personalized screen that reveals the status of one's portfolio, yield curve data, upcoming events, and business news. In addition to this basic information, it allows one to negotiate with multiple suppliers of money market and interest rate products, in order to secure the best possible terms. The suppliers currently available through this site are Bank of America, ABN/Amro, AIG, BNP/Paribas, and Standard-Chartered. The results of these transactions can be linked to a company's in-house treasury management systems with the XML standard.

At this time, there is no charge for the use of any CFOWeb services. However, charges will be added for premium services that are still being configured for the web site.

A final benefit to the use of this service is that no software except an Internet browser is needed to access it—no other software, hardware, or maintenance personnel are needed. In short, this approach reveals a great many benefits and no particular shortfalls, except that it is a very new service that will evolve and reconfigure itself as it develops its market, which may improve or reduce the level of utility that each user experiences.

USE WEB BROADCASTING FOR PUBLIC REPORTING

Publicly held companies are supposed to issue financial information to the public through the quarterly reporting process. However, this has, until recently, only required the issuance of standard quarterly financial statements and an annual meeting. Any further information was frequently limited to meetings with selected Wall Street analysts. This reduced level of information dispersal has now come to an end, thanks to the Securities and Exchange Commission's new Regulation FD (for Fair Disclosure). This new rule requires companies to make a broad disclosure, through a press release at a minimum, whenever company officers release important information about the company to *any* outsiders. Though the traditional press release is sufficient for compliance with the regulation, it is also possible to generate much broader distribution of this information through the use of a webcast.

A webcast is simply a conference call that is posted on the Internet for general access. It allows virtually anyone to listen in on the discussions between company managers (usually the chief executive officer or chief financial officer) and outside analysts regarding company-specific information. This is a very inexpensive approach to disseminating information. It also keeps analysts from getting access to tidbits of company information that they can in turn send out to their clients as hot tips (especially since their clients may have been listening to the same webcast), unless the webcasts are issued on a time-delayed basis.

A provider of webcasts is Corporate Communications Broadcast Network, whose web site can be reached at *www.ccbn.com*. This company facilitates webcasts by setting up basic audio webcasts for quarterly conference calls, and also offers an enhanced audio webcast that is set up through a separate web page that looks like a page from a company's regular web site, but which has special features, such as a time delay on the broadcast and access to detailed audience reporting, in order to find out who has monitored the webcast. The company also offers an advanced feature called "Virtual Presentations" that synchronizes audio presentations with PowerPoint slides, using its TalkPoint[TM] technology. This option can be used for other purposes, such as training presentations, product demonstrations, and advertising.

Chapter 12

Financial Statements Best Practices

This chapter covers the best practices that can be used to issue financial statements more rapidly. This creation process can be one of the most convoluted and time-consuming of all activities, with a long time needed to complete a quality set of statements. When a long interval is regularly required to complete financial statements, it has two significant impacts: not allowing any time for the accounting staff to complete other activities, and an irate management team that never receives its information on time. These are serious problems that can be completely eliminated by the best practices noted in this chapter.

The primary purpose of the two dozen improvement suggestions in this chapter is to streamline the entire process of financial statement production. This is done in a variety of ways, such as completing some tasks before the end of the month, avoiding the bank reconciliation, and automating the month-end cut-off process. Most of these steps are simple ones and can be quickly and easily inserted into the existing process. A few, however, such as automating the period-end cut-off, require a significant amount of extra work and may carry some risk of providing imperfect financial information. Consequently, it is necessary to review each recommended best practice carefully and only use those that will most easily be inserted into the existing system without causing either a stoppage in financial statement production or a reduction in their quality.

This chapter begins with a brief analysis of the level of implementation difficulty for each of the best practices, proceeds to a detailed review of each one, and finishes with an overview of how most of them can be grouped together into a highly efficient financial statement production process.

IMPLEMENTATION ISSUES FOR FINANCIAL STATEMENTS BEST PRACTICES

This section notes the relative level of implementation difficulty for all of the best practices that are discussed later in this chapter. The primary source of information is contained in Exhibit 12.1, which shows the ease, duration, and cost of implementation for each best practice (which are listed in alphabetical order). For this group of improvements, the table makes it clear that in most cases, changes are of little duration, easy to implement, and have little or no cost. The reason is

Exhibit 12.1.   Implementation Issues for Financial Statements Best Practices

Description	Ease of Implementation	Duration of Implementation	Cost of Implementation
Assign Closing Responsibilities	Easy	Short	Inexpensive
Automate Recurring Journal Entries	Easy	Short	Inexpensive
Automate the Cut-Off	Difficult	Long	Expensive
Avoid the Bank Reconciliation	Moderate	Short	Inexpensive
Complete Allocation Bases in Advance	Easy	Short	Inexpensive
Conduct Daily Review of the Financial Statements	Moderate	Short	Inexpensive
Conduct Transaction Training	Moderate	Medium	Medium
Continually Review Wait Times	Easy	Short	Inexpensive
Convert Serial Activities to Parallel Ones	Moderate	Medium	Inexpensive
Create a Closing Schedule	Easy	Short	Inexpensive
Defer Routine Work	Easy	Short	Inexpensive
Document the Process	Easy	Short	Inexpensive
Eliminate Multiple Approvals	Moderate	Medium	Inexpensive
Eliminate Small Accruals	Easy	Short	Inexpensive
Move Operating Data to Other Reports	Moderate	Short	Inexpensive
Post Financial Statements in an Excel PivotTable on the Internet	Easy	Short	Inexpensive
Reduce Investigation Levels	Easy	Short	Inexpensive
Restrict the Level of Reporting	Easy	Short	Inexpensive
Restrict the Use of Journal Entries	Easy	Short	Inexpensive
Train the Staff in Closing Procedures	Moderate	Medium	Medium
Use Cycle Counting To Avoid Month-End Counts	Difficult	Long	Medium
Use Internal Audits To Locate Transaction Problems in Advance	Moderate	Medium	Medium
Use Standard Journal Entry Forms	Easy	Short	Inexpensive
Write Financial Statement Footnotes in Advance	Easy	Short	Inexpensive

that most alterations are confined to a small number of people within the accounting department, which makes it a simple matter to alter the tasks of just that small group. Also, these are mostly procedural changes, ones that do not require expensive and problematic computer programming alterations. Further, there is little need for the participation of other departments. Thus, for all these reasons, the risk and investment associated with most of these best practices are low.

The two glaring exceptions are automating the period-end cut-off and using inventory cycle counting to avoid month-end inventory counts. In the first case, there is a need for programming, and in both cases, the complete cooperation of the warehouse staff is required. Given these two additional variables, these best practices become not only the most expensive and time-consuming ones to implement, but also the ones that are most likely to fail.

However, with these two exceptions, best practices for the production of financial statements are generally easy to implement.

ASSIGN CLOSING RESPONSIBILITIES

The typical financial statement preparation process can be a jumbled affair. It is not clear who is completing which task or when anything needs to be completed. This leads to disarray in the ranks of the accounting staff whenever the financial statements are to be produced.

A simple best practice is to produce a document that clearly states exactly who is responsible for each task required to produce financial statements. As noted in Exhibit 12.2, it states the job position that must complete each task. In order to fully utilize this document, it is necessary to have a staff meeting prior to each closing period so the controller can go over the closing responsibilities. This reinforces the need for each person to complete each task exactly on time, so the accounting team can reliably issue financial statements every period. When combined with a detailed closing schedule, as described later in this chapter under the

Exhibit 12.2.   Statement of Responsibilities for the Production of Financials

Task	Controller	Assistant Controller	General Ledger Accountant
Calculate Depreciation		✓	
Calculate Interest Accrual		✓	
Compare to A/P Detail			✓
Compare to A/R Detail			✓
Compare to F/A Detail			✓
Do Recurring Journal Entries			✓
Prepare Bank Reconciliation		✓	
Prepare Footnotes	✓		
Review Cut-off		✓	

"Create a Closing Schedule" section, a controller has a complete set of documentation on hand for producing the financial statements.

AUTOMATE RECURRING JOURNAL ENTRIES

The average financial statement many require several dozen journal entries before it is completed. Some of these entries can be quite large, perhaps to re-distribute payroll costs to a large number of departments, or to allocate occupancy costs in a similar manner. If they are substantial, it is easy to incorrectly enter them occasionally, resulting in revenues and expenses being sent to the wrong accounts, making the financial statements very difficult to compare from month to month. If the journal entries have been highly inconsistent over time, it may even be necessary for the general ledger accountant to review all of them and create new journal entries to correct the original entries. All of this work takes time, of course—and time is in short supply during the financial statement closing process.

Many general ledger accounting software packages have a feature that allows one to avoid the continual re-entry of journal entries every month by setting up recurring journal entries which the system will automatically generate every month, with no further manual interference. This type of entry is only for those situations where the exact amounts of the entries do not change from month to month (e.g., for the allocation of occupancy costs), so it will only apply to a portion of the total number of journal entries. Nonetheless, by setting up recurring entries in the computer, there are fewer journal entries to make.

The only problem with using recurring entries is that they will change at long intervals, necessitating a periodic update. To use the earlier example, occupancy costs may be re-allocated based on changes in the square footage occupied by each department, so the closing schedule should include an annual review and updating of the amounts used in this entry. Another way to update recurring entries is to create a schedule of entry updates, so a controller knows the exact month or year in which a recurring entry is scheduled to change and can ignore it in the meantime. Either approach gives a sufficient amount of control over this type of journal entry, while still reducing the total amount of accounting time allocated to it.

AUTOMATE THE CUT-OFF

The single most difficult issue at the time of each financial statement closing is the cut-off. This involves matching the invoices from suppliers with receipts to ensure that all expenses carry with them a corresponding benefit within the same period. The main problem in this area is the cost of goods sold, where large quantities of goods are received every day, usually comprising the bulk of all expenditures. If even a single high-value delivery is recorded in the wrong period, the cost of goods sold can be off significantly, either too high, because an expense is recorded without the corresponding receipt, or vice versa. To exacerbate the problem, the incorrect entry will reverse itself in the following accounting period, resulting in a continual fluctuation in the cost of goods sold, one period being too high and the next too low. This can be very embarrassing for a controller and is a grave matter for publicly held companies, which can be sued by shareholders for incorrectly reporting financial results. To avoid this problem, most controllers allocate an inordinate amount of manpower to the comparison of accounts payable and inventory records.

To avoid the entire cut-off problem, it is absolutely mandatory that a company strictly adhere to a policy of turning away from the receiving dock any deliveries that do not have an accompanying purchase order number. By closely following this policy, it is possible to entirely automate the period-end cut-off. The reason why automation then becomes easy is that by immediately logging in all receipts against purchase orders in the computer system (thus the additional need for immediate data entry), it is possible to generate a computer report that compares all inventory receipts to the purchase orders entered into the computer system as well as all received supplier invoices which match up against the purchase orders. The net result of this report is a complete list of all receipts for which there are no supplier invoices, making it a simple matter to accrue for all missing invoices. This carries with it the double benefits of not only avoiding the manual labor of determining a clean cut-off, but also eliminating the wait time that would otherwise be required before supplier invoices arrive.

Unfortunately, there are several problems with this excellent approach that limit a controller's ability to install it. One is that it requires the cooperation of the computer services and warehousing departments—the first to program the changes needed to make it run in the computer system and the latter to agree to reject all items without purchase orders, as well as to enter all receipts in a computer at the receiving dock. Whenever additional departments are involved, the chances of completion drop, since there are more supervisors who can interfere with it. Also, due to the programming needs, this is an expensive implementation (unless there is already a packaged software solution on hand that contains the appropriate features). Further, the purchasing department must be persuaded to enter all purchase orders into the computer system in a timely manner. All of these issues, particularly the involvement of multiple departments, makes this a difficult and expensive best practice to implement, though it is also one of the most rewarding ones to have in place.

AVOID THE BANK RECONCILIATION

The last item completed before issuing financial statements is usually the bank reconciliation. A company's bank takes a few days to compile bank statements for all of its customers following the end of the month, then a few more days pass while the statement travels through the mail. The typical company then receives it on about the fifth business day of the month and someone in the accounting department must scramble to complete the bank reconciliation. Usually, there are bank fees noted on the statement that must be recorded on a company's books, as well as any unrecorded checks (always manual ones that were never entered into the computer system) that must be recorded. Because of the delay built into receiving the statement and the time needed to complete the bank reconciliation, many companies cannot reduce the time needed to complete their financial statements to less than five or six days.

To reduce the time needed to produce financial statements, one must not include the bank reconciliation in the month-end closing procedure. By doing so, there is no need to wait for the bank statement to arrive, nor is there any last-minute rush to complete the bank reconciliation.

However, there is a significant risk to consider, which can be greatly mitigated. The risk is that there is an expense located on the bank statement that, if not recorded, will have a major impact on the level of reported profits in the financial statements. For example, a large manual check representing a major expense is listed on the bank statement as having been processed; this check will eliminate all monthly profits when recorded in the general ledger. This possibility is the main reason why many controllers insist on waiting for the bank reconciliation to be completed before they will consider issuing financial statements. Luckily, there are several steps one can take to reduce this risk. One is to accrue banking fees. These are usually about the same amount each month and so can be accrued and then reversed after the actual bank statement arrives. Second, one can call the bank and advance the date on which the bank statement is issued, say to the 25th day of the month, which allows the accounting staff to complete the bank reconciliation much sooner, though there is still a risk that the final few days of the month may contain an unrecorded expense that will not be found until the following month's bank statement. Also, the outside auditors will object to a bank statement that does not extend to the last day of the month, so the final statement of the year must be converted back to the traditional month-end variety. Third and best, the accounting staff can subscribe to its bank's on-line transaction review system (assuming it has one), which allows someone to review all checks received every day and to maintain a running bank reconciliation. By using this final approach, the bank reconciliation is always perfect and all expenses are spotted on the same day they are recorded by the bank. As a result, there is no need to worry about unexplained expenses appearing on the bank statement and the reconciliation can safely be shifted out of those few frenzied days when the financial statements are being produced. Though any of the three variations noted in this paragraph can be used, only the last one is a completely foolproof way to avoid missing something on a bank statement that should be recorded as a current expense.

COMPLETE ALLOCATION BASES IN ADVANCE

A number of expenses must be allocated among departments. These can include occupancy, telephone, insurance, and other costs. For each allocation, there is usually an allocation base. For example, occupancy may be based on the square footage occupied by each department, while telephone costs are allocated based on the number of employees in a department. For each allocation base, someone in the accounting department must update all of the information based on the latest financial results, prior to creating a journal entry to allocate the costs to various departments. Because an allocation base usually includes the latest financial information before a final cost allocation is made, it tends to be one of the last action items the accounting department completes before it issues the financial statements. Because it falls so late in the process, it can have a direct impact on the total time required to issue financial statements.

The best practice that solves this issue is a straightforward one—use information from the previous month as an allocation base. By doing so, there is no allocation base to update in the midst of the frantic release of financial statements. Instead, the update can be completed at everyone's leisure, since it does not have to be ready until the next month's financial statements are put together. In case there are any concerns regarding the relationship between the previous month's allocation base and the current month's expenses to be distributed, one can always release a study that shows the (almost invariably) minor changes in the allocation base from month to month. An alternative approach that may quash any fears of this sort is to use a three-month averaging allocation so that any unusual variations in the monthly allocation base can be spread out. The only remaining problem is the outside auditors, who may insist on an allocation base that uses information from the end of the year; if so, the allocation base can be updated for the final month of the fiscal year, but the system can revert to a previous-month system for all other months of the year. This is an easy way to shift some of the workload away from the busy days immediately following the end of an accounting period.

CONDUCT DAILY REVIEW OF THE FINANCIAL STATEMENTS

Sometimes the initial review of the period-end financial statements comes as quite a shock—the revenues or expenses may be wildly off from expectations. This results in a great deal of frantic research, while the controller investigates possible causes, rapidly makes changes, and issues bland statements to the rest of the management team that the financial statements might be issued a bit late this month. If the financials are indeed substantially different from what management has been led to expect, the blame may even be pinned on the controller, who may lose his or her job as a result.

The best way to avoid this problem is to conduct a daily review of the financial statements. Yes, this means *prior* to the end of the month. By doing so, a controller can review revenues as soon as they are billed and expenses as soon as they are incurred so that any obvious discrepancies can be resolved right away. In addition, if there is a real problem with the financial results, the controller will know about it immediately, rather than being taken by surprise at month-end, which carries the additional benefit of being able to warn the management team immediately, setting their expectations for the period-end financial results. Also, by finding and correcting problems well in advance, there are hardly any issues left to deal with by the end of the month, so the financial statements can be issued much more quickly. Thus, a daily review enhances the controller's knowledge of how the financial statements are likely to appear and gives advance warning of problems.

Many controllers would say that a daily review of the financial statements is an excessive use of their time, since a review on each business day of the month piles up into a formidable block of time. This is true, so the time must be used wisely. For example, if there are repeated accounting problems with just the revenue-recording part of the financial statements, it may be sufficient to review only the sales each day. Similarly, if transactions are only posted into the general ledger once a week, then the financial statements will only be updated once a week, reducing the number of times when it is necessary to review the statements. Also, if there are lots of minor problems throughout the financial statements, the daily review chore can be assigned to a financial analyst, with instructions to only notify the controller of major issues. By selecting a review interval that meets the needs of the specific situation, a controller can reduce the amount of labor assigned to this task.

CONDUCT TRANSACTION TRAINING

Once the preliminary financial statements have been completed, the controller must carefully review all expense, revenue, and balance sheet items to see if there are unusual variances, investigate all of them, and make corrections that result in an accurate financial statement. Depending on the number of errors and the time it takes to research them, this error checking phase can seriously extend the time required before financial statements are produced.

The best practice to eliminate a large number of these errors is conducting detailed transaction training for all employees who have a role in entering transactions into the computer system (typically a sizeable group). The reason for doing this is that the controller's final review of the financial statements is only a method for removing errors after they have already been made; by eliminating these errors before they happen through proper training, the number of errors that the controller must later research will drop dramatically.

The training must be very specifically targeted at eliminating recurring errors. This is done through a feedback loop. All errors discovered in the financial statements should be noted in a log, along with the name and position of the person most likely to have caused the error. This information is reviewed each month and a short training program is created, targeted both at the specific person who made the mistake and the type of error that occurred; if the error appears to be a common one for many employees to make, the training can be given to everyone who enters the same transaction. Also, the training programs may be used to update the initial training that all employees receive in transaction processing, thereby avoiding errors in the initial training program. Mandatory reinforcement training is also useful, both as a reminder for experienced staff and as a part of the core training for new recruits, thereby keeping the focus on error reduction over the long term.

The main problem with this approach is the cost of training. If there are many people entering transactions, the training required to cover all of them can be considerable. In these cases, it may be necessary to scale back to a small number of seminars per year, or else to issue bulletins describing problems, or to use on-line training through the computer system. All of these approaches are less expensive than comprehensive and frequent training, but are also less effective. At worst, there should be a follow-up program with the specific individuals who make errors so the worst offenders can be targeted for immediate improvement. Also, some of the people who need training may work for other departments, so the controller may have to exercise some tact in asking other department heads for permission to repeatedly train their employees. However, these issues are minor ones, given the benefits of reduced transaction error rates.

CONTINUALLY REVIEW WAIT TIMES

A lengthy financial statement completion process has a number of spots built into it where there are long wait times. For example, the typical company waits five days before it receives a bank statement from the bank for each of its accounts necessary to complete a bank statement. Also, there is usually a wait of a few days while supplier invoices arrive, just to make sure that all expenses have been properly recorded. It is pauses like these that make it nearly impossible to issue financial statements in a rapid manner, no matter how quickly all other tasks are completed. For example, it may be possible to blaze through a bank reconciliation in an hour, but if you are still waiting five days to receive the bank statement, you are focusing on the speed of the wrong activity.

The best practice that helps to resolve this issue is a continual review of wait times. This focuses attention on those activities a controller should really be attempting to reduce in size or eliminate. To review wait times, the best tool is a Gantt chart. This shows the typical start and stop dates for each closing activity. By closely examining the start dates for each activity and questioning why those dates cannot be accelerated, it brings attention to bear on any activities that are dependent on the prior completion of other activities. However, this is only a tool for pointing out where there are problems; it does not actually resolve them. To use the example from earlier in this section, a Gantt chart will only tell a controller that there is a substantial wait involved before all supplier invoices are received—the controller must still *do* something about it (that particular item is addressed in the "Automate the Cut-Off" section).

There are no problems with using this best practice, for it is easily implemented, requiring only a brief review by the controller after each financial statement closing to determine if there have been any wait time changes. It also needs no programming and does not involve other departments. In short, it is a simple best practice to install and provides valuable information for the targeting of further improvements.

CONVERT SERIAL ACTIVITIES TO PARALLEL ONES

A common problem, especially in smaller accounting departments, is that a considerable amount of wait time is built into the process because there are too many activities being conducted in a serial manner—that is, one process does not start until another is finished. A good example is in a small organization where just one person is in charge of completing several processing steps and does not have time to advance to additional tasks until the first one is complete. The same problem occurs in large organizations but usually not due to a lack of manpower. Instead, the information that flows into one process must be supplied by another task, so the preceding step must be completely finished before the next one can be started. These issues create a great deal of difficulty in reducing the time needed to complete financial statements.

The best practice that eliminates serial activities is to convert them into parallel ones. A parallel activity is one which can be completed without any need for data from a preceding process. An example of several parallel closing activities is shown in Exhibit 12.3, which depicts the accounts receivable, accounts payable, fixed assets, and payroll processes. Only in one case, where the final detail of the accounts payable process is needed as the starting point for the fixed assets process, is there any linkage between the separate processes. The trick to making this best practice work is to separate the individual processes that make up a financial statement closing so that they can be independently processed. An example of this is using a preliminary set of financial statements as the input into an allocation base from which occupancy costs are allocated to various departments. By using older information in the allocation base (see the "Complete Allocation Bases in Advance" section in this chapter), there is no longer a linkage between the two processes, so that they can now be processed as parallel activities. Similarly, the accounts payable function is not normally closed until several days have passed, while the company waits for a few supplier invoices to arrive. This serial processing issue is readily avoided by using computer systems and real-time entry of receipts at the warehouse (see the "Automate the Cut-Off" section in this chapter) to create an accrual for all missing supplier invoices without waiting for the actual

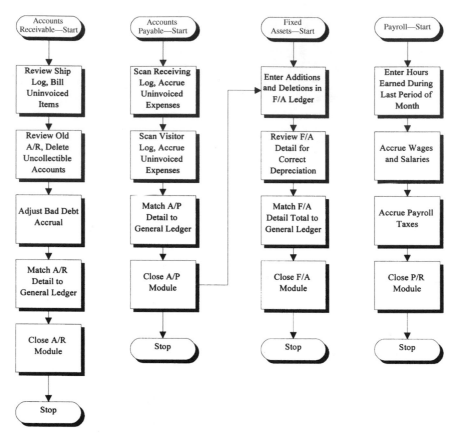

Exhibit 12.3.   Example of Parallel Closing Activities

Reprinted with the author's permission: Steven Bragg, *Just-in-Time Accounting,* (New York: John Wiley & Sons, 1996), 334.

invoices to arrive. Conducting a comprehensive review of all closing activities and systematically converting serial activities into parallel ones is one of the best ways to reduce the time needed to produce financial statements.

CREATE A CLOSING SCHEDULE

The worst enemy of a financial statement process is a disorganized closing. Without a sufficiently detailed procedure, no one will know when any deliverables are needed, or if some deliverables are needed at all. Further, there is no sequence to the process so some steps are waiting for the completion of previous steps that no one is working on. For example, the accounts payable module must be completed before anyone can complete the fixed assets module since it is possible to overlook last-minute fixed asset additions if some of the accounts payable have not been entered. A disorganized closing can drastically delay the completion of financial statements.

The best practice that resolves this issue is to create a closing schedule such as the one shown in Exhibit 12.4. This schedule itemizes all tasks that must be completed during each day of the closing process. By creating such a schedule, it is immediately obvious when all tasks must be completed so that the controller can follow up with employees and apply extra resources to those tasks which are falling behind the schedule. Please note that a number of activities scheduled in Exhibit 12.4 should be completed *prior* to the end of the reporting period, leaving

Exhibit 12.4.   Sample Closing Schedule

- *Four days prior to period-end.*
    1. Revise the closing schedule and distribute to staff.
    2. Verify that recurring journal entries are still correct for the current reporting period.
    3. Review financial statements with the most recent information and investigate any unusual variances.
- *Two days prior to period-end.*
    1. Review the contract schedule and verify that all contractual agreements have been either paid out to suppliers or billed to customers.
    2. Complete all allocation bases.
    3. Review financial statements with the most recent information and investigate any unusual variances.
- *One day prior to period-end.*
    1. Conduct an audit of the inventory to determine the accuracy level.
    2. Complete footnotes.
    3. Review financial statements with the most recent information and investigate any unusual variances.
    4. Go on-line with the bank and complete a preliminary bank reconciliation.
- *Day of period-end.*
    1. Process the period-end closing program in the computer.
    2. Print all period-end reports.
- *First day after period-end.*
    1. Compare all period-end reports to general ledger balances and reconcile differences.
    2. Accrue for unpaid payroll.
    3. Close the accounts receivable module.

(continues)

Exhibit 12.4. Continued

- *Second day after period-end.*
  1. Review cut-off information and accrue for any missing supplier invoices.
  2. Close the accounts payable module.
  3. Update the fixed assets schedule and calculate depreciation.
  4. Complete all remaining accruals.
- *Third day after period-end.*
  1. Update detailed schedules for all balance sheet accounts.
  2. Complete all operating data for inclusion in the financial statements.
  3. Complete a preliminary set of financial statements.
- *Fourth day after period-end.*
  1. Finalize the financial statements and issue.
  2. Calculate the borrowing base certificate and send it to the bank, along with a set of financial statements.

---

much less work to do at the end of the process. This schedule is most effective when combined with a schedule of responsibilities, such as the one noted earlier in Exhibit 12.2. The two schedules can even be combined so that the name or title of the responsible person is listed at the beginning of each activity in the closing schedule.

The only issue with creating a closing schedule is that it is a constantly changing document requiring regular updating and communication to the accounting staff. The reason for the regular updates is that the schedule will initially allow for a substantial number of days before statements are completed, but management will gradually shrink the number of days, requiring a constant reshuffling of tasks and responsibilities. The accounting staff will only follow changes to the schedule if the alterations are clearly communicated to them. In particular, the controller must listen to their objections regarding a reduction in the time to complete tasks so their requirements can be incorporated into the schedule. As long as these factors are considered, the closing schedule becomes the foundation document that drives the timely completion of the financial statements.

DEFER ROUTINE WORK

An accounting department is usually overwhelmed by its ongoing volume of work, without the extra crushing load of creating and distributing the periodic financial statements. Many of these tasks, such as payments to suppliers, invoicing to customers, daily or weekly reports to management, or the processing of cash, are vital ones, and cannot be delayed for long. As a result, the accounting staff is accustomed to working long overtime hours during the first week of each month, not to mention a blackout on vacation time during this period. Also, the following week is sometimes a frenzied one as well, since the accounting department must catch up on the necessary work it did not quite have a chance to complete in the previous week. In short, producing the financial statements is a hard lump for the accounting department to swallow.

The solution is to carefully review the tasks currently scheduled for completion during the first week of the month and see if there are ways to eliminate them or shift them into a (much) later week. For example, management may be accustomed to receiving a daily report of sales and cash receipts; it may be possible to completely eliminate this report for a few days during the beginning of the month so that the workload is completely eliminated, rather than being shifted into the next week. Completely avoiding work is always the best option, but for some tasks, there is no alternative to shifting it forward a few days. Examples of this kind are paying suppliers or billing customers—this must be done, but a judicious delay of a few days will not do an excessive amount of harm to these basic processes. However, there may be a few cases, such as invoicing very large dollar amounts or paying suppliers in order to take a large early payment discount, where it pays to go ahead with the work in the current period, but only for key items; the remaining smaller items can still be deferred for a short time. This solution is an easy way to reduce the amount of overtime required to complete the financial statements.

DOCUMENT THE PROCESS

Some organizations have created closing procedures and established responsibilities for those accounting people who are involved with the production of financial statements, which helps them to some degree in organizing the flow of work. However, they meet with great resistance when they take the next step and mandate reductions in the time needed to complete the statements. Employees grouse that there is not enough time to complete their work, that upstream work is not completed on time (which does not allow them to start *their* tasks on time), and that management does not know all the details required to complete their tasks. As a result, though the process appears to be more organized, there is no way to reduce the time and resources allocated to it.

The underlying reason why this problem arises is that the employees are right—the managers who are driving for shorter completion dates do not really know the process and cannot understand the plethora of additional necessary changes before the process will become truly streamlined. The only way to avoid this quagmire is to document the process thoroughly. This means that a team must interview all employees who are involved in the reporting process, write down detailed descriptions of what they do, and flowchart all activities. Only after these steps are completed can one see the bottlenecks in the process that must be eliminated. For example, an employee may be using a painfully slow allocation method for spreading occupancy costs which can be easily altered by switching to a simpler method—but a controller will never know this without a complete documentation of exactly how the current allocation calculation is made. The documentation process can be a slow one, especially for a multi-division company including many employees and locations in the process. Nonetheless, it is the only way to gain a better understanding of the process, which leads to better decisions regarding how other best practices can be inserted to ensure better results.

It is possible to short-circuit some of the documentation process. The best way is to determine which people in the process are the obvious bottlenecks, since the work seems to pile up at their desks. Their work should be documented and acted on first, while the efforts of others, whose work products are clearly coming in on time, can wait until any changes alter the process enough to make *them* the new bottlenecks. By using this variation on the documentation process, it is possible to more rapidly institute changes to the overall process.

ELIMINATE MULTIPLE APPROVALS

A typical problem when financial statements are produced is to have employees wait for approvals before they are allowed to complete their tasks, or to pass along work to other employees, who cannot begin until the approvals are given. When there are many approvals to obtain, especially in areas where the approvals are holding up key work products, there can be a substantial impact on the speed of financial statement completion. Typical spots in the financial statement process that include approvals are journal entries, footnotes, the final version of the statements, and the final results from all of the major accounting modules: accounts payable, accounts receivable, payroll, and fixed assets. Given the number of approvals in some companies, it is a wonder that the financial statements are ever produced in less than a month.

There are several solutions that bypass the approvals problem. When reviewing them, one must consider the underlying reason for using approvals, which is to ensure that information is correctly processed. Without an approval, there must be a countervailing system in place to ensure that accurate information is still transmitted to the financial statements. Some solutions to the approvals dilemma are as follows:

- *Designate a back-up approver.* If there is a continuing problem with finding the person who is allowed to issue approvals, then there should be a back-up approver available. This should still be a person who has a sufficient level of technical expertise, and so is only a viable option for those companies with some extra employees on hand who are sufficiently qualified.

- *Increase training levels.* An excellent way to avoid approvals is to train the accounting staff in the closing procedures so that they all become experts in their jobs. After heavy and repeated training, it is quite common to find that the staff is more technically proficient in their tasks than their bosses, with little need for any approval. Also, newcomers to the accounting department must receive similarly high levels of indoctrination.

- *Issue ranges within which approvals are not required.* The best way to handle the approval problem is not to require approvals at all. To do so, determine the comfort level of the controller in regard to how much an accountant is allowed to do without any supervisory review. For example, one can establish a limit of $2,500 for any journal entry, above which approvals are still required. This approach usually eliminates the bulk of the approvals, while still reserving the oversight privilege for those transactions that are large enough to truly warrant a review. This method usually requires a periodic review of all transactions to ensure that the pre-set ranges are being observed.

- *Reduce to one approver.* In cases where there is more than one approver, there is rarely a need for it. For example, if a journal entry for more than $5,000 must be approved by an assistant controller, but anything over $25,000 requires the approval of the controller, it is usually sufficient to give the assistant controller a much higher sign-off authority, reserving only the most unusual situations for the involvement of the extra person. If a controller still insists on requiring a secondary review of all approvals, then either the controller is a certifiable micromanager (which may require counseling), or else the person issuing the first approval is not sufficiently qualified to give it (in which case he should have no approval authority at all).

- *Shift the approver to an available person.* A common occurrence is that a high-ranking person is the only one allowed to approve certain transactions. If that person is commonly traveling or in meetings, then a process cannot be completed until the person becomes available to give an approval. Consequently, the best approach is to re-assign the approval to a different person who is always on site, usually an assistant controller or accounting manager.

All of these approaches are targeted at reducing the processing time required to track down a designated approver. Given a company's individual circumstances, especially involving the risks of not approving a processing step, the ultimate solution to this problem will be a mix of the above solutions. The key issue to remember is that some situations do indeed require some kind of supervisory control, so there is always some approval requirement for at least a few key deliverables.

ELIMINATE SMALL ACCRUALS

In some companies, there is a focus on achieving perfectly accurate financial statements, no matter how many extra accruals are needed to ensure that expenses are recorded absolutely perfectly. Though there is a certain degree of professional satisfaction in issuing a set of absolutely accurate financial statements, this can use up a considerable amount of accounting resources which could be better used elsewhere. For example, it may require twenty extra accruals, along with the attendant analysis, review, and approval effort, to yield financial statements that now have a profit altered by one or two percentage points. Realistically, such a slight change in the financial results will not have a noticeable impact on the decision making of the managers, stock analysts, or creditors who review the financial statements. So, despite an inordinate amount of extra effort, no one really cares about the slightly more accurate results.

The answer to this problem is to review all existing accruals and throw out all of the ones that result in only very small accrual amounts. By doing so, less time is needed to produce the financial statements, opening up resources for other uses. However, when conducting the accrual review, it is important to check on a number of past journal entries to ensure that each accrual is always a small one— if there is even a slight chance of an accrual occasionally being a large one, it is best to keep it in place on the grounds that financial statement accuracy could be severely impacted by its absence at some point in the future. Thus, as long as an appropriate degree of caution is used when eliminating accruals from the financial statement closing procedure, it is reasonable to permanently eliminate the use of small accruals.

MOVE OPERATING DATA TO OTHER REPORTS

A major factor in the delay in sending financial statements is the inclusion of operating data in the statements. The reason is that this information, such as scrap rates or employee turnover, is not contained in the financial information that the accounting staff normally deals with, nor is it readily obtained by creating ratios or comparisons of the financial data. In short, this information can be hard to obtain. The situation is worsened by the lack of control of the accounting staff over who tracks the information, as well as its accuracy once it is obtained. For example, a subsidiary may forward information about its customer backlog that seems suspiciously high; the controller has the options of including the provided data in the financial statements or of holding off on the financial statement distribution while requesting and waiting for a review of the numbers by the subsidiary—which is under no obligation to do the review. Thus, including operating data in the financial statements can not only delay the issuance of the statements, but also does nothing to ensure the accuracy of the operating information.

An easy way to avoid these problems is to separate all operating information from the financial statements so the statements can be issued in a timely manner, with the operating information sent out later in a separate document. By using this approach, there are fewer steps to complete when issuing financial statements, leaving fewer steps to delay the overall process. Also, if there are problems with the operating data, the controller can review the information at his leisure and verify that the information is correct before releasing it. Not only is this an easy best practice to implement, but it is also one that has no associated expense.

POST FINANCIAL STATEMENTS IN AN EXCEL PIVOTTABLE ON THE INTERNET

A number of companies have found that an effective way to increase investor knowledge of their activities is to post their financial statements on their web sites. These tend to be a summary-level duplication of the most recent quarterly or annual results, as well as any accompanying financial notes. Though this is certainly a good way to communicate with investors, the concept can be taken a step further by loading the financial information into an Excel PivotTable, which is essentially a three-dimensional spreadsheet that reveals different layers of information to the user. By using a PivotTable, a reader of a financial statement can access the results for multiple years, or even different lines of business, within a summary-level financial statement. A good example of this layout can be found in the Investor Relations section of the Microsoft web site. This is a relatively easy best practice to implement. The only downside is that investors must download the file, which creates the highly unlikely, yet possible, risk of importing a computer virus through the spreadsheet file.

REDUCE INVESTIGATION LEVELS

Before issuing the financial statements, they are subject to an intensive review by the controller, who compares each line item to the budgeted level and thoroughly investigates each item that varies significantly from the budget. This is an admirable and necessary practice, since it catches errors and also prepares the controller for any questions from the management team regarding those same variances. However, the practice can be taken too far. For example, it is almost impossible for any revenue or expense line item to match exactly the budgeted amount (unless it is related to a long-term contract that ensures totally predictable amounts), so a controller who investigates virtually all variances will be doomed to review every line item in the general ledger. This is an enormous task and also an unnecessary one, for the vast majority of variances are so small that there is no point in reviewing them—even if there is an error somewhere, the total impact is so insignificant that there will be no noticeable impact on corporate profitability.

A very simple best practice that eliminates the bulk of this review work is to reduce investigation levels to the point where only the largest variances are checked for accuracy. This can take several forms. For example, a minimum dollar amount, such as $10,000, can be set for the amount of a variance that a controller will bother to investigate. Alternatively, it can be on a percentage basis, such as anything over a 30 percent variance. Also, there may be some accounts, such as payroll, that are better reviewed by checking headcount figures each month, thereby entirely eliminating them from the variance analysis. The best approach is usually a combination of all three techniques, which means that anything over a specific dollar variance is always reviewed, plus any large percentage variances that may fall under the pre-set dollar level, with the exception of certain accounts reviewed in other ways. This system can then be modified over time to allow for changes in the controller's comfort level with variance investigation, as well as to cover new accounts that may be added. By creating such a system of variance review levels, it is possible to greatly reduce the amount of review work that must be completed prior to issuing financial statements.

RESTRICT THE LEVEL OF REPORTING

Over time, many older companies have gradually gotten into the habit of demanding (and receiving) immensely detailed financial statements from the accounting department. Besides the usual balance sheet and income statement, as well as departmental reports, there can be a plethora of additional schedules, such as sales by customer or region, inventory levels by type of inventory, and a complete activity-based costing analysis of every customer. Though some of these reports may be set up to run automatically as part of the regular package of financial statements (and thereby requiring no additional work), other reports may require the transfer of information to a different format, such as an electronic spreadsheet, for further analysis and re-grouping into a customized report. In this case, the amount of time required to assemble and independently prepare the reports may exceed the time needed to create the primary financial statements. Thus, the more reports included in the financial statements, the more time it takes to issue the statements.

The best way to avoid this problem is to make a list of all the reports included in the financial statements, ignore those that are automatically created by the accounting software, and focus on eliminating or delaying those that are created separately. It may be possible to strip these reports out of the basic financial reporting package, allowing the accounting staff to issue the basic underlying statements much more quickly. To achieve this goal, it may be necessary to explain to management that the reports will no longer be provided at all (which is normally not received well). Other variations are to issue the reports separately and at a later date, or to issue them less frequently, such as once a quarter or year. Usually, there is some combination of methods that will be agreeable to management, thereby allowing a controller to restrict the level of reporting in the financial statements to only the most basic information.

RESTRICT THE USE OF JOURNAL ENTRIES

Journal entries can be the bane of the general ledger accountant who is desperately trying to issue accurate financial statements. The reason is that in the midst of cleaning up the general ledger in preparation for the issuance of financial statements, this person will sometimes find that a journal entry has miraculously appeared in the ledger, requiring a hurried investigation to determine who made the entry, why it was made, and whether the entry was already duplicated by the general ledger accountant. After this added work, there is always the chance that even more entries will be made prior to the closing of the books for the reporting period. A particularly irritating problem is when a journal entry is made between the time when the financial statements are issued and the accounting period is closed in the computer system, since the change appears in the beginning balance for the next month, but does not show up in the financial statements! This can be an exceedingly difficult item to trace. Thus, allowing multiple people to create journal entries can lead to significant delays during the production of financial statements.

A much simpler approach is to restrict the use of journal entries to a single person, the general ledger accountant. Even the controller should not be allowed to create journal entries. By using this approach, there is a single easily controlled point of entry into the general ledger, ensuring that the information entering the ledger has been verified in advance. The inevitable result will be fewer problems with the production of financial statements.

There are a few problems with this approach. Some accounting personnel will probably complain that they are entitled to make journal entries, while there may also be a problem if the general ledger accountant is not available at month-end to make entries; if so, there should be a back-up person on hand authorized to handle journal entries. Another issue for larger corporations is what to do if there are a number of general ledger accountants, all of whom must make entries at the same time, simply because of the volume of entries required. In this case, it is necessary to maintain a log, either manually or in the computer, in which every accountant must record all entries. By referring to other entries already in the log, any of the general ledger accountants can easily see what entries have already been made and can thereby avoid any duplicate entries.

TRAIN THE STAFF IN CLOSING PROCEDURES

One of the biggest problems with a new accounting staff, or one in which the responsibilities for producing financial statements have changed recently, is that they do not know what they are supposed to do. This results in a general level of confusion regarding responsibilities, as well as the slow completion of deliverables and their probable inaccuracy even when they *are* done. This is a nightmare situation for a controller, who must review everyone's work in great detail and check on everyone's progress to make sure that they will complete their assigned tasks on time. This scenario is almost guaranteed to result in the late production of financial statements, and probably ones with errors, as well.

A key factor that will reduce the level of confusion is proper training of the accounting staff. By doing so, error rates will decline, while the time needed to complete assigned tasks will drop dramatically. To achieve this end result, one must first have an adequate set of procedures from which to conduct training (see the "Document the Process" section in this chapter). Once these procedures are written, one can use them to conduct personalized training of every person who is involved in the creation of financial statements. It is important to conduct training prior to the end of the reporting period so that the training can be done in a leisurely manner, giving everyone time to ruminate over the information and to have their questions answered thoroughly. If the training is conducted in the midst of the closing process, there will not be enough time for an adequate level of training. Also, once the initial training is complete, the controller must still monitor the progress of all the people on the accounting team and provide follow-up training as needed to ensure that they have fully absorbed what they have been taught and that any errors are corrected. Finally, the procedures that were used as a training tool must be given to the accounting staff for referral purposes, as well as being updated at once to reflect any ongoing changes to the closing procedure. Training is an extremely cost-effective method for ensuring that the accounting staff completes the financial statements in an efficient and effective manner.

USE CYCLE COUNTING TO AVOID MONTH-END COUNTS

A common effort for companies with poor inventory record-keeping systems is to count the inventory at the end of every reporting period. By doing so, the controller is assured of a reasonably accurate cost of goods sold figure, though at the cost of shutting down the business while the counting process goes on (since this may interfere with accurate inventory counts), which not only runs the risk of losing some business, but also requires paying some employees to conduct the decidedly *not* value-added inventory counting activity. Over the course of a year, this represents either a major loss of revenue, addition to expenses, or both.

The solution is to stop taking periodic inventory counts. By doing so, there is no stoppage of sales activities, nor is there any need to re-direct anyone's activities to counting inventory. In addition, the accounting staff no longer has to spend valuable time during the end of the month to participate in the inventory count, which gives the staff more time to complete the financial statements more quickly. Unfortunately, this happy state of affairs brings with it some risks. The main one is that inventory may become quite inaccurate over time, resulting in cost-of-goods-sold numbers in the financial statements that will, over time, depart quite a long way from the actual situation. If this number is inaccurate,

the borrowing base information a company presents to the bank will also probably be wrong, which may give the bank grounds for withholding additional borrowings. A final problem is that if the financial statements are incorrect, the controller may pay for this oversight by losing his job. The best way to avoid all of
these issues is to use cycle counting. This process involves a continual count of
the entire inventory so that all items, especially the high-value or high-usage
ones, have their quantities verified frequently. In addition, a trained cycle-
counter is much more likely to obtain accurate inventory figures than the less
knowledgeable group of counters typically employed for period-end counts. A
good cycle-counter is trained to investigate *why* there are counting variances,
resulting in changes to the underlying systems that originally caused the errors.
By using this approach, it is very unlikely that the inventory will be very far off
at any time, which gives a controller much better confidence that the inventory
figures at the end of the month are accurate, without the need for a periodic
physical inventory count.

USE INTERNAL AUDITS TO LOCATE TRANSACTION PROBLEMS IN ADVANCE

The financial statement is, in a manner of speaking, the cesspool into which all
corporate information flows—that is to say, all transaction errors will wend their
way into this final repository of corporate information. This means that there can
be a large concentration of incorrect data in the general ledger, which unfortunately is the only source of information from which the financial statements are
created. Accordingly, poorly completed transactions upstream from the general
ledger will eventually appear in the financial statements. This causes a great deal
of extra work for the accounting staff, which must frantically research all of the
problems that were caused upstream from the financial statements and issue journal entries to correct them—all in the few days during which the statements must
be completed and issued. This problem will occur month after month unless
something is done to find out where these problems are occurring and why.

The internal auditing staff can be brought in to discover where these problems are occurring, why they are happening, who is causing the problems, and
what can be done to fix them. By using the internal auditing staff, the controller
can determine the exact nature of all the problems plaguing the financial statements. Though this best practice does not solve the problems, it at least identifies them, making it much easier for a controller to determine an appropriate
response to each one. The long-term result of this approach is a gradual reduction in the number of errors in the financial statements, resulting in much less
analysis time by the accounting staff to correct the preliminary version of the
financial statements.

The main problem with this best practice is the internal audit department and
its controlling audit committee. The department recommends to the audit com-

mittee (which is usually composed of members of the Board of Directors) a set of investigative projects for the upcoming year, which the committee typically approves without much discussion. The department creates this list based on the perceived payback from each potential audit, or because they are in potentially high-risk areas. If the controller cannot get the transaction review audit onto this annual project list (and repeatedly so, since this audit must be repeated time and again), there is no way that the best practice can ever be completed. It may take a considerable amount of influence with the internal audit manager or the audit committee to make sure that these audits are regularly conducted.

USE STANDARD JOURNAL ENTRY FORMS

The production of a typical set of financial statements requires the entry of a large number of journal entries. These must be made for a variety of reasons that even the best-run accounting department cannot avoid, such as cost allocations, accrued expenses for which a supplier invoice has not yet arrived, or the shifting of an expense to a different account than the one into which it was initially recorded. Recording each one of these entries can take a considerable amount of time, for a great deal of thought must go into which accounts are used, their account numbers, the amounts of money to be recorded in each account, and whether or not there will be a debit or credit entry. Consequently, the use of journal entries can take up a significant amount of the total time required to produce financial statements.

One way to reduce the amount of time devoted to journal entries is to create a standard set of journal entry forms. These are used for the recording of standard journal entries where the amount of money to be recorded will vary, but the account numbers will stay the same most of the time. An example of such an entry is noted in Exhibit 12.5. This type of entry is a common one and probably applies to a majority of the journal entries every month. This type of journal entry standardization can also be taken a step further by creating recurring journal entries, which can be used for any entries that have the exact same amount of money in the entry every time. For more information on this approach (see the "Automate Recurring Journal Entries" section in this chapter).

WRITE FINANCIAL STATEMENT FOOTNOTES IN ADVANCE

There are many footnotes that accompany a well-documented set of financial statements. These typically include an executive summary, notes on the accounting methodologies, the amount of long-term debt (as well as the years in which it comes due), a commentary on insurance coverage, any customers with a high preponderance of a company's sales, and a historical comparison of the current results to prior years. Depending on the number of footnotes added to the financial statement package, this can be a considerable amount of work to update every period.

Exhibit 12.5.   Sample Journal Entry Form for the Allocation of Occupancy Costs

Account Description	Debit	Credit
Rent Expense	XXX	
Utility Expense	XXX	
Building Maintenance Expense	XXX	
Accounting Department Occupancy Expense		XXX
Engineering Department Occupancy Expense		XXX
Logistics Department Occupancy Expense		XXX
Marketing Department Occupancy Expense		XXX
Production Department Occupancy Expense		XXX
Sales Department Occupancy Expense		XXX

The best way to avoid much of the work required to create footnotes is to separate them into two categories: boilerplate information that is rarely changed, and information that is closely linked to current financial results, requiring a great deal of updating. All footnotes in the first category should be clustered together to the greatest extent possible, reviewed prior to the end of the month, and even printed out and ready for inclusion with the remainder of the financial statements. By handling these items well in advance, there is less work to be done during the crucial period immediately following the end of a reporting period, when there is little time available for such work. Unfortunately, many footnotes *do* require updates based on current financial results and so cannot be completed in advance. In these cases, it is still possible to highlight those portions of each footnote that must be changed, either with different font sizes, underlining, or color changes in the computer, so that everything requiring examination can be spotted and checked easily. In addition, it is a good idea to create a checklist containing all of the data to be updated in each footnote. This checklist is an excellent way to avoid situations where footnotes are distributed that have not been updated to account for the most recent results.

TOTAL IMPACT OF BEST PRACTICES ON THE FINANCIAL STATEMENTS FUNCTION

This section gives an overview of how and when the best practices described in this chapter should be implemented, and the total impact of these changes on the financial statement reporting function.

The "how" of implementing best practices in this area is answered by, "do them in big blocks." The reason is that, in general, these best practices are very easy to implement and can be installed in clusters. Given their minimal impact on department operations, they rarely have much of an impact on employee morale, so there is no restriction on multiple implementation projects at the same time. A key issue to consider is that a number of these implementations do not have a clear beginning and end. For example, training the staff in closing procedures, or reviewing wait times, will always require continuing review, because the state of the art will continually change, making it necessary to go back to these items constantly. Thus, the best approach is multiple best practice implementations, which are constantly reviewed.

The other key issue is the timing of the implementations. For most of these best practices, it is best to conduct an implementation outside of the period when financial statements are prepared. This point is best illustrated by perusing Exhibit 12.6. This exhibit clusters all of the best practices into the time either before the end of the reporting period, in the midst of it, or after it. The vast majority of the practices fall into the first category. This means that most financial statement best practices can be completed at leisure, when there is not a rush to produce financial information. The main benefits of this timing issue are that implementations can be completed more smoothly, there is time to correct mistakes, and if there is an implementation problem, it can be deferred in favor of the procedure it is replacing. Therefore, timing of the changes tends to be a minor issue.

The overall impact of best practices on the financial statements function falls into two areas. One is that financial statements can be completed much more quickly, efficiently, and with fewer errors, all of which are greatly appreciated by upper management. The standard for world-class companies with multiple subsidiaries is to issue financial statements in two working days, while single-location companies have been known to issue them in as little as one day. These benchmarks are quite attainable if all of the best practices noted in this chapter are not only installed, but also constantly reviewed to ensure that they are being used in the most efficient manner. The other impact of best practices is that the workload for producing financial statements partially shifts into the week prior to the end of the reporting period from the week following it. The evidence of this shift is amply illustrated in Exhibit 12.6, where there are sixteen listed activities that can be completed prior to the end of the reporting period. All accounting managers should integrate this shift in workloads into the schedules of their staffs, ensuring that there are no excessively high or low work periods resulting from the change in systems.

SUMMARY

This chapter covered a variety of techniques for improving the speed with which financial statements can be distributed. These methods vary from shifting the work of the closing process to before the end of a reporting period to avoiding

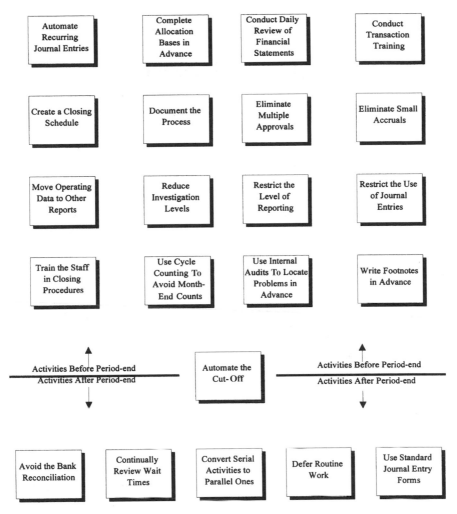

Exhibit 12.6. Impact of Best Practices on the Financial Statements Function

some of the closing work entirely. Most of the suggestions noted here will work in all companies, irrespective of the closing systems they already have in place. A few items require a careful appraisal of the current situation, however, such as avoiding the completion of the bank reconciliation and using an automated cut-off system—these require either special training or new computer systems and must be used with an eye to the risk of system or training failures and their impact on the accuracy of the financial statements. No matter which best practices are chosen from the list in this chapter, one overriding issue remains constant—this is a carefully choreographed dance of many people working together, requiring a good manager to control.

Chapter 13

General Best Practices

There are a number of best practices that do not fall into any of the categories listed in the other chapters of this book. They can be clustered into three primary areas: activities related to processes, personnel, and reporting, as shown later in Exhibit 13.9. These are all key areas that deserve special management attention to ensure that they operate properly. Examples of best practices related to processes include process centering and consolidating accounting functions, while examples of best practices for personnel include policies and procedures manuals and training programs. Finally, examples of best practices related to reporting include the use of on-line and balanced scorecard reporting. A review of this array of best practices allows one to enhance a number of key activities.

IMPLEMENTATION ISSUES FOR GENERAL BEST PRACTICES

This section covers the general level of implementation difficulty that will arise when installing the best practices discussed later in this chapter. This information is primarily contained in Exhibit 13.1, which shows the ease, duration, and cost of implementing each best practice.

The best practices noted in this chapter tend to require larger levels of management time than those noted in other chapters, as well as a longer project duration and higher cost. Examples of this are the consolidation of accounting functions and switching to on-line reporting, which require a great deal of planning and programming work, as well as (in the first case) the geographical transfer of employees.

Even if these difficult best practices are excluded, the remainder will at least require some advance planning, along with a week or more of work before they are fully operational. The biggest problem with most is that they are *systems*—they require their own procedures, training, and measurements to ensure that they work properly. Examples of systems best practices are the continual review of process cycles, training, and process centering. Due to the extra work required to create and maintain an entire system, one must be aware of the time and effort needed before some payback will be realized.

Finally, a few best practices are simple to initiate and complete, require minimal management attention, and need only a modest amount of follow-up work from time to time. These best practices include the creation of a contract terms database, issuing activity calendars, and outsourcing tax form preparation. How-

Exhibit 13.1. Implementation Issues for General Best Practices

Description	Ease of Implementation	Duration of Implementation	Cost of Implementation
Avoid Over-Auditing of Internal Audits	Easy	Short	Inexpensive
Complete All Internal Audit Workpapers in the Field	Easy	Short	Inexpensive
Consolidate All Accounting Functions	Difficult	Long	Expensive
Continually Review Key Process Cycles	Moderate	Medium	Inexpensive
Create a Contract Terms Database	Moderate	Short	Inexpensive
Create an On-Going Training Program for all Accounting Personnel	Moderate	Medium	Moderate
Create an On-Line Internal Audit Library	Moderate	Medium	Moderate
Create an On-Line Tax Policy Listing	Moderate	Medium	Moderate
Create a Policy and Procedure Manual	Moderate	Medium	Moderate
Create Computer-Based Training Movies	Moderate	Medium	Inexpensive
Implement Cross-Training for Mission-Critical Activities	Moderate	Medium	Moderate
Implement Process-Centering	Moderate	Medium	Moderate
Issue Activity Calendars to All Accounting Positions	Easy	Short	Inexpensive
Outsource Tax Form Preparation	Easy	Short	Moderate
Outsource the Internal Audit Function	Moderate	Medium	Moderate
Post the Policies and Procedures Manual on the Company Intranet Site	Moderate	Medium	Medium
Scan Data with Modified Palm Computing Platform	Difficult	Long	Medium
Scan Fingerprints at User Workstations	Moderate	Short	Inexpensive
Schedule Internal Audits Based on Risk	Easy	Medium	Inexpensive

(continues)

Exhibit 13.1.   Continued

Description	Ease of Implementation	Duration of Implementation	Cost of Implementation
Sell the Shared Services Center	Moderate	Medium	Inexpensive
Switch to a Limited Usage Application Service Provider	Easy	Short	Inexpensive
Switch to an Application Service Provider	Moderate	Medium	Medium
Switch to On-Line Reporting	Difficult	Long	Expensive
Track Function Measurements	Moderate	Medium	Inexpensive
Use Balanced Scorecard Reporting	Moderate	Medium	Inexpensive

ever, restricting one's implementation of best practices to just these items would be a mistake, for the level of accounting efficiency will rise dramatically when the more difficult implementations are successfully completed.

The remainder of this chapter is grouped into sections, each of which covers one best practice. In each section, there is a discussion of the problems that a best practice can alleviate, how the best practice works, and any implementation problems that may arise.

AVOID OVER-AUDITING OF INTERNAL AUDITS

Many internal audits involve the repetitive review of the same topical areas, if only because these areas are perceived to have the highest degree of financial risk to a company, and so are worthy of constant review. When internal audits are repeated on a regular basis, the managers of these audits will usually pull out the workpapers from the last audit that was conducted on the same area, and simply copy out the same auditing requirements. This can result in over-auditing, because the internal audit manager never questions why each of the tasks needs to be completed a second time. Many of the audit procedures noted in the workpapers may have been intended to be one-time reviews to investigate perceived problems that have since been overcome with new control systems, rendering the original audit steps no longer valid. Given this constant tendency to copy previous audits, a non-essential audit step may have been repeated dozens of times, simply on the grounds that if it was done before, it should be done again.

A better approach is to conduct a brief, formal review of the upcoming internal audit with the internal audit team assigned to do the work. This group should review the results of the last internal audit, pore over the control chart (if any) for the area to be reviewed, and come up with a new audit plan for every engagement. By doing so, the team avoids the mindless repetition of early audit steps that are no longer valid, and concentrates on the key issues that will result in the most valuable audit results. Also, by including the entire audit team in this review, a company will find that there is much better buy-in to and understanding of the work being done, which may increase both employee efficiency and reduce long-term turnover in the internal audit staff.

COMPLETE ALL INTERNAL AUDIT WORKPAPERS IN THE FIELD

The objective of an internal audit is to complete a report that describes any control issues found. However, one would think that, from the perspective of the internal audit team, the objective is to move on to the next internal audit as quickly as possible. There is a preference by internal auditors to continually meet the upcoming schedule to work on the next audit, rather than to complete the one currently being conducted. This results in a long trail of incomplete audits that requires constant badgering by senior management to have completed, frequently requiring weekend work by the internal audit teams. To avoid this problem, the standard procedure for all internal audits should be that the workpapers should be fully completed in the field before an internal audit team is allowed back to the main office or to proceed to the next audit. If this results in delays in the completion of subsequent internal audits, then fine—it will also yield much more rapid completion of the final audit reports, which was the objective when the audits were scheduled. This point can be made to the audit teams more forcefully by even issuing a small bonus for all the internal audits that are wrapped up in the field.

CONSOLIDATE ALL ACCOUNTING FUNCTIONS

A company with many locations will frequently have a separate accounting staff in each location. By doing so, the overall cost of accounting tends to be much higher than the industry average because there is a great deal of staff duplication. For example, each location requires its own controller, assistant controller, and accounting manager. Also, transaction volumes may not be great enough to fill the time of the accounting staff in each location, leading to underutilized personnel. Also, the quality of management may vary significantly between locations, resulting in differences in the level of efficiency, with locations experiencing the same transaction volume requiring significantly different volumes in the number of required accounting staff. Further, with accounting conducted in many locations, a well-run company must schedule a large number of internal audits in all of those locations to ensure that procedures are completed in accordance with corporate standards. Finally, extra labor is needed at corporate headquarters to consolidate all of the accounting records for financial reporting purposes. This formidable array of inefficiencies results in a significant increase in accounting expenses.

The best practice that resolves this tangled web of accounting problems is to consolidate all or most of the functions into the smallest possible number of locations. By doing so, fewer accounting managers are needed, while procedures can be standardized and enforced much more easily. Also, given the smaller number of locations, the work of consolidating financial results is much easier. The only case in which this solution does not work well is if a company has an extremely diversified set of subsidiaries. For example, the accounting operations of a railroad, an oil refinery, and a cement plant are so different that consolidating these functions would be extremely difficult. Conversely, the consolidation task becomes much easier for those companies who do business in a single industry and just have many locations that conduct the same kind of business using approximately the same procedures.

Here are the most common areas in which companies have had success in centralizing into shared services centers:

- Accounts receivable collections
- Cash application
- Cost accounting
- Employee expense report processing
- Inter-company accounts payable and receivable processing
- Inventory accounting
- Invoice processing
- Payroll processing

The difficulty with this best practice is that it requires a great deal of management skill and money to consolidate accounting operations. For example, combining the accounts payable functions of many locations requires the construction of a central processing facility, along with the transfer of staff to that location, retraining, the design of new systems, new audit procedures, and the orderly transfer of supplier invoices from many locations to a single one—and in the midst of this massive change, suppliers must still be paid on time so there is no disruption of deliveries to the company from suppliers. Given the size of this task, the major factors needed to ensure success are the appointment of an excellent manager to the consolidation process, the complete support of this project by top management, and sufficient funding to see it through to completion. In addition, given the amount of disruption involved, it would be wise to consolidate only one function at a time so that most activities are not interrupted at the same time. By taking these steps, the odds of successfully finishing a consolidation project are greatly enhanced.

CONTINUALLY REVIEW KEY PROCESS CYCLES

As a general rule, any system will begin to degrade as soon as it is created. For example, a new purchasing process cycle will begin almost immediately to encounter exceptions to the rules as well as special situations that spawn a subset of extra procedures which do not appear anywhere in the procedures manual. Further, the process will not be maintained very well, resulting in lots of excess data in the system, such as the records of suppliers who have not been used in years, perpetually open purchase orders, even though the orders were filled long ago, and supplier invoices that have a permanent "hold" slapped on them so that they cannot be paid. The example is only for accounts payable, but the same problem applies to all processes. Thus, over time, all of an accounting department's processes will be in desperate need of a tune-up.

That tune-up is provided by a rarely used best practice in which a designated employee is in charge of constantly reviewing process cycles. In some companies, this person is called the "process owner," with responsibility for the flow of information through a specific process and for any changes to it. When someone is assigned to review process cycles, there should be a very detailed set of tasks to be reviewed. To use the previous example, the process owner should review the list of suppliers in the computer to see who can be deleted, check on open purchase orders to see what can be closed, review the list of suppliers with early payment discounts to verify that discounts are taken, check with the receiving staff to make sure that they receive only goods labeled with valid purchase order numbers, and review payment packets to verify that all payments were only for items authorized by the purchasing department. If the process is large enough, one or more people may be assigned to it—otherwise, one person may be assigned multiple cycles and rotate through a review of them all so all primary cycles receive a tune-up several times a year.

One advantage of constantly reviewing process cycles is that few exception transactions will occur, resulting in far less research work to correct problems. Another factor is that employees who are involved in creating transactions will receive constant advice from the process owner regarding how they are supposed to be conducting their work, resulting in much better standardization of output. Further, the process owner constantly reviews why old transactions have not yet been completed, tracks down the reasons for the problems, and corrects them at the source. None of these changes are major, but when taken as a whole, they represent a considerable improvement in the way a company's key processes operate. This work is well worth the effort.

The main disadvantage of this best practice is that the process owner is a new position and adds to overhead. However, the number of mistakes this person finds and corrects will frequently pay back his or her salary. For example, finding and fixing a hole in the revenue cycle that lets shipments disappear from the system may keep a company from missing billings to customers. Similarly, keeping the accounts payable staff from making unapproved payments to suppliers will also save money. Another problem is that this position tends to step outside the boundaries of the accounting department since the processes being reviewed are impacted by other departments, such as the shipping and receiving departments and the purchasing department. Because this may be looked on as interference by the accounting department, a process owner must be a very tactful person and strongly supported by upper management. If these issues can be overcome, the process owner becomes a major contributor to the smooth functioning of any company.

CREATE A CONTRACT TERMS DATABASE

It is a common occurrence for the accounting department to forget about the terms of various agreements other departments of a company entered into, resulting in missed billings to customers or payments to suppliers. Due to the special nature of these agreements, which usually fall outside of the usual accounts payable and receivable systems, it is easy for them to be forgotten. Examples of these contracts are billings for the sub-lease of company equipment, rebates, and maintenance agreements. The typical result of these problems is either missing revenue, because customers were not billed, or irate suppliers who were not paid. In the latter case, missing payments to suppliers may also result in the failure of key services to the company, such as failed maintenance agreements for key equipment. Thus, a lack of attention to the terms of a company's various contractual arrangements can result in lost revenues or services.

The solution to this problem is to create a database of all current contractual agreements, along with a central file containing copies of all the contracts. An example of a contract terms database is shown in Exhibit 13.2. This database lists all of the key information about each contract, including the due date on which billings or payments are supposed to occur, the termination date of the contract, the frequency with which activities are required, the amounts involved, and any extra details to clarify the nature of each transaction—in short, a brief but thorough summarization of all the activities needed to fulfill the terms of all contracts. In case there are questions about the terms of each agreement, the accounting department should maintain copies of all agreements, as well as an extra file containing any agreements which have expired in the last few years. This arrangement will quickly bring order to the administration of any contracts which are the responsibility of the accounting department.

CREATE AN ON-GOING TRAINING PROGRAM
FOR ALL ACCOUNTING PERSONNEL

The efficiency and effectiveness of an accounting department are based on many factors, but a crucial one all too many controllers ignore is training. Many accounting managers simply assume that their staffs have acquired all the knowledge they need in college and in subsequent work experience and need no further training of any kind. This belief is based on the erroneous assumption that all accounting practices are the same, no matter where accountants work, and

Exhibit 13.2.   Sample Contract Terms Database: ABC Company
Agreements Summary

Due Date	Termination Date	Frequency	Amount	Name	Details
Last Day	7/31/03	Monthly	$90	Smith, Joseph	Lease on Pickup Truck
Mid-Aug.	Ongoing	Annual	$.01 per lb.	English Polymers	Rebate of $.01 for Every Pound Purchased in Previous 12-Month Period
After Mtg.	Ongoing	Quarterly	$250	Board of Advisors	Advisory Fee Paid to These People Immediately After Each advisory meeting
End of Quarter	2012	Quarterly	$12,500	Limited Partner	$50,000 pd. in Quarterly Installments, But Not to Exceed 10% of Pretax Income (Less Cost of Health Insurance) + Out-of-Pocket Expenses
None	7/15/01	Quarterly	Varies	Frontage Plastics	5% of 1st Year Sales Generated by FP Accounts, 5% of 2nd Yr. Sales, 3% of 3rd yr. Sales, Max Pay of $250,000
None	8/31/01	Annual	$980	E-Net Cellular	Service Plan for Portable Phones
None	6/30/02	Annual	$80	Dept. of Agriculture	License Fee for Scales 1 × 2,001 lb. 12 × 50 lb. Scales
None	5/31/03	Annual	$2,700	Masterson	Annual Extended Warranty
None	5/20/01	Annual	N/A	E Prime	5% Reduction in Natural Gas Prices
None	4/1/99	Annual	$2,208	NowComm	Phone Maintenance
None	10/1/00	Monthly	$1,248	Rogers Mechanical	Building Preventive Maintenance
None	9/30/07	Monthly	$1,000	Single Source	Bill Them for Monthly Lease of Space
None	None	Quarterly	$202	Pitney Bowes	Lease on Postage Machine

(continues)

Exhibit 13.2. Continued

Due Date	Termination Date	Frequency	Amount	Name	Details
None	None	Semi-Annual	$150	Overhead Door	Overhead Door Maintenance
None	None	Monthly	$1,150	Local Janitorial	Daily Janitorial Services
None	10/24/00	Monthly	$265	Forklift Specialists	Maintenance on 3 Fork-lifts
None	4/30/00	Monthly	$29,339	Dean, Struthers, Markson	Building Lease

employees can be neatly swapped between jobs and companies with no additional training of any kind. Over the long term, this can have a major impact on the accounting staff, for the following reasons:

- *Accounting rule changes.* The accounting profession is constantly reviewing changes in how accounting transactions are completed and reported, resulting in a multitude of rule changes, especially in the area of financial reporting. Anyone who has not received formal training in these changes within the past few years must receive training in all rules updates, while those not having been trained in a decade or more will require comprehensive retraining.

- *Computer-specific knowledge.* There are many accounting software packages in use, all with their own quirks and foibles. Each of these packages requires special training before employees will fully comprehend how to use them most effectively, as well as (perhaps more importantly) what *not* to do, since some systems require expert usage to run properly.

- *Lack of management training.* Accounting is not just clerical—it requires an excellent knowledge of how to manage processes in a multitude of functional areas, frequently including employees in outlying locations. Without proper management training, there will almost certainly be gross inefficiencies and errors in the department.

- *Lack of process training.* The accounting function, above all others, deals with processes, such as the revenue cycle or the purchasing cycle. All employees in this department must have a clear knowledge of exactly how these processes work so they can process information through them most efficiently, as well as make modifications that will further increase the level of efficiency. Though some of this knowledge can be gleaned through many years of experience, it is best to cut short this interval through a training program that imparts both the fundamentals and the detailed steps involved in all key company processes.

- *Lack of training for advanced positions.* Though employees may be adequately trained in their existing jobs, this does not mean that they are in any way prepared to take over positions higher in the accounting hierarchy. Without the necessary training to prepare them for these positions, employees may become frustrated and leave for other companies willing to provide the training for more advanced and higher-paying jobs.

- *Practices that are industry-specific.* Many industries have accounting practices that are completely unique. An example of this is the gambling industry, which has an extreme orientation toward the collection, handling, and recording of cash coming from the gambling floor. In these industries, it is dangerous to bring in people from other industries without first giving them a sufficient degree of training in industry-specific accounting practices.

The types of training classes administered may vary considerably from the rote accounting topics that are covered in a traditional business college. For example, Allied-Signal includes the following topics in its accounting and finance curriculum:

- Accounting for business combinations
- Activity-based management
- Business controls
- Cash-flow management
- Coaching and career management
- Controllership
- Diversity
- E-commerce
- Financial planning and analysis
- Global finance
- Management accounting
- Mergers and acquisitions
- Six sigma
- Supply-chain management
- Taxation
- Revenue-chain management

All of these reasons sum up strongly in favor of a detailed and prolonged training program for the entire accounting department covering such areas as software, processes, new pronouncements by the Financial Accounting Standards Board (FASB), industry-specific issues, and general management training.

The best way to set up a training program is to make a list of all positions in the accounting department and determine the training strengths and weaknesses of every person occupying those positions. Then a master list of all possible training must be assembled, with the required training for each person noted on the master list. An example of such a list is shown in Exhibit 13.3, which lists the training program for a variety of software modules in an accounting software package. It is also useful to maintain a list of credit hours for continuing professional education, in case employees want to pursue or maintain professional accreditation.

The main problem with training programs is that employees usually must be forced to complete their scheduled training, since they find that there is not enough time in the midst of their other activities to fit it in. To avoid this issue, the controller should schedule a monthly review of completed training to ensure that all employees are meeting their training goals. Also, one should incorporate training goals into the targets that employees must meet each year in order to be given pay raises or bonuses. Further, the internal audit staff may also schedule an occasional review of all training records to ensure that employees are indeed completing their training work and not falsely reporting training hours that never happened. When combined, all of these measures will ensure a thorough and comprehensive training program that will improve employee knowledge, especially in regard to improving and managing systems, while also reducing the risk of employee turnover.

CREATE AN ON-LINE INTERNAL AUDIT LIBRARY

An internal audit team will go on most audit engagements without a great deal of company expertise to back them up. If they encounter an unusual problem in the field, they have no one to turn to for advice. Similarly, if they encounter a control problem, they have no way of knowing if it is an isolated issue, or if it has been uncovered in other places within the company. These problems can be reduced by setting up an on-line internal audit library that contains records from previous completed audits, as well as who worked on them, and how they can be accessed. Further, the library can hold updates on all of the most recent accounting standards, as well as cross-indexed data on problems or unusual audit scenarios encountered during other company audits. By accessing this information, audit teams can save a great deal of research time that would otherwise be spent combing through the company directory or the paper-based audit files to find the same information.

Setting up such a system requires each internal audit manager to create an electronic summary-level report on each audit as it is completed, which is then forwarded to the company web master for inclusion in the library. Also (and involving much more time), staff must be assigned to the same task for all previous audits for at least the past few years, and preferably for at least the last five (in order to build up a reasonable base of information). This can be a substantial

Accounting Department Training

[Lists dates of completion for modules with 80+% scores]

	Abdullah, B.	Bronson, C.	Cavez, T.	Dingle, D.
General Ledger Account Structure				
Maintaining a chart of accounts	8/1/00			6/15/99
Entering a new organization	8/1/00			
Maintaining account groups	8/1/00		6/30/99	6/15/99
Using organization groups	8/1/00		6/30/99	
Setting up the bank master	8/1/00		6/30/99	
General Ledger Transaction Processing				
Entering new journal entries		12/12/99		
Changing existing journal entries		12/12/99		
Creating journal entry template		12/12/99		
Using journal entry template		12/12/99		5/29/99
Creating recurring journal entries		12/12/99		
Deleting a journal entry		12/12/99		
Approving batches		12/12/99		
Posting batches to journal entries		12/12/99		
Using statistical journal entries				
Period close	5/31/99			5/29/99
Budgeting				
Budget definitions	11/30/99			
Updating a budget	11/30/99			
Printing a budget	11/30/99			
Copying a budget	11/30/99			
Product costing				
Establishing item standard costs				8/31/99
Establishing standard costs for assemblies				8/31/99
Inquiry screens				8/31/99
Accumulating order costs with average actual costing				8/31/99
Managing order costs with average actual costing		3/1/00		8/31/99
Managing mfg. order costs using standard costing		3/1/00		8/31/99
Managing purchase order costs with standard costing		3/1/00		8/31/99
Inventory value reporting		3/1/00		8/31/99
Accounts Payable Invoice Entry				
Entering an invoice			4/7/00	
Matching an invoice to a PO receipt			4/7/00	
Entering an invoice not associated with a PO			4/7/00	
Tools to use for vendor inquiries			4/7/00	
Approving an invoice for payment			4/7/00	
Placing an invoice on hold			4/7/00	
Taking vendor discounts			4/7/00	
Miscellaneous disbursements			4/7/00	
Accounts Payable Processing				
Setting up a payment run			4/9/00	
Recording a manual payment			4/9/00	
Voiding a payment			4/9/00	
Tools to use in a bank reconciliation			4/9/00	

Exhibit 13.3. Sample Master Training Schedule

effort. Finally, accounting standards can be easily obtained from various CD-based products for posting on the on-line library. Be sure to obtain an accounting standards product that contains an index search capability, so that users can easily search for items of particular interest.

CREATE AN ON-LINE TAX POLICY LISTING

The accounting staff does not always have a clear grasp of the tax implications of various accounting transactions. Examples of these problem areas are transfer pricing, capital movements, and employee contracts and benefits. When a question arises in regard to such a problem, either it is put on hold while a question is run past the legal or tax staffs, or else it is processed in ignorance of the answer—which frequently leads to a lack of consistency in the handling of transactions, and a large headache for the tax staff. These problems can be avoided by installing a clear set of tax policies on-line.

By itemizing the most current tax policies on-line, anyone in the accounting department can readily research problems and expect to find answers within a few minutes of a tax-related question being posed. If the answer is not there, then the site can also include an e-mail linkage to the tax or legal department, so that the problem can then be properly researched and posted on-line for the next person who has the same problem. Also, because the posting is on-line, there is no need to issue a cumbersome mailing to a list of approved recipients every time a change is made to the policies—instead, the change can be readily made to the on-line posting, which makes it available to anyone at once. There will be complex transactional situations that are so unique that only the advice of a trained tax person will yield the correct answer to a query. Nonetheless, the majority of tax problems can be resolved for the accounting staff by this simple means.

CREATE A POLICY AND PROCEDURE MANUAL

As is noted several times in this chapter, an unorganized accounting department is inefficient, suffers from a high transaction error rate, and does not complete its work products on time. While other best practices noted in this chapter, such as general training, cross-training, and calendars of events will contribute to a more structured environment, one of the very best ways to create a disciplined accounting group is to create and maintain a policies and procedures manual.

This manual should list the main policies under which the accounting department operates, such as those listed in Exhibit 13.4. These are the key issues that confront each functional area and are usually limited to just a few pages. Anything longer probably indicates an excessive degree of control or some confusion in the difference between a policy and a procedure.

A good example of a policy is one that sets a boundary for an activity. The first policy noted in Exhibit 13.4 states that an accounts payable clerk is allowed to process any supplier invoice within 5 percent of the amount listed on the original purchase order. By doing so, this policy clearly defines what the clerk is allowed to do. A procedure, on the other hand, defines the precise activities that take place within the boundaries the policies create. An example of a procedure is

Exhibit 13.4.   Sample Policies Page

Accounts Payable:
- Any supplier invoice within five percent of the price indicated on the buyer's purchase order requires no additional authorization to pay.

Document Archival:
- Use the following format to determine when to dispose of old records:

Type of Record	Retention
Accounts Payable Ledgers/Schedules	7 Years
Advertisement for a Job Opening	1 Year
Capital Stock Records	Permanent
Checks (Canceled)	7 Years
Deeds, Mortgages, Bills of Sale	Permanent
Earnings Per Week	3 Years
Financial Statements	Permanent
General Ledgers (Year-End)	Permanent
Hiring Records	1 Year from Date Record Made or Personnel Action Taken, Whichever Is Later
Insurance/Pension/Retirement Plans	1 Year after Termination
Invoices to Customers	7 Years
Minute Books, including Bylaws and Charter	Permanent
Payroll Records—employment data	3 Years from Termination
Physical/Medical Examinations	Duration of Employment, plus 30 Years
Property Records	Permanent
Sales and Purchase Records	3 Years
Stock and Bond Certificates (Canceled)	7 Years
Subsidiary Ledgers	7 Years
Tax Returns	Permanent
Time Cards	3 Years

Fixed Assets:
- The minimum dollar amount above which expenses are capitalized is $2,000.
- Any member of the Management Committee can approve an expenditure for amounts of $5,000 or less if the item was already listed in the annual budget.

(continues)

Exhibit 13.4. Continued

- Any capital expenditure exceeding $5,000 requires the approval of the President, plus all expenditures not already listed in the annual budget, regardless of the amount.
- Every molding machine shall be assigned a salvage value of 25 percent of the purchase price.

Logistics:
- Any items arriving at the receiving dock without a purchase order number will be rejected.

Travel and Entertainment:
- All reimbursements require a receipt.
- Must show all receipts for travel advances within one week of travel, or the advance will be considered a salary advance.
- Only coach fares will be reimbursed.
- There is no movie reimbursement.
- There is no reimbursement for commuting miles.
- There is no reimbursement for lunch mileage.

shown in Exhibit 13.5, where there is a definitive listing of the exact steps one must follow in order to create and issue the annual budget. A procedure is usually sufficient to use as a guideline for an employee who needs to understand how a process works. When combined with a proper level of training, the policies and procedures manual is an effective way not only to increase control over the accounting department, but also to enhance its efficiency.

Though there are few excuses for not having such a manual, there are some pitfalls to consider when constructing it, as well as for maintaining and enforcing it. They are as follows:

- *Not enough detail.* A procedure that does not cover activity steps in a sufficient degree of detail is not of much use to someone who is using it for the first time; it is important to list specific forms used, computer screens accessed, and fields on those screens in which information is entered, as well as the other positions that either supply information for the procedure or to which it sends information. It may also be helpful to include a flowchart, which is more understandable than text for some people.
- *Not reinforced.* A procedures manual does not do much good if it is immediately parked on a remote shelf in the accounting department. Instead, it should be made an integral part of all training programs and included in peri-

Exhibit 13.5. Sample Procedure Page

Procedure: Update the annual budget
Responsibility: Controller
Steps:

1. *Expense update.* **As of mid-November,** issue each department a listing of its expenses, annualized based on actual expenses through October of the current year. The listing should include the personnel in each department and their current pay levels. Request a return date of 10 days in the future for this information, which should include estimated changes in expenses.

2. *Revenue update.* **As of mid-November,** issue the sales manager a listing of revenue by month by business unit, through October of the current year. Request a return date of 10 days in the future for this information, which should include estimated changes in revenues.

3. *Capital expenditure update.* **As of mid-November,** issue a form to all department heads, requesting information about the cost and timing of capital expenditures for the upcoming year. Request a return date of 10 days in the future for this information.

4. *Automation update.* **As of mid-November,** issue a form to the engineering manager, requesting estimates of the timing and size of reductions in headcount in the upcoming year due to automation efforts. Request a return date of 10 days in the future for this information. Be sure to compare scheduled headcount reductions to the timing of capital expenditures, since they should track closely.

5. *Update the budget model.* **This task should be completed by the end of November,** and includes the following steps:

   • Update the numbers already listed in the budget with information received from the various managers. This may involve changing "hard-coded" dollar amounts or changing flex budget percentages. Be sure to keep a checklist of who has returned information so you can follow up with those personnel who have not returned it.

   • Update the "Prior Year" cells on the left side of the budget model with estimated year-end balances (primarily for the balance sheet).

   • Update the "Last Year" cells on the right side of the budget model, using annualized figures.

   • Verify that the indirect overhead allocation percentages shown on the budgeted factory overhead page are still accurate.

   • Verify that the Federal Insurance Contributors Act (FICA), State Unemployment Tax (SUTA), Federal Unemployment Tax (FUTA), medical, and workers' compensation amounts listed at the top of the staffing budget page are still accurate.

(continues)

Exhibit 13.5. Continued

- Add job titles and pay levels to the staffing page as needed, along with new average pay rates based on projected pay levels made by department managers.

- Run a depreciation report for the upcoming year, add the expected depreciation for new capital expenditures, and add this amount to the budget.

- Revise the loan detail budget based on projected borrowings through the end of the year. Be sure to list only loan balance reductions based on principal pay-downs, not interest payments.

6. *Review the budget.* Print out the budget and circle any budgeted expenses or revenues that are significantly different from the annualized amounts for the current year (do this by comparing the last two columns on each page). Go over the questionable items with the managers who are responsible for them.

7. *Revise the budget.* Revise the budget, print it again, and review it with the president. Incorporate any additional changes.

8. *Issue the budget.* Bind the budget and issue it to the management team.

9. *Update accounting database.* Enter budget numbers into the accounting software for the upcoming year. **All tasks should be completed by mid-December.**

---

odic discussions regarding the updating and improvement of key processes. Only through constant attention will the manual be used to the fullest extent.

- *Not updated.* Even the best manual will become obsolete over time, as changing circumstances alter procedures to the point where the manual no longer describes conditions as they currently exist. When this happens, no one bothers to use the manual. Accordingly, it is necessary to update the manual whenever changes are made to the underlying systems.

- *Too many procedures.* A common problem is that the manual is never released because the controller is determined to include a procedure for every conceivable activity the accounting department will ever encounter. However, the main principle to follow is that the manual must be issued soon, so it is better to issue it quickly with procedures that cover the bulk of accounting activities and address the remaining procedures at a later date. This approach gets the key information to those employees who need it the most, and does so very quickly.

The single most important factor in the success of a policies and procedures manual is an active accounting manager. This person must reinforce the use of the manual with the staff so it is not simply ignored as a one-time report gathering dust on a shelf. Only through continual attention by the entire staff will it become the foundation of how all key accounting processes are completed.

CREATE COMPUTER-BASED TRAINING MOVIES

There are several major problems with any in-house training program. It must be carefully scheduled so that the maximum number of people can attend (which means that some people will *not* be able to attend, or at least will be seriously inconvenienced). Also, an expensive trainer and training facility must be used. Furthermore, people must travel to the training site for classes, which may entail great expense. All of these problems can be avoided through the use of computer-based training movies.

A computer-based training movie is one that replicates on-screen the actions of someone who is walking through a standard set of activities, while explaining each action through a microphone. The resulting movie will show a user exactly what is being done to process a transaction (or some other activity) while the accompanying voice recording explains what is going on. Just as is the case with a movie that is inserted into a video cassette recorder, this movie format contains on-screen buttons for rewind, pause, play, and fast forward. Each movie is easily created—just plot out the steps to be followed during the movie, practice them a few times, and then press the "record" button and start recording the movie. The audio portion of the movie can be added concurrently, or at a later time.

By storing computer-based training movies at a central intranet location, a company can make it available to all employees at all company locations. Employees can download it at their leisure, and review those portions about which they are uncertain. When training movies are made for a wide range of company functions, they can be set up in an index format on the intranet site, so that an entire training program can be made available to employees on a wide range of topics. The only problems with computer based movies are that they take up a large amount of computer storage space, and that all accessing computers require audio cards and speakers. However, these are minor cost issues.

The software that is currently available for making computer-based movies includes ScreenCam by Lotus (*www.lotus.com*), HyperCam by Hyperionics (*www.hyperionics.com*), Camtasia™ Recorder and Producer by TechSmith® (*www.techsmith.com*), and CameraMan™ by Motion Works (*www.mwg.com*). Even the most expensive of these packages costs only $150

IMPLEMENT CROSS-TRAINING FOR MISSION-CRITICAL ACTIVITIES

There are a number of crucial accounting activities that will cause a significant amount of disturbance within a company if they are not completed on time, every time. Examples of these activities are payroll, since employees will refuse to work unless they are paid, and accounts payable, for suppliers will refuse to provide additional goods and services unless *they* are paid. In these cases and others, the greatest risk is that only one person knows how to process transactions. If that person leaves the company or is incapacitated for any reason, there can be a serious system failure that will quickly bring the entire company to a grinding halt.

The best way to avoid this dependency on a single person is to implement cross-training, using other accounting employees. By doing so, there is far less risk that mission-critical activities will not be performed in a reliable manner, which greatly reduces the chance that any key activity will not be completed on time. To do so, there should be a schedule of key activities for which there is a listing of required training elements. The controller should identify those personnel who are most qualified to act as back-ups, put them through the training regimen, and ensure that they receive continual retraining, so they can easily step into the needed jobs. A small pay hike for those employees receiving cross-training will ensure their enthusiastic participation in this system. The key factor to remember is that training alone does not make for a good back-up person—only continual hands-on practice under the direct tutelage of the person who is currently responsible for the work will ensure that this best practice will work.

The only people who ever oppose this practice are those who are currently in charge of mission-critical functions. This is because they feel more valuable if they are the only ones who can complete a task and will feel less useful if there is someone else who can also do the same work. To overcome this problem requires a great deal of tact and diplomacy. Sometimes they continue to be hostile to the concept and must be removed to other positions while their replacements figure out the system without any support at all. These are difficult alternatives, but must be followed through if there is to be an adequate degree of cross-training in key functional areas.

IMPLEMENT PROCESS-CENTERING

A major problem at many companies is the inordinate amount of time it takes to complete a process. For example, insurance companies are famous for spending many weeks to review an insurance claim and issue a payment check, when the total amount of work required is under an hour. The long time period from the beginning to the end of the process is usually due to the number of transfers between employees. For example, the insurance branch office may forward a claim to an insurance adjuster, who passes it along to a manager if the amount exceeds a set level, or who hands it off to another person who checks to see if the claim may be fraudulent or if the claimant has an unusually long history of claims, then moves the paperwork to another person who issues checks, and then returns the entire packet to the insurance branch office. Insurance is just an example—upon further investigation, it is common to find that all companies invest a shocking amount of time in moving paperwork between a multitude of employees. A related problem is that transactions can be lost when they are moved between employees. Further, it is difficult to pin blame on anyone when a transaction is improperly completed because there are so many people involved in the process. Thus, spreading work among too many people opens a virtual Pandora's box of troubles.

The best practice that resolves this problem is called process-centering. Its underlying principle is to cluster as many work tasks for a single process as possible with a single person. By doing so, there are fewer transfers of documentation, which reduces the amount of time lost during these movements, while at the same time eliminating the risk that paperwork will be lost. Further, employees have much more complete and fulfilling jobs since they see a much larger part of the process and have a better feeling for how the entire process works. And best of all for a company, the time needed to complete transactions drops drastically, sometimes to less than 10 percent of the amount previously needed.

The main problem with process-centering is employee resistance. This is a *re-engineering* best practice, which means that the old process is ripped up and replaced with an entirely new workflow, which makes many employees nervous about their jobs, or if they will even have a job when the changes are complete. Accordingly, they are usually not pleased with the prospect of a new system and resist vigorously, or at least will not be of any assistance. Only excellent communications and a strong commitment by top management to completing the project will make this best practice operational, given the likely level of resistance to it.

ISSUE ACTIVITY CALENDARS TO ALL ACCOUNTING POSITIONS

The bane of any accounting department is disorganization. This department, above all others, is responsible for consistently completing the same tasks, day after day and year after year, with a great deal of reliability. If the employees cannot organize themselves properly so key tasks are completed on time, the entire function can fall into disarray, resulting in payments and billings not being completed on time. Also, financial statements, the most subject to delays if there is disorganization, will be released much later than expected, possibly containing a large number of errors. Clearly, some instrument of organization must be found.

An excellent tool for straightening out the timing of accounting work is the calendar. One can create a calendar on the computer, either with a scheduling software package or an electronic spreadsheet, and load it with all of the tasks that must be completed each day. An example of such a calendar is shown in Exhibit 13.6. Though some employees are naturally well-organized and will already have it in place, many others will be in desperate need of this simple organizational tool. The best way to distribute these calendar schedules is to keep the schedules for all employees in a single location, update them at the end of each month, and have a staff meeting to distribute them so the controller can emphasize all calendar changes. It is then a simple matter to refer to copies of all employees' calendars each day and follow up with them to ensure that they are completing the scheduled tasks.

The calendar is only one way to assist in managing the operations of the accounting department. Another excellent tool is the policy and procedure manual, which was discussed earlier in this chapter, in the "Create a Policy and Procedure Manual" section.

Monthly Calendar						
Sunday	Monday	Tuesday	Wednesday	Thursday	Friday	Saturday
		1 Issue Prior-Month Sales Figures	2 Review Receivables	3 Annual Review with A. Smith	4 Managers Meeting Back up Computers	5
	Measurements					
6	7 Measurements Issue Financial Statements	8 Review Accounting Expenses	9 Review Receivables	10 Pizza Party	11 Managers Meeting Back up Computers	12
13	14 Measurements	15 Review Bad Debts	16 Review Receivables	17 Review Procedures	18 Managers Meeting Back up Computers	19
20	21 Measurements	22 Meet with Outsourcing Consultants	23 Review Receivables	24 Meet with Auditors	25 Managers Meeting Back up Computers	26
27	28 Measurements	29 Annual Review with J. Doctorow	30 Review Receivables	31 Go over Tasks for Issuing Next Months' Financial Statements		

Exhibit 13.6. Sample Monthly Activities Calendar

OUTSOURCE TAX FORM PREPARATION

For smaller firms, the accurate and timely preparation of tax forms is a monumental pain that frequently results in missed filing dates, incorrect payments, and penalties. The reason is that a smaller organization cannot afford the services of a full-time tax accountant, which means that incoming tax forms are routed to whomever has time to complete them. No one likes to do tax forms and so they end up at the bottom of someone's work pile, which results in a last-minute rush to complete them without much regard to accuracy or filing dates. Larger organizations do not have this problem, since they have specialists on staff who can organize a steady stream of tax work resulting in accurate tax filings mailed out precisely on time which are supported by fully documented work papers that can be easily audited. Thus, the controller of a small company needs to find a better way to prepare tax forms.

The solution is to outsource the bulk of the tax filings to one or more suppliers, usually with a few tax returns remaining in-house. A common situation is for a company's audit firm to take over all federal and state income tax returns. These are among the most complex returns to file and these are precisely the forms that most audit firms specialize in filing. In addition, many companies outsource their payroll so the payroll-processing suppliers will handle all of the tax return information related to payroll. This leaves local returns, which are best kept in-house—the reason is that these documents are usually so specialized that suppliers do not have any experience in filing them and so are no more efficient (and much more expensive) than the accounting employees who can do the same work. Thus, there are opportunities to divest an accounting department of the majority of its tax form preparation work.

There are two factors to consider when outsourcing tax work. One is that some suppliers will charge an inordinate amount to prepare a tax return. To avoid this problem, it is wise to first inquire about the hourly rates of the supplier's staff who are most likely to prepare taxes and the likely time required to complete each return. If the expected amount is too high, it may be useful to comparison shop against the rates of other tax preparation firms. It may also be possible to institute a fixed fee for each tax return, thereby capping the expense. The other problem is that there is some inefficiency in separating the tax filing work from the outside auditors a company already uses. The reason is that the auditor must copy the workpapers and send them to the tax supplier, which is not only an extra expense, but also slower than leaving all of the work with the auditor. Despite these problems, it is a very good idea for a smaller firm to outsource the preparation of its tax returns.

OUTSOURCE THE INTERNAL AUDIT FUNCTION

Some organizations have their internal audit function report to the controller or chief financial officer. In these situations, the manager of the accounting function has the additional burden of selecting auditing targets, planning for audit teams to review them, managing the teams, and acting on their findings. For a larger organization, this management work can be a considerable additional burden, for there may be many auditors.

Though it is not possible to completely eliminate all management of the internal audit function, a controller or chief financial officer can outsource the function, which removes selected management tasks. For example, giving all internal audit work to an outside supplier keeps a manager from having to plan each audit or review the teams as they conduct their work. It still leaves a manager with selecting audit targets and acting on the results of audits, but at least some activities have been eliminated. Using an outside auditor carries with it the additional advantage of reduced travel time to outlying company locations, since an audit firm with many locations can assign local staff to each company facility. Further, outside auditors do not have to be paid if they are not working on company-specific projects, nor does a company have to pay for their ongoing training. These advantages have pushed a number of companies into the arms of outside auditors.

However, there are problems with this best practice that have raised some ire in the ranks of internal auditors. One issue is that many companies use their internal auditing departments to groom new managers for senior-level positions. This is an excellent approach, for not only does it give auditors a wide-ranging view of company operations, but it also allows the managers of functions being audited to see them and to provide feedback to the human resources department regarding the wisdom of promoting them to more senior positions. Another problem is that outside auditors will sometimes assign junior staff personnel to internal audits, which allows them to charge less per hour. However, these junior personnel frequently have less experience than the internal auditors and also have no experience with specific details of company operations, making them doubly inefficient. Consequently, one must weigh the advantages and disadvantages of this approach closely before handing over the internal audit department to a supplier.

POST THE POLICIES AND PROCEDURES MANUAL ON THE COMPANY INTRANET SITE

When the accounting staff is widely scattered through many locations, it is difficult to make available to them a current version of the accounting policies and procedures manual. This can be a real problem, for the accounting department is much more procedurally driven than any other department, and operating with antiquated procedures can cause significant differences in operations between various locations. Traditionally, this problem has been addressed by creating an internal procedure-writing and publishing department that constantly updates documents, maintains a list of authorized recipients, and mails the changed documents to them. This group is expensive, and does not always result in updated manuals at outlying locations, especially if those outlying personnel take a dim view of spending their valuable time replacing pages in their procedures manuals.

A significant improvement on this method is to convert each page of the manual into an HTML or Adobe Acrobat format, so that it can be posted directly to the corporate intranet site. By doing so, there is no need to publish and distribute any more paper-based documents. In addition, an on-line index can allow users to quickly search through the database to find the exact procedural references they need. In addition, there is no longer a need to gradually compile a lengthy list of procedure changes, and then issue all of the changes at the same time—instead, a procedure writer can quickly make any change and immediately post it to the intranet site. The only problem with this approach is that all accounting personnel must have ready access to the site where the documents are posted. This requires a reasonably advanced level of networking ability within a company.

SCAN DATA WITH MODIFIED PALM COMPUTING PLATFORM

There are a number of applications in which accounting department personnel can scan bar codes that store data about various items, such as personnel, fixed assets, or inventory, and then either compare this information to a central database for accuracy, or input new data to a database that is at least partially comprised of this bar coded data. For example, the accounting staff should verify the existence of all fixed assets in the company at least once a year. To do so, they can scan the bar coded identification tags that are attached to each asset. This task is typically accomplished with a bar code scanner that either transmits the data directly to the central accounting computer, or stores it internally for an upload at a later date. These scanners can be quite expensive. An alternative to this approach has just been developed by Symbol Technologies.

Symbol has developed a variation on the popular Palm computing platform that contains a bar code scanner that can scan and translate nearly all of the major bar code methodologies. The product descriptions can be found on the Internet at *www.symbol.com/palm*. With this product, one can scan and store bar codes in the Palm computer, and then upload this data at the user's leisure into the central accounting database. It is also possible to first download data to the Palm, and then use the scanning option to bring in and compare additional data to the downloaded data. For example, inventory information can be dumped into the Palm, so that the user can take it to the warehouse and scan in product quantities during an inventory count. A program stored in the Palm can then compare the quantities scanned to the inventory information. Any differences can be investigated on the spot.

The initial pricing for these Palm products are in the range of $500 to $700, depending on the amount of RAM added to them. These prices are roughly double the rate at which a Palm computer without the scanning feature can be purchased. The software for these products are still being developed, so it may be easier to purchase developer software from the manufacturer in order to create internal applications. At this time, the main development effort has been made by Stevens Creek Software, which has developed the "On Hand" program that allows one to conduct inventory counts and asset tracking. A similar product, called "Pocket Inventory," has been developed by PC America.

A unique possibility is the ability to create invoices in the field with the Symbol Palm computer. By using either the "Route Accounting Automation" software, written by Remote Data Systems, or else the "Route Salesman 3" software, written by PalmX Route Accounting, one can scan shipping information in the field, such as product codes, prices, and quantities, and create an invoice on the spot for immediate delivery to the customer. This option requires the use of portable printer that can receive information from the infrared port on the Palm computer.

This new device may become a superior tool that supplants the more traditional bar code scanning devices that have been available for many years, because it also includes a miniature computer that results in more computing capability. However, the software needed to link it to one's accounting systems is still in its infancy, and will therefore probably require some degree of customization, if not a complete software writing project, before it can be tightly integrated. Consequently, the effort required to make the Symbol Palm computer a major new accounting tool may be considerable.

SCAN FINGERPRINTS AT USER WORKSTATIONS

Security is always an issue in the accounting department, where the staff is constantly reviewing confidential materials. It is a real problem trying to keep unauthorized personnel from accessing accounting terminals, unless the entire department is to be locked up behind a fence.

A unique new approach to solving the security problem is to use a variety of input devices that scan one's thumbprint or fingerprint and transmits the scan to a central file for verification. If the scanned image matches that of an on-file thumbprint, then the user is allowed access to the terminal.

A scanner mouse, called the "EyeD Mouse™," is available from Secugen Corporation (*www.secugen.com*). The same company also sells a keyboard, called the "EyeD KeyBoard™," that contains a scanner for fingerprints. Yet another option that it sells is the "EyeD Hamster™," which is a separate scanning device that is used by those who do not wish to replace their existing mice or keyboards.

There are a few downsides to the use of this technology. The main one is that some software reconfiguration will be necessary to ensure that selected databases are covered by this security feature. A lesser issue is the cost of the new scanning equipment; prices are roughly double the amount that one would spend on mice or keyboards that do not contain these biometric security features.

SCHEDULE INTERNAL AUDITS BASED ON RISK

The scheduling of various areas within a company for internal audits is usually an arcane process, involving pressure from the audit committee to have a few "pet" areas investigated. Some department managers may demand audit reviews of particular areas, while other managers put forth considerable effort to avoid audits on the grounds that they take up too much staff time. The internal audit manager is caught in the midst of this maelstrom, trying to please everyone while still scheduling audits for those areas in which he or she feels some problems may lurk. A simple way to revise this scheduling process is to base all audits on the concept of risk to the company.

To schedule based on risk, a company must devise a ranking for risk levels, with number one being any potential control problem that could place the company in grave financial danger, while lesser levels of risk can be assigned a lesser category. Then the internal audit manager can assign a risk ranking to each requested audit, while also conducting a review of other control areas to see if there are other areas of risk that are not currently being addressed. The upshot of this process is a clear ranking of audit reviews that is highly defensible, and which will focus the bulk of company audit attention on those few key control processes that are at the most risk of causing financial trouble.

The main issue to be aware of is that the internal audit committee should formally approve of this scheduling process, so that the internal audit manager can use that committee's support when telling other company managers that their requested audits will not occur quite so quickly as they would like.

SELL THE SHARED SERVICES CENTER

Larger corporations have been working for the last decade to centralize their far-flung transaction processing operations, on the grounds that increasing the transaction volume in a single location will reduce the cost per transaction processed. This theory has proven to be true, resulting in the centralization of such functions as accounts receivable, accounts payable, payroll, and cash application. It is even listed earlier in this chapter as a recommended best practice.

As a result of this intense focus on efficiency, many organizations have achieved remarkably low costs per transaction. However, one must ask if the focus of company management should be centered on activities that are generic transactions, or on value-added activities—in short, has the drive toward excellent operations been in the wrong area of the company? If the answer to this question is "yes," then perhaps the next step is to sell the shared services center.

By selling the center to a supplier who specializes in outsourced services, a company can realize a cash gain from the sale for a one-time jump in profits and cash flow, while also writing into the sale agreement a clause that requires the buyer to continue to use the center to provide services to the company for a designated period of time and at pre-specified rates. This approach eliminates the management time invested in the process, continues to result in low transaction costs, and yields a cash payment. Why would a supplier agree to such a deal? Because it gains a large block of business from the seller for a period of years, while also gaining the expertise of the employees running the center. The supplier can then sell the services of this group to other customers, thereby expanding the scope of the shared services business. Consequently, this best practice is one that enhances the position of all involved parties.

SWITCH TO A LIMITED USAGE APPLICATION SERVICE PROVIDER

The last best practice was designed for larger companies that are willing to pay a fairly large monthly subscription fee in exchange for the use of a comprehensive accounting package that is based on the Internet. But what about small organizations with only a limited number of employees that cannot afford such service? There are Internet sites that deal with this type of companies.

A good example is found at *www.openair.com*. This web site offers free access to time sheets and expense reporting functions that are quite useful for the most simplistic accounting operations—and they are free. These features can also be carried over to one's Palm computer, for later uploading to the web site. It also exchanges data with the QuickBooks Pro accounting software. Add-on services, such as the printing and mailing of invoices, as well as payroll calculations, cost extra. This option is particularly useful for those organizations, such as small consulting firms, where the staff is constantly on the move, and wants direct access to a common web site from which they can update information and issue their own invoices. Similar web sites can be found at *www.us.sage.com* and *www.onthegosoftware.com*.

A more expansive view of the applicability of the Internet to this type of solution can be found at *www.eality.com*. This web site provides on-line software applications that employees can use for purchase requisitions, check requests, personnel action notifications, new employee set-up, performance reviews, educational reimbursements, and even such office management applications as office supply provisioning for business cards, credit cards, and equipment. This approach makes available a download to several popular in-house software packages, so that employees located away from the main office can interact directly with the main company administration and accounting databases. If the future direction of business is smaller size and greater employee mobility, then perhaps the number of people utilizing this option will grow in the near future.

SWITCH TO AN APPLICATION SERVICE PROVIDER

The typical accountant has a great deal of training and experience in how to process accounting transactions, but much less in how to select, install, and maintain an accounting software package. Despite this shortcoming, often an accountant will be called on at some time to either fix or maintain an existing accounting software package or select and install a new one. The most common issue of all is the continuing addition of software upgrades, and dealing with the technical issues caused by them. Not far behind is dealing with the problems that arise when a software system crashes. Given the lack of expertise in this area, it is no surprise that many accountants do not show a high degree of competence when this happens, which can have a significant impact on their careers.

Luckily, it is now possible to leave the software problem to someone else through the use of an application service provider (ASP). This is a company that maintains accounting (or other) software on its own computer system, and is responsible for its upkeep and reliability. Users of the ASP's services simply log in to process their transactions, and depart when they are done—leaving all system maintenance worries to the ASP's staff.

This is a particularly fine option for smaller companies that cannot afford the cost of purchasing and implementing their own accounting software and hardware, which can run over $100,000 for even a modest installation. It is also a good alternative for any company that needs to switch to a new system in a hurry, since the existence of a functioning software system eliminates the many implementation steps associated with system installation and testing. Further, any organization that wants to focus its attention on its key strategic values will like this option, since it can use it to avoid investing valuable management time in the oversight of the information systems department.

A good example of the uses to which ASP software can be put is the order entry function. Traditionally, the sales staff mails, calls, or faxes orders to the accounting staff, which then enters this information into the accounting system. This approach results in lost or miskeyed orders, and therefore unhappy customers. However, with an ASP, the sales staff can directly access the order entry system over the Internet and enter their orders directly into it, without worrying about any of the just-noted problems.

There are a few problems with ASPs. One is that they do not want to customize their software for any but the largest customers, since their business model depends on selling the same type of software product to as many companies as possible. This is a particular problem for those companies who have so extensively modified their computer systems for competitive purposes that a change to a more "vanilla" package may seriously jeopardize their profitability. Another issue is that most ASPs do not offer a complete solution that covers the functions of all key areas of a company (as is now the case with enterprise resource planning systems that are installed in-house). At the moment, the most comprehensive software offerings are by Usinternetworking, which has available software for accounting, finance, human resources, sales force automation, and human resources.

Another issue is the security of the company data that is stored at the ASP location. There may be many companies using the software, and there should be no way that anyone from one company can accidentally access the data owned by someone else; these issues should be addressed by a set of security provisions and guarantees that are outlined in a service level agreement (SLA). A final concern is that any stoppage in the Internet connection to an ASP will bring down a company's computer access to its ASP-based software; this will become less of a problem as Internet connections become more reliable.

More than 300 companies offer ASP services. Examples of this group are Oracle Business Online, Asera, Applicast, AristaSoft, Breakaway Solutions, eOnline, Usinternetworking, Corio, Xpedior, and mySAP.com. When deciding on which one to select, a key factor is the range of different software systems offered by each one. If a supplier only maintains software that has limited applicability in a company's field of operations, then a different supplier may be the answer.

SWITCH TO ON-LINE REPORTING

In organizations that occupy a large geographical area, the accounting staff faces the chore of somehow sending financial and operational reporting information to many locations. This can mean a mass mailing once a month, or perhaps more frequently if daily or weekly reports are required. If there is some urgency to this information, overnight express mail delivery may be necessary, which is quite expensive, especially when used many times a year for many locations. Faxing this information is frequently not an allowable option, for the information being transmitted may be so sensitive that there is too great a risk that the wrong person will retrieve the information from the fax machine. Thus, sending paper reports throughout a company, and especially a large one, is a major hassle.

An effective means for eliminating the problems with paper-based reports is to switch to electronic transmission. By doing so, there is no need to send any paper documents and there is also no transmission time interval before the information is available to recipients. The only difficulty with this approach is that a few of the more formal documents, such as audited financial statements, with their accompanying footnotes and graphics, cannot be sent easily by electronic means. However, for the bulk of all reports, this remains an effective approach.

Information can be sent electronically in either a passive or "push" mode. In the passive mode, the accounting department simply posts the information in a file and waits for employees to go to the file to scan the data. The "push" method involves sending information to employees by e-mail. The "push" method is generally more effective, since there is no way for employees to avoid the data, unless they are in the habit of deleting their e-mail without first reading it.

This approach can be an expensive one with a long implementation interval, but only under certain implementation approaches. It is certainly more expensive if a special file structure is created to contain the on-line reports, especially if the data is to be contained in a data warehouse (a *major* undertaking that is not recommended). Even the less difficult approach of sending out reports by e-mail requires the previous installation of a company-wide e-mail system, which can be a problem if there are many locations that must be linked. However, the distribution of data is made vastly easier by the presence of the Internet; any company location can now obtain an e-mail address from a third-party e-mail provider at minimal cost and receive electronic transmissions through this electronic mailbox. Another alternative is to spend a moderate amount on a corporate intranet site, on which financial reports can be posted under an icon. Though an effective and easy-to-use approach, it does require access to the intranet from outlying locations. Consequently, there are a range of implementation alternatives for all possible budgets, starting with distribution by the Internet, progressing through an intranet site, and ending with a custom-made file structure with comprehensive user access. The best approach will depend on a company's budget, existing systems, and information distribution requirements.

TRACK FUNCTION MEASUREMENTS

The role of the accounting department does not just include completing daily transactions and issuing financial statements. In addition, it must issue periodic measurements to the rest of the company that show the results of key activities. A poorly organized accounting department may issue this information only grudg-ingly when senior management demands it and then stop immediately once the complaints cease. This approach does not allow the accounting staff to derive a set of standard procedures for the collection of measurement information, nor does it build up much goodwill with the management team.

A better approach is to create a standardized set of performance criteria that the accounting staff will calculate and distribute at set intervals. An example of such a report is shown in Exhibit 13.7. By using this report, management can spot operational problems at once and correct them. Also, the controller can play a key role in determining which measurements are used; this can be a pivotal item in some situations, for other department managers may not want to have their poor performance measured and reported. Also, with a standardized set of measure-ments, the controller can build the measurement task into the accounting depart-ment's daily work schedule in a manner that does not interfere with other opera-tions, while also allowing for the construction of a procedure that standardizes the calculation of each measurement (ensuring the consistency of calculations from period to period). These are all good reasons for implementing a reporting system for key corporate measurements.

USE BALANCED SCORECARD REPORTING

The typical controller only reports on the financial situation of a company. Unfor-tunately, this is the information that is the result of many other activities that the accounting department does not normally have anything to do with. For example, profits are impacted if the customer is not satisfied (impacted by quality, pricing, and on-time delivery), if internal business processes do not function properly (which are impacted by such issues as machine utilization and the level of automation), and if employees are not well trained in their jobs (which is impacted by training and any factors leading to high employee turnover). A con-troller is not accustomed to reporting on any of these issues, but they all impact company profitability, the controller's primary reporting responsibility.

Robert S. Kaplan and David P. Norton have addressed this issue in their landmark book, *The Balanced Scorecard.* In it, they argue a strong case in favor of an entirely new method of reporting that itemizes the key factors that impact company profitability. An example of such a report is shown in Exhibit 13.8, where measurements are clustered into blocks, each one concerned with a differ-ent aspect of key success factors: financial, customer, internal business processes, and employee learning and growth. Kaplan and Norton feel that these four areas must be closely managed as a whole in order to attain truly exceptional levels of profitability.

Where does this leave a controller? This person is the one whom most of a company relies on to issue reports regularly on company status, even though those reports are only concerned with finances. Since reporting is already a part

Company Measurements (Issued on Mondays)

		Current Month				Nov.	Oct.	Sep.
		Week 5	Week 4	Week 3	Week 2	Week 1			
Cash	Available Debt (000s)	$267	$258	$242	$242	$442	$550	$500	$150
	Cash Burn Rate/Mo (000s)	$186	$186	$186	$186	$214	$214	$182	$190
	Months Cash Available	1.4	1.4	1.3	1.3	2.1	2.6	2.7	0.8
Working Capital	Days Accounts Receivable	35	37	40	43	43	39	48	53
	Days Total Inventory	41	41	42	43	41	40	43	47
	Days Accounts Payable	40	39	38	36	37	39	33	45
Financial	Breakeven, 2 Mo. Rolling (000s)	—	—	—	—	—	$850	$839	$821
	Net Profits Before Tax (000s)	—	—	—	—	—	$228	$234	$127
Sales	Sales (weeks are cumulative) (000s)	$1,055	$792	$540	$393	$123	$1,031	$899	$1,175
	Backlog (000s)	$1,602	$1,620	$1,599	$1,498	$1,397	$1,779	$988	—
	Backlog/Sales Ratio	—	—	—	—	—	173%	110%	—
Production	Machine Utilization	67%	61%	58%	52%	44%	46%	40%	35%
	$ Not Shipped by Promise Date (000s)	$28	$29	$31	$42	$50	$37	$24	—
	% Actual Labor Hrs over Standard	8%	15%	12%	13%	22%	3%	8%	15%
	Scrap Percentage	1.6%	1.7%	1.7%	2.0%	1.2%	2.5%	1.9%	2.7%
Quality	Returns $$$ (000s)	$15	$0	$0	$0	$0	$15	$16	$14
	Returns Percentage	—	—	—	—	—	1.5%	1.8%	1.2%
Logistics	Finished Goods Inv. Accuracy, IP	68%	64%	62%	62%	36%	27%	0%	0%
	Finished Goods Inv. Accuracy, Ass'y	19%	17%	15%	0%	0%	11%	0%	0%

Exhibit 13.7 Sample Measurements Report

ABC Company
Balanced Scorecard

Goal: To spin off enough cash flow to build new facilities and acquire competitors.

Financial:	Actual	Goal		**Customer:**	Actual	Goal
Net Profits		22%		*Customer Satisfaction*		95%
This Month	18.0%			This Month	82.0%	
This Quarter	16.0%			This Quarter	67.0%	
Last Year	11.0%			Last Year	41.0%	
F/G Turns		20		*On-time Shipments*		99%
This Month	22.8			This Month	88%	
This Quarter	17.6		<	This Quarter	75%	
Last Year	12.0			Last Year	63%	
A/R Turns		9.0				
This Month	6.9					
This Quarter	6.5					
Last Year	8.1					

Learning and Growth:				**Internal Business Processes:**		
	Actual	Goal			Actual	Goal
Employee Turnover		2%		*Scrap Percentage*		1.5%
This Month*	12%			This Month	2.2%	
This Quarter*	14%			This Quarter	2.4%	
Last Year*	18%			Last Year	2.4%	
* All turnover figures				*Direct Labor Percentage*		10.0%
are annualized.			>	This Month	16.9%	
				This Quarter	17.7%	
Employee Training (Hours/Year)		40		Last Year	15.1%	
This Month*	37					
This Quarter*	35			*Machine Utilization*		75%
Last Year*	32			This Month	58.0%	
				This Quarter	42.0%	
* All training figures are annualized.				Last Year	76.0%	

Exhibit 13.8.   Sample Balanced Scorecard

of this person's job, it only makes sense to expand the range of information covered to include those Kaplan and Norton advocate. This will require new reporting systems, as well as direction from senior management, since the exact measurements selected will require some thought by that group. In addition, the company will certainly want to see the traditional set of financial information as well, so this will be an added task for the controller—but one that management can use to track the performance of many more key functions than were previously covered by any sort of accounting reports.

TOTAL IMPACT OF BEST PRACTICES ON GENERAL ACCOUNTING FUNCTIONS

This section covers the impact of the best practices described in this chapter on the general administration of the accounting department.

Accounting processes attract most of the attention in this chapter, since there are best practices here for outsourcing some processes, using process-centering in other cases, and consolidating others. They are noted in Exhibit 13.9. The manner in which these best practices should be installed is that all outsourcing opportunities should be identified and completed first, followed by any needed consolidation of activities into the smallest number of locations. By taking these steps first, a company does not waste time reviewing existing processes that are about to be eliminated or moved elsewhere. After these tasks are completed, it is time to conduct a thorough review of all processes, increase the number of process tasks assigned to individual employees (i.e., process-centering), and then set up a continual process review system so that they are constantly analyzed for further improvements. By taking this approach, one can achieve a remarkable improvement in the efficiency of all accounting processes.

There are also four best practices related to accounting personnel, which involve training and job standardization. They are shown in the middle of Exhibit 13.9. By implementing them all, one can not only arrive at a department that knows exactly what to do and when to do it, but also one that experiences a much lower degree of turnover. The smaller number of employee departures is caused by the reduced level of anxiety that goes hand in hand with the reduced number of problems that are the end result of standardizing jobs and increasing the level of training.

Finally, there are a few best practices related to measurements, shown at the bottom of Exhibit 13.9. Though these have only a modest impact on the accounting department, they are quite useful to the rest of the corporation. On-line measurement reporting puts key operating data in the hands of all authorized employees, while balanced scorecard reporting shows how the company is performing in a wide array of crucial areas which have a direct impact on its current and future success. Also, there are internal measurements a controller can use to track the performance of the accounting and other departments. All of these best practices combine to greatly enhance the self-awareness of a corporation, giving it more information regarding how it can continually improve itself.

SUMMARY

This chapter covered a number of best practices that address problems in three main areas—processes, personnel, and reporting.

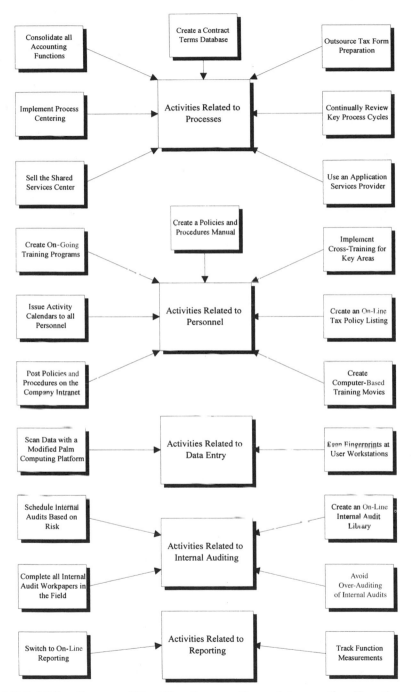

Exhibit 13.9. Impact of Best Practices on General Accounting Functions

Six best practices covered issues in the area of accounting process, with principal recommendations covering the outsourcing of smaller functions, consolidating accounting functions, setting up a database of contract terms, and focusing closely on the organization of employees around processes. These changes can bring about a major improvement in the efficiency of accounting processes.

Four best practices focused on accounting employees. A highly focused and organized training program is needed, especially when combined with cross-training for key activities, a policies and procedures manual, and a calendar of activities. These improvements will help to convert the accounting department into a highly knowledgeable and well-coordinated group.

Finally, three best practices target changes in the reporting function. One uses on-line reporting to ensure that information is disseminated as inexpensively and widely as possible, while balanced scorecard and function measurements are needed to determine the progress of the corporation as a whole and of individual departments, respectively, in achieving their goals. Though the reporting changes will not have an immediate impact on the efficiency of the accounting department, they will assist in informing management of company-wide activities, resulting in better control over overall operations.

Chapter 14

General Ledger
Best Practices

In most of this book, the primary basis for best practices is simplification in order to achieve an enhanced level of efficiency. Though there are best practices that can streamline the general ledger in a similar manner, this is one of the rare cases where pursuing a higher degree of complexity will achieve a greater overall benefit for the entire company. The two best practices which follow this approach are restructuring the general ledger to allow for the use of activity-based costing, and using it as a data warehouse. In both cases, there are significant start-up costs and much more work for the accounting staff, but the level of information that this practice provides to the rest of the organization is greatly enhanced. Thus, there are a few situations where greater cost and complexity can be beneficial.

In addition, there are the usual streamlining actions to reduce the work needed to maintain the general ledger. These best practices include restricting the use of journal entries, automating interfaces with subsidiary ledgers, and simplifying the chart of accounts. Though all of these measures will certainly reduce the work of the general ledger accountant, one should strongly consider adding the best practices for activity-based costing and data warehousing, which will increase that person's work, because it will be so beneficial to the remainder of the company.

This chapter covers ten best practices for the general ledger function, as well as a series of implementation issues for each best practice, which are discussed in the next section.

IMPLEMENTATION ISSUES FOR GENERAL LEDGER
BEST PRACTICES

This section describes the general level of implementation difficulty for all of the best practices discussed in this chapter. Three levels of implementation difficulty are covered in Exhibit 14.1, which shows the general level of ease, duration, and cost to implement each best practice.

In general, the level of implementation difficulty is higher for general ledger best practices than for other functional areas because changes in this area either

Exhibit 14.1.   Implementation Issues for General Ledger Best Practices

Description	Ease of Implementation	Duration of Implementation	Cost of Implementation
Construct Automated Interfaces to Software That Summarizes into the General Ledger	Difficult	Long	Expensive
Create General Ledger Drill-Down Capability	Difficult	Long	Expensive
Eliminate Small-Balance Accounts	Easy	Short	Inexpensive
Modify Account Code Structure for Storage of ABC Information	Moderate	Medium	Inexpensive
Overlay the General Ledger with a Consolidation and Reporting Package	Difficult	Medium	Expensive
Reduce the Chart of Accounts	Easy	Medium	Inexpensive
Restrict Use of Journal Entries	Easy	Short	Inexpensive
Subsidiaries Update Their Own Data in the Central General Ledger	Moderate	Medium	Medium
Use Automated Error-Checking	Difficult	Long	Expensive
Use Data Warehouse for Report Distribution	Difficult	Long	Expensive
Use Forms/Rates Data Warehouse for Automated Tax Filings	Difficult	Long	Expensive
Use Identical Chart of Accounts for Subsidiaries	Difficult	Long	Medium
Use the General Ledger as a Data Warehouse	Moderate	Medium	Inexpensive

involve major programming work or significant alterations to the way in which a company conducts its business. For example, one best practice is to switch the chart of accounts over to a structure that will allow a company to accumulate information for an activity-based costing system more easily; however, altering the chart of accounts always involves setting up new methods for collecting data, which can require major procedural changes throughout a company. In short, since the general ledger is the core data collection point in a company, alterations to it will have a ripple effect that may impact distant corners of the organization that the change initiator never anticipated.

Though many of the implementations listed in Exhibit 14.1 are described as being of long duration or expensive, many of them can still be cost-effective ways to improve the efficiency of the accounting department. However, given the potential costs, it is mandatory, in this functional area above all others, that a controller conduct a thorough investigation and comparison of the costs and benefits associated with any best practice-related changes. An implementation should proceed only after this step has been taken.

CONSTRUCT AUTOMATED INTERFACES TO SOFTWARE THAT SUMMARIZES INTO THE GENERAL LEDGER

A large number of transactions must be moved from subsidiary ledgers to the general ledger at the end of each accounting period. In most cases, there is some reasonable degree of integration so that this transfer of information occurs automatically. However, the majority of organizations have a few outlying ledgers that are not directly connected to the general ledger; for example, the fixed assets register or payroll. In these instances, the general ledger accountant must wade through a considerable pile of information to determine the correct amounts to shift into the general ledger. This is a time-consuming process and one that is subject to error.

It may be possible to construct an automated interface between these outlying ledgers and the general ledger. By doing so, there is a considerable advantage in eliminating the time required to move data to the general ledger manually, particularly important if an accounting department is committed to reducing the time needed to issue financial statements. Unfortunately, because of the programming required, this can be both a difficult and expensive best practice to implement. The company's programming staff must analyze the interface requirements, design the interface, program it, and test it, all of which can add up to a cost that greatly exceeds the benefit of having the automation. The best cases in which this is still a viable option are for a large company that can afford the cost, an organization that faces a very difficult manual transfer of information, or (best of all) where a third-party interface is already on the market, which can be quickly layered on top of the existing software to make the interface a reality. If any of these cases are present, then the automated interface best practice should be completed.

CREATE GENERAL LEDGER DRILL-DOWN CAPABILITY

A common problem for the general ledger accountant is the relative degree of effort required to extract information from the general ledger. For example, if someone makes an inquiry regarding the exact nature of the expenses recorded in the office supplies expense account, the accountant reviews the information listed in the general ledger, which probably shows no more than the total amount of accounts payable posted on a given day attributable to the office supplies account, then goes to the accounts payable register to obtain information about the exact invoices that were charged to office supplies, and then pulls the invoices from the filing cabinet in which they reside—all this to answer the simple question, "give me the detail for the office supplies account." Given the number of steps involved, it is obvious that a number of information requests of this kind (which are especially common right after the financial statements are distributed) can completely overload the general ledger accountant.

Installing a drill-down capability in the general ledger software is the best way to surmount this problem. The drill-down system allows one to position the cursor on the field on the computer screen for which the user wants to find additional information; the user then presses a button, and the next most detailed level of information appears on the screen. There may be several levels of information that can be accessed in this manner, allowing a user to "drill down" through the various levels until the needed information is obtained—hence the name of this best practice.

Though an obvious godsend for anyone who must research detailed information through the general ledger, this is not an easy item to install in an existing computer system. In essence, the computer programming staff must re-design large portions of the general ledger programming code so that the field in a high-level screen is automatically linked to a screen that contains more detailed information, requiring a web of cross-indexes to a multitude of screens (which may be located in other software packages) before users have a comprehensive drill-down capability. This is a major programming project, especially if the drill-down capability is given to a large number of data items, which means that there will be a large number of cross-indexes. This option is virtually impossible to implement if a company is using a third-party software package since any periodic update of the packaged software by the supplier will automatically wipe out all custom programming that the local programming staff has done since the last update was installed.

In short, the drill-down capability greatly increases a general ledger accountant's overall level of efficiency, but it requires either a large amount of internal programming time or the purchase of packaged accounting software that already contains this feature.

ELIMINATE SMALL-BALANCE ACCOUNTS

If the general ledger accountant is in the habit of maintaining a record of all the transactions in all accounts, there can be a considerable workload in store if there are many accounts. This practice is particularly common for balance sheet accounts, where it is necessary to keep track of all asset and liability records so that they can be reviewed during the year-end audit. If there are fewer accounts, there is less maintenance work needed to update a listing of the detailed records in each account.

Accordingly, a minor and easily implemented best practice is to periodically review the balances in the balance sheet accounts and merge them into larger accounts (or expense them) if the current balances are quite small. This task can be included in the financial statement preparation procedure as a standard item so that someone reviews the size of accounts on a regular basis and eliminates a few as necessary. There are no downsides to this best practice since it requires minimal work, reduces the clutter in the balance sheet, and does not interfere with the proper recording of information.

MODIFY ACCOUNT CODE STRUCTURE FOR STORAGE OF ABC INFORMATION

The general ledger accountant is frequently drawn into any activity-based costing (ABC) project because of his or her knowledge of the existing account structure. This accountant is commonly asked to set up a mapping program that translates the regular chart of accounts into a different (sometimes *much* different) chart of accounts that will be used to compile information for an ABC analysis. This analysis then compiles the costs of various products or activities throughout the company, which usually results in better management decisions and a greater level of profitability. Though this sounds like a reasonable task, involvement in an ABC project requires a startlingly large amount of time, perhaps even full-time participation for a number of months. The reason for such a heavy involvement is that the existing chart of accounts rarely accumulates data in the same way that an ABC analysis requires. For example, a traditional chart of accounts stores expense information by department, whereas an ABC system needs to have this information stored by activity center (such as a machine). Thus, when an ABC system is installed, the general ledger accountant may not only expect a considerable increase in the current workload, but may even require a replacement to fill in for all previous work while the ABC project is continuing.

A possible solution to this change in workload is to alter the chart of accounts, at least in part, so that information is stored in the manner the ABC system uses. By storing information in the ABC format right away, there is no need for the general ledger accountant to spend additional time re-formatting it. This can be quite a difficult best practice to implement, for several reasons. First, it requires the transfer of expense information from old accounts to new ones, as well as the alteration of all entries to the general ledger, so that all new information is re-directed in a similar manner. Also, all reports derived from the general ledger must be altered so that they draw information from the new accounts instead. The greatest problem of all is that the recipients of the revised reports may not be at all pleased to find that the information that they are accustomed to receiving has been substantially altered. For example, a department manager may find that there is no longer a department expense report, but instead an expense report grouped by machine. This alteration is not usually taken well by company management. The best way around all of these difficulties is to set up automatic distributions within the general ledger so that

expenses are still routed to the same accounts, but the accounts are then allocated out to a different set of ABC accounts for further ABC analysis. Unfortunately, the account allocation feature is not normally available in less expensive
general ledger accounting software packages, so this option is usually only
available to larger corporations. A lesser alternative is to alter just a small portion of general ledger accounts so that they can be used for ABC work, leaving
the main accounts as they are and relying on a manual conversion of data for
these accounts. This approach has the advantage of not altering the existing
financial reports to any significant degree, but still requires a considerable
amount of work by the general ledger accountant.

Despite all of the problems with converting the general ledger format to
accommodate an ABC system, this is still worthwhile in many cases. The reason
is that though there is no increase in efficiency for the general ledger function
(quite the contrary), there will be a rapid and smooth flow of information into the
ABC system, which will result in better management decisions, which in turn
will have a direct impact on the profitability of the entire organization.

OVERLAY THE GENERAL LEDGER WITH A CONSOLIDATION AND REPORTING PACKAGE

It can be extremely difficult to report on the consolidated results of a distributed
company, since there may be a number of different general ledger software packages in use, some of which run in different computer environments. Though it is
possible to manually consolidate this information, it is a tedious and error-prone
process that also requires a considerable lag time before consolidated reports can
be generated. Also, if anyone has a question about the resulting report, the
accounting staff must research the details in the underlying general ledgers and
then create another manual report—all of which takes yet more time. There are
two ways to avoid this problem. One approach is to create customized interfaces
from each general ledger to a centralized data warehouse, as is discussed later in
this chapter under the "Use a Data Warehouse for Report Distribution" heading.
This method is expensive to implement, and requires a considerable amount of
programming time. An alternative is to overlay the general ledger with packaged
consolidation and reporting software.

This type of software is sold by Hyperion, and is called the Hyperion Enterprise software, as well as the ancillary Hyperion Financial Analysis Solutions
software. These packages can be found on the company's web site at *www.hyper-
ion.com.* The software can be linked to any number of general ledgers through
published application programming interfaces, as well as through Hyperion's
integration tool, Hyperion Application Link. Once the data is combined in the
Hyperion Enterprise software, it can conduct automatic currency translations,
inter-company eliminations, European Monetary Union dual currency reporting,
and consolidation tracking. When combined with the Hyperion Enterprise

Reporting software, it can also allow users to drill down through the data in issued reports to the underlying transactional detail, as well as export reports to electronic spreadsheets, to the PDF (Portable Document Format) or HTML file formats, or post them directly to a web site for general access.

All of these advantages are available through a packaged system, rather than a custom-designed data warehouse whose roll-out time and cost is much higher. The primary issues with the Hyperion solution are that some interfaces with outlying general ledgers will likely require customized programming, and the cost of the software.

REDUCE THE CHART OF ACCOUNTS

All too many organizations are burdened with an immense chart of accounts. Instead of having a short list of accounts in which to store information—such as one or two hundred accounts—many organizations have a convoluted and lengthy chart of accounts that covers many pages. The sheer length of such a list introduces a number of problems into the general ledger function. One is that it is difficult to put numbers into the same accounts consistently time after time. Instead, they are recorded in different accounts, resulting in very poor comparability of information across time. Another issue is that it can be very difficult to train a new general ledger accountant in the use of a very complicated chart of accounts; during the training period, it is very likely that the accountant will make mistakes in recording financial information into the correct accounts, resulting in inaccurate financial statements. It is also more expensive to audit a long chart of accounts since the outside auditors must spend more time reviewing more accounts. Furthermore, writing a new report with general ledger information is quite difficult if the information is being drawn from a veritable maze of accounts. In short, a plague of problems accompanies an excessively long chart of accounts.

The best practice that resolves this problem is one that takes a fair amount of work to implement. Though it seems simple—just reduce the number of active accounts in the chart of accounts—there are ancillary issues that require additional work. One problem with reducing the chart is that users may still continue to code expenses to the old accounts, if only out of habit. To stop this from happening, the old accounts that are being retired must be blocked from further use in the computer system. Though most computer systems now have this blocking feature, it is useful to determine its presence before proceeding further with an implementation. Another issue is that when the chart is reduced, it is much more difficult to create historical reports to compare account balances to those of previous periods. For example, if five accounts are merged into one consolidated account, it becomes impossible to show how the balance in the new account compares to the old balances in five accounts, unless the general ledger copies all of the information to an electronic spreadsheet and manually re-groups the information, a time-consuming task. There is no good way around this problem, unless the existing accounting software has a reporting feature that allows old accounts to be grouped for comparison purposes (a rare feature). This is a particular problem if the accounts are merged in the middle of a company's reporting year so that it is not even possible to compare financial results from month to month. The best solution to this problem is to undertake major chart of account conversions only at the very beginning of a reporting year so that there is no intra-year reporting problem. Another way to resolve the problem is to fix the chart of accounts over a number of years by eliminating only a small number of accounts each year, which does not impact the comparability of accounts in any one year to any great degree. A final issue with reducing the chart of accounts is that information may be stored in an account strictly for inclusion in a report that has some special purpose. If the account is discontinued, the report can no longer be completed, which may be a source of irritation to the report recipient. To avoid this issue, it is necessary to review all reports generated from the general ledger and determine which accounts are used to create them. If the information in these special accounts is truly indispensable, they should be left alone.

Though a number of problems have been noted that can arise when the chart of accounts is streamlined, this is still a best practice immensely worthy of consideration. It is especially useful for older companies with many departments or subsidiaries, for these have frequently accumulated a large number of stray accounts over the years that should certainly be researched and eliminated. By doing so, it is much easier to maintain the general ledger.

RESTRICT USE OF JOURNAL ENTRIES

Many general ledger accountants spend a large part of their time researching why journal entries have been made. This is an especially galling problem if journal entries were made by someone else because there may be no record of why they were entered or even of who made the entry. Also, if the computer system has a "drill-down" capability for researching general ledger information in detail (see the "Create General Ledger Drill-Down Capability" section in this chapter), an information search may end at the journal entry, with no explanation for why the entry was made. This is an uncomfortable state of affairs for a general ledger accountant, who must report back to anyone requesting information from the general ledger saying that he or she does not know the nature of an account balance. Besides being embarrassing, it also takes time to research.

An easy best practice to implement is to totally restrict the use of journal entries to the general ledger accountant. By doing so, this person can research each request for a journal entry to verify that it is valid, make sure that the correct accounts are debited and credited, and include a description with the journal entry. This approach virtually eliminates all stray or undocumented journal entries from the system. Though it should not cause any problems, it may be difficult to implement if the computer system does not allow the journal entry feature to be restricted to one person—this depends on the type of computer security system included in the software.

Restricting the use of journal entries leads to cleaner and more fully documented general ledger information that is maintained much more easily.

SUBSIDIARIES UPDATE THEIR OWN DATA
IN THE CENTRAL GENERAL LEDGER

A lengthy task for any general ledger accountant who must consolidate the results of subsidiaries is to input the general ledger of each one into the general ledger of the corporate parent. This can be a lengthy and arduous task, as well as one that is easily subject to error. The typical consolidation requires a very large journal entry for each subsidiary, possibly requiring over a hundred accounts. If there is any problem with the data entry, the entire entry must be reviewed to find the mistake. If there are many subsidiaries, there are many entries to make; if there is a time crunch associated with producing financial statements, it is extremely likely that all of the data-entry work required of the general ledger accountant will be a bottleneck for the timely production of those statements.

The solution to this quandary is to hand the data-entry chore over to the subsidiaries. They can be given access to the computer system of the corporate parent with modems, as well as password access to the general ledger, and then enter their financial results directly into the computer system. The general ledger accountant thereby avoids all data-entry work related to the subsidiaries and only has to analyze his or her own data inputs to see if there are any unusual items. By having each subsidiary enter its own information, the data can be entered much more quickly, resulting in the elimination of the work flow bottleneck associated with this task. In short, a relatively simple system change can improve the efficiency of periodic corporate consolidations.

There are a few issues to consider before attempting this best practice, however. First, there is a minor expense associated with giving modems to all subsidiaries. This expense will include the cost of a direct phone line for each computer so equipped (though this also makes those computers useful for other modem-related tasks, perhaps justifying the cost in this manner). Also, there must be password protection for anyone dialing into the main computer system, since there is always a risk of someone hacking into the computer and destroying or accessing sensitive data. Another issue is that, by giving access to many people, the number of users accessing the system at one time may rise, which may require the purchase of additional user licenses (if the system is a third-party package that uses a licensing fee arrangement). Finally, all the new users must be trained in how to make a journal entry in the corporate computer system, which may require nothing more than an instruction sheet, but which may require travel to all locations to conduct a short training class. If all of these issues can be dealt with at minimal cost, then having subsidiaries enter their own data into the corporate general ledger can improve the efficiency of that function.

USE AUTOMATED ERROR-CHECKING

Despite the best possible training and experience, it is still possible, if not likely, for a general ledger accountant to enter incorrect information into the general ledger, or to not catch incorrect information others have entered. This information may not be caught until it appears in the preliminary financial statements, necessitating a hurried investigation and correction, which delays the completion and delivery of the statements. Given the volume of transactions summarized in the general ledger, it would take a miraculous accountant to catch all possible irregularities before they are reported for the rest of the company to see in the financial statements.

The best practice that helps to eliminate some of these irregularities is using automated error-checking. This approach can take a variety of forms. One is that the journal entry input screen can contain controls over the size of entries that are allowed or the accounts to which entries are made. For example, any entry over $1 million may be automatically rejected, as would any entry to retained earnings (though with an override by a person with the appropriate password, since sometimes these pre-set boundaries *will* be exceeded). Another option is for the system to allow only a pre-approved set of journal entries, all with pre-set accounts to which changes will be allowed. All other journal entries will require a special password to enter. Yet another approach is to use a report writer to explore all of the transactions that have been entered into the general ledger, sort through the ones that exceed pre-set boundaries, and issue them in a report. For example, a report could extract all travel expenses of more than $5,000 dollars, or all fixed asset additions less than the minimum capitalization limit. A report can also compare all expenses to year-to-date or period-budgeted amounts and only show those that exceed their budgeted amounts. By running these reports regularly, the general ledger accountant can quickly spot those transactions that may be wrong or placed in the wrong account.

The main problem with incorporating automated error-checking into the general ledger is that many accounting software packages do not have this feature built into them. If this is the case, the expense of programming the alterations is probably so great that it will exceed any possible benefit. In this situation, the best alternative is to use a report writer to create reports showing problems that have already been entered into the general ledger. This is a much easier alternative, since most computer systems have a report writer. In other words, if it is not possible to stop bad information from entering the general ledger, it may still be possible to spot it once it is there and subsequently make corrections.

USE DATA WAREHOUSE FOR REPORT DISTRIBUTION

Larger organizations, especially those with multiple locations or subsidiaries, commonly expend a great deal of time compiling and distributing reports to employees. This problem arises because each location frequently has its own general ledger, from which the information is drawn. If any of the information from multiple locations is to be combined to create summary-level reports, then either a custom interface must be built to combine the data, or else it must be manually combined and inserted into a new report.

An excellent method for avoiding this trouble is to dump selected data from all of the general ledgers into a central data warehouse. This involves the use of many customized interfaces that frequently pull the data out of outlying locations and push it into the data warehouse, so that it contains only the most current information. Then a set of reporting programs frequently (perhaps every few minutes, depending on how it would downgrade system performance) accesses the data warehouse to refresh the information stored in a set of standard reports, which in turn are made available to employees through the company intranet.

This elaborate shifting and recompiling of data results in very "fresh" data that employees can use at once, and also takes the accounting department completely out of the business of repetitively compiling reports—though it may still be asked to create new reports for posting to the intranet site. A key change after this system is installed is that the accounting staff will find itself spending much more time cleaning up the data that goes into the data warehouse. The reason is that manually compiled reports give the accounting staff time to review the data and fix any obvious anomalies before they reach the user; however, this automated reporting system does not allow the accounting staff this luxury, so now its focus must change toward ensuring that the data is always correct.

A different approach to the data warehouse is noted in the "Use the General Ledger as a Data Warehouse" section in this chapter, where we see that extra data can be added to an existing general ledger, rather than exporting the general ledger to another location. This alternative is more usable in situations where there is only one general ledger in use, and so is more applicable to smaller companies.

USE FORMS/RATES DATA WAREHOUSE
FOR AUTOMATED TAX FILINGS

Any organization that operates in a number of states will find that an inordinate number of sales and income tax returns must be filed, not to mention a plethora of lesser forms. The traditional way to meet these filing requirements is to either keep a staff of tax preparation personnel on hand, or else outsource some or all of these chores to a supplier. Either approach represents a significant cost. An alternative worth exploring is to store tax rates and forms in a database that can be used to automatically prepare tax returns in conjunction with other accounting information that is stored in either a general ledger or a data warehouse.

To make this best practice operational, there must first be a common database containing all of the information that would normally be included on a tax return. This may call for some restructuring of the chart of accounts, as well as the centralization of company-wide data into a data warehouse (see the preceding best practice). This is no small task, since the information needed by each state may vary slightly from the requirements of other states, calling for subtle changes in the storage of data throughout the organization that will yield the appropriate information for reporting purposes.

The next step is to obtain tax rate information and store it in a central database. This information can be manually located by accessing the tax agency web sites of all fifty states, but is more easily obtained in electronic format from any of the national tax reporting services. This information can then be stored in the forms/rates data warehouse. An additional step is to create a separate program for each of the tax reports, so that a computer report is issued that mimics the reporting format used by each state. Then the information can be manually transferred from the computer report to a printout of the PDF file of each state's tax from. For those programming staffs with a large amount of available time, it is also possible to create a report format that exactly mirrors each state tax form, and which can be printed out, with all tax information enclosed within it, and immediately mailed out.

The trouble with this best practice is the exceptionally high programming cost associated with obtaining a complete automated solution. There are so many tax forms to be converted to a digital format that the development task is considerable. Accordingly, it is more cost effective to determine those tax forms that share approximately the same information, and to develop an automated solution for them first. Any remaining tax forms that would require special programming to automate should be reviewed on a case-by-case basis to determine if it is cost-beneficial to complete further programming work, or to leave a few stray reports for the tax preparation staff to complete by hand.

USE IDENTICAL CHART OF ACCOUNTS FOR SUBSIDIARIES

If a company has a number of subsidiaries, the general ledger accountant will have a much more difficult time at the end of the financial reporting period, because the results of each subsidiary must be translated into the chart of accounts structure of the corporate parent. This can involve an enormous amount of work, because the information the subsidiaries send in may be in a chart of accounts structure that is so different from the one the parent uses that it is a matter of pure guess work by the accountant to determine the correct accounts into which the subsidiary data should be recorded. This is a particularly galling problem if the subsidiaries are in an entirely different line of business, for this means that the chart of accounts may be substantially different; thus, consolidating account numbers is more of a problem if a company acquires disparate companies, as opposed to acquiring companies that are in the same industry.

There are several variations on the same best practice which will resolve this problem, as noted in the following bullet points. They range from merely requiring the permission of the corporate parent before a subsidiary alters its chart of accounts any further, to requiring the substitution of the existing chart with the one the corporate parent uses. The bullet points are listed in ascending order of conformance, with the least amount of conformance being the easiest to implement and complete conformance being the most difficult to install. The particular variation selected may be dependent on the speed with which a company is buying other companies, since a complete replacement of a chart of accounts can be a major undertaking and may not be possible if the rate of acquisition is extremely rapid. The best practice options are as follows:

- *Require permission to make account changes.* It may be necessary to leave the current situation alone, perhaps because there are too many subsidiaries and too few resources available to re-set the chart of accounts structure across all subsidiaries. In this situation, the easiest step is to issue a blanket order to all subsidiaries that they cannot make further changes to their charts of accounts without permission from the corporate parent—in other words, the main action is not to make the situation any worse than it already is. This is an extremely minor action to take, since it is a rare event for a company to create new accounts once the basic chart of accounts has been completed.

- *Use a written map to lay out how accounts are linked.* A more advanced level of activity, which can also incorporate the first bullet point, is to create a map that traces each account number used by every subsidiary to the corresponding account number in the corporate parent's chart of accounts. Though only a manual tool, not an automated one, this is still a very important way to create consistent entries through many accounting periods. To make this approach even more effective, there should be a standardized journal entry form for each subsidiary that lists both sets of account numbers so that the general ledger accountant only has to fill in the form and enter it into the computer.

- *Have subsidiaries convert results to corporate parent's chart of accounts.* An excellent approach for organizations that do not like to impose an excessive level of control onto their subsidiaries is to let them use any account code structure that they want and just require them to make the conversion to the parent's chart of accounts when submitting period-end information. This approach is a benign one many companies use, for it avoids the effort of a complete standardization while still ensuring that the parent company receives the information that it needs. It can also be completed in short order, merely requiring a visit from corporate headquarters to work with the local accounting staff to create an account code conversion table the local staff will use to submit data to the corporate parent.

- *Have subsidiaries enter their data directly into the parent's general ledger.* This approach is similar to the preceding one in that the subsidiaries can keep their own charts of accounts but must submit their reporting information in the corporate parent's format. The difference here is that the subsidiaries are given dial-up computer access to the corporate parent's general ledger, into which they are expected to enter the period-end data themselves. This approach presents the risk of someone entering incorrect information into the computer system but avoids the need for extra data-entry work by the corporate general ledger accountant. Instead, the people entering the information are the ones who know the most about it, which means that there is less likelihood of a conversion or data-entry error being made. This best practice is described in more detail in the section "Subsidiaries Update Their Own Data in the Central General Ledger."

- *Convert all subsidiaries to a common chart of accounts.* The best way to ensure complete standardization is to impose the chart of accounts of the parent onto the subsidiaries. This can involve a massive amount of work, for each accounting system must be re-set to use the new accounts. This will also probably destroy all historical reporting comparisons, which must use the old account numbers. Some subsidiaries may also be in such a different line of business that the new chart of accounts is quite unsuitable for recording information, requiring the accounting staff to "shoehorn" data into accounts that do not agree exactly with the account descriptions. Many companies find this approach to be much too difficult and expensive to be worthwhile and will use one of the preceding options instead.

Thus, there is quite a range of options available for converting the chart of accounts of a subsidiary to that of the parent. The exact option taken will depend on the level of effort and resources that the parent is willing to put into this effort. Some of the easier options are quite as reliable as the most difficult, making them worthy of careful consideration when picking from the range of options presented here.

USE THE GENERAL LEDGER AS A DATA WAREHOUSE

When issuing financial reports, a controller draws all of the financial information from a single source, the general ledger. However, there are usually a number of operating statistics, such as headcount, turnover percentages, scrap, and the like that must be accumulated from a variety of sources before they can be brought together into a coherent group and inserted into the financial statements. These can be quite difficult to accumulate at the last moment and must be added manually to the financial statements since they are not stored in the general ledger, the primary source from which the statements are drawn. The reporting problem becomes worse if management is accustomed to printing financial reports on its own, for any operating statistics will not appear on them, necessitating a sudden and unscheduled accumulation of this information by the accounting staff in order to supplement the existing reports. Thus, non-financial data can introduce some inefficiency into the production of financial statements.

The best practice that resolves this issue is to create additional records in the general ledger for the storage of non-financial information. This is more commonly known as a data warehouse, since data of all kinds can be stored there. When in place, this arrangement allows a company to store all the operating data it desires in the same place as its financial data, which means that any reports accessing one can just as easily access the other so all possible information can be *automatically* included in the existing financial reports. Since all possible information is listed on the reports, there is no need to supplement them with additional, manually compiled reports. This is a much more satisfactory state of affairs since all information and reporting is centralized.

There are some problems with changing a general ledger into a data warehouse. One is that the existing software may not allow for this arrangement; if the software is provided by a third party and regularly updated, there may be no way to alter the situation without an appeal to the supplier to include a data warehousing feature in its next update of the software. Another problem is that the existing financial reports must be altered to include the new information that will now be stored in the general ledger. Yet another issue is deciding who will update the operations information and how it will be added to the general ledger. For example, if it is deemed necessary to record the monthly inventory turnover rate at each of a dozen facilities, who will collect and input this data? The answer is usually either to allow each department or facility to forward this information, have the internal audit team (which is more objective in reporting disappointing results) do it, or have the former do it with periodic reviews by the latter. It may also be possible either to give these people direct access to the statistics accounts in the general ledger so that they can make these entries themselves, or (best of all) to construct automated interfaces to whatever local systems are already accumulating this information.

Thus, the main problem is not having a general ledger that will accommodate the data warehousing concept; the other problems are either surmounted during the implementation or can be eliminated through automation or bringing in the assistance of the internal audit department. If these problems can be overcome, using the general ledger as a data warehouse becomes an effective way to manage and report on all kinds of key management information.

TOTAL IMPACT OF BEST PRACTICES ON THE GENERAL LEDGER FUNCTION

This section describes how the best practices described earlier in this chapter can be brought together as a group to achieve a more efficient general ledger function that also provides better information to management.

The best practices can be clustered into three groups: those that impact the chart of accounts, those that impact the general ledger, and those that modify the general ledger to improve the reporting of information. These clusters are shown in Exhibit 14.2. The first cluster focuses on streamlining the chart of accounts, as well as various methods for incorporating the charts of accounts of subsidiaries into those of the parent organization. These best practices focus on improving the efficiency of the general ledger function. The second cluster uses a number of techniques not only to improve the ability of the general ledger accountant to

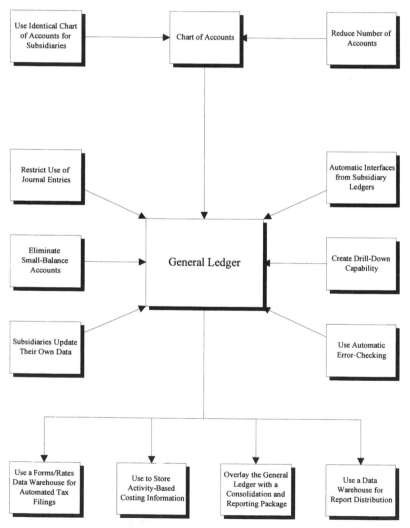

Exhibit 14.2.   Impact of Best Practices on the General Ledger Function

research information in the general ledger (such as with drill-down inquiries or restricting the use of journal entries), but also to reduce the amount of work needed to maintain it. In this latter category are such best practices as having subsidiaries load their own financial results into the master general ledger, using automated error-checking, and automating the interfaces with subsidiary ledgers. When coupled with the previously noted improvements to the chart of accounts, these best practices can result in a significant enhancement to the overall efficiency of the general ledger function. Finally, the third cluster of best practices actually *increases* the complexity of the general ledger, but does so in order to provide more information to other parts of the company, either by way of an activity-based costing analysis or through a data warehouse. Thus, there is a logical grouping to the best practices which may be useful in designating which clusters of them are implemented first.

If a controller can designate the order in which all of these best practices are implemented, it is best to work on streamlining the function first and adding the data warehousing and ABC functions later. Otherwise, reversing this order of implementation will result in adding complexity to a situation that is already not entirely efficient, which may result in a great deal of confusion and a complete failure to implement *any* best practices.

For more information on each of the best practices noted in Exhibit 14.2, refer back to each section in this chapter noted as a separate activity in the flow chart.

SUMMARY

This chapter discussed a variety of best practices for the general ledger function. Though many of them will reduce the workload of the general ledger accountant by streamlining the work flow and reducing the number of errors that can enter into the process, a few can be both difficult and expensive to implement. Some, such as using the general ledger to support activity-based costing, will even make the general ledger accountant's job more difficult, rather than less. Accordingly, for most general ledger best practices, it is necessary to ensure that there will be sufficient payback in exchange for installing a new best practice. The payback is not just greater accounting efficiency, but in a few cases the provision of better information to the rest of the company.

Chapter 15

Inventory Best Practices

This chapter describes a variety of best practices that are tightly focused on improving the accuracy of the existing inventory, as well as on all ongoing inventory transactions. Though these improvements most directly assist other departments, such as the production, warehouse, and purchasing employees, the accounting staff is deeply interested as well. The reason is that the accuracy of the financial statements is largely driven by the accuracy of the inventory—if it is off by even a few percent, the variance flows through the cost of goods sold, resulting in a considerable amount of inaccuracy in reported profits.

The best practices shown in this section are different from those listed elsewhere in this book in that the controller must obtain the approval and active participation of the warehouse and engineering managers for most of them. Without their help, such best practices as improving the bills of material, moving inventory to floor stock, and segregating customer-owned inventory will not be accomplished.

The remainder of this chapter consists of a review of implementation issues for inventory best practices, followed by a detailed discussion of each one, and ending with notes on the impact of best practices on the inventory function.

IMPLEMENTATION ISSUES FOR INVENTORY BEST PRACTICES

This section describes the levels of implementation difficulty for each of the best practices detailed in this chapter. Each one is noted in Exhibit 15.1, alongside a listing of the relative level of implementation ease, duration, and cost. Most of these best practices are not simple ones to install because they involve one or more other departments, usually warehousing and engineering. Whenever another manager is brought into the implementation process, the chances of success drop rapidly, since this additional person must be convinced of the efficacy of the change.

A few of the best practices noted here rarely succeed at all, though world-class companies have installed them—these are the elimination of the warehouse and the receiving function, which can only be accomplished through a time-consuming process of inventory elimination and supplier qualification. However, for those companies who are well along in accomplishing these tasks, the best practices should be considered, given the resulting reduction in costs and elimination of inventories.

Most of the other best practices are relatively inexpensive to install, since they generally involve changes to procedures, which have no attendant expense at

Exhibit 15.1. Implementation Issues for Inventory Best Practices

Description	Ease of Implementation	Duration of Implementation	Cost of Implementation
Audit All Inventory Transactions	Moderate	Short	Inexpensive
Audit Bills of Material	Easy	Short	Inexpensive
Compare Recorded Inventory Activity to On-Hand Inventories	Moderate	Short	Inexpensive
Eliminate the Physical Count Process	Difficult	Long	Inexpensive
Eliminate the Receiving Function	Difficult	Long	Expensive
Eliminate the Warehouse	Difficult	Long	Expensive
Lock Down the Warehouse Area	Moderate	Short	Moderate
Modify the Bills of Material Based on Actual Scrap Levels	Moderate	Short	Inexpensive
Move Inventory to Floor Stock	Moderate	Medium	Moderate
Review Inventory Returned to the Warehouse	Moderate	Short	Inexpensive
Segregate Customer-Owned Inventory	Moderate	Medium	Moderate
Streamline the Physical Count Process	Easy	Short	Inexpensive
Track Inventory Accuracy	Moderate	Short	Inexpensive
Verify That All Receipts Are Entered in the Computer at Once	Moderate	Short	Inexpensive

all. A few best practices require the installation of fencing or different bin systems, but even these expenses are not considerable, unless the warehouse in question is a very large one.

The remainder of this chapter separately discusses each of the best practices shown in Exhibit 15.1, and does so in alphabetical order

AUDIT ALL INVENTORY TRANSACTIONS

For any manufacturing organization, there are a myriad of transactions associated with the receipt of goods, their transfer to locations in the warehouse, and additional movement to the production floor, as well as the return of any excess items to the warehouse. Given the inordinate volume of transactions, some are bound to be done incorrectly. When this happens, the recorded quantities of inventory on hand and used will be incorrect, resulting in incorrect financial results. The problem impacts other departments too, since inaccurate inventory volumes impact the purchasing, production, and warehouse departments.

One best practice that targets inventory transaction problems is auditing them. By doing so, one can spot problems, research why they happened, and take actions to keep the transaction errors from occurring again. For example, if an audit uncovers a lack of operator training that results in receiving not being completed in the computer, either a comprehensive or focused training session with that person, along with follow-up reviews, will eliminate the error.

Auditing can be assigned to the internal audit department. However, continual review work may be necessary, which the audit department may not have sufficient manpower to provide; the accounting department is well advised to take on this chore itself, if no other approach will work. Once the entity doing the work has been determined, the next step is to find the best way to spot transaction problems among the hundreds or thousands of inventory-related transactions that occur every month. A simple random selection of transactions will eventually discover a reasonable quantity of mistakes to review, but there are ways to improve one's chances of finding them. For example, a transaction that results in a negative inventory on-hand quantity is certainly worthy of a review, as is any transaction that takes more out of stock than is actually there. The same exception rules can be applied to transactions with inordinately large quantities. Further, transactions can be compared to the production schedule to see if any of the items received in the warehouse are scheduled to be used in production in the near future. Any of these issues are indicative of a problem and should be reviewed first. Though many of them may be valid, the odds of finding an error are greatly enhanced.

The next step in the auditing process is discovering the nature of the problem that caused the transaction error. Since the only two possibilities are systems or people problems, it is wise to assign a team with exceptional systems knowledge and people skills to this task. Since most employees will not admit to an error if they have made one, the single most important auditing skill is carefully dealing in a non-threatening manner with the people involved in these transactions. Finally, there must be a follow-up routine established that reviews previously uncovered problems to verify that they have been fixed. Only if *all* of these steps are followed will errors in the recording of inventory-related transactions be fixed.

As several departments are involved in the recording of transactions related to inventory, the controller must be able to deal carefully with the managers of these other departments to ensure that the auditing process does not degrade into a situation where discovered problems are used to attack each other. Thus, interpersonal skills are critical to the success of this best practice.

AUDIT BILLS OF MATERIAL

Some companies use back flushing as the means of recording changes to inventory. Under this methodology, inventory is taken from the warehouse without any associated picking transactions put into the computer. Then, when production is completed, the total amount of production by item is entered into the computer and the software automatically removes the associated inventory amounts from the warehouse records, using bills of material as the basis for doing so. Though this is a very simple method for keeping warehouse paperwork to a minimum, an incorrect bill of material will quickly alter the on-hand inventory balances to such an extent that inventory accuracy will plummet. In addition, the accounting department uses the bills of material to determine the cost of any finished goods; an inaccurate bill will also impact the accuracy of this costing. Thus, the accuracy of a company's bills of material impact not only the records for inventory quantities, but also their cost.

The best practice that keeps the bill of material errors to a minimum is an ongoing audit of them. This practice keeps inventory quantities from becoming too inaccurate in a back-flushing environment, while making the costing of finished goods more precise. To do so, a person who is knowledgeable about the contents of bills of material must be assigned to a regular review of them. Any problems must be corrected at once. To be the most effective, it is best to concentrate the efforts of the reviewer on those bills that are used the most, or which are expected to be included in upcoming production runs. By focusing on those bills receiving the most usage, a company can be sure of maintaining a high degree of bill accuracy for the bulk of its products.

The only difficulty in implementing this approach is that it requires the cooperation of the engineering manager, who must assign a staff person to the reviewing process. This assistance is critical, since engineers are the ones with the best knowledge of bills of material.

COMPARE RECORDED INVENTORY ACTIVITY TO ON-HAND INVENTORIES

Some industries deal with extremely expensive materials. In these situations, it is critical to ensure that recorded inventory levels are completely accurate, since even a small quantity variance can lead to a large impact on profitability. This is a particular concern when dealing with precious metals or gemstones, not to mention a variety of electronic components.

Many of the other best practices noted in this chapter will help to keep inventory accuracy within reasonable limits, such as auditing inventory transactions or cycle counting, but to be absolutely sure that quantities are correct, the best way is to compare recorded inventory activity to on-hand inventories. This approach varies from auditing because it assumes a 100 percent review of all transactions for selected items. Because it is a highly labor-intensive approach, one must confine it to a minimum number of especially expensive or critical inventory items.

To use this method, one should conduct a *daily* comparison of on-hand quantities to every transaction associated with them, such as receipts, inventory moves, scrap, production, returns from the production floor, and shipments. Of particular interest during this review process is any transaction that is not made, is made twice, is made in the wrong amount or on the wrong date, or which involves the wrong part number or unit of measure. Only by conducting this complete review every day can a company determine where there are problems in the stream of transactions and fix them immediately. One should also try to spot trends in or concentrations of transaction errors, such as a number of receiving or scrap errors, which allows one to target a specific problem and fix it.

This best practice is strongly supported by those other departments that rely on accurate inventory levels, such as the warehousing, production, and purchasing departments. However, they support this because they do not have to provide the significant amount of staff time required to ensure its success. Accordingly, a controller should be extremely careful to use it only with a very small minority of the inventory items, monitor it carefully, and eliminate items from the review process as soon as it becomes apparent that there are no transactional errors occurring.

ELIMINATE THE PHYSICAL COUNT PROCESS

As noted in the last section, there are a variety of problems associated with having any sort of physical count at all. This section outlines how to use cycle-counts to completely avoid any physical count.

One must use cycle-counting as the primary way to eliminate the physical counting process. To do so, there are a set of carefully defined steps to follow before inventory reaches an accuracy level sufficiently high to allow one to avoid the physical count. One should read through all of the following steps and make a realistic assessment of a company's ability not only to complete them, but also to maintain the system over a long period. If it is not realistically possible, then do not run the risk of wasting up to a year of work on this project—there are other best practices in this chapter that pose a much higher chance of success. The steps are as follows:

- *Throw out the trash.* The warehouse must first be cleaned up before spending a great deal of time on counting parts. Accordingly, trash, obsolete parts, and old supplies or tools must either be thrown out or moved to an outlying location.

- *Identify the remainder.* The first step reduces the amount of inventory items to be reviewed for part numbers. This is now the main task—review all remaining inventory and post a part number on it.

- *Consolidate inventory.* Once all parts are identified, it is time to cluster them together for easy counting, rather than leaving them in a variety of locations. This takes several iterations before all inventory is completely consolidated, but do not worry about it—the main reason for consolidating at this stage is to make it easier to count and box the inventory in the next step, so a few unconsolidated items will not present much of a problem later on.

- *Count and box the remainder.* Count all the inventory and then box or bag it. There should be a seal on each container, with the quantity marked on the seal, so that a glance at the container will reveal the complete quantity of the part. This is of vast benefit to cycle-counters, who can now cycle-count hundreds of items very quickly. Please note that it is not necessary at this point to correct all inventory balances in the computer, for the cycle-counters will soon take care of this problem when they start to methodically review the entire warehouse.

- *Create warehouse locations.* Clearly mark every bin location. The location should include the aisle, rack, and bin number, so there is no question about where an inventory item is located. This step is crucial for cycle-counting, since one cannot cycle-count if one cannot first find the part.

- *Assign inventory to specific locations.* Go into the computer and assign a location code to every inventory item. This may require special programming to put a location field into the computer database.

- *Create a cycle-counting report.* Create a computer report that lists all on-hand inventory, sorted by location code. The cycle-counters must have this available as their main tool for reviewing inventory.

- *Segregate the warehouse.* Put up a fence around the warehouse and lock the gate! Now that cycle-counting is about to begin, there should be no way for non-warehouse staff to enter the warehouse in order to take parts off the shelf.

- *Initiate cycle-counts.* Assign cycle-counters a section of the warehouse to count. Issue them the latest cycle-counting report. They must carefully count all the items in every bin location and make corrections to the report to ensure that the computer database is correct. The warehouse manager should monitor their progress every day to ensure that they are completing their counts on time. A good initial cycle-counting frequency is to review the entire inventory six times a year; this high volume of counting can drop later, when accuracy levels increase.

- *Audit inventory accuracy.* Audit the inventory once a week. A small sample of the total inventory is sufficient to determine the total accuracy of the inventory, which should be posted for the review of the warehouse staff. It may be necessary to post accuracy by aisle, in case some sections of the warehouse are particularly prone to mistakes. If so, the best cycle-counters should be assigned to these aisles.

- *Use a bonus program.* The entire warehouse staff should receive a bonus at the end of each month, based on the audited accuracy of the inventory. A good measure above which bonuses should be given is 95 percent accuracy, with any item being defined as accurate if the counted quantity is within 2 percent of the amount listed in the computer (though this may not be a good measure in some industries, such as diamond processing). This is an extremely effective way to maintain the interest of the warehouse staff in the continuing accuracy of the inventory records.

Though cycle-counting will certainly allow one to avoid a physical inventory count, it is equally important to investigate why errors are occurring, not just to change inventory balances if they are wrong. If one can get to the bottom of a transaction problem and fix the underlying error, it is possible to greatly increase record accuracy and require less work by the cycle-counting staff to keep it that way.

ELIMINATE THE RECEIVING FUNCTION

Similar to the last section with the warehouse, the receiving function is responsible for entering receipts into the computer system, and occasionally does not do a good job in this capacity. For example, the late or inaccurate data entry of receiving information can lead to inaccurate financial statements, as well as inaccurate information for the production planning and purchasing staffs to procure and assemble materials for the production department to use.

As was also the case in the last section, the solution is to eliminate the function. And, as was the case before, this is an extremely difficult best practice to implement. The concept that only a relatively small number of companies have fully implemented is to fully qualify suppliers in terms of their ability to ship goods of high quality, precisely on time, and to do so directly to the production process. This requires a great deal of advance work by the purchasing staff to find suppliers who are willing to do this, as well as supplier inspections to company engineers to ensure that supplier quality standards match or exceed those of the company. Only after this work has been done can a company convert to the direct delivery of goods to the production department, bypassing the receiving area.

A final problem to overcome is how to account for receipts if there is no receiving staff. The answer is to assume that parts were received if the products in which they are used as components were built. Accordingly, production records are exploded into their component parts in the computer to determine whose parts were used, and to then pay those suppliers based on these usage records. Subsidiary problems to resolve before this payment system will work are to centralize component sourcing with one supplier per part and to eliminate all scrap from the production process. Supplier centralization is necessary because the computer system will not know which supplier to pay once it backs into the number of parts used. Similarly, there can be no scrap in the production process, or else suppliers will not be paid for the full number of parts delivered, since these parts were not included in finished products; the only alternative that will work here is to set up a scrap reporting system, from which suppliers can also be paid.

Clearly, there are a large number of major issues to overcome before the receiving department can be eliminated. Though this does result in fewer transaction errors for the accounting department to worry about, this improvement is dwarfed by the changes needed to bring it about. Accordingly, this best practice should only be attempted if there are a number of other reasons, probably involving other departments, for eliminating the receiving function.

ELIMINATE THE WAREHOUSE

The source of many accounting-related transactions is the warehouse. This department records entries for the receipt, movement, and issuance of parts to and from stock. If any of these transactions are incorrect, the inventory quantities used to derive the cost of goods sold, as well as of on-hand inventory will be incorrect. In addition, there is probably a fair amount of obsolete inventory somewhere in the warehouse, which the accounting staff must identify and cost out. These are major issues that can seriously impact the accuracy of the financial statements.

A very difficult best practice to implement is the complete elimination of the inventory, which in turns means the elimination of the warehouse. Several world-class companies have achieved this best practice by switching to just-in-time receiving and production, which allows them to bypass the storage of all parts in a warehouse. By doing so, a company can avoid all of the transactions needed to log something in and out of the warehouse, not to mention avoiding all the staffing, space, insurance, and inventory obsolescence and damage costs that go along with having a warehouse. From the perspective of the accounting staff, this is the ultimate best practice in inventory accounting, since there is *no* inventory to account for besides the relatively minor amounts in work-in-process.

Unfortunately, this is a goal that very few companies achieve, for a variety of reasons. First, just-in-time receiving and production are very difficult concepts to fully implement, given the difficulty of changing both internal processes and the delivery systems of suppliers. Further, there may be some parts that are shipped from long distances, or which are difficult to obtain, and which *must* be kept in some sort of warehousing facility. Finally, the existing amount of inventory may take years to reduce to zero, unless a company is willing to take write-downs to eliminate some stock or return it to suppliers at a loss. Nonetheless, if a company can convert even some of its systems to just-in-time, it is possible to send received parts directly to the production facility without spending any time in the warehouse; this reduces the number of inventory transactions that can be made in error, resulting in an overall increase in the level of accounting accuracy.

LOCK DOWN THE WAREHOUSE AREA

The single most important cause of inventory inaccuracy is parts "walking out of the warehouse." This means that the physical layout of the warehouse allows anyone to wander in and take any parts they need for the production process. When this happens, there is no record that any item was taken from stock, so no one knows what is left on the shelf, or even if there is *anything* left, which renders any automated reordering system useless. From the accountant's perspective, the physical inventory count will probably be significantly different from what the accounting records show, resulting in a large inventory variance at the end of the year.

All of these problems can be eliminated by segregating the warehouse. This is done by setting up a fence around the entire storage area and locking the gate when there are no warehouse personnel on hand. In addition, there must be iron-clad rules about who has a key to this gate. If too many keys are handed out, anyone will still be able to enter the warehouse after hours. To prevent this, there should be no more than one key given to the production personnel, and then only to the most responsible person, who will faithfully mark down anything taken from the warehouse. If possible, even this should be avoided by pre-positioning any needed parts outside of the warehouse for use by the production staff when the warehouse staff is not available. Further, the warehouse staff must be carefully instructed in why no one but them is allowed in the warehouse, should receive additional training in how to process inventory transactions, and then be given a bonus plan based on reaching high inventory accuracy levels. Only by taking all of these steps will there be a good chance that non-warehouse personnel can be kept out of the warehouse, and that the warehouse personnel are committed to a high level of inventory accuracy.

This best practice is always opposed by the production department, which claims that either it will be too time consuming to wait for the warehouse department to pick parts from the shelf, or else that they will not be able to get any parts at all if the warehouse staff is not available. The best way to allay these fears is to have all systems in place and fully functional before locking down the warehouse. By doing so, the production staff will find that there are no problems with the new system and will have no complaints left to make.

MODIFY THE BILLS OF MATERIAL BASED ON ACTUAL SCRAP LEVELS

The typical company relies heavily on its bills of material to determine the cost of its products. They can be used not only as a reference tool to quickly look up a cost, but also as the primary means of calculating the remaining on-hand inventory balance if back-flushing is used. Under the back-flushing concept, a company simply enters the amount of its production for the day, and the computer will automatically clear this inventory from stock, based on the amount of materials that should have been used, as noted in the bills of material. Though this approach is remarkably easy to use, given the reduced volume of paperwork, it can quickly lead to very inaccurate inventory balances if the underlying bills of material are incorrect. This is a particularly difficult problem if the true scrap level is not reflected in the bills of material. If this is the case, the amount of materials listed in each bill will be too small, resulting in an inadequate amount being back flushed out of inventory, which leaves inventory balances too high.

The best practice that resolves this situation is to ensure that the correct scrap levels are included in each bill of material. By doing so, the amount of material back-flushed out of the inventory will be much more accurate, resulting in a more accurate inventory, cost of goods sold, and fewer (if any) material stock-outs to interfere with production.

To add accurate scrap rates to the bills of material, there must be a scrap reporting system already in place that notes the precise quantities of scrap that occur whenever a product is produced. With this information in hand, one can easily update scrap rates with a great deal of precision. Also, access to the information in the bills of material must be severely restricted to ensure that no one but an authorized user is allowed to change the scrap rates in bills; without this security point, there is no way to ensure that the most accurate scrap rates are indeed in the computer system. In addition, there must be constant attention to the scrap rates, for they will change over time as production practices and machinery change. Without this continual review process, the existing scrap rates in the bills of material will gradually depart from actual rates. Finally, there should be a provision in the computer system for automatically changing large blocks of scrap rates in many bills of material; given the time needed to alter individual scrap line items in all existing bills, this is an extremely helpful labor-saving device to have on hand. If all of these issues are addressed, the accuracy of the bills of material should rise markedly, along with the accuracy of the inventory and cost of goods sold.

MOVE INVENTORY TO FLOOR STOCK

The typical inventory contains an enormous number of small parts, many of which are difficult to track, are not stored in easily countable containers, and which require a large amount of paperwork in proportion to their size and frequency of usage. In short, they are a pain for the warehouse staff to handle. Likewise, they represent a minor irritation for the accounting staff, since they must all be counted during the physical inventory counting process, and, because of the difficulty of counting them, they take up an inordinate amount of time. Further, they can easily represent one-third of the total number of inventory items, which is one-third more costing documentation than the accounting staff wants to track. Accordingly, it is safe to say that the smallest and most inexpensive parts in inventory are the root cause of a great deal of extra work for the employees of several departments.

A moderately easy best practice that takes care of this problem is shifting the small inventory items out of the warehouse and onto the shop floor, where they are treated as supplies. This approach carries the multiple benefits of requiring far less inventory handling work from the warehouse staff, fewer inventory counts during the physical inventory process, and much less inventory costing work from the accounting staff. In addition, it brings more inventory close to the shop floor, where the production staff appreciates the readier access, as well as not having to go to the parts counter to requisition additional parts. This is one of the rare best practices that is greeted with universal approval by a multitude of personnel, not just those in the accounting department.

Though this step can be taken quickly, one should be mindful of the danger of issuing a quantity of expensive parts to the shop floor that may quickly disappear, resulting in a significant loss. For these few costly items, it may be better to leave them in the warehouse. Also, there must be a tracking system in place on the shop floor, whereby someone can check part bins and quickly determine which parts must be re-ordered. There are a variety of simple systems available that accomplish this, such as painting a re-order fill line in each storage tray, or using a two-bin system, where parts are re-ordered as soon as one bin is emptied. A manual re-order system is necessary for shop supplies, since it is no longer in the inventory database, where re-ordering can be done automatically, based on recorded inventory levels. Also, some of the parts being pulled from the warehouse may be listed in bills of material, which can be a problem if a company uses back-flushing. In this instance, items will be automatically withdrawn from the quantity shown in the computer system as soon as production is recorded, so the system will show negative usage of items that are no longer there. One should carefully consider and resolve all of these problems before moving parts out of inventory and into floor stock.

REVIEW INVENTORY RETURNED TO THE WAREHOUSE

Most organizations that produce any sort of tangible product will be familiar with this scenario: the warehouse staff uses a computer-generated picking list to pick a number of items from the shelf for use in an upcoming manufacturing order, delivers these items to the production facility, and then finds after the job is completed that a number of items are returned to the warehouse, even though the pick list it used was intended to completely use up all items picked. Any returns of this type indicate that the bills of material used to compile the pick lists are incorrect. When this happens, the bills of material are listing too high a quantity of materials; if these bills are also used to calculate the amount of items to be purchased, this results in an excessive number of purchases being made. From an accounting perspective, an inaccurate bill of material leads to inaccurate product costs, which results in an inaccurate finished goods valuation.

The best way to avoid this issue is to create a procedure for closely examining the parts returned to the warehouse, in order to determine exactly which line items in the bills of material are inaccurate. This may require the assistance of the engineer who is responsible for each bill of material, since this person has the most knowledge of what is supposed to be contained in each product. By making changes to the bills, one can improve the accuracy of purchases, eliminate the labor of the warehouse staff in logging parts back into the warehouse, and be assured of accurate finished goods costs.

The only problem with installing this procedure is that it requires the active cooperation of the warehouse manager, who will most likely try to avoid the hassle of investigating product returns and just put items back on the shelf with no further investigation. However, explaining that a proper amount of up-front investigation will lead to a smaller number of part returns in the future may sway this person to be of more assistance.

This best practice can also be used in reverse, so that any additional parts issuances to the production floor are investigated. In this situation, the quantities listed on the bills of material are too low, resulting in parts shortages that will probably lead to incomplete production runs, on the grounds that the production staff runs out of parts before completing the scheduled quantity of products.

SEGREGATE CUSTOMER-OWNED INVENTORY

A dangerous problem for many controllers is incorrectly valuing inventory too high because customer-owned inventory is mixed into it. This problem is especially common in cases where customers frequently ship components to a company for inclusion in finished products. This situation arises when a customer has the rights to a proprietary product component, prefers to do some finishing work on selected components, or only wants a company to do final assembly work on its products. When any of these situations arise, the receiving staff commonly makes the mistake of recording receipts as company-owned stock and storing it alongside all other inventory in the warehouse. As a result, the inventory can be massively overvalued, leading to incorrectly reported profits.

The best way to eliminate this problem is to institute procedures and set up segregated areas that allow one to promptly identify customer-owned products at the receiving dock and shunt them immediately to the segregated area. By doing so, one can be assured of having much more accurate inventory quantities and costs. To implement this best practice, it is critical to require a purchase order on all items arriving at the receiving dock. With this procedure in place, the receiving staff can quickly identify all receipts that the purchasing department has previously noted on a purchase order as being owned by a customer. With this information in hand, the receiving staff can easily record the entry in the computer system and then move the items to a separately marked-off area. This approach results in the storage of item quantity information in the computer system so the warehouse staff can easily find the parts, but at a zero cost, meaning the accounting staff does not make the mistake of increasing the amount of company-owned inventory.

The main problem with using this methodology is that the purchasing and warehousing departments must get used to issuing purchase orders for *all* items received, while also rejecting all items shipped to the company without attached purchase orders. Only by closely following these procedures can one be sure of identifying all customer-owned inventory at the point of acceptance.

STREAMLINE THE PHYSICAL COUNT PROCESS

Some companies find that they are unable to produce anything for several days while count teams perform a physical count of all on-hand inventory. When this happens, a corporation loses sales, since it cannot produce anything. In addition, the resulting inventory is not entirely accurate, since the counting process is frequently conducted by people who do not have a thorough knowledge of what they are counting, which results in incorrect counts and misidentified parts. Also, key people are taken away from their other work to conduct the count, resulting in little or no attention to customers for the duration of the count. Finally, the accounting staff usually stops all other work in order to devote itself to the processing of count tags. Thus, the physical count is a highly disruptive and inaccurate process.

For those organizations that cannot entirely dispense with the physical count, it is still possible to streamline the process so that fewer resources are assigned to it, while keeping the accuracy level relatively high. The improvements are as follows:

- *Eliminate some inventory from the count with cycle-counting.* For situations where a company has just started cycle-counting (see the "Eliminate the Physical Count Process" section in this chapter) but has not yet brought accuracy levels up to a sufficiently high level, it may still be possible to concentrate the cycle-counting effort on a few key areas. By doing so, the accuracy of the inventory in these locations will be so high that there is no need to conduct a physical count.

- *Enter location code on tags.* When counters are entering information on count tags, they should also enter a location code. With this information, it is much easier for the accounting staff to later locate where a tag was used to record information, rather than wandering through the warehouse in a frustrated search for the information. This approach is even better than the common practice of tracking blocks of tags that are assigned to teams counting specific locations; though this brings a review person to the general vicinity of an inventory item, it does not precisely identify the location, which leads to lost time while someone searches for the part.

- *Enter tags directly into the computer.* It is much more efficient to directly enter tag information into the computer system, rather than entering it into an electronic spreadsheet for manual comparison to a computer-generated inventory report. This approach allows the computer to automatically issue a comparison of the counted quantities to the quantities already stored in the computer, so that one can quickly determine where there may be counting errors. Most good computer software packages contain this feature; if not, one must evaluate the cost of programming the feature into the system.

- *Identify all items in advance.* A team should review the warehouse well in advance of the physical count to spot all items that lack identifying part numbers. By researching these items and correctly marking them in advance, the counting teams do not have to address this task while also trying to count inventory, thereby shortening the counting process.

- *Only allow warehouse staff to count.* Warehouse employees have an excellent knowledge of all the parts stored in the warehouse and so are the most qualified to identify and count inventory in the most efficient manner possible. If other, less knowledgeable people are brought into the counting process, it is much more likely that there will be counting problems, resulting in wasted time at the end of the physical count, when extra counting teams must be dispatched to research potential miscounts.

- *Only conduct one count.* Do not count something more than once! Though some companies conduct a double count of all inventory items and then conduct a comparison of the two counts to spot errors, it is much easier and faster to complete a single count and compare this to the book balances already stored in the computer system. Conducting a double count adds to the time and effort needed to complete the counting process.

- *Pre-count the inventory.* A team should begin counting the inventory days or weeks in advance of the formal physical inventory count. This group's job is to gather inventory into single locations, count it, seal it into containers, and mark the correct quantity on the containers. By doing so, it is much easier for the physical count teams to complete their work in an efficient and accurate manner. Though this may seem like an considerable amount of advance work (it is), it results in a much shorter interval for the physical count, which allows a company to be shut down only for the briefest possible time.

When these suggestions are implemented together or individually, a company will experience significant reductions in the effort needed to complete a physical inventory, while increasing the accuracy of the resulting information. For a more comprehensive best practice that entirely eliminates the need for a physical count, continue on to the next section.

TRACK INVENTORY ACCURACY

A controller is always concerned about the accuracy of the inventory. If it is off by even a few percent at the end of the year, the annual physical count may result in a large alteration in profits that will cost the controller his or her job on the grounds that inaccurate financial statements have been issued. Furthermore, the purchasing staff cannot properly order replacement parts if it does not have an accurate idea of what is currently in stock, while the production department never knows when parts that it needs for current jobs will not be in stock. Thus, all these departments are deeply affected by the accuracy of the inventory.

The way to gain some assurance about overall levels of accuracy is to track inventory accuracy with periodic audits. By doing so, one can determine if there is an accuracy problem, resulting in further steps as outlined elsewhere in this chapter, such as locking down the warehouse and shifting inventory into the floor stock area. To review accuracy, one must be able to print out a report from the computer system that shows the inventory in each warehouse location. Then an accounting person should take a sample of items from this list and verify that the items listed on it are indeed in stock in the correct quantities, and that they are stored in the correct locations. Similarly, a small sample of items should be traced from the shelf to the computer report to verify that all items are being tracked in the computer system. The total of all correct items should be divided by the total amount sampled to determine the accuracy percentage. For even the largest warehouse, a sample size of thirty items is usually sufficient to determine the accuracy of the entire facility. This information should be reported to management and posted for the warehouse staff to see. By showing this information to the warehouse staff and tying a series of bonus payments to it, one can be assured of an improvement in the overall level of accuracy.

There is little resistance by anyone to tracking inventory accuracy, though there are two systemic problems that may interfere with it. One is that the computer system must be able to produce a report that sorts inventory by location—if not, the auditing person will not be able to find items in the warehouse without a long search, turning the audit into a tedious affair that can last hours. The other problem is that the computer system must store location information for each part. If parts are scattered throughout the warehouse with no record of their precise location, it will be exceedingly labor-intensive to track down anything. If these two problems can be overcome, the auditing process becomes a simple and mechanical one that only takes an hour or so to complete.

VERIFY THAT ALL RECEIPTS ARE ENTERED IN THE COMPUTER AT ONCE

There is nothing that throws a wrench into a company's production planning and accounting more than the delayed entry of warehouse receiving into the computer system. When this happens (or rather, when it does *not* happen), the purchasing staff does not know if materials have arrived and they begin a series of frantic calls to suppliers to determine when items are to be shipped. Likewise, the production scheduling staff decides not to produce something because it does not see any receipt in the computer system. Finally, the accounting staff has a very difficult time determining what was really received at the end of the accounting period, resulting in the reporting of inaccurate inventory figures in the financial statements. All this because someone in the warehouse is slow in entering receipts.

The obvious best practice is to make the warehouse staff make their receiving entries as soon as they receive any parts, but the solution is not quite so simple. The underlying reason why receipts are not being entered at once is probably because the staff is too busy to do it, and so this chore waits until a slow period, perhaps at the end of the day. Thus, to make them enter receipts more quickly, one must find a better way to enter the receipts, one that is so simple and easy there is no excuse to delay the process. One way is to require all suppliers to attach a bar-coded sheet to all shipments, allowing the receiving staff to scan this sheet directly into the computer system, thereby recording the entry. This is a quick and easy way to approach the receiving data-entry task. Another is to restructure the receiving data-entry screen so that one only needs to enter the purchase order number upon which any receipt is based. The purchase order then comes up on the screen, and the receiver quickly notes the quantity received. This latter approach is also a good way to pay customers without the extra effort of using the accounts payable staff (see Chapter 3). The latter approach carries with it the added benefit of forcing suppliers to provide only the purchase order number with their shipments— many suppliers resist having to bar-code the information on their shipments. Either technique is an effective way to reduce the time needed to enter receipts, thereby eliminating a host of downstream problems.

TOTAL IMPACT OF BEST PRACTICES ON THE INVENTORY FUNCTION

The impact of the fourteen best practices described in this chapter on the inventory function is a considerable increase in the accuracy of inventory information. They are not designed to directly improve the functions of the warehouse, since this book only deals with accounting improvements. Nonetheless, it would be strange if the warehouse personnel were not to experience a much easier existence if they had certain knowledge of the exact quantities and locations of all the parts located in the warehouse. As for the accounting staff, improved inventory accuracy leads to much less concern about the accuracy of the inventory and cost-of-goods-sold figures noted in the balance sheet and income statement, respectively. Further, the purchasing staff has a much easier time ordering parts, since it has much better knowledge of the accuracy of the on-hand inventory balances and no longer needs to make a trip to the warehouse to verify this information. Finally, the production department will no longer experience parts shortages due to inaccurate inventory balances, resulting in the timely completion of more production runs. Thus, the best practices shown graphically in Exhibit 15.2 are unique among the best practices listed in this book in that their beneficial impact spreads far beyond the accounting department.

Two of the best practices noted in Exhibit 15.2 are mutually exclusive, so one would not need to implement both—just one or the other. One cannot lock

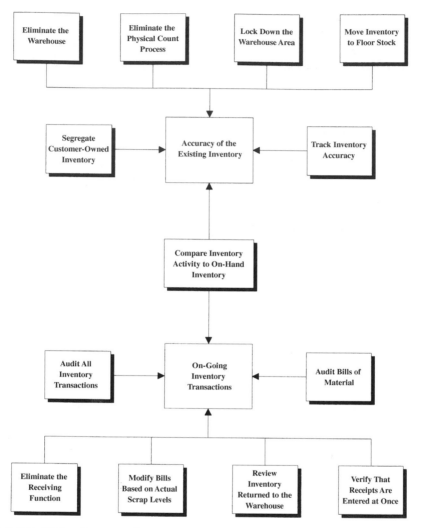

Exhibit 15.2. Impact of Best Practices on the Inventory Function

down the warehouse while eliminating the entire function at the same time. The choice of which one to use is up to the individual company, though most choose locking down the warehouse. The reason is that this approach is vastly easier to implement than the complete elimination of all inventory, which is the only way in which the warehouse can be eliminated. Alternatively, the latter approach requires a long-term commitment to just-in-time production and purchasing principles, and usually takes years to implement.

SUMMARY

This chapter covered a number of best practices that honed in on improving the accuracy of the inventory database. By doing so, the accounting department can be assured of much better accuracy in the inventory valuation figures it records in the financial statements, which has the related benefit of reducing any chance of error in the reported level of profitability.

Unfortunately, the bulk of the best practices noted here are ones that must be implemented and maintained by the warehouse and engineering departments, which means that the controller cannot use any direct authority to ensure their completion and use. Instead, this is a case where active persuasion is the key component of the implementation effort on the part of the controller.

Chapter 16

Payroll Best Practices

The payroll function involves a large clerical workload occuring shortly before and at the end of each pay period. For example, the typical payroll department collects time cards, calculates the amount due, plus overtime premiums, checks with supervisors regarding questionable time cards, subtracts deductions of various kinds, cuts the checks, issues them, and reconciles any differences when employees bring in their paychecks with questions. After this frenetic time period, there is little for the department to do—until the end of the next pay period arrives. This highly predictable surge and drop in the payroll staff's workload can be a difficult one for a controller to manage because it requires either large amounts of overtime by the payroll staff during the heaviest work periods, or else a re-distribution of the accounting department staff to assist in the effort from time to time. It is best to avoid the problems associated with periodic strains on the staffing of the accounting department by examining each step of the payroll process and streamlining it to reduce the overall workload. This chapter contains a number of best practices that assist in doing so.

Another problem with the payroll function is that it is very error-prone. For example, it is easy to miss a pay raise, a vacation accrual, or a deduction. Every time this happens, an employee will arrive with questions he or she wants answered on the spot, which seriously impairs the efficiency of the department. In addition, these problems create concern on the part of employees that their paychecks are not being correctly calculated, which causes them to review pay data even more carefully, which in turn brings even more employees to the payroll department, requesting investigation of their problems. Thus, payroll errors not only require valuable time to fix, but also bring about a decline in employee confidence in the accounting department. This chapter contains several best practices that will reduce or eliminate many payroll errors.

Though this chapter reveals many techniques for *reducing* the workload and error rate of the payroll staff, there are no methods for entirely sidestepping the process, as is the case in the accounts payable area, so most of the best practices described here are incremental in nature. The remainder of this chapter describes the implementation problems associated with each best practice, followed by a description of each one.

IMPLEMENTATION ISSUES FOR PAYROLL BEST PRACTICES

For the reader to understand which of these best practices is the right one for a specific situation, it is useful to review the table shown in Exhibit 16.1. This table lists a number of key implementation issues for each best practice. It notes the ease of implementation, which is a crucial point for those people trying to implement changes as quickly as possible. It also points out the likely duration and cost

Exhibit 16.1.   Implementation Issues for Payroll Best Practices

Description	Ease of Implementation	Duration of Implementation	Cost of Implementation
Automate Fax-Back of Payroll Forms	Difficult	Long	Expensive
Automate Vacation Accruals	Easy	Short	Cheap
Avoid Job Costing through the Payroll System	Easy	Short	Cheap
Consolidate Payroll Systems	Difficult	Long	Expensive
Disallow Pre-Payments	Easy	Short	Cheap
Eliminate Personal Leave Days	Easy	Short	Cheap
Give Employees Direct Access to Deduction Data	Difficult	Long	Expensive
Link Payroll Changes to Employee Events	Difficult	Long	Expensive
Link the 401(k) Plan to the Payroll System	Moderate	Long	Medium
Link the Payroll and Human Resources Databases	Difficult	Long	Expensive
Minimize Payroll Cycles	Difficult	Long	Cheap
Outsource the Payroll Function	Difficult	Medium	Medium
Prohibit Deductions for Employee Purchases	Easy	Short	Cheap
Send Remittances as E-mail Messages	Difficult	Long	Expensive
Switch to Salaried Positions	Moderate	Medium	Cheap
Use Bar-Coded Time Clock	Moderate	Medium	Medium
Use Biometric Time Clocks	Moderate	Short	Medium
Use Direct Deposit	Moderate	Medium	Cheap
Use Honor System To Track Vacation and Sick Time	Easy	Short	Cheap
Use Web-Based Payroll Outsourcing	Moderate	Medium	Inexpensive

of implementation, which is of concern to those companies that may have a short time and cost budget for improvements. The table is an effective approach for quickly determining which projects to work on and which ones to avoid.

A danger of using the table in Exhibit 16.1 to pick only the easiest best practices is that these are primarily "quick hits" that will generally have a relatively small impact on the overall level of efficiency of the payroll function. Accordingly, it is important to insert changes that require greater implementation effort and which have a correspondingly higher payback. For example, adding direct deposit is an easy and popular improvement, but a more fundamental change that requires much persuasion and more time to implement is reducing the number of payroll cycles. Creating a mix of both easy and difficult projects is key to showing continuing successes, while working toward greater levels of efficiency over the long term.

The reader should use Exhibit 16.1 to select the best practices listed in the remainder of this chapter that most closely match specific company requirements.

AUTOMATE FAX-BACK OF PAYROLL FORMS

A payroll clerk is the unofficial keeper of the payroll and human resources forms. Employees come to this person to collect these sheets, which can vary from a request to change a payroll deduction to a request to change a 401(k) deduction amount. If a company has many employees, or if there are many company locations, which necessitates putting a form in an envelope and mailing it, the chore of handing out forms can take up a large amount of staff time.

To avoid distributing forms to employees, it is possible to set up an automated fax-back program. This best practice involves having employees contact a computer, either using a Touch-Tone phone or through the computer system, and request that the appropriate form be sent to a fax number close to the employee. The computer has all the forms digitized and stored in its memory, and can make the transmission with no human intervention. For example, an employee accesses the system through a computer, scrolls through a list of available forms, highlights the needed item, enters his or her fax number, and logs off. The form arrives a few moments later. The process is noted in more detail in Exhibit 16.2.

Besides the obvious advantage of eliminating some effort by the payroll staff, an automated fax-back system also has the advantage of always distributing the most recent forms, which means that forms employees submit to the payroll staff never have to be thrown out and re-submitted, since employees always obtain the correct ones. Under a manual distribution system, it is common practice to issue large quantities of forms to outlying locations, so that employees do not constantly call and ask for more forms; however, these forms end up being used for a long time, frequently past the date when they are obsolete. Using an automated fax-back system eliminates this problem. In addition, the system can automatically send along an extra instruction sheet with each distributed form so that employees can easily fill out forms on their own, with no need to bother the

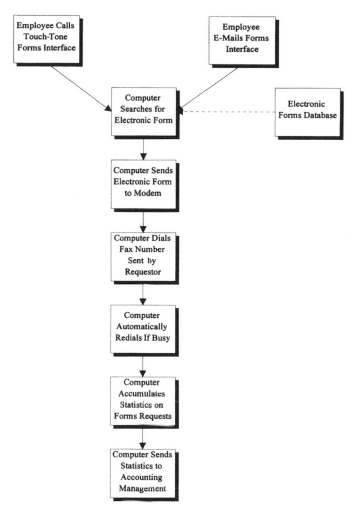

Exhibit 16.2.   Automate Fax-Back of Payroll Forms

payroll staff for help. These extra advantages will tip the scales in favor of the system for many companies.

An automated fax-back system can be rather expensive, so it is necessary to determine all costs prior to undertaking an implementation. The system includes a separate file server linked to one or more phone lines (for receiving Touch-Tone phone requests, as well as for sending forms out to fax machines), plus a scanner for digitizing payroll forms. The best way to justify these added costs is if there are a large number of employees to be serviced, which saves a significant portion of staff time. If there are not enough employees to justify the system, it should not be installed.

AUTOMATE VACATION ACCRUALS

The topic that is of the most interest to the most employees is how much vacation time they have left. In most companies, this information is kept manually by the payroll staff, so employees troop down to the payroll department once a month (and more frequently in the prime summer vacation months!) to see how much vacation time they have left to use. When employees are constantly coming in to find out this information, it is a major interruption to the payroll staff, because it happens at all times of the day, never allowing them to settle down into a comfortable work routine. If there are many employees who want to know about their vacation time, it can be a considerable loss of efficiency for the payroll staff.

A simple way to keep employees from bothering the payroll staff is to include the vacation accrual in employee paychecks. The information appears on the payroll stub, and shows the annual amount of accrued vacation, net of any used time. By feeding this information to employees in every paycheck, there is no need for them to inquire about it in the payroll office, eliminating a major hindrance. However, there are several points to consider before automating vacation accruals. The first one is that the payroll system must be equipped with a vacation accrual calculation option. If not, the software must be modified with custom programming to allow for the calculation and presentation of this information, which may cost more to implement than the projected efficiency savings. Another problem is that the accrual system must be set up properly for each employee when it is originally installed, or else there will be a number of outraged employees crowding into the payroll office, causing more disruption than was the case before. This startup problem is caused by having employees with different numbers of days of vacation allowed per year, as well as some with carry-over vacation from the previous year. If this information is not accurately reflected in the automated vacation accrual system when it is implemented, employees will hasten to the payroll area to correct this problem at once. Another problem is that the accruals must be adjusted over time to reflect changes. Otherwise, once again, employees will interrupt the staff to notify them of changes, thereby offsetting the value of the entire system. For example, an employee may switch from two to three weeks of allowed vacation at the fifth anniversary of his hiring. The payroll department must have a schedule of when this person's vacation accrual amount changes to the three-week level, or the employee will come in and complain about it. If these problems can be overcome, using vacation accruals becomes a relatively simple means of improving the efficiency of the payroll department.

AVOID JOB COSTING THROUGH THE PAYROLL SYSTEM

Some controllers have elaborate cost accounting systems set up that accumulate a variety of costs from many sources, sometimes to be used for activity-based costing and more frequently for job costing. One of these costs is labor, which is sometimes accumulated through the payroll system. When this is done, employees use lengthy time cards where they record the time spent on many activities during the day, resulting in vastly longer payroll records than would otherwise be the case. This is a problem when the payroll staff is asked to sort through and add up all of the job-costing records, since this increases the workload of the payroll personnel by an order of magnitude. In addition, the payroll staff may be asked to enter the job-costing information that it has just compiled into the job-costing database, which is yet another task that gets in the way of processing the payroll.

The obvious solution is to not allow job costing to be merged into the payroll function, thereby allowing the payroll staff to vastly reduce the amount of work it must complete, as well as shrink the number of opportunities for calculation errors. However, this step may meet with opposition from those people who need the job-costing records. There are several ways to avoid conflict over the issue. One is to analyze who is charging time to various projects or activities and see if the proportions of time charged vary significantly over time; if they do not, there is no reason to continue tracking job-costing information for hours worked. Another possibility is to split the functions so that the payroll staff collects its payroll data independently of the job-costing data collection, which can be handled by someone else. Either possibility will keep the job-costing function from interfering with the orderly collection of payroll information.

CONSOLIDATE PAYROLL SYSTEMS

A company that grows by acquisition is likely to have a number of payroll systems—one for each company that it has acquired. This situation may also arise for highly decentralized companies that allow each company location to set up its own payroll system. Though this approach does allow each location to process payroll in accordance with its own rules and payment periods, while also allowing for local maintenance of employee records, there are several serious problems that can be solved by the consolidation of all these systems into a single, centralized payroll system.

One problem with having many payroll systems is that employee payroll records cannot be shifted through a company when an employee is transferred to a new location. Instead, the employee is listed as having been terminated in the payroll system of the location that he is leaving and is then listed as a new hire in the payroll system of the new location. By constantly re-entering an employee as a new hire, it is impossible to track the dates and amounts of pay raises; the same problem arises for the human resources staff, who cannot track eligibility dates for medical insurance or vesting periods for pension plans. In addition, every time employee data is re-entered into a different payroll system, there is a risk of data inaccuracies that may result in such embarrassments as wrong pay rates or mailing checks to the wrong address. Also, a company cannot easily group data for company-wide payroll reporting purposes. For all these reasons, it is common practice to consolidate payroll systems into a single, centralized location that operates with a single payroll database.

Before embarking on such a consolidation, one must consider the costs of implementation. One is that a consolidation of many payroll systems may require an expensive new software package that must run on a large computer, which entails extra capital and software maintenance costs. In addition, there is probably a significant cost associated with converting the data from the disparate databases into the new consolidated one. In addition, there may be extra time needed to test the tax rates for all company locations, in order to avoid penalties for improper tax withholdings and submissions. Finally, the timing of the implementation is of some importance. Many companies prefer to make the conversion on the first day of the new year so that there is no need to enter detailed pay information into the system for the prior year to issue year-end payroll tax reports to the government. The cost of consolidating payroll systems is considerable and must be carefully analyzed before the decision to convert is reached.

Switching from many payroll systems to a single one is an excellent best practice to implement, with many long-term benefits. However, due to the conversion cost, it is important to weigh the costs and benefits of the project and to insert the project into a company's capital budget only when the funds are definitely available.

DISALLOW PRE-PAYMENTS

Many employees do not have the monetary resources to see them through until the next payday. Their solution is to request a pay advance, which is re-paid at the time of the next payday. It is a humane gesture on the part of the payroll manager to comply with such requests, but it plays havoc with the efficiency of the payroll department. Whenever such a request is made, the payroll staff must manually calculate the taxes to take out of the payment, then manually cut a check and have it signed. However, the inefficiencies are not yet over! In addition, the staff must manually enter the pay advance in the computer system so that the amount is deducted from the next pay check. For larger advances, it may be necessary to make deductions over several paychecks, which requires even more work. Clearly, paycheck pre-payments do not help the efficiency of the payroll department. This is a particularly large problem in companies where a large proportion of the employees are paid at or near the minimum wage, since these people do not receive enough money to meet their needs.

The best practice that solves this problem seems simple, but can be surprisingly difficult to implement. One must create a rule that no paycheck pre-payments will be handed out, which effectively ends the extra processing required of the payroll personnel. The trouble with this rule is that a needy employee can usually present such a good case for a pay advance that exceptions will be made, which grinds away at the rule over time until it is completely ignored. Other managers will assist in tearing down the rule by complaining that they will lose good employees if advances are not provided to them. The best possible way to stand firm with the rule is for a company to form an association with a local lending institution that specializes in short-term loans. Then, if an employee requests an advance, he can be directed to the lending institution, which will arrange for an interest-bearing loan to the employee. When this arrangement exists, it is common for employees to tighten their budgets rather than pay the extra interest charged for use of the lender's money. This improves employee finances while increasing the processing efficiency of the payroll staff. In short, this best practice involves two steps: prohibiting pay advances while at the same time arranging for alternative financing for employees.

ELIMINATE PERSONAL LEAVE DAYS

A common task for the payroll staff is to either manually or automatically track the vacation time employees earn and use. Depending on the level of automation, this task can require some portion of staff time every week on an ongoing basis. Some companies then take the additional step of accruing and tracking the usage of personal leave days, which are essentially the same thing as vacation time, but tracked under a different name. By having both vacation and personal leave days, the payroll staff is reduced to tracking data in both categories, which doubles the work required to simply track vacation time.

A reasonable, and easily implemented, best practice is to convert personal leave days into vacation days and eliminate the extra category of time off. By doing so, the payroll staff can cut in half the time it devotes to analyzing employee vacation time. The only resistance to this change usually comes from the human resources department, which likes to offer a variety of benefits to match those other companies offer; for example, if a competitor offers personal leave days, then so should the company. Though only a matter of semantics, this can cause a problem when implementing the simpler system.

GIVE EMPLOYEES DIRECT ACCESS TO DEDUCTION DATA

A major task for the payroll staff is to meet with employees to go over the effect of any deduction changes they wish to make, calculate the changes, and enter them into the payroll database. This can be a particularly time-consuming task if the number of possible deduction options is large, if employees are allowed to make deduction changes at any time, or if employees are not well educated in the impact of deduction changes on their net pay.

A particularly elegant best practice that resolves this problem is to give employees direct access to the deduction data so they can determine the impact of deduction changes themselves and enter the changes directly into the payroll database. To do so, one must construct an interface to the payroll database that lists all deductions taken from employee paychecks (with the exception of garnishments, which employees would be tempted to reduce to zero). However, this is not enough, for most deductions are usually tied to a benefit of some kind. For example, a deduction for a medical plan can only be changed if the underlying medical plan option is altered. Accordingly, an employee needs access to a "split screen" of information, with one side showing benefit options and the other side showing the employee's gross pay, all deductions, and net pay. This view allows one to modify deductions and watch the impact on net pay. Examples of deductions for which this data view will work are:

- Federal tax deductions
- State tax deductions
- Medical plan coverage
- Dental plan coverage
- 401(k) deductions

An example of this approach is a dental plan. On one side of the computer screen, an employee is presented with five dental plan options, all with different costs. The employee can scroll through the list and select any option, while watching the selection automatically change the payroll calculation on the other side of the screen. Once the employee finds a selection that works best, he presses a button and the change is entered into the payroll system. Such a system usually includes some selection blocks so that an uncertain employee does not constantly change deductions. For example, the software may contain a limitation of one health plan change per year.

This approach completely eliminates all work by the payroll staff to enter deduction changes into the computer. An added benefit is that employees are responsible for their own data-entry mistakes. If they make an incorrect entry, they can go into the system themselves and correct it. The system can also be expanded to include other data items, such as employee addresses and phone numbers. In addition, the deduction modeling system just noted allows employees to determine precisely what their net pay will be, eliminating any surprises. In a more traditional system, an employee might make a deduction change without realizing the full impact of the change on his net pay and end up back in the payroll office, demanding a reversion back to the old deduction level. By using the modeling system, the payroll staff can eliminate such multiple visits from employees.

This system is extremely useful for eliminating several payroll processing tasks, but it will only work if a company is willing to invest in the custom design of an employee interface, as well as the provision of computers to all employees who want to access the payroll system in this manner. Given the cost of the system, it is most commonly found only in larger companies with many employees, where the cost-benefit tradeoff is very clear cut.

In short, using a special payroll interface to give employees direct access to their own payroll deduction information is an excellent way to lessen the work of the payroll department, while also giving employees greater control over the benefit plans they want.

LINK PAYROLL CHANGES TO EMPLOYEE EVENTS

There are many payroll changes that must be made when certain events occur in an employee file. Many of these changes are never made, because either the payroll staff is so busy with the standard, daily processing of information that it has no time to address them, or the payroll staff does not possess enough knowledge to link the payroll changes to the employee events. For example, when an employee is married, this should trigger a change in that person's W-4 form, so that the amount of taxes withheld will reflect those for a married person. Automation can create many of these linkages. Here are some examples:

- As soon as an employee reaches the age of fifty-five, the system issues a notification to the pension manager to calculate the person's potential pension, while also notifying the employee of his or her pension eligibility. These notifications can be by letter, but a linkage between the payroll system and the e-mail system could result in more immediate notification.

- As soon as an employee has been with a company for ninety days, his or her period of probation has been completed. The system should then automatically include the employee in the company's dental, medical, and disability plans, and include deductions for these amounts in the person's paycheck. Similarly, the system can automatically enroll the employee in the company's 401(k) plan and enter the deductions in the payroll system. Since these pay changes should not come as a surprise to the employee, the system should also generate a message to the employee, detailing the changes made and their net payroll impact.

- When a company is informed of an employee's marriage, the computer system generates a notice to the employee that a new W-4 form should be filled out, while also sending a new benefit enrollment form, in case the employee wishes to add benefits for the spouse or any children. Finally, a notification message can ask the employee if he or she wants to change the beneficiary's name on the pension plan to that of the spouse.

- When an employee notifies the company of an address change, the system automatically notifies all related payroll and benefit suppliers of the change, such as the 401(k) plan administrator and health insurance provider.

- When a new employee is hired, the system sends a message to the purchasing department, asking that business cards be ordered for the employee. Another message goes to the information systems department, requesting that the appropriate levels of system security be set up for the new hire. Yet another message goes to the training department, asking that a training plan be set up for the new employee.

Many of these work flow features are available on high-end accounting and human resources software packages. However, this software costs more than a million dollars in most cases, and so is well beyond the purchasing capability of many smaller companies. An alternative is to customize an existing software package to include these features, but the work required will be expensive. Accordingly, these changes should only be contemplated if there are many employees, since this would result in a sufficient volume of savings to justify the added expense.

LINK THE 401(K) PLAN TO THE PAYROLL SYSTEM

A common activity for the payroll staff is to take the 401(k) deduction information from the payroll records as soon as each payroll cycle is completed, enter it into a separate database for 401(k) deductions, copy this information onto a diskette, and send it to the company's 401(k) administration supplier, who uses it to determine the investment levels of all employees, as well as for discrimination testing. This can be a lengthy data-entry process if there are many employees, and it is certainly not a value-added activity when the core task is simply moving data from one database to another one.

The best way to avoid re-typing 401(k) payroll deductions is to link the payroll system directly into a 401(k) plan. This is done by outsourcing the payroll processing function to a supplier who also offers a 401(k) plan. A good example of this is Automated Data Processing (ADP), which offers linkages to a number of well-known mutual funds through its payroll system. When a company uses ADP's payroll and 401(k) services, a payroll department can record a 401(k) payroll deduction for an employee just once and ADP will then take the deduction and automatically move it into a 401(k) fund, with no additional bookkeeping required from the payroll staff. For those companies with many employees, this can represent a significant reduction in the workload of the payroll staff.

There are two problems with this best practice. One is that a company must first outsource its payroll function to a supplier that offers 401(k) administration services, which the company controller may not be willing to do (see the "Outsource the Payroll Function" section in this chapter). The second problem is converting to the new 401(k) plan. To do so, all employees in the old plan must be moved to the new plan. The associated paperwork may be great enough to not make the transition worthwhile; also, the old 401(k) administrator may require a separation fee if the company is terminating its services inside of a minimum time interval, which may involve a small penalty payment. These issues should be considered before switching to a centralized payroll and 401(k) processing system.

Linking the 401(k) plan to the payroll system is worth considering for those companies who have already outsourced their payroll processing, since it eliminates the manual movement of data from the payroll database to the 401(k) database.

LINK THE PAYROLL AND HUMAN RESOURCES DATABASES

The payroll database shares many data elements with the human resources database. Unfortunately, these two databases are usually maintained by different departments—accounting for the first and human resources for the second. Consequently, any employee who makes a change to one database, such as an address field in the payroll system, must then walk to the human resources department to have the same information entered again for other purposes, such as benefits administration or a pension plan. Thus, there is an obvious inefficiency for the employee who must go to two departments for changes, while the accounting and human resources staffs also duplicate each other's data-entry efforts.

The obvious best practice here is to tie the two databases together. This can be done by purchasing a software package that automatically consolidates the two databases into a single one, but the considerable cost of buying and implementing an entirely new software package will grossly exceed the cost savings obtained by consolidating the data. A less costly approach is to create an interface between the two systems that automatically stores changes made to each database and updates the other one as a daily batch program. Creating this interface can still be expensive, since it involves a reasonable amount of customized programming work. Consequently, consolidating the payroll and human resources databases is an expensive proposition and is usually done only when both computer systems are being brought together for more reasons than a simple reduction in data-entry work.

MINIMIZE PAYROLL CYCLES

Many payroll departments are fully occupied with processing some kind of payroll every week and possibly even several times in one week. This situation arises when different groups of employees are paid for different time periods. For example, hourly employees may be paid every week, whereas salaried employees may be paid twice a month. In addition, the employees of acquired companies can be paid in accordance with the pay periods that were in existence prior to their acquisition. Processing multiple payroll cycles eats up most of the free time of the payroll staff, leaving it with little room for cleaning up paperwork or researching improvements to its basic operations.

An excellent best practice that eliminates a considerable amount of inefficiency is to consolidate the payroll cycles into a single, company-wide cycle. By doing so, the payroll staff no longer has to spend extra time on additional payroll processing, nor does it have to worry about the different pay rules that may apply to each processing period—everyone is treated exactly the same. To make payroll processing even more efficient, it is useful to lengthen the payroll cycles. For example, a payroll department that processes weekly payrolls must run the payroll fifty-two times a year, whereas one that processes monthly payrolls only does so twelve times a year, which eliminates 75 percent of the processing that the first department must handle. These changes represent an enormous reduction in the payroll-processing time the accounting staff requires.

Prior to reducing the number of payroll cycles, however, one must bring up the issue with employees, who may have a considerable number of objections. The main complaint will be that employees have structured their spending habits around the old pay system. For example, employees who currently receive a paycheck every week may have a great deal of difficulty in adjusting their spending to a paycheck that only arrives once a month. If a company were to make a switch from a short to a long pay cycle, it is extremely likely that the payroll staff will be deluged with requests for pay advances well before the next paycheck is due for release, which will require a large amount of effort to handle. To overcome this problem, many companies will only lengthen their pay cycles incrementally, usually to once every two weeks or twice a month, and make it clear to employees that pay advances *will* be granted for a limited transition period. By making these incremental changes, a company can keep the level of employee discontent to a minimum.

Another implementation point is to make sure that the rest of the management team is supportive of the length of the new payroll cycle. They must buy into the program because all of their employees will be impacted by the change. If they receive an inordinate volume of complaints from their employees about this issue, they may argue against the change; if enough of them do that, this best practice may never succeed.

In short, consolidating and lengthening payroll cycles is an excellent method for making a significant improvement to the efficiency of the payroll staff, but it must be done with the full approval of the management team and with adequate forewarning of all company employees.

OUTSOURCE THE PAYROLL FUNCTION

A typical in-house payroll department has many concerns. Besides the task of issuing paychecks, it may have to do so for many company locations, where tax rates differ, employees are paid on different dates, and tax payments must be made to state governments by different means (e.g., direct deposit, bank deposit, or mail), and W-2 forms must be issued to all employees at the beginning of each year. Of all these issues, the one carrying the heaviest price for failure is a government tax deposit—missing such a payment by just one day can carry a large penalty that rapidly accumulates in size. All of these problems and costs can be avoided by handing over some or all portions of the payroll function to an outside supplier.

Payroll is one of the most commonly outsourced company functions. There are several good reasons for this. First, a supplier will undertake to pay all payroll taxes without troubling the company. The savings from avoiding government penalties for late tax payments will, in some cases, pay for the cost of the payroll supplier! In addition, the supplier can usually process payroll for all company locations; several suppliers are based in all major cities, so they can handle paycheck deliveries to nearly any location. Other smaller suppliers get around not having multiple locations by sending checks to company locations with overnight delivery services—either approach works well. Another advantage is that nearly all payroll suppliers can deposit payments directly into employee bank accounts, which is something that many in-house payroll systems, especially the smaller ones, are incapable of performing. In addition, the time-consuming task of stuffing checks into envelopes is one that many suppliers will handle, thereby freeing up the internal staff for less mundane work. A typical supplier also provides a wide array of reports, usually including a report-writing package that can address any special reporting needs. Once again, many smaller in-house payroll systems lack a report-writing package, so this can be a real benefit. If these advantages are not enough, one must also remember that payroll suppliers are staffed with a large team of experts who know all about the intricacies of payroll. They can answer payroll questions over the phone, provide specialized or standard training classes, or come out to company locations for hands-on consulting. The wide array of benefits has convinced thousands of companies to switch to an outsourced payroll solution.

However, before jumping on the outsourcing bandwagon, one must consider a few reasons for not using a payroll supplier. One is that outsourcing is generally more expensive than an in-house solution. The reason is that the supplier must spend funds on marketing its services and must make a profit—two items that an in-house payroll staff does not have to include in its budget. A supplier will usually sell its services to a company by offering an apparently cheap deal with a small set of baseline services, and then charge high fees for add-on services, such as direct deposit, check stuffing, early check deliveries, report-writing software, and extra human resources additions to the payroll software. As long as a company is well aware of these extra fees and budgets them into its initial cost-benefit calculations, there should be no surprises later on, as more supplier services are added and fees continue to rise. The other main problem with outsourcing is that the payroll database cannot be linked to a company's other computer systems. Since a company's payroll data is usually located in a mainframe computer at an off-site supplier location, it is nearly impossible to create an interface that will allow for user access to payroll data. The best alternative (though a poor one) is to either keypunch the most important data into a company payroll database from payroll reports printed by the supplier or to download data from the supplier's computer. Because of this missing database linkage, a number of larger companies prefer to keep their payroll-processing work in-house.

In short, there are many good reasons for a company to outsource its payroll function to a qualified supplier. The only companies who should not do so are those that are either highly sensitive to the cost of payroll processing, or those who must link their payroll data to other computer databases.

PROHIBIT DEDUCTIONS FOR EMPLOYEE PURCHASES

Many companies allow their employees to use corporate discounts to buy products through them. For example, a company may have obtained a large discount on furniture from a supplier. Its employees buy at the discounted rate and then have the deductions subtracted from their paychecks in convenient installments. Some employees make excessive use of this benefit, purchasing all kinds of supplies through the company; accordingly, it is common to see a very small minority of employees making up the bulk of these purchases. The problem for the payroll staff is that it must keep track of the total amount that each employee owes the company and gradually deduct the amount owed from successive paychecks. If an employee has multiple purchases, the payroll staff must constantly recalculate the amount to be deducted. Depending on the number of employees taking advantage of purchases through the company, this can have a measurable impact on the efficiency of the payroll department.

The apparently easy solution to the employee purchases problem is to prohibit purchases. By doing so, all the extra paperwork associated with employee purchases is immediately swept away. Though a good best practice for most companies to implement, this is one that should first be cleared with senior management. The reason is that some employees may be so accustomed to purchasing through the company that they will be rudely surprised by the change, which may be something that management wants to avoid (especially if valuable employees will be irritated by the change). Also, some companies have valid reasons for allowing employee purchases. The most common situation is when employees buy products that are meant to be used at work, such as work boots or tools. In these cases, the reasons in favor of maintaining a purchasing program may outweigh the reduced efficiency of the payroll department. A possible alternative approach that will still eliminate payroll deductions is to still allow employee purchases, but on condition that either the purchases are billed straight to them, or that the employees pay the company in full as soon as the goods are received.

In short, eliminating employee purchases that require deductions is a simple best practice to implement, though there are employee relations issues that may keep it from being implemented.

SEND REMITTANCES AS E-MAIL MESSAGES

A company may go to a great deal of trouble to install a direct deposit option in order to avoid sending checks to employees, only to find that it must still send a remittance advice, which lists the amounts paid and incidental data such as vacation or sick time earned. Because a company must send its employees some evidence of payment, it is difficult to avoid this distribution step.

A possible solution is to send remittances as e-mail messages, though there are some problems with this approach. This system works by having the payroll system compile a set of electronic messages after each payroll run, which are then loaded into a company's e-mail system for distribution to employees. Though this seems like a relatively simple approach, there are a number of issues to overcome before it will work in a reliable manner. They are as follows:

- *Custom programming.* The existing payroll software must be modified to allow for automated e-mail transmissions. The amount of programming required can be considerable, depending on the complexity of the software. Also, if the software is a "canned" package that is periodically upgraded by a supplier, the custom programming may not work after the next upgrade, since the underlying software code will change.

- *Outsourced payroll.* If a company's payroll is outsourced to a supplier, then the payroll software is probably off-site, at the supplier's computer center. If so, it is highly unlikely that the supplier will agree to customize its payroll software to transmit e-mail messages.

- *Existing e-mail system.* It is impossible to send e-mail messages to employees if there is not a pre-existing e-mail system in place to which all employees are connected. Such a system must be installed before e-mailing payroll remittances can be considered.

- *Employee access to computers.* An obvious problem is having employees, such as production workers, without ready access to computers on which they can check their e-mail. It is possible to avoid this issue by installing free-standing kiosks where all employees can check their e-mail. Another option is to send remittances to the e-mail of employee supervisors, who can then print out the messages and distribute them. Yet another option is to send printed remittances to those employees without e-mail and e-mail remittances to those who can receive them in this manner.

- *Lost e-mail.* It is all too easy to press the "delete" button and see an e-mail message disappear forever. This can be a problem if the deleted e-mail happens to contain a payroll remittance. To avoid this problem, it may be necessary to allow employees to send an e-mail request to the payroll department to request either a new e-mail remittance or a hard copy of the remittance (which may be necessary for other reasons, such as mortgage applications that require a payroll remittance). It may even be possible to have employees contact the payroll database themselves to have a remittance printed out on a local printer, but this option carries the risk of having an employee discover the passwords for other employees, and then print out their payroll remittances, too.

Despite the number of complications that can arise when installing this best practice, it is still useful under certain situations. It is of most use in such service industries as insurance, where nearly all employees have computers, and probably ill-advised in most production industries, where too few employees have ready access to this form of communication. Thus, the distribution of computers among employees is critical to the success of e-mailed payroll remittances.

SWITCH TO SALARIED POSITIONS

When processing payroll, it is evident that the labor required to process the payroll for a salaried person is significantly lower than the labor needed to process payroll for an hourly employee. The reason is that there is no change in the payroll data from period to period for a salaried person, whereas the number of hours worked must be recomputed for an hourly employee every time the payroll is processed. Therefore, it is reasonable to try to shift as many employees as possible over to salaried positions from hourly ones in order to reduce the labor of calculating payroll.

Implementing this best practice can be a significant problem. One issue is that it is not under the control of the accounting department—it is up to the managers of other departments to switch people over to salaried positions, so the controller must rely on persuasion of other managers to make the concept a reality. Another problem is that this best practice tends to run into opposition from unions. They prefer to keep the employees they represent on hourly pay, since this gives employees the opportunity to earn overtime. If a union has a strong presence in a company, this will almost certainly keep a company from switching people to salaried positions for at least those employees who are represented by the union. Finally, there may be legal issues that get in the way of making this conversion work. There are frequently regulations at the state level that prohibit converting employees to salaried positions, with the main determining criterion being that a salaried person must be able to act with minimal supervision—this situation will vary by state, depending on local laws. All of these issues can impede the implementation of a complete conversion of employees to salaried pay.

Given the number of implementation problems just mentioned, it may seem impossible to implement this best practice. However, it is quite possible in some industries. The main factor for success is that the industry have few hourly workers to begin with. For example, a company with many highly educated employees, or one that performs limited manufacturing, may already have so many salaried employees that it becomes a minor cleanup issue to convert over the few remaining hourly employees to salaried positions with a minimum of difficulty. Consequently, it is only possible to completely implement this best practice in certain industries—it should not be attempted in those cases where there is already a high proportion of hourly workers who are spread through many departments, especially when their hourly pay status is protected by a union or local laws.

USE BAR-CODED TIME CLOCKS

The single most labor-intensive task in the payroll area is calculating hours worked for hourly employees. To do so, an accounting clerk must collect all the employee time cards for the most recently completed payroll period, manually add up the hours listed on the cards, and research missing hours with supervisors.

This is a very lengthy process and usually has a very high error rate, due to the large percentage of missing start or stop times on most time cards. The errors are usually found by employees as soon as they are paid, resulting in a loud and (sometimes) boisterous visit to the payroll department, demanding an immediate adjustment to the paid amount with a manual paycheck. This disrupts the payroll department and introduces additional inefficiencies to the process. Improving the process would create a grateful payroll staff!

A common solution to these problems is to install a computerized time clock. This is a clock that requires an employee to "swipe" an employee-specific plastic card through the clock. The card is encoded with an employee-identifying number, using either a bar code or a magnetic stripe. Once the swipe occurs, the clock automatically stores the date and time, and downloads this data upon request to the payroll department's computer, where special software automatically calculates hours worked and highlights any problems for additional research (such as missed swipes). Many such clocks can be installed throughout a large facility, or at outlying locations, so that employees can conveniently record their time, no matter where they may be. The more advanced clocks also track the time periods when employees are supposed to arrive and leave, and require a supervisor's password for card swipes outside of that time period—this feature allows for greater control over employee work hours. Many of these systems also issue absence reports at any time, so that supervisors can easily tell who has not shown up for work. Thus, an automated time clock eliminates much low-end clerical work, while at the same time providing new management tools for supervisors.

Before purchasing a bar-coded time clock, it is important to recognize its limitations. The most important one is cost. This type of time clock usually costs $2,000 to $3,000, or can be leased for several hundred dollars per month. If several clocks are needed, this can add up to a substantial investment. In addition, outlying time clocks that must download their information to a computer at a distant location require their own phone lines, which represents an additional monthly payment to the phone company. There may also be a fee for using the software on the central computer that summarizes all the incoming payroll information. Given these costs, it is most common for bar-coded time clocks to be used only in those situations where there are so many hourly employees in a company, there is a significant time savings in the payroll department resulting from their installation.

USE BIOMETRIC TIME CLOCKS

The bar-coded time clocks noted in the last best practice represent a wonderful improvement in the speed and accuracy with which employee time data can be collected. However, it suffers from an integrity flaw—that employees can use each other's badges to enter and exit from the payroll system. This means that some employees may be paid for hours when they were never really on-site at all.

A division of Ingersoll-Rand has surmounted this problem with the use of biometric time clocks.

Recognition Systems is a company that sells the punch biometric time clock
(as shown at *www.handreader.com*). It requires an employee to place his or her
hand on a sensor, which matches its size and shape to the dimensions already
recorded for that person in a central database. The time entered into the terminal
will then be recorded against the payroll file of the person whose hand was just
measured. Thus, only employees who are on-site can have payroll hours credited
to them. The company sells a variation on the same machine, called the HandKey,
which is used to control access to secure areas. These systems have a secondary
benefit, which is that no one needs an employee badge or pass key; these tend to
be lost or damaged over time, and so represent a minor headache for the accounting or human resources staffs, who must track them. In a biometric monitoring
environment, all an employee needs is a hand.

USE DIRECT DEPOSIT

A major task for the payroll staff is to issue paychecks to employees. This task
can be subdivided into several subsidiary steps. First, the checks must be
printed—though it seems easy, it is all too common for the check run to fail,
resulting in the manual cancellation of the first batch of checks, followed by a
new print run. Next, the checks must be signed by an authorized check signer,
who may have questions about payment amounts which may require additional
investigation. After that, the checks must be stuffed into envelopes and then
sorted by supervisor (since supervisors generally hand out checks to their
employees). The checks are then distributed, usually with the exception of a few
checks that will be held for those employees who are not currently on-site for
later pick-up. Finally, the person in charge of the bank reconciliation must track
those checks that have not been cashed and follow up with employees to get them
to cash their checks—there are usually a few employees who prefer to cash
checks only when they need the money, surprising though this may seem. In
short, there are a startlingly large number of steps involved in issuing payroll
checks to employees. How can we eliminate this work?

Converting to direct deposit is a simple way to eliminate the distribution of
paychecks. This best practice involves issuing payments directly to employee
bank accounts. Besides avoiding some of the steps involved with issuing paychecks, it carries the additional advantage of putting money in employee bank
accounts at once, so that those employees who are off-site on payday do not have
to worry about how they will receive their money—it will appear in their checking accounts automatically, with no effort on their part.

Implementing direct deposit can be somewhat more difficult than one may
first realize. It requires an ability to transfer payment information to the company's
bank in the correct direct deposit format, which the bank uses to shift money to

employee bank accounts. This information transfer can be accomplished either by purchasing an add-on to a company's in-house payroll software, or by paying extra to a payroll outsourcing company to provide the service—either way, there is an expense associated with starting up the service. Also, it can be difficult to get all employees to switch over to direct deposit. Though the benefits to employees may seem obvious, there will be a large proportion of employees who prefer to cash their own checks, or who do not possess bank accounts. To get around this problem, a company can either force all employees to accept direct deposit, or only do so with new employees, with existing employees being allowed to still take paper checks. If employees are forced to accept direct deposit, the company can make the issue less onerous by working with a local bank to provide a free bank account to each employee. Also, there will be the inevitable start-up problems for the first few weeks, resulting in some direct deposits not going through to employees on time. All of these issues make implementing direct deposit somewhat more difficult and expensive than would first appear to be the case.

Besides implementation issues, there are a few other problems to consider before using direct deposit. One is the fee charged by the bank or payroll service to do it—a common charge is one dollar to make a direct deposit to each employee's account, which can add up if there are many employees and frequent pay periods (e.g., once a week). Also, some paper-based form of notification must still be sent to employees so that they know the details of what they have been paid. This means that using direct deposit does not eliminate the steps of printing, envelope stuffing, or check distribution (though there is no need to sign the pay notifications or hold them for stray employees, nor is there any further trouble with tracking payroll checks that have not been cashed). Finally, most companies find that they end up with a dual system— some employees take direct deposit and some go with paper checks—so that they have a *more* complicated system with two forms of payment. However, do not let all these problems shoot down an initiative to use direct deposit. If one follows through on it properly, then most or all employees can still be converted to it over the long term. Despite its disadvantages, direct deposit can be a clear advantage to both the accounting department and employees if properly implemented.

USE HONOR SYSTEM TO TRACK VACATION AND SICK TIME

It is common for the payroll staff to be in charge of tracking the vacation and sick time used by employees. This involves sending out forms for employees to fill out whenever they take time off, usually requiring their supervisor's signature. Upon receipt, the payroll staff logs the used time in the payroll system and files the forms away in employee personnel folders. If the payroll staff does not account for this information correctly in the payroll system, employees will probably spot the problem on their remittance advices the next time they are paid and will go to the payroll office to look into the matter—these inquiries take up accounting staff time, as does the paperwork tracking effort.

When used with some control features, it is possible to completely eliminate the tracking of vacation and sick time by the payroll staff. Under this scenario, employees are placed on the honor system of tracking their own vacation and sick time. Though this system keeps the payroll staff from having to do any tracking of this information, there is also a strong possibility that some employees will abuse the situation and take extra time. There are two ways to avoid this problem. One is to institute a company-wide policy that automatically wipes out all earned vacation and sick time at the end of each calendar year, which has the advantage of limiting the amount of vacation and sick time to which an employee can claim that he is entitled. This step mitigates a company's losses if a dishonest employee leaves the company and claims payment for many hours of vacation and sick time that may go back many years. The other way to avoid the problem is to switch the tracking role to employee supervisors. These people are in the best position to see when employees are taking time off and can track their time off much more easily than can the payroll staff. In short, with some relatively minor control changes, it is possible to use an honor system to track employee usage of vacation and sick time.

USE WEB-BASED PAYROLL OUTSOURCING

Payroll processing has been the most common accounting function to outsource for many years. However, it suffers from several deficiencies, such as having to send in information to the payroll supplier only on certain days, or (if the amount of information is minimal) waiting for a supplier representative to call, so that the information can be conveyed over the phone. In addition, any information that is verbally conveyed to the supplier runs the risk of being incorrect, since an additional person is involved in the data entry. Yet another problem is that the supplier will typically run the payroll in a batch processing run that evening, and then deliver the completed payroll to the company one or two days later, which is the earliest point at which the accounting staff knows the exact amount of its payroll liability, which it needs for cash management purposes.

To get around these problems, it is now possible to process one's payroll over the Internet. This involves accessing a supplier's web site, entering payroll and time card information on the spot, and gaining access to fully processed payroll information immediately. This approach also allows one to enter payroll information at any time of the day or night, and to avoid additional data-entry problems that are caused by the use of an extra data-entry person by the supplier.

A particularly fine benefit to this approach is the lack of need for any software that must be installed on a computer in the accounting department. This software is needed for traditional outsourced payroll processing, where the data-entry is conducted by an accounting clerk into a local computer, and then uploaded to the supplier through a modem. This software may be incompatible with other operating or application software on the computer, generally requires that the computer be reserved for payroll use (since it contains sensitive information), must be updated as the supplier issues new software versions, and also costs money—payroll suppliers will charge several hundred dollars to give participating companies the "privilege" of using it.

The main downside to web-based payroll processing is that it can be difficult to access or process if there is a poor Internet connection. Also, as is the case for any outsourced payroll, the payroll information is kept separate from other accounting information in the company's central database, so it is difficult to combine payroll information with other types of information for reporting purposes.

This type of payroll processing is offered by PayMaxx Inc. (*www.paymaxx. com*), Ceridian Corp. (*www.ceridiansmallbusiness.com*), and the Emerging Business Services division of Automatic Data Processing Inc. (*www.ebs.adp.com*).

TOTAL IMPACT OF BEST PRACTICES
ON THE PAYROLL FUNCTION

This section selects many of the preceding best practices and merges them into a sample payroll department, in order to show the overall impact of best practices on the payroll function. Not all of the best practices are shown here because some are mutually exclusive. Though the solution presented would work well for most companies, a careful controller should review *all* of the best practices presented in this section and modify the payroll system discussed in this section, thereby arriving at a system that fits the particular needs of his or her company more exactly.

When selecting those best practices from the previous list in order to construct a more efficient system, it rapidly becomes apparent that the overall trend of the best practices is to streamline the existing payroll system by paring away unnecessary functions. Accordingly, this section notes a number of tasks that can be completely dispensed with. These items are noted down the left side of Exhibit 16.3 with a line through them, denoting processes that have been eliminated from the payroll processing system.

As noted in Exhibit 16.3, a fully streamlined payroll function should avoid any additional tracking time for job costing, avoid special entries for employee advances, not include additional calculations for personal leave days, eliminate deductions for employee purchases, and avoid manual vacation accruals, as well as the manual tracking of vacation and sick time—in short, one must strip this function down to the single key task of calculating employee pay, which is what it was originally intended to do.

Even the simple task of calculating pay can be further reduced so that more automation and fewer paychecks keep the amount of manual intervention to a minimum. As noted in Exhibit 16.3, a bar-coded time clock can be used to avoid

Eliminated Tasks   Streamlined Process Flow

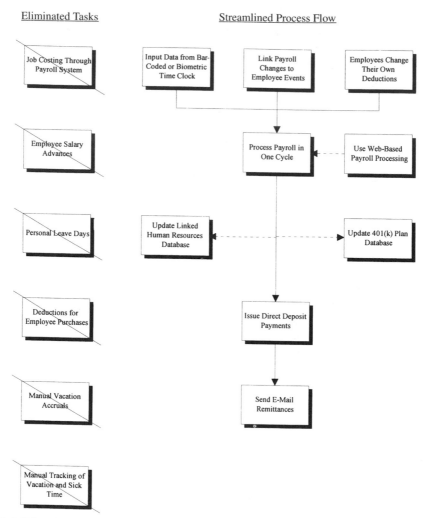

Exhibit 16.3. A Modified Payroll System

the manual entry of employee time cards, while employees can be allowed direct access to their deduction information so that they can enter this information on their own. Once payroll processing is completed, the payroll system can be automatically linked to the human resources and 401(k) databases, which further reduces the work needed to update multiple databases. Additional automation includes issuing direct deposit payments, as well as payment remittances by e-mail. All of these extra levels of automation reduce the labor of the payroll staff to a bare minimum.

An additional improvement is to consolidate all of the diverse payrolls that a company may have into a single payroll processing run that covers the pay of all employees, which avoids having the payroll staff get bogged down in constant payroll calculations, check printings, and distributions. A further enhancement is to stretch out the time between payroll processing runs by changing the payroll frequency from as low as once a week to possibly as long as once a month. These steps will keep the payroll staff from spending all its time processing payroll data.

The sum total of all these changes can transform an overwhelmed payroll department into one that focuses on a minimal number of tasks, handles far fewer transactions, experiences a minimal number of errors requiring correction, and which probably needs fewer employees—in short, we arrive at a low-cost and very efficient payroll processing engine.

SUMMARY

This chapter primarily dealt with a variety of techniques for streamlining an existing payroll system. Central to the recommended changes were the concepts of reduced manual labor and centralized systems, both of which have the net impact of greatly reducing the workload of the payroll staff. Examples of reducing the amount of manual labor are shifting deduction changes to employees, as well as automating vacation accruals. Examples of centralized systems include merging all payroll systems into one system and combining the human resources database with the payroll database. Though few companies would implement all of the best practices listed in this chapter, given the variations in how payroll is processed in some industries, there are still many techniques listed here that a payroll manager should strongly consider installing.

Some of the best practices noted in this chapter work to the detriment of employees. For example, in order to streamline the payroll function, a company may do away with employee purchases and payroll advances, since these require extra monitoring work from the payroll staff. However, if a company is in an industry or geographical region where qualified employees are in short supply, it may be a reasonable decision by the management team to allow these inefficiencies to continue, rather than to run the risk of losing employees over such minor streamlining changes. Because of the impact on employees of many payroll best practices, it is wise to consult with senior management prior to making any significant changes and not to be surprised if the decision handed back is to leave the payroll situation as it is, despite the higher levels of inefficiency.

Appendix A

Suggested Readings

Ansar, Shaid L., and Jan E. Bell. *Target Costing.* New York: McGraw-Hill, 1997.

Banham, Russ. "Champions of Change," *CFO,* December 1997, 35–54.

"Best Practices for E-Commerce Self-Defense," *Journal of Accountancy,* April 2000, 12.

"Better Returns Via the Web," *CFO,* February 2000, 19.

Bogan, Christopher, and Michael English. *Benchmarking for Best Practices.* New York: McGraw-Hill, 1994.

Boggs, Scott. "Accounting—The Digital Way," *Journal of Accountancy,* May 1999, 99–108.

Bragg, Steven. *Advanced Accounting Systems.* Altamonte Springs, FL: Institute of Internal Auditors, 1997.

Bragg, Steven. *Just-in-Time Accounting.* New York: John Wiley & Sons, 1996.

Bragg, Steven. *Outsourcing.* New York: John Wiley & Sons, 1998.

Bruttig, Dana. "What Automated Expense Reporting Management Can Do for You," *Management Accounting,* February 1998, 38–43.

"Cash? Who Needs Cash These Days?" *Business Week,* June 29, 1998, 136.

"Champions of Change," *CFO,* December 1997, 35–54.

Cheney, Glenn. "T&E Technology: Don't Leave Home Without It," *Strategic Finance,* August 1999, 70–76.

Danilewicz, Dennis. "The Payroll Function," *Management Accounting Human Resources/Payroll Supplement,* June 1997, 6.

Dennis, Anita. "Best Practices for Audit Efficiency," *Journal of Accountancy,* September 2000, 65–68.

Enzweiler, Al. "Raising the Bar," *Management Accounting,* December 1997, 26–30.

Fryer, Bronwyn. "Straight from the Screen," *CFO,* November 1998, 83–92.

Garrison, Randall D., and James A. Weisel. "Cut and Deal New Savings with Procurement Cards," *Management Accounting,* April 1997, 16–22.

Harris, Roy. "Slow Connection," *CFO,* June 2000, 99–108.

Hertenstein, Julie H., and Marjorie B. Platt. "Why Product Development Teams Need Management Accountants," *Management Accounting,* April 1998, 50–55.

Hornyak, Steve. "Budgeting Made Easy," *Management Accounting,* October 1998, 18–23.

John, Lauren. "Automatic 401k Plans," *CFO,* September 1998, 30.

Klimas, Anthony J. "Reengineering in the Real World," *Management Accounting,* May 1997, 30–35.

Leibs, Scott. "Shop Till You Drop," *CFO,* June 2000, 33–34.

Lenning, Jeff. "Financial Reports in a Snap," *Journal of Accountancy,* April 2000, 31–35.

LeRouge, Cynthia. "21st Century Technology Issues," *Strategic Finance,* January 2000, 55–60.

Lobaugh, Jean L. "Paperless Payables Pays Off," *Management Accounting,* September 1996, 31–35.

Lobaugh, Jean, "Paperless Payables Take Off," *Management Accounting,* September 1996, 31–35.

Mahoney, Lois S., and Judith K. Welch. "PC Movies Get Two Thumbs Up for Computer Application Training," *Strategic Finance,* September 2000, 74–78.

Mandelker, Jeannie. "Empowered Employees," *CFO,* April 1999, 73–80.

McKinney, "The Station Never Sleeps," *Journal of Accountancy,* January 2000, 63–71.

Mello Jr., John P. "E-Payroll, Anyone?" *CFO,* November 1999, 29.

Mello Jr., John P. "Fly Me to the Web," *CFO,* March 2000, 79–84.

Nyberg, Allan. "Bad News for Bic," *CFO,* September 2000, 38.

Mello, Jr, John P. "Economy Class," *CFO,* July 1998, 67–70.

Palmer, Richard J. Leland D. Green, and Marie T. Ventura, " Are Corporate Procurement Cards for You?" *Management Accounting,* September 1996, 22–30.

Palmer, Richard J., and Walter D. Ward. "Charge It!" *Journal of Accountancy,* July 1997, 51–54.

Pitta, Julie. "Requiem for a Bright Idea," Forbes, November 1, 1999, 390–392.

Reason, Tim. "Share Where?" *CFO,* September 2000, 101–108.

Roehl-Anderson, Jan, and Steven Bragg. *Controllership,* Sixth Edition. New York: John Wiley & Sons, 1999.

Skinner, Robert. "Are You Really Managing Your Corporate Resources?" *Management Accounting,* August 1998, 31–36.

Spinner, Karen. "Going with the Flow," *CFO,* August 1997, 53–57.

Stern, Gary. "Digital Dunning," *e-CFO,* April 2000, 29.

Stewart, Thomas A. "Making Decision in Real Time," *Fortune,* June 26, 2000, 332–334.

Weber, Joseph. "Full Disclosure for All," *Business Week,* September 18, 2000, EB106–EB110.

Zerega, Blaise. "Knocked on Their ASPs," *Forbes ASAP,* May 29, 2000, 79–84.

Summary of Best Practices

This appendix itemizes all of the best practices that are described in greater detail in the preceding chapters of this book. They are listed by title in alphabetical order, which is the same order in which they are listed in each chapter. This appendix is meant to give the reader a rapid overview of the available accounting best practices, which can then be used to locate them in the relevant chapter, where more information is available about the advantages, disadvantages, implementation issues, and costs of each one. The best practices are as follows:

ACCOUNTS PAYABLE BEST PRACTICES—CHAPTER 3

Audit expense reports

Automate expense reporting

Automate payments for repetitive invoicing

Automate three-way matching

Automate value-added tax analysis

Centralize the accounts payable function

Create direct purchase interfaces to suppliers

Create on-line purchasing catalog

Digitize accounts payable documents

Directly enter receipts into computer

Eliminate manual checks

Fax transmission of accounts payable documents

Have suppliers include their supplier numbers on invoices

Internet-based monitoring of credit card purchases

Issue standard account code list

Link corporate travel policies to an automated expense reporting system

Link supplier requests to the accounts payable database

Outsource the accounts payable function

Pay based on receiving approval only

Receive billings through electronic data interchange
Reduce required approvals
Request that suppliers enter all invoices through a web site
Shift incoming billings to an EDI data-entry supplier
Shrink the supplier base
Substitute petty cash for checks
Substitute wire transfers for checks
Transmit expense reports by e-mail
Use blanket purchase orders
Use procurement cards
Use signature stamp

BILLING BEST PRACTICES—CHAPTER 4

Add carrier route codes to billing addresses
Automatically check errors during invoice data entry
Computerize the shipping log
Delivery person creates the invoice
Delivery person delivers the invoice
Early billing of recurring invoices
Eliminate month-end statements
Issue electronic invoices through the Internet
Issue single, summarized invoices each period
Offer customers secure Internet payment options
Print separate invoices for each line item
Reduce number of parts in multi-part invoices
Replace inter-company invoicing with operating transactions
Track exceptions between the shipping log and invoice register
Transmit transmissions via electronic data interchange
Use automated bank account deductions

BUDGETING BEST PRACTICES—CHAPTER 5

Automatically link the budget to purchase orders
Budget by groups of staff positions
Clearly define all assumptions

Clearly define all capacity levels

Create a summarized budget model for use by upper management

Establish project ranking criteria

Establish the upper limit of available funding

Identify step-costing change points

Include a working capital analysis

Issue a budget procedure and timetable

Link to performance measurements and rewards

Reduce the number of accounts

Simplify the budget model

Store budget information in a central database

Use activity-based budgeting

Use flex budgeting (use cost drivers)

Use on-line budget updating

Use video conferencing for budget updating

CASH MANAGEMENT BEST PRACTICES—CHAPTER 6

Area-concentration banking

Consolidate bank accounts

Controlled disbursements

Electronic funds transfer

Lockbox collections

On-line access to bank account information

Positive pay system

Proliferate petty-cash boxes

Utilize an investment policy

Zero-balance accounts

COLLECTIONS BEST PRACTICES—CHAPTER 7

Access to customer assets database

Access to customer orders database

Automatic bankruptcy notification

Automatic fax of overdue invoices

Automatic issuance of dunning letters

Collection call database

Collection call stratification

Customer order exception tracking

Grant percentage discounts for early payment

Immediate review of unapplied cash

Linkage to comprehensive collections software package

Lockbox collections

Outsource collections

Pre-approved customer credit

Pricing structure simplification

Standardized credit level determination system

Write off small balances with no approval

COMMISSIONS BEST PRACTICES—CHAPTER 8

Automatically calculate commissions in the computer system

Calculate final commissions from actual data

Construct a standard commission terms table

Include commission payments in payroll payments

Lengthen the interval between commission payments

Only pay commissions from cash received

Periodically audit commissions paid

Periodically issue a summary of commission rates

Post commission payments on the company Intranet

Show potential commissions on cash register

Simplify the commission structure

COSTING BEST PRACTICES—CHAPTER 9

Audit bills of material

Audit labor routings

Eliminate high-leverage overhead allocation bases

Eliminate labor variance reporting

Follow a schedule of inventory obsolescence reviews

Implement activity-based costing

Implement target costing

Limit access to unit of measure changes

Review cost trends

Review material scrap levels

Revise traditional cost accounting reports

FILING BEST PRACTICES—CHAPTER 10

Add digital signatures to electronic documents

Adopt a document-destruction policy

Archive canceled checks on CD-ROM

Archive computer files

Document imaging

Eliminate attaching back-up materials to checks for signing

Eliminate reports

Eliminate stored paper documents if already in computer

Extend time period before computer records are purged

Extend use of existing computer database

Improve computer system reliability

Move records off-site

Reduce number of form copies to file

FINANCE BEST PRACTICES—CHAPTER 11

Access bank account information on the Internet

Automatic 401(k) plan enrollment

Avoid delays in check posting

Centralize foreign exchange management

Consolidate insurance policies

Grant employees immediate 401(k) eligibility

Install a treasury workstation

Negotiate faster deposited check availability

Optimize cash management decisions through the Internet

Use Internet-based cash flow analysis software

Use Internet-based options pricing services

Use Internet-based risk measurement services

Use Internet-based technical analysis services

Use Internet-based treasury management services

Use web broadcasting for public reporting

FINANCIAL STATEMENTS BEST PRACTICES—CHAPTER 12

Assign closing responsibilities

Automate recurring journal entries

Automate the cut-off

Avoid the bank reconciliation

Complete allocation bases in advance

Conduct daily review of the financial statements

Conduct transaction training

Continually review wait times

Convert serial activities to parallel ones

Create a closing schedule

Defer routine work

Document the process

Eliminate multiple approvals

Eliminate small accruals

Move operating data to other reports

Post financial statements in an Excel PivoTable on the Internet

Reduce investigation levels

Restrict the level of reporting

Restrict the use of journal entries

Train the staff in closing procedures

Use cycle counting to avoid month-end counts

Use internal audits to locate transaction problems in advance

Use standard journal entry forms

Write financial statement footnotes in advance

GENERAL BEST PRACTICES—CHAPTER 13

Avoid over-auditing of internal audits

Complete all internal audit workpapers in the field

Consolidate all accounting functions

Continually review key process cycles

Create a contract terms database

Create an ongoing training program for all accounting personnel

Create an on-line internal audit library

Create an on-line tax policy listing

Create a policy and procedure manual

Create computer-based training movies

Implement cross-training for mission-critical activities

Implement process-centering

Issue activity calendars to all accounting positions

Outsource tax form preparation

Outsource the internal audit function

Post the policies and procedures manual on the company Intranet site

Scan data with modified palm computing platform

Scan fingerprints at user workstations

Schedule internal audits based on risk

Sell the shared services center

Switch to a limited usage application service provider

Switch to an application service provider

Switch to on-line reporting

Track function measurements

Use balanced scorecard reporting

GENERAL LEDGER BEST PRACTICES—CHAPTER 14

Construct automated interfaces to software that summarizes into the general ledger

Create general ledger drill-down capability

Eliminate small-balance accounts

Modify account code structure for storage of ABC information

Overlay the general ledger with a consolidation and reporting package

Reduce the chart of accounts

Restrict use of journal entries

Subsidiaries update their own data in the central general ledger

Use automated error-checking

Use data warehouse for report distribution

Use forms/rates data warehouse for automated tax filings

Use identical chart of accounts for subsidiaries

Use the general ledger as a data warehouse

INVENTORY BEST PRACTICES—CHAPTER 15

Audit all inventory transactions

Audit bills of material

Compare recorded inventory activity to on-hand inventories

Eliminate the physical count process

Eliminate the receiving function

Eliminate the warehouse

Lock down the warehouse area

Modify the bills of material based on actual scrap levels

Move inventory to floor stock

Review inventory returned to the warehouse

Segregate customer-owned inventory

Streamline the physical count process

Track inventory accuracy

Verify that all receipts are entered in the computer at once

PAYROLL BEST PRACTICES—CHAPTER 16

Automate fax-back of payroll forms

Automate vacation accruals

Avoid job costing through the payroll system

Consolidate payroll systems

Disallow pre-payments

Eliminate personal leave days

Give employees direct access to deduction data

Link payroll changes to employee events

Link the 401(k) plan to the payroll system

Link the payroll and human resources databases

Minimize payroll cycles

Outsource the payroll function

Prohibit deductions for employee purchases

Send remittances as e-mail messages

Switch to salaried positions

Use bar-coded time clocks

Use biometric time clocks

Use direct deposit

Use honor system to track vacation and sick time

Use web-based payroll outsourcing

Index